KINSHIP AND GENDER

KINSHIP AND GENDER

An Introduction

FIFTH EDITION

Linda Stone
Washington State University

WESTVIEW PRESS

An Imprint of Perseus Books

Published by Westview Press,
An imprint of Perseus Books, LLC, a subsidiary of Hachette Book Group, Inc.

Every effort has been made to secure required permissions to use all images, maps, and other art included in this volume.

Find us on the World Wide Web at www.westviewpress.com.

Westview Press books are available at special discounts for bulk purchases in the United States by corporations, institutions, and other organizations. For more information, please contact the Special Markets Department at Perseus Books Group, 2300 Chestnut Street, Suite 200, Philadelphia, PA 19103, or call (800) 810-4145, ext. 5000, or e-mail special.markets@hbgusa.com.

Library of Congress Cataloging-in-Publication Data

Stone, Linda, 1947–
  Kinship and gender : an introduction / Linda Stone, Washington State University.—Fifth edition.
     pages cm
  Includes bibliographical references and index.
  ISBN 978-0-8133-4861-2 (pbk.)—ISBN 978-0-8133-4862-9 (e-book) 1. Kinship. 2. Sex role. 3. Human reproduction. 4. Matrilineal kinship. 5. Patrilineal kinship. I. Title.
  GN487.S76 2013
  305.3—dc23
                        2013004579

Contents

Illustrations

Figures

Preface

Kinship is often a difficult concept to grasp—but as I learned through many years of undergraduate teaching, the idea of kinship came alive in a new way for students when we focused on the issue of gender. Similarly, students more easily understood the nuances of gender in different cultural contexts when they had a cross-cultural knowledge of kinship.

This book, then, is designed to provide an accessible yet comprehensive introduction to kinship for use in undergraduate classes on kinship, on gender, or, as with my own course, on the two combined. Most chapters adopt a historical perspective, giving a sense of how ideas in this field have developed over time. The book also includes fifteen ethnographic case studies to give students a strong sense of the intricate interconnections between kinship and gender as a lived experience and among a variety of cultural groups.

The book may be used as a supplementary text in courses that focus on gender or families cross-culturally but do not otherwise deal with anthropological kinship. However, in these courses, instructors might wish to skip over Chapter 5 ("Double, Bilateral, and Cognatic Descent"), since the material there on kinship is more technical and complex than in other chapters.

When I began the first edition of this book in the 1990s, I could not have chosen a more difficult time to write an introductory text on kinship. At that time, kinship, possibly the most tortured topic in anthropology, nearly slipped off the edge of professional interest. Yet, particularly when linked with gender, kinship has since seen a revival, as briefly covered here in Chapter 1. There are many current issues and debates related to kinship that are of keen interest to professional readers, but that I could not delve deeply into in this introductory text. I have, however, tried to give students a sense of the directions that contemporary investigations of kinship and gender are taking. The "suggested further reading" and references concluding each chapter will guide readers in search of greater detail.

Along with general updating, this fifth edition of the book contains a new chapter, "The Globalization of Kinship." Here I discuss some interesting twists and turns in kinship and the family under the impact of urbanization, transnational migration, and international adoption. This chapter includes a new case study on child circulation in Peru. In Chapter 4 ("Through the

Mother") I have expanded the case study about "visiting husbands" to cover the Mosuo of southwest China as well as the Nayar of India. Chapter 7 ("A History of Euro-American Kinship and Gender") also contains a new case study on "breadwinning women" in the United States. Here I consider changes in gender relations and family life that are occurring as increasing numbers of women outearn their male husbands or partners. In this edition I have also expanded the list of websites at the end of each chapter; these were last accessed in February 2013.

For their helpful comments on earlier editions of the book, I thank Karen Sinclair, Barry S. Hewlett, Jessica Lynch Alfaro, Andrew Strathern, Jeannette Mageo, and Nancy P. McKee. I am grateful to Lynn Bennett, Bernard Chapais, Alma Gottlieb, Diane King, Jessaca Leinaweaver, Nancy E. Levine, and Miranda Warburton for their assistance with particular chapters or specific case studies. This fifth edition of the book benefited from very useful suggestions from Westview Press's developmental reviewers, including William Donner, Lina Fruzzetti, Raymond Hames, Robert H. Lavenda, Nancy E. Levine, and Shane J. Macfarlan; I extend a special thanks to all of them. For his considerable help and support during the preparation of the book through all editions, I am deeply grateful to my husband, Paul F. Lurquin. Finally, I thank Karen Sinclair's undergraduate students at Eastern Michigan University and my undergraduate students at Washington State University, who gave me valuable feedback on particular chapters.

LINDA STONE
NOVEMBER 2012

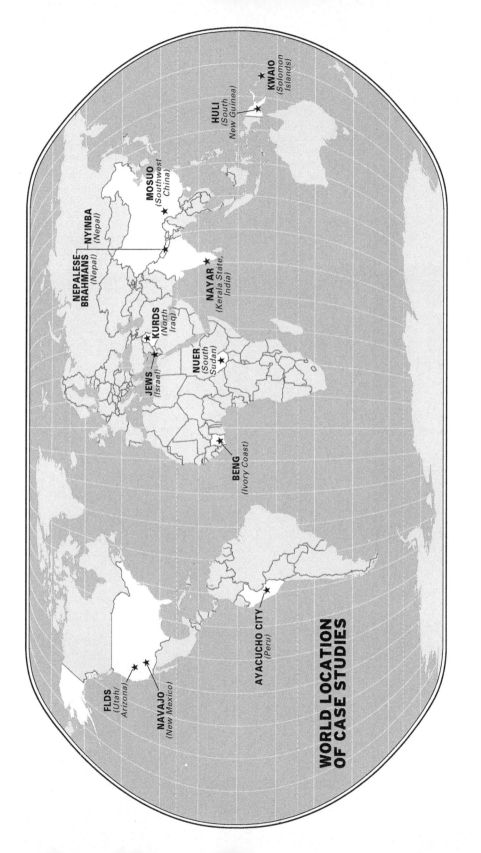

**WORLD LOCATION
OF CASE STUDIES**

KWAIO
*(Solomon
Islands)*

HULI
*(South
New Guinea)*

MOSUO
*(Southwest
China)*

NYINBA
(Nepal)

NEPALESE
BRAHMANS
(Nepal)

NAYAR
*(Kerala State,
India)*

KURDS
*(North
Iraq)*

NUER
*(South
Sudan)*

JEWS
(Israel)

BENG
(Ivory Coast)

FLDS
*(Utah/
Arizona)*

NAVAJO
(New Mexico)

AYACUCHO CITY
(Peru)

1

GENDER, REPRODUCTION, AND KINSHIP

Women and men today are raising new questions about gender identity and status. In the process of forming these questions, we have seen a growth of interest in approaching the subject both cross-culturally and historically. This approach has been essential in that it allows us to address some of the larger concerns, such as whether and to what extent women have been universally subjugated to men or treated as "second-class citizens." In addition, many students have sought to look beyond the confines of their own cultures and times to gain a broader perspective on particular gender issues in their own societies.

As a field of study, gender refers not only to people's understandings of the categories "male" and "female" but also to the ways in which these understandings are interwoven with other dimensions of social and cultural life. The latter include the social roles that women and men play, the values surrounding male and female activities, and people's particular conceptions of the nature and meaning of sexual differences.[1] All of these aspects of gender vary widely from culture to culture.

In this book I explore gender cross-culturally through the framework of kinship. Specifically, I seek to introduce new ways in which some cross-cultural variations in gender can be understood. Kinship is an old, established specialization in anthropology, noted more for its difficult jargon and tortuous diagrams than for the light it sheds on gender. Indeed, Michael Herzfeld (2007: 313) notes that "students who have never confronted [kinship's] more technical aspects still profess boredom with the topic and relief that they do not have to deal with it." Of course, my intention is not to bore yet another generation of students but, instead, to show that kinship, when stripped of certain of its more advanced complexities and focused on the subject of gender, can be both interesting and illuminating.

There are many areas in which the study of kinship and the study of gender intersect (for example, in religion or in political organization), but the one I emphasize in this book is reproduction. In all societies, human offspring are a vital concern; in fact, the very survival of any society depends on successful reproduction. And in all societies, human reproduction is regulated. Laws, norms, and cultural ideologies define where, when, and in what contexts heterosexual intercourse is permitted or prohibited, encouraged or discouraged. When intercourse results in reproduction, a whole host of laws, norms, and values come into play to define this situation, especially as it relates to the allocation of children to particular individuals or groups. The meanings of "marriage" and "divorce," and the idea of child "legitimacy," are all a part of how different human groups handle reproduction. Kinship is everywhere a part of the social and cultural management of reproduction and, as such, is intimately interlinked with gender. A primary concern of the book, then, is the sexual and reproductive roles of women and men. We will see how kinship shapes these roles and, in the process, affects gender.

Both ambivalence and controversy have surrounded the discussion of reproductive roles in relation to gender status. We know that, biologically speaking, women play a special role in reproduction—that they, and not men, undergo pregnancy and childbirth. Some scholars hold that gender is rooted in these biological facts of life, or that gender is rooted in sex differences. Consider Alice Rossi's (1985) work, which focuses on uncovering the influences of biological factors on women's behavior, showing, for example, how pregnancy stimulates certain maternal responses in women. Or consider the many studies suggesting that even at very young ages, males are more aggressive than females and exhibit greater competition and dominance striving (MacIntyre 2009). Yet many social scientists feel that studies of biology do not go very far in accounting for differences in gender, as these differences vary considerably across cultures and, in their view, are largely learned. Barbara Miller (1993: 22) summarizes this view: "A simple rule of science is that variables (sex and gender hierarchies) cannot be explained by constants (genitals and chromosomes)." In other words, if male/female biological differences are everywhere constant, then we cannot refer to those differences to account for the variable gender patterns we see around the world.

Other scholars have linked gender with biology by focusing on what they propose all human groups do have in common with regard to reproduction. For instance, evolutionary social scientists have suggested that human males and females have evolved different mating strategies, as have all other animal species. Thus males and females are biologically oriented to maximize their genetic "fitness," or reproductive success—that is, they pursue strategies to ensure that their genes will be maximally transmitted to and represented in subsequent generations (see Chapter 2). Men's best strategy is to mate with a plurality of females. Women, by contrast, do not seek to become pregnant and give birth as often as possible (this would only weaken them and lessen the survival chances of their many children) but rather seek fewer offspring who can be well cared for and so themselves survive and eventually reproduce. A woman does not need many sexual partners to maximize her fitness, but only one good mate, or perhaps a few, to impregnate her. Thus, as expressed by one evolutionary ecologist, males go for "mate quantity" whereas females go for "mate quality" (Smuts 1995: 5). In the end, then, men seek sexual activity with a number of partners, or are inherently more promiscuous than women, since this will help maximize their fitness.

An additional idea along these lines is that men and women also differ in parental investment, or how and how much they care and provide for offspring to help the offspring's survival and reproduction. For a woman the situation is simple since a woman always knows who her offspring are. Investing in her offspring will directly increase her fitness, although some circumstances may alter her strategies. For example, if the woman has poor resources and cannot provide well for all of her children, she may favor those of her children who are more likely to survive, and neglect the others. But for men the situation is very different: Their parental investment depends on "paternity certainty," or the extent to which a man can be assured that a particular child is biologically his. Paternity certainty will be higher where there are greater restrictions on female sexuality. Some have argued, then, that many practices around the world (female seclusion, a sexual double standard, etc.) developed to increase paternity certainty (Smuts 1995). Women may also support these restrictions because they know, however unconsciously, that higher paternity certainty will increase the chances that men will help provide for the women and their children.

Evolutionary psychologists maintain that these different male and female strategies for mating and parental investment evolved during a particular period in time (the Environment of Evolutionary Adaptation, or the Paleolithic period of human prehistory) but they continue to shape human behavior. David Buss (1994) claims that as a result men everywhere are attracted to women who look young and healthy, as these are signs of good fertility. By contrast women care less about looks and youth (older, less attractive men may still be good impregnators) but are instead attracted to men who exhibit wealth and power, as these men are likely to be good providers. Buss also argues that men evolved greater sexual jealousy than women: A man's female mate's infidelity threatens a man's fitness since it reduces his paternity certainty, whereas a man's infidelity does not really threaten his mate's fitness. These ideas from evolutionary social science remain controversial. Some writers charge that they merely justify male infidelity, ideas about female dependence on male resources, restrictions on female sexuality, and hence female subordination (Tang-Martinez 1997).

Evolutionary ecologists have used these ideas on human mating strategies, or more generally strategies for reproductive success, to address questions about women's status and life options. Here, attention is given to ecological and social factors (such as marriage forms and subsistence systems) that shape reproductive and parenting strategies. In this approach some cross-cultural generalizations emerge. For example, Bobbie Low (2005) has shown how, across cultures, male and female children tend to be raised differently in accordance with the strategies for reproductive success of each gender. "Cross-culturally, sons are more strongly trained than daughters in behaviors useful in open competition, while daughters are more strongly trained in such values as sexual restraint, obedience, and responsibility—traits widely sought by men in their wives" (2005: 74). Low also found that in those societies where women do control important resources, daughters are less likely to be raised to be submissive.

Other scholars have avoided or discounted discussion of gender and biological reproduction, not wishing to fuel the notion that "biology is destiny." They are concerned that these approaches can be used to justify the subordination of women as "natural," inevitable, and unchangeable. By contrast, their approach minimizes the difference in men's and women's reproductive roles (Rothman 1987). They stress, for example, that just because women get pregnant and give birth, it does not necessarily follow that they must be the primary caretakers of children, remain confined to the home, or be excluded from important political and economic pursuits. In particular, these writers argue that a subordinate status of women is not biologically rooted but socially imposed (or imposed by men).

Still other writers reject the idea that biology determines gender but nevertheless hold that women's reproductive roles do work as an instrument of their oppression or subordination to men. For example, Michele Rosaldo (1974) claimed in her earlier writing that women's reproductive roles confine them to the home and to domestic tasks. She argued that this domestic, "private sphere" of women is everywhere less valued than the "public sphere" of men, or the broader male world of politics and extra-domestic authority. The idea was that the male public sphere is superior because it encompasses the female domestic realm and involves economic and political activities of concern to larger social groups. However, critics countered that not all societies exhibit such a sharp division between private and public spheres, that women in some societies do have public roles, and that female domestic activities are not necessarily everywhere devalued. Rosaldo (1980) later came to agree with many of these criticisms; in particular, she concurred that gender conflicts in relation to a private/public dichotomy may be a characteristic of Euro-American society rather than a human universal.

In contrast to Rosaldo, others argued that women are generally oppressed not because their reproductive and domestic roles are devalued but precisely because their reproduction is highly valued socially and thus controlled by men (Moen 1979). Men have power over women because men are in greater control of the political and economic forces that control human reproduction

(Robertson 1991: 41). Faye Ginsburg and Rayna Rapp (1995) also look at human reproduction in terms of the forces regulating it and the effects of this control on individuals and groups. They suggest many ways in which global processes perpetuate social inequalities through the international politics of reproduction (see Chapter 10).

More recently, many have come to question not only whether a subordination of women is universal but also along what criteria such a claim could ever be made. How should we define the "status" of women, especially cross-culturally? Women in a particular society might be seen as "oppressed" by outsiders and yet have a very different view of their own situation and status. A good example is the veiling of women in public, as practiced in several Islamic areas of the Middle East and Southwest Asia. Outsiders may see these practices as "oppressive" to women, but women within these societies may have an entirely different view. They may see veiling as a good and necessary protection of their persons in the world outside the home and as a symbol of their own self-respect. To what extent, then, can we define "female oppression" in a way that is free of our own cultural biases?

In addition, it has become clear that women, even within one society, can differ widely in their perceptions of gender, depending on factors such as class position. Also, any woman's status will vary according to the different roles she plays within her society and the different situations she encounters over her life course. Faced with these kinds of considerations, studies of gender have subsequently moved somewhat away from the issue of whether and in what sense there is a universal subordination of women, focusing instead on the different interests and strategies of women and men in the performance of gender in everyday life and on gender in relation to other social divisions such as race, ethnicity, class, and age (di Leonardo 1991: 18; Lamphere 1993: 72; Lamphere, Ragoné, and Zavella 1997). There is still great interest in cross-cultural studies of gender; although many of these do not invoke the idea of a universal subordination of women, they do compare societies in terms of their level of equality between men and women in different spheres of life, as will be seen throughout this book.

ENACTING AND EMBODYING GENDER

How do women and men come to play the gender roles that they do in any society? One set of ideas on this issue focuses on socialization (or enculturation), that is, how we internalize certain culturally specific behaviors and attitudes as we grow from infants to adults. A simple example concerns the effects of parents in the United States giving Barbie dolls to girls and toy military weapons to boys. Later in life peer groups become powerful forces behind gender construction and role performance. This internalization of ideas about gender and gender roles is often unconscious. While socialization theory is still used in studies of gender and gender roles, some scholars came to feel that this approach went too far in characterizing culture as a static set of ideas and practices and depicting human actors as passive recipients of culture; that is, it downplayed human agency. A more contemporary approach sees culture and human action in dynamic interaction with each other. In this view we are influenced by our culture (we internalize it through socialization) but at the same time we act within it (sometimes conforming, sometimes resisting) and so affect it, potentially bringing about culture change in the process.

Another question for gender studies has been: Through what common forms is gender expressed? Here, anthropologists and others have come to see the human body as among the most powerful and prominent of such forms. Ideal male and female bodies, body adornment, body language, posture, clothing, medical handling of bodies, and so on resound with gender messages in any culture. Bodies are sites for the expression and negotiation of gender. One has only to look at some historical transformations in the United States to see how body ideals and manipulations of bodies encode gender. Here, in the nineteenth century, the ideal male body was "lean and wiry" (Bederman 1995: 15) and the ideal man had a "pale complexion and languid air" (Kimmel 1996: 28). Over the twentieth century (and increasingly so into the twenty-first) this ideal shifted to a large, muscular body. Historians have analyzed how this shift reflected a transition away from a cultural concern with "manliness" (focused on nineteenth-century ideas of male honor and self-restraint) toward a concept of "masculinity" (focused on virile male power). These historians have shown how this shift coincided with nineteenth- and early twentieth-century challenges to middle-class male security and bread-winning capacity—economic depressions, political challenges from lower-class males and immigrants, and the women's suffrage movement (Bederman 1995, Kimmel 1996). As a result middle-class men lost confidence in the earlier image of manly self-control and adopted a rougher, tougher ideal body exuding raw power.

Over the same period there were changes in the ideal female body as well. In the nineteenth century women's bodies were perceived as frail and vulnerable to breakdown at the slightest physical or mental challenge; perhaps to counter this inherent tendency to break down, the ideal female body was relatively plump and voluptuous (McKee and Stone 2007). Today the ideal is an extremely thin female body, variously interpreted as symbolic of self-discipline and control. Reflecting this trend, even Barbie lost weight in 1997 when her new model came out with slimmer hips and reduced breasts (Reischer and Koo 2004: 298). Also interesting is that women in the United States are now strongly focused on other body modifications—tummy tucks, Botox, face-lifts—to say nothing of daily regimens of skin care and hair treatment, all of which is leaving many women with a sense of perpetual inadequacy as they fall short of impossible ideals (Bordo 1997). Even more recently, a slightly muscular female ideal body has come into vogue. This has been seen as echoing women's substantial and yet problematic entry into the workforce, where barriers to gender equality are still experienced. For some women, muscles, symbolizing strength and discipline and previously considered unfeminine, are now to be seen as equally characteristic of women and men (Reischer and Koo 2004). In many ways, then, bodies both reflect and challenge the dominant social order and power relationships.

Today we study gender as a social process. Cultural constructions of gender are considered to be something that we as human actors ourselves continually generate in our everyday lives. And yet our actions do take place within specific social and cultural structures. One of those structures is kinship.

GENDER AND REPRODUCTION

Human reproduction is clearly important to social life, yet its connections to gender remain controversial. We will encounter some additional debates in subsequent chapters. For now, however, I offer my own position, at least with respect to biology: Although biology is not destiny, a male/female difference in reproduction is universal and everywhere affects gender. But the way in which this difference is related to gender is not everywhere the same. Local conceptions of and interests in reproduction, and the meaning it has to and for men, women, and social relations generally, do show considerable variation across time and place.

Thus I do not follow Sylvia Yanagisako and Jane Collier (1987), who argue that the study of kinship and gender should not be positioned with reference to biological "facts" of reproduction. These authors hold that biological "facts of life" are themselves culturally constructed and therefore cannot be taken for granted in a study of kinship or gender in any society.[2] They emphasize that different cultures may have different ideas about what counts as sexual differences between males and females, as well as different notions about the nature of human reproduction itself, and hence that each culture must be approached on its own terms in the study of kinship and gender. Their points are valuable and they raise fundamental issues that must be considered seriously. But my view is that a male/female difference in reproduction is universal (however varied the cultural constructions of this difference might be) and that on the basis of this fact we can begin to make meaningful cross-cultural comparisons.

In drawing out the connections between kinship and gender in the chapters ahead, I focus on two dimensions of reproduction with regard to women. One is women's sexuality, and the other is women's fertility or reproductive capacity. My aim is not only to show how various human groups perceive, evaluate, or negotiate these two dimensions of womanhood but also, more

specifically, to consider how cultural ideas about female sexuality and reproductive capacity are related in different societies. In some, female sexuality
is given relatively free rein while rights over a woman's children are established by rules unrelated to her sexual behavior; in others, a woman's sexual
behavior can devalue her reproduction (Chapter 4). In Euro-American culture,
female sexuality and fertility historically seem to have been at odds with each
other (Chapter 7). Meanwhile, new reproductive technologies have resulted
in further divisions and conflicts (Chapter 9).

   This relationship between female sexuality and fertility will affect another
important dimension in women's lives, namely their reproductive autonomy.
To what extent and in what ways does a woman in any particular culture or
society have reproductive options and to what extent can she exert relatively
unfettered control over her reproduction? As we will see, societies vary in
the extent to which social and cultural constraints govern women in their
roles as producers of children. We will also see that in general terms, in societies where women's reproductive autonomy is high, there is greater gender
equality in other spheres of life.

   Men and women not only play different roles in reproduction, they may
also have different reproductive goals, as we have already seen with respect
to evolutionary theory. This difference is sometimes dramatically enacted. In
one township in Oaxaca, Mexico, men tell tales of their collective destruction
of a "birth control" tree, an actual tree whose bark was locally believed to
work as a contraceptive. Men believed that many women who wished to prevent conception were secretly drinking tea prepared from this bark. "The
women weren't having babies. They were lazy and didn't want to produce,"
said one man, and so eventually "a group of men banded together one day
and tore the tree down" (Browner and Perdue 1988: 93–94).

   Relationships among female sexuality, fertility, and reproductive autonomy
are defined largely by the concerns of families and kin groups. The remainder
of this chapter presents some basic terms and concepts in the study of kinship
that I use as a foundation for exploring gender.

WHAT IS KINSHIP?

Kinship is conventionally defined as relationships between persons based on
descent or marriage. If the relationship between one person and another is
considered by them to involve descent, the two are *consanguineal* ("blood")
relatives. If the relationship has been established through marriage, it is *affinal*.
Thus, in the United States, relatives such as one's mother, father, brother,
sister, cousin, grandparent, and grandchild are consanguineal relatives,
whereas one's father-in-law, sister-in-law, and so on are affinal relatives. In
America, one's uncle is a consanguineal relative if he is one's father's brother
or mother's brother, but if the uncle is a father's sister's husband or mother's
sister's husband, he is an affinal relative.

Societies vary in the extent to which kinship connections form the basis of their social, economic, and political structure. In some, kin groups are political groups, and economic relationships between people are kinship relationships. The whole fabric of such societies is woven with strands of kinship. In others, the major groups in the society are formed on other bases, and socioeconomic or political institutions are, at least technically speaking, separated from kinship. Yet even in these latter cases, kinship may play a powerful (if unofficial) role in economic and political life. It may be that a person lands a job or gets into a school because he or she is qualified "on paper," but, in fact, nearly everything valuable in society is distributed through links of kin. In the United States there is little tolerance for the use of kinship to achieve positions in public or professional life, but we are all aware of cases of this sort.

Although the official and other roles played by kinship vary considerably across societies, kinship relations in general entail the idea of rights and obligations. Some of these are codified in law, as when legal rules specify the order of succession to property when a person dies without a will. It is this aspect of kinship that gives it social force.

Kinship involves much more, however, than relations through descent and marriage, social structure, and rights and obligations between kin. Indeed, kinship is also an ideology of human relationships; it involves cultural ideas about how humans are created and the nature and meaning of their biological and moral connections with others. This dimension of kinship, its cross-cultural variations, and the implications for gender are reflected in different people's ideas about human procreation. For example, in her study of a group of people in Malaysia, Carol Laderman (1983, 1991) encountered the local belief that a baby begins not in the mother's womb but in the father's brain, where it exists in liquid form. She writes (1991: 1x):

> When I asked my midwife-teacher what that meant, she was equally startled. Imagine a grown, highly educated woman not knowing that a baby develops within its father's brain for forty days before its mother takes over! She pointed to her husband as an example, reminiscing about the time he carried their youngest child, and how he had craved sour foods during his pregnancy.

The liquid fetus is thought to pass through the father's body and into the mother through sexual intercourse, a belief that has an important connection with gender. These people consider that in the process of their creation as humans, they acquire a rationality that distinguishes them from animals and, furthermore, that men have more rationality than women. "It makes sense, therefore, for a baby to begin life within its father's brain . . . where it acquires rationality from a developed source" (Laderman 1991: 92). This example is but one of many illustrating the considerable variation among cultural beliefs about the nature and extent of male and female contributions to conception and fetal development.

Connections between gender and ideas about procreation can also be seen in Euro-American societies, despite the popular notion that Euro-Americans think about procreation only in a modern, scientific way. For instance, Carol Delaney (1991: 8) writes about the procreative metaphor of active, generative, male "seed" implanted in a passive, nurturing, female "soil." This is a metaphor emphasized by the Western Christian tradition and other monotheistic traditions that portray a male God as creator of the world. This metaphor, which attributes a special life-giving force to males, continues to exist alongside our scientific understanding of human conception.

The ways in which a society defines and uses relations of kinship can collectively be called its kinship system. Along with ideas about reproduction, this system encompasses the rights and obligations recognized between kin or groups of kin, the categories into which kin are linguistically classified, and the rules, or norms that specify modes of descent, patterns of residence, and forms of marriage. To understand these concepts, and to follow the discussions of kinship and gender throughout this book, the reader needs to become familiar with a basic tool of kinship studies: the Kinship Code.

THE KINSHIP CODE

Anthropologists use the elements of the Kinship Code to diagram kin relationships. The elements applicable to this book are presented in Figure 1.1. Note the term *ego* at the bottom of the figure. This term refers to the discrete individual upon whom a particular kinship diagram is centered. In Figure 1.2 and other such "egocentric" diagrams, it is conventional to shade in ego symbols.

FIGURE 1.1   The Kinship Code

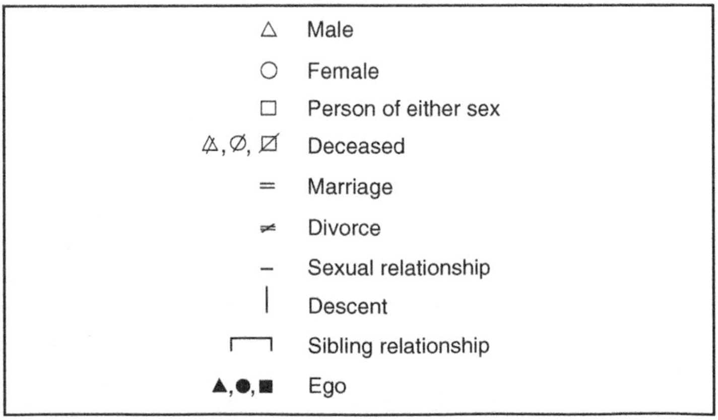

△	Male
○	Female
□	Person of either sex
⚰, ∅, ⊠	Deceased
=	Marriage
≠	Divorce
–	Sexual relationship
|	Descent
⌐¬	Sibling relationship
▲, ●, ■	Ego

FIGURE 1.2   An Illustration of the Kinship Code

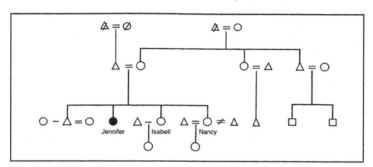

Figure 1.2, which focuses on a female ego, shows how all the symbols of the Kinship Code can be used. Here we see that Jennifer has two living parents. She has grandparents, too, but only one of them is still living. Her father was an only child, but her mother has a sister who has a son, Jennifer's cousin. Her mother also has a brother, who in turn has children. Jennifer herself is unmarried. She has two sisters, Isabell and Nancy. Nancy was married but then divorced and remarried. She has a daughter by her second marriage. The other sister, Isabell, is not officially married, but she has a partner and, through this union, a daughter. Jennifer's brother is married, and the diagram tells us that he is having some kind of affair on the side. (It does not specify whether others know of this affair; rather, it shows only that the person who constructed the diagram presumes to know.)

This egocentric diagram readily presents Jennifer's *kindred*, or a set of relatives traced to one particular ego. Although the diagram appears to suggest some biological relationships, it (and other diagrams) should not be understood as representing actual biological or genetic connections. On the contrary, it represents what these people are claiming to be the relationships between them or, more precisely, what the person who drew the diagram understood and wanted to show about these people in terms of their kinship. Based on the diagram, then, we cannot say, for example, that Jennifer's father is or is not her actual biological father. Possibly her father himself believes he is but in fact is not. The point is that kinship diagrams show kinship relationships that may or may not also involve biological relationships.

There are some things this diagram does not show. For example, it does not show whether any of Jennifer's siblings are older or younger than she. Nor does it show whether Jennifer was adopted. But if we wanted to represent such details, it would be easy to do, so long as we specified what is meant by the new notations we are using. For example, Figure 1.3 shows us that a particular female ego was adopted and that she has one younger sister and two younger brothers.

FIGURE 1.3 One Way to Show Adoption and Sibling Order on a Kinship Diagram

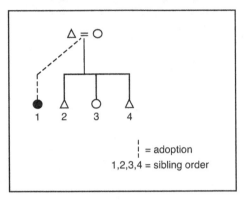

Another convention in kinship notation involves a very simple set of symbols, as follows:

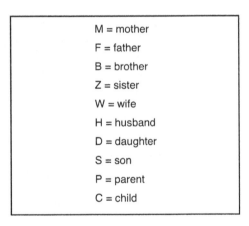

These letters can be used as a shorthand system for designating relationships. They also can be strung together to indicate the paths of a relationship. For example, we can indicate that a particular male ego has a relative who is his MFBSD. This connection could be diagrammed as shown in Figure 1.4.

Kinship diagrams can, and should, be tailored to show only what the diagram drawer feels is necessary to make his or her key points. For example, Figure 1.4, showing an ego's MFBSD, could be more simply and efficiently presented as shown in Figure 1.5. If our only objective is to trace the connection between an ego and his MFBSD, we need not indicate that ego has a father as well as a mother or that his MF and MFB have spouses, even if all of these relationships also exist.

FIGURE 1.4 A Kinship Diagram Connecting Ego to an MFBSD

FIGURE 1.5 A Simplified Diagram Connecting Ego to an MFBSD

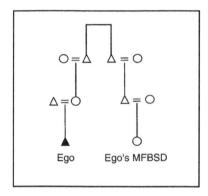

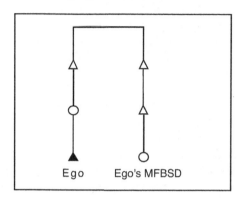

Not all kinship diagrams are egocentric. Some diagrams can be used simply to show relationships between sets of people or groups. In Figure 1.6, for example, there is no ego as a reference point, nor is an individual's kindred depicted. The diagram merely indicates that two sisters have married two brothers.

I will continue using these triangles, circles, letters, and other symbols throughout the book, beginning with the following section, which introduces some of the key concepts involved in the study of kinship.

FIGURE 1.6 Two Sisters Married to Two Brothers

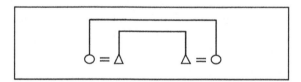

KEY CONCEPTS

Descent

Humans live in groups. To survive, they must be able to construct and maintain more or less cohesive groups. One reason kinship became and remains important in human societies is that it serves as a means of group formation. Indeed, kinship can be used efficiently to form discrete, stable groups that persist over time, beyond the lives and deaths of the people of a single generation. In Chapter 2 we will examine the evolution of human kinship more fully. But for now, to appreciate how kinship can be used to form groups, we can picture a hypothetical early human population seeking to utilize an area's natural resources in an organized way. There is no government and no mechanism to regulate who gets to use which resources when. Nor are there rules regulating who gets to live where, so these humans are engaged in a struggle to establish occupancy of land and use of resources. They do, however, recognize kinship links among themselves; many are related to one another in some way, and many others are not. Figure 1.7 shows a fraction of this population of humans, along with the kinship relations that they acknowledge.

These people have kinship but, as yet, no groups based on kinship or, for that matter, on anything else. Now let's assume that one woman, Z, in the figure forms a group with herself as its point of reference. She calls together all of the people related to her by any kinship connection (her siblings, cousins, nephews, nieces, and so on). She then stakes a claim to a section of land and a set of resources and establishes the right of members of her group to occupy the land and use the resources. A problem would immediately arise here whenever another person (for example, the man R in Figure 1.7) tries to implement the same strategy. There is no mechanism to regulate who can or should be the central node of a group; even if only a few people try to set themselves up as central nodes, many others will eventually find that they are potential members of two or more groups. Which group, for example, should the man F join, that of Z or that of R, given that he is equally related to both? In fact, this early human population could never form discrete groups on the basis of ego-centered kin groups, or kindreds, since membership in these groups would always be overlapping. And even if, say, Z managed to pull together a group for a while, it would collapse upon her death and the next generation would have to start all over again.

FIGURE 1.7   Kinship Connections in a Hypothetical Early Human Population

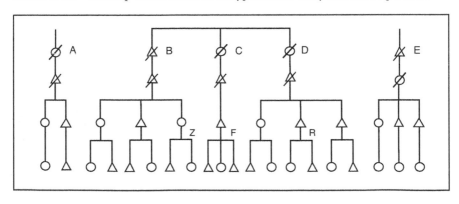

But there is another possibility: the formation of groups on the basis of ancestors rather than living persons. The woman Z could pick her grandfather, B, and establish a group consisting of all the descendants of B. This way will work. The population could now have stable, discrete groups based on descent, as illustrated in Figure 1.8. Everybody now knows to which group he or she belongs, and the groups themselves can persist through generations yet unborn. Even F knows with which group to affiliate; he is a member of the group that traces descent from the ancestor C. In short, these humans now have stable, ongoing descent groups.[3] The descent groups are now able to stake territorial and other claims, and to transmit these claims or rights to their descendants. This hypothetical example demonstrates how the notion of descent from a common ancestor can be used to form stable human groups that persist over time (Keesing 1975: 17). In fact, most of the societies we will be examining in this book use descent as the basis for forming important groups.

The tracing of descent from a common ancestor is found in many, though not all, human societies. And among societies that do trace this descent, not all base the formation of groups on descent from a common ancestor. Still, all societies reckon descent in some way or another, whether or not they make use of common ancestors or the kin groups traced from them. Basically, there are three modes of descent in human societies.

1. Cognatic descent, which is based on links through both men and women.
2. Patrilineal descent (also called agnatic descent), which is based on links through males only.
3. Matrilineal descent (also called uterine descent), which is based on links through females only.

FIGURE 1.8   The Formation of Descent Groups from Common Ancestors

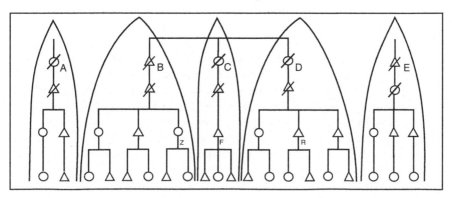

Cognatic descent is the mode that the woman Z used to form her descent group and that the other groups of the population later adopted. Euro-Americans also tend to conceptualize descent as traceable through males and females; however, the term *cognatic* is best reserved for societies that actually use this mode of descent to form groups. Most Euro-American societies do not use descent to form groups. In America, for example, people are not divided up or organized according to their membership in descent groups, although many Americans individually recognize their ancestors and consider that they are descended from them. In this book the term *bilateral society* refers to a society that traces kin connections over the generations through both males and females, *but without the formation of descent groups.*

Cognatic societies are further discussed in Chapter 5, and the Euro-American system and its history are covered in Chapter 7. Patrilineal and matrilineal descent are cases of *unilineal* descent, traced through only one sex. Examples of both are provided in Chapters 3 and 4. There is also a fourth mode, called double descent. This is a very rare form and is covered in Chapter 5.

Labeling two or more societies patrilineal, matrilineal, or cognatic does not indicate that they necessarily have much in common aside from mode of descent. Indeed, these modes are employed in different ways and to different ends by the groups that use them. In later chapters we will see how modes of descent are interwoven with gender in different ways. Chapters 3 and 4 reveal specifically how patrilineal and matrilineal descent work and how discrete groups are formed using a rule of unilineal descent. But here we need to discuss the idea of descent groups a bit further.

With reference to kinship, Roger Keesing (1975: 9–11) drew attention to the distinctions among category, group, and corporate group. The term *category* refers to things that are classed together. All the items included in a particular category have something in common. Thus "opera lovers of San Francisco" refers to all those people who share (1) a love of opera and (2) residence in San Francisco. This is a category of people, but it is not a group. Those included in the category may never meet; they need not even know of one another's existence. But suppose there is a real organization, called Opera Lovers of San Francisco, that consists of actual members who meet every year or so to discuss and celebrate opera. This organization would be considered a group. A social group refers to human beings who not only have something in common but regularly interact with one another. Now suppose that the people in this group decided to collect dues from members, set up a common treasury, and use the money to provide fellowships for young, gifted people to study opera. The people of this group now own something in common, the money in their treasury. We would consider them a corporate group; their organization is a corporation. Should the organization then purchase property—say, an opera house—it becomes even more strongly corporate. When the organization must pay taxes or when it is sued by an individual, its members become very aware of their corporate existence. A corporate group, then, is a group of persons who collectively share rights (usually rights to some property or resource), privileges, and liabilities.

In the context of the societies discussed in this book, we will encounter kinship categories, kinship groups, and kinship corporations, so it is important to keep these distinctions among category, group, and corporation in mind. Societies have a way of reckoning descent; hence, they can construct descent categories, such as "all the descendants of ancestor X." But not all societies form real groups on this basis. And within those that do, the groups so formed may or may not be actual corporate groups.

In many societies, corporate groups are formed on the basis of descent. Corporate descent groups operate very much like businesses or other kinds of corporations in society, and they may be very powerful in terms of regulating the lives of their members. They may not only hold corporate property or assets but may also function as political units and as religious cults. Like all corporations, they are, legally speaking, single entities and can persist despite the loss of individual members.

We saw earlier that society in the United States is not organized on the basis of descent groups. Yet it would be possible for a particular set of kin to establish themselves as a descent group within this society. For example, if one set of kin decides that all the descendants of some common ancestor will regularly meet once a year to honor this person, we would have to say that this is a descent group. We could even say that some prominent American families, such as the Rockefellers, whose members collectively own property or share some rights on the basis of descent, are corporate descent groups. But apart from these exceptions, descent groups are not relevant to American social organization.

Residence

In any society, descent needs to be considered in conjunction with residence patterns, since the physical closeness of people related by descent has a lot to do with the strength of the ties between them. There are many different possibilities. For example, the people of one descent group may all live in the same area. If this is the case, they are likely to be quite a solid group. Alternatively, the descent group may have grown too large, prompting some subgroups to move elsewhere. Over time, migrations of this sort may result in descent groups that are highly dispersed. Two possible outcomes are shown in Figure 1.9. (For additional variations, see Keesing 1975: 39–43.) The two descent groups at the top of the figure are localized. As they grow and expand over time, their members continue to reside adjacent to one another. By contrast, the three descent groups at the bottom are dispersed. As time passes, the various branches of each group split up geographically, such that each residence area eventually contains members of different descent groups.

Whatever the outcome, the combination of descent and residence patterns affects the texture of life in communities. In many cases, people's ties to and identification with a locality may be as strong and as important as their ties of descent. For example, among the Nuer people (see Case 2 in Chapter 3), villages consisted of members of different descent groups. Each village was itself a corporate group, owning common rights to the use of certain resources. Among these people, loyalty to one's descent group was strong, but so was loyalty to one's village.

FIGURE 1.9   Localized and Dispersed Descent Groups

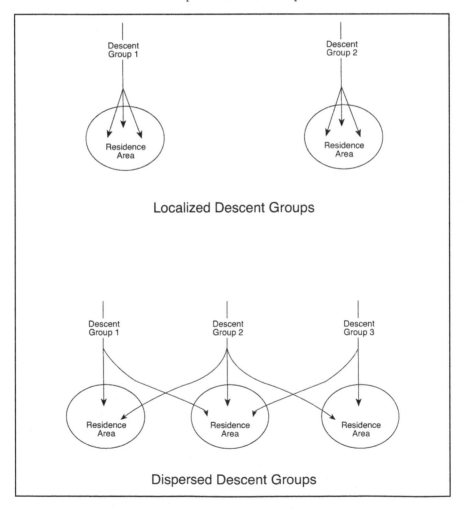

Residence is also important in terms of how it affects the structure of a domestic group, which consists of people who live together and share resources for their subsistence. Here we need to consider types of postmarital residence. All societies have conventions or norms specifying where or with whom couples should live after marriage. The standard postmarital residence patterns are as follows:

1. Patrilocal (also called virilocal), whereby a married couple lives with or near the groom's kin.
2. Matrilocal (also called uxorilocal), whereby a married couple lives with or near the bride's kin.
3. Ambilocal, whereby a married couple can choose to live with or near the kin of either the groom or the bride.
4. Neolocal, whereby a married couple moves to a new household or location, living neither with kin of the groom nor the bride.
5. Natolocal, whereby a wife and husband remain with their own natal kin and do not live together.
6. Avunculocal, whereby a married couple moves to or near the residence of the groom's mother's brother(s).

A given society may have one dominant mode of postmarital residence but will at the same time show exceptions to it. For example, a society may be largely patrilocal, but some couples may live matrilocally or neolocally under certain circumstances at different times in their lives. In the United States different types of postmarital residence are possible, but the norm, and the ideal, is neolocal residence. Avunculocal residence may seem a bit curious, but its significance will become clear in Chapter 4 when we examine matrilineal descent.

Domestic Cycles

Whatever the norms of residence, domestic groups or households are never static; they change composition over time as new members are born or recruited and as other individuals marry, die, or disperse. All domestic groups are best seen as in flux. To capture this dynamic nature of domestic groups, Meyer Fortes (1949, 1958) developed the concept of the domestic cycle. As individuals go through their "life cycles"—marked by stages such as birth, puberty, marriage, reproduction, and death—so too will domestic groups in all societies show cyclical development as they move through different stages of family reproduction, or phases of establishment, growth, and decline. Thus at any one time within a society, there will be various forms or types of households because the households are at different stages in a general domestic cycle pertaining to that society.

In the United States, a new household will typically start with the marriage of a couple; it then expands with the birth of children, later shrinks down with the dispersal of these children during adulthood, and finally ends with the death of the founding couple. Variations and additional fluctuations may be brought about by divorce and remarriage, but the overall pattern of the establishment of new households at marriage in each generation remains. Throughout much of patrilineal/patrilocal South Asia, by contrast, one household may endure over many generations and the flow of people in and out of households is quite different. A married couple reproduces; their daughters will disperse out and brides of their sons will move in. The domestic group at some point may become quite large as brothers born into it stay together and each produces additional offspring. Theoretically, this could go on for generations (and this is the cultural ideal in many areas), but typically the household will split with the death of the oldest senior male (usually a grandparent to the resident children), with most or all of the remaining married couples moving out with their dependent offspring, setting up new households and starting the cycle over again.

The concept of domestic cycles has been applied very usefully to cross-cultural studies of family systems (Harrell 1997) and studies of the social organization of human reproduction (Robertson 1991). Different domestic cycle patterns found around the world can be studied in relation to political and economic factors, the use of human and natural resources for subsistence, the transmission of property, and other cultural and historical factors. The domestic cycle of the so-called stem family pattern, for example, can be seen in relation to particular economic interests. This pattern once existed (and sometimes still does) in particular rural farming areas of Europe and Japan. In these areas, the household operated as an economic unit, and farmland had to be kept at a certain size to remain viable. Fragmentation of household farmland was seen as economically disastrous. In this pattern, only one son (or if there were no sons, a daughter) married and inherited the land. He and his wife then lived with his parents, cared for them in old age, gradually took over the farm, and raised children of their own. This heir's siblings all moved out and sought their livelihood in some other way, usually with some initial financial contribution from the stem household. This system, although often challenging for the nonheirs, kept the farmland intact and prevented its continual fragmentation, as would have occurred if all children or all sons inherited separate plots.

Marriage

Aside from relations based on descent, kinship concerns affinal relationships, or relationships established through marriage. Marriage is found in some form or other in all societies, and it is widely (though not universally) associated with the legitimization and allocation of children. Yet there is great diversity among institutions of marriage, and among the ways in which marriage both reflects and influences gender. There are three basic marriage forms: (1) monogamy, or marriage between two persons, generally a man and a woman; (2) polygyny, or marriage of a man to two or more women at the same time; and (3) polyandry, or marriage of a woman to two or more men at the same time. On a world scale, monogamy is the most common form of marriage. Even within societies that permit polygyny, most marital unions are monogamous. Polyandry is the rarest form.

With regard to marriage, two other important terms are *exogamy* and *endogamy*. Exogamy refers to the rule whereby persons must marry outside a certain social category or group. In many societies, descent groups are exogamous. Another example would be a society that imposed a rule of village exogamy. In this case, all persons of one village would be prohibited from marrying within it and would have to find spouses from other villages. Conversely, endogamy refers to the rule whereby persons must marry within a certain social category or group. For example, societies that are stratified by caste usually have rules prescribing caste endogamy, or marriage within the caste. In the United States, there are no exogamy or endogamy rules as such. But some states prohibit marriages within a certain range of kin (for example, between first cousins), thus imposing a kind of kindred exogamy. And although there is no rule, we do see a norm of class and ethnic-group endogamy in the United States.

As we will see in the next chapter, exogamy (specifically descent-group exogamy) is not just a common marriage rule or practice but is also important to the evolutionary origins of human kinship. It is widely believed that our human ancestors "invented" exogamy as a way of promoting peaceful relationships between groups and avoiding conflict. Descent-group exogamy forces the group to depend on other groups for marriage partners. Intermarriage between or among different local groups may have indeed prevented these groups from hostile, fatal encounters. There is little doubt that descent-group endogamy, which is practiced among some people today, came later in human history. It probably emerged in some contexts as a means of keeping wealth within a descent group (see Chapter 6).

KINSHIP THEORY

Anthropologists have been researching and analyzing kinship and marriage around the world for over a century. For many of these decades, kinship was at the core of anthropology, reflecting the major theoretical currents in the field. Then interest in kinship waned for about a twenty-year period covering the 1970s and 1980s. Beginning in the 1990s, kinship study saw a revival and it has been gaining momentum ever since. This contemporary study of kinship is quite different from that of earlier times. Taking just the period from the mid-twentieth century to the present, there have been, among many changes, three major shifts.

1. From Social Structure to Culture

Anthropologists once saw kinship as important primarily because it was understood to constitute social structure; kinship was seen to play a fundamental role in the formation of many societies' social groups and was as well a key to many peoples' political, economic, and religious organizations. By the mid-twentieth century, anthropological models of kinship systems in relation to social structure had become quite complex; the field was highly technical, and its concepts a bit static and rigid. Anthropologists debated how particular kinship systems worked, or the function of certain widespread features of kinship systems. They argued over whether relationships based on descent or relationships formed through marital alliances were more fundamental to social organization.

Meanwhile field research was showing that there was often a less-than-perfect fit between anthropologists' abstractions about kinship and the way that local people themselves were conceptualizing and using their own kinship systems. Some felt it was almost as though anthropologists had become so fixated on systems, definitions, and diagrams that they had lost sight of the real people experiencing their own systems of kinship. This helped to bring about a shift of focus. The question moved somewhat away from "How do kinship systems organize societies?" (a question of social structure) and toward "What does kinship mean to people in different cultures?" and "How do individuals use their own cultural understandings of kinship, and to what ends?" (questions of culture). All this is not to say that an interest in kinship in relation to social structure has disappeared. It is rather that understanding the connection of kinship with social structure has been modified considerably by greater attention to the internal cultural meanings of kinship.

2. Back and Forth with Biology

To what extent should "kinship" relations be understood to involve biological relationships between people? Is kinship everywhere inseparable from human procreation? These questions have been fundamental to debates within the field and, as discussed earlier with gender, the study of kinship has seen a tense and unsettled relationship with biology that continues to this day. In the nineteenth and early twentieth centuries, anthropologists very much saw kinship relationships as connected with acts of birth and human understandings of procreation. The idea was that people are linked together through biological ties that form the basis of their kinship systems, and this appeared to some to be a human universal. These scholars recognized, of course, that not every kinship tie was necessarily a true biological (genetic) link. All societies also had, in this view, what came to be known as "social kinship," relationships formed, for example, through adoption. Still, behind all of this, in the view of these anthropologists, was the notion that all societies recognized genealogical links among their members and these either were presumed to be true biological links or were "as-if" kin links that, for all practical purposes, amounted to the same thing. Behind social kinship was, in any case, the idea of links formed through acts of birth, or procreation. Social kinship was modeled on ideas of biological kinship.

By the 1970s this view of kinship was severely challenged, most notably by David Schneider (1984). Schneider charged that what anthropologists understood as "kinship" did not necessarily exist cross-culturally. He said that anthropologists had been following a Euro-American notion of kinship as based on or modeled on presumed biological connections between people. Other people, however, may base their own ideas of their own connections on common residence, feeding, and nurturing or on the performance of certain rituals. Schneider went so far as to pronounce that "kinship," as conceived by anthropologists, was not a tenable or valid cross-cultural category. Many agreed and, with that pronouncement, kinship studies suffered a twenty-year decline.

The study of kinship was kept alive and later revived in part through feminist anthropology, and it is here that we see a growing interest in connecting kinship with gender. Feminist anthropologists of this period sought to study kinship/gender in each culture separately to understand how notions of relatedness, sexual difference, and gender are culturally constructed from within (Yanagisako and Collier 1987). The result was a richer ethnography of both kinship and gender in different cultures.

When kinship began to revive in the 1990s, no one any longer blindly assumed that what might look to an outsider as biological or genealogical "kinship" in a given society is locally understood to be (or even modeled on) biological relatedness, and this approach has continued to the present time. The emphasis on uncovering local conceptions of human relationships, whatever those may be, has continued. Nowadays a locally perceived notion of biological relatedness is understood to be just one of a number of possible bases for local "kinship" constructions, although it is the most common basis worldwide.

And yet, even with the sharp severing of kinship and biology in anthropological kinship studies, biology did not go away; indeed, in some respects biology is now seeing a revival with respect to the study of kinship. First, one current approach is to see human biology not just as one common basis for local kinship constructions but as, evolutionarily speaking, a force behind the construction of kinship in the first place. In this view, humans have

evolved a propensity to construct kinship to enhance their survival and reproduction. In other words, human evolutionary biology is seen to lie behind
the cultural construction of kinship. A kind of "capacity for kinship" then
becomes comparable to the human capacity for language. In this light certain
patterns in human kinship systems are analyzed in relation to, for example,
mating strategies and reproductive success. Second, growing evidence shows
that a variety of nonhuman primates exhibit many of the basics of humanlike
kinship systems. This finding supports the idea that human kinship is a part
of our primate heritage and that it is best understood in relation to primate
and human evolution. Both of these issues will be covered in Chapter 2.

3. Kinship as Process

By the 1980s most anthropologists came to agree that among many people
and in many different cultural contexts, "kin" were often made, not born.
This realization opened the way for another shift in kinship studies, one that
sees kin relations as not necessarily established once and for all (for example,
through acts of birth) but as processual, as established or maintained over
time through various actions. The work of Janet Carsten (1995), for instance,
shows how among Malays on the island of Langkawi, people are not born
once and for all into kinship positions, but rather kinship emerges over time
through acts of receiving and giving food and through sharing of hearth space.
These actions can create "kinship" between people who are not considered
biological kin. In turn, if these acts are discontinued, even among biologically
related people, the sense of "kinship" between them is likewise seen to lapse.
With the work of Carsten and many others on relatedness as process, kinship
is now seen as more fluid and dynamic than previously assumed.

KINSHIP AND GENDER

With this brief introduction to kinship we have covered the distinction between consanguineal and affinal kin, the idea of an individual's kindred, and
the concept of descent from ancestors as a basis for forming groups. We have
also noted the importance of residence, as well as the various forms of postmarital residence and marriage. All of these dimensions of kinship combine
in different ways in different societies and influence social structure to varying
degrees. The same dimensions of kinship are also interwoven with gender relationships. But before delving into the subject of human societies and cultures, we must address some more basic questions: How did the recognition
of kinship come about? When, where, and with what consequences did humans first come to think of one another as kin or nonkin? To what extent
do our primate cousins "recognize" one another as kin or nonkin? When
and why did human groups first begin to use kinship to form groups, or first

begin to "invent" marriage and follow residence rules? And what can the study of the evolution of human kinship tell us about human gender? Not all of these questions can be precisely answered, but the next chapter presents what we know so far.

DISCUSSION QUESTIONS

1. What is your own position on the question of whether women are universally subordinate to men? What evidence or reasoning lies behind your position?

2. Using the Kinship Code and yourself as "ego," construct a kinship chart showing your relatives over as many generations as possible. Compare your chart to those of other students. Do you see any patterns over the generations? For example, many students' genealogies may show that over the generations, cases of divorce and remarriage increase. Do you find other patterns? Discuss what might account for the patterns you find.

3. What examples of nonbiologically based kinship do you find in your own society? Do you think these types of kinship bonds are as strong as biologically based ones?

SUGGESTED FURTHER READING

Fox, Robin. 1980 [orig. 1967]. *Kinship and Marriage: An Anthropological Perspective*. Cambridge, England: Cambridge University Press. This is the classic kinship text. Although now an older work, it remains amazingly current in terms of basic definitions and concepts. It is highly entertaining and user-friendly.

Parkin, Robert. 1997. *Kinship: An Introduction to the Basic Concepts*. Oxford, England: Blackwell. Covers basic terms, provides a good history of the topic, and discusses ethnographic examples.

Pasternak, Burton, Carol R. Ember, and Melvin Ember. 1996. *Sex, Gender and Kinship: A Cross-Cultural Perspective*. Upper Saddle River, NJ: Prentice Hall. This text does not provide much coverage of kinship, but it is an excellent introduction to the anthropology of sex, gender, marriage, and the family.

Strathern, Andrew, and Pamela J. Stewart. 2011. *Kinship in Action: Self and Group*. Upper Saddle River, NJ: Prentice Hall. This text provides an introduction to the field by focusing on kinship as social process.

SUGGESTED CLASSROOM MEDIA

The Yucatec Maya: A Case Study in Marriage and the Family. 1983. KOCE-TV (Television station: Huntington Beach, CA); produced by Coast Community College in cooperation with Holt, Rinehart, and Winston. Faces of Culture (series) No. 10. Thirty minutes. This video follows the lives of members of an extended family among the Maya of the Yucatan region of Mexico. Close family relationships are important in the operation of slash-and-burn horticulture. The video shows how this family responds to new forces of change affecting its community. The importance of kinship and family to these Mayan people and the connection between kinship and the local economy is well portrayed.

Kinship and Descent. Pt. 1. 1983. KOCE-TV (Television station: Huntington Beach, CA); produced by Coast Community College in cooperation with Holt, Rinehart, and Winston. Faces of Culture (series) No. 11. Thirty minutes. This program gives a good introduction to the basics of kinship and descent. It contrasts kinship/descent in the United States with that of the matrilineal Trobriand Islanders.

WEBSITES

www.ancestry.com/default.aspx. For students wishing to search their own genealogies online, Ancestry.com is a good place to start. Some searches through this source may require a paid subscription.

www.as.ua.edu/ant/Faculty/murphy/436/kinship.htm. *A Kinship Glossary: Symbols, Terms, and Concepts.* Department of Anthropology, University of Alabama. This site provides a useful and comprehensive glossary of terms used in the study of kinship.

NOTES

1. It was once common to distinguish "gender," understood as a cultural construct that varied from culture to culture, from "sex," or the biological facts of life, presumed to be the same everywhere (Oakley 1972). But some scholars have more recently suggested that different cultures have different ways of constructing sex as well as gender (Laqueur 1990) and that this variation must be taken into account in the study of gender. For this reason, Yanagisako and Collier (1990) suggest that the distinction between sex and gender should not be maintained.

2. Yanagisako and Collier (1987) build upon the earlier work of David Schneider (1984) in kinship. Schneider argued that anthropologists influenced by Western culture perceive kinship in terms of biological or biogenetic relationships, but that such relationships cannot be assumed to apply to other cultures in the same way or to the same extent. Collier and Yanagisako direct a similar critique against the concept of gender. For a critique of their position, see Scheffler (1991).

3. Strictly speaking, this way of forming descent groups would not necessarily produce discrete, nonoverlapping groups. For example, if members of any of these descent groups intermarry, their children would be members of two groups at once. This matter will be taken up in Chapter 5.

REFERENCES

Bederman, Gail. 1995. *Manliness and Civilization: A Cultural History of Gender and Race in the United States, 1880–1917*. Chicago: University of Chicago Press.

Bordo, Susan. 1997. The Body and Reproduction of Femininity. In Katie Conboy, Nadia Medina, and Sarah Stanbury, eds., *Writing on the Body: Female Embodiment and Feminist Theory*, pp. 90–110. New York: Columbia University Press.

Browner, C. H., and Sondra T. Perdue. 1988. Women's Secrets: Bases for Reproductive and Social Autonomy in a Mexican Community. *American Ethnologist* 15(1): 84–97.

Buss, David. 1994. *The Evolution of Desire: Strategies of Human Mating*. New York: Basic Books.

Carsten, Janet. 1995. The Substance of Kinship and the Heat of the Hearth: Feeding, Personhood, and Relatedness Among Malays in Pulau Langkawi. *American Ethnologist* 22: 223–241.

Delaney, Carol. 1991. *The Seed and the Soil: Gender and Cosmology in Turkish Village Society*. Berkeley: University of California Press.

di Leonardo, Micaela. 1991. Gender, Culture and Political Economy: Feminist Anthropology in Historical Perspective. In Micaela di Leonardo, ed., *Gender at the Crossroads of Knowledge: Feminist Anthropology in the Postmodern Era*, pp. 1–48. Berkeley: University of California Press.

Fortes, Meyer. 1949. Time and Social Structure: An Ashanti Case Study. In Meyer Fortes, ed., *Social Structure: Studies Presented to A. R. Radcliffe-Brown*. Oxford, England: Clarendon Press.

———. 1958. Introduction. In Jack Goody, ed., *The Developmental Cycle in Domestic Groups*. Cambridge, England: Cambridge University Press.

Ginsburg, Faye D., and Rayna Rapp. 1995. Introduction: Conceiving the New World Order. In Faye D. Ginsburg and Rayna Rapp, eds., *Conceiving the New World Order: The Global Politics of Reproduction*, pp. 1–17. Berkeley: University of California Press.

Harrell, Stevan. 1997. *Human Families*. Boulder, CO: Westview Press.

Herzfeld, Michael. 2007. Global Kinship: Anthropology and the Politics of Knowing. *Anthropological Quarterly* 80(2): 313–323.

Keesing, Roger M. 1975. *Kin Groups and Social Structure*. Fort Worth, TX: Holt, Rinehart, and Winston.

Kimmel, Michael S. 1996. *Manhood in America: A Cultural History*. New York: Free Press.

Laderman, Carol. 1983. *Wives and Midwives: Childbirth and Nutrition in Rural Malaysia*. Berkeley: University of California Press.

———. 1991. *Taming the Wind of Desire: Psychology, Medicine, and Aesthetics in Malay Shamanistic Performance*. Berkeley: University of California Press.

Lamphere, Louise. 1993. The Domestic Sphere of Women and the Public World of Men: The Strengths and Limitations of an Anthropological Dichotomy. In Caroline B. Brettell and Carolyn F. Sargent, eds., *Gender in Cross-Cultural Perspective*, pp. 67–77. Englewood Cliffs, NJ: Prentice Hall.

Lamphere, Louise, Helena Ragoné, and Patricia Zavella. 1997. Introduction. In Louise Lamphere, Helena Ragoné, and Patricia Zavella, eds., *Situated Lives: Gender and Culture in Everyday Life*, pp. 1–19. New York: Routledge.

Laqueur, Thomas. 1990. *Making Sex: Body and Gender from the Greeks to Freud.* Cambridge, MA: Harvard University Press.

Low, Bobbie S. 2005. Women's Lives There, Here, Then, and Now: A Review of Women's Ecological and Demographic Constraints Cross-Culturally. *Evolution and Human Behavior* 26: 64–87.

MacIntyre, Matthew H. 2009. The Early Development of Gender Differences. *Annual Review of Anthropology* 38: 83–97.

McKee, Nancy P., and Linda Stone. 2007. *Gender and Culture in America*, 3rd ed. Cornwall-on-Hudson, NY: Sloan Publishing.

Miller, Barbara Diane. 1993. The Anthropology of Sex and Gender Hierarchies. In Barbara Diane Miller, ed., *Sex and Gender Hierarchies*, pp. 3–31. Cambridge, England: Cambridge University Press.

Moen, Elizabeth W. 1979. What Does "Control over Our Bodies" Really Mean? *International Journal of Women's Studies* 2(2): 129–143.

Oakley, Ann. 1972. *Sex, Gender, and Society.* New York: Harper & Row.

Reischer, Erica, and Katheryn S. Koo. 2004. The Body Beautiful: Symbolism and Agency in the Social World. *Annual Review of Anthropology* 23: 297–317.

Robertson, A. F. 1991. *Beyond the Family: The Social Organization of Human Reproduction.* Berkeley: University of California Press.

Rosaldo, Michele Z. 1974. Woman, Culture, and Society: A Theoretical Overview. In Michele Z. Rosaldo and Louise Lamphere, eds., *Woman, Culture, and Society*, pp. 17–42. Stanford, CA: Stanford University Press.

———. 1980. The Use and Abuse of Anthropology: Reflections of Feminism and Cross-Cultural Understanding. *Signs: Journal of Women in Culture and Society* 5(3): 389–417.

Rossi, Alice. 1985. *Gender and the Life Course.* New York: Aldine.

Rothman, Barbara Katz. 1987. Reproduction. In Beth B. Hess and Myra Marx Ferree, eds., *Analyzing Gender: A Handbook of Social Science Research*, pp. 154–170. Newbury Park, CA: Sage Publications.

Scheffler, Harold. 1991. Sexism and Naturalism in the Study of Kinship. In Micaela di Leonardo, ed., *Gender at the Crossroads of Knowledge: Feminist Anthropology in the Postmodern Era*, pp. 361–382. Berkeley: University of California Press.

Schneider, David M. 1968. *American Kinship: A Cultural Account.* Englewood Cliffs, NJ: Prentice Hall.

———. 1984. *A Critique of the Study of Kinship.* Ann Arbor: University of Michigan Press.

Smuts, Barbara B. 1995. The Evolutionary Origins of Patriarchy. *Human Nature* 6(1): 1–32.

Tang-Martinez, Zuleyma. 1997. *The Curious Courtship of Sociobiology and Feminism: A Case of Irreconcilable Differences.* In Patricia Adair Gotway, ed., *Feminism and Evolutionary Biology: Boundaries, Intersections and Frontiers*, pp. 116–150. New York: Chapman and Hall.

Yanagisako, Sylvia Junko, and Jane Fishburne Collier. 1987. Toward a Unified Analysis of Gender and Kinship. In Jane Fishburne Collier and Sylvia Junko Yanagisako, eds., *Gender and Kinship: Essays Toward a Unified Analysis*, pp. 14–50. Stanford, CA: Stanford University Press.

———. 1990. The Mode of Reproduction in Anthropology. In Deborah L. Rhode, ed., *Theoretical Perspectives on Sexual Difference*, pp. 131–141. New Haven, CT: Yale University Press.

2

THE EVOLUTION OF KINSHIP AND GENDER

In this chapter we briefly depart from human society to enter the world of the nonhuman primates. How much of what we see in human kinship systems is really unique to our species? After exploring kinship and gender among nonhuman primates, we will consider some ideas on the evolution of kinship, and the implications for gender, in humans.

Primates are a natural grouping (an order) of mammals that include prosimians (that is, tree-dwelling animals such as lemurs and tarsiers), monkeys, apes, and humans. Some of the physical characteristics that distinguish primates from other mammals are binocular vision and the grasping hand with mobile digits and flat nails. Evolutionary trends characteristic of the primate order and most pronounced in humans also include lengthening of gestation of the fetus, prolongation of the period of infant care, and expansion and elaboration of the brain.

Some primates—for example, gibbons and many prosimians—live in "monogamous" units. Others, such as gelada baboons, live and mate "polygynously" in units consisting of one adult male and several females. Still others, including chimpanzees, live in multimale, multifemale units where mating is largely promiscuous. There are even cases of "polyandrous" primates, such as the saddle-backed tamarins in South America, where two to four males stay and copulate with one female. Nonhuman primates also show different dispersal patterns that resemble human patterns of postmarital residence (as reviewed in Chapter 1), although the human patterns are more varied. In most nonhuman primate species females stay put and males typically disperse out at maturity to join and breed within other groups. But in some species (for example, chimpanzees), females disperse and in still others (for example, gibbons and orangutans) both females and males disperse at maturity. These dispersal patterns are important because they determine what types of kin are left within local groups.

A significant feature in the social life of many nonhuman primates is dominance and the formation of dominance hierarchies. Primatologists consider a "dominant" animal to be the one who usually wins in an aggressive encounter with another (Silk 1993). Very often (but not always) the dominant animal will have greater access to resources such as food, water, or sexual partners. In some primate groups the dominance hierarchy is fairly clear-cut; in others it is difficult to discern or varies considerably by context. And at any one time dominance relationships may be in flux. Also noteworthy is that there are egalitarian primate species, such as the muriqui monkeys, with no dominance hierarchies (Strier 1992).

Nonhuman primates are fascinating in their own right, but many researchers study them primarily to gain perspectives on human behavior and evolution. In this respect certain trends in the study of primates are important to bear in mind. First, research has shown that nonhuman primates are far more intelligent and skilled, and live in vastly more complicated social orders, than was previously supposed. Not so long ago, particular adaptations, such as tool manufacture and use, food sharing, and cooperative hunting, were believed to be uniquely human. Then came Jane Goodall's (1988) reports of chimps in Tanzania's Gombe National Park that were modifying and using twigs to extract termites and using leaves as sponges to soak up water for drinking. Other reports from the Taï forest (Ivory Coast) showed chimps using wooden clogs and stone hammers to crack open nuts (Boesch and Boesch 1990). Goodall also observed food sharing among Gombe chimps: Not only do mothers share food with infants, but adults share meat with one another, especially males with males (Goodall 1986: 374). Moreover, forms of cooperative hunting were observed among the chimps of Gombe, where a few females hunt along with the males (Goodall 1986: 286). Year-round sexual receptivity was long thought to be unique to human females, but research now reveals that certain nonhuman female primates can and do mate outside their estrous periods. Young female bonobo chimpanzees (a species closely related to the common chimpanzee) are almost continually receptive (Kano 1992: 154). In addition to these findings came the startling discoveries about the vocal communicative abilities of wild chimps and the learning of human sign language among captive chimps. And today scholars are even discussing how the evolutionary roots of human morality are expressed in primates (de Waal 2006).

Second, in the past, humans were often directly compared with only one or a few major primate species. For example, some types of baboons (such as hamadryas baboons and savannah baboons) were once favored for comparison because, like our ancestors, they left the trees during their evolution and made adaptations to open country. Research later focused on chimpanzees in comparison with humans, since analyses of chromosomes, blood proteins, and DNA confirm that chimps are our closest evolutionary "cousins." By these measures, humans and chimps are evolutionarily more closely related than chimps and gorillas. Although comparisons between chimpanzees and humans are still popular, human behavior is currently often analyzed in relation to the whole spectrum of primate behavior and social organization. Only such broad comparisons among many species can allow researchers to distinguish the effects of ecological pressures from the effects of close common ancestry in bringing about similar behaviors among human and nonhuman primates (Strier 2002).

A third trend in recent decades has been the recognition of a far greater behavioral diversity among and within primate species than was previously presumed. For example, studies of the bonobo chimpanzees in the Democratic Republic of Congo (formerly Zaïre) show important contrasts with common chimpanzees, such as those of the Gombe National Park in Tanzania. In terms of mating behaviors, wild bonobo chimpanzees not only copulate more frequently but also engage in ventro-ventral copulation, in contrast to the ventro-dorsal copulation seen among common chimpanzees (Kano 1992: 140). Male dominance over females, evident among common chimpanzees, is not expressed among bonobos (Kano 1992; de Waal 2002). And most notably the bonobos—now famous as the "make love, not war" primates—use sexual behavior (including homosexual behavior) as a mechanism to curtail aggression and reduce social tension (de Waal 2002).

Finally, primate observers are now able to precisely determine genetic relationships among individuals. Previously it was hard to tell, beyond mother-child and maternal sibling connections, which animals were related and in what ways. Particularly among primate groups where mating is promiscuous, one could not tell who the father was or who was related to whom through the father. Then one study at Gombe devised a handy technique for discovering genetic connections within chimpanzee groups by collecting hair samples for DNA analysis from the abandoned sleeping nests of chimps (Morin et al. 1994). These and similar noninvasive techniques of collecting DNA samples have considerably enhanced the study of primate kinship and have allowed for the testing of many hypotheses about primate behavior (Morin and Goldberg 2004; Woodruff 2004).

KIN RECOGNITION

Kin recognition is known to be widespread among insects, birds, and mammals. In many species, behavior toward kin is markedly different from that toward nonkin. Thus, for example, mole rat aunts will care for nieces and nephews but not for nonrelated young, and Japanese quails show a clear preference for mating with first cousins (Wilson 1987). And in the case of the desert isopod, an insect who lives in burrows in nuclear family units but wanders about outside for food, any family member will drive out a non-family stranger who comes to the burrow embankment (Linsenmair 1987).

Nonhuman primates, too, are known to be able to recognize close kin. There is evidence that some primates are able to recognize not only their own kin but also those of others as well. This trait has been observed among baboons, for example (Smuts 1985). And among pigtailed macaques, nonrelated individuals in aggressive encounters later "reconcile" not just with each other but also with each other's close kin (Judge 1983). In one interesting experiment with vervet monkeys, researchers played tape-recorded vocalizations of infants' calls to their mothers from a hidden speaker. Not only did individual mothers recognize their own infants' voices—as evidenced by the fact that they looked directly at the source of the call—but other nearby females looked directly at a particular mother when her own infant's calls were being played (Cheney and Seyfarth 1980). Subsequent studies have confirmed this ability to recognize one another's kin among other primate species (Cheney and Seyfarth 2004).

Other behaviors in primates suggest additional expressions of kin recognition. One is incest avoidance, which will be discussed later. Another is that among some primate species, when groups grow too large, they tend to split up along lines of kinship, specifically matrilineal segments (Chapais 2008: 278–279). In species such as rhesus monkeys, in which males emigrate to join other groups, related males sometimes leave together, joining the same new group; males also tend to transfer to new groups into which a male relative has previously immigrated (Gouzoules and Gouzoules 1987: 302). There is also the adoption of orphaned infants by older female siblings, as observed among Gombe chimps (Goodall 1986: 101) and other primate species.

Nonhuman primates recognize their kin, but how exactly do they do so? Regrettably, this is not known, and as yet we have no way to probe into their consciousness. But with primates we know that something more than the innate mechanisms of mole rats and desert isopods is involved. Some research suggests the possible existence of recognition mechanisms based on phenotypic matching, that is, visual or olfactory recognition of "family resemblances."[1] Another, and more certain, possibility is an association mechanism whereby an infant primate simply grows up forming a definite recognition of and a close bond with the mother, and gradually learns to distinguish, or classify, others on the basis of their interaction with the mother and him- or herself (Bernstein 1991; Silk 2001). The implication is that what exists inside the minds of primates are not "categories of kinship" as such but various learned "categories of association."

Let us assume, then, that primate kin recognition develops through association mechanisms focused on the mother. For most primates paternal kin will not be recognized, at least not through an association mechanism, since

IMAGE 2.1 Chimpanzee kin.

Drawing by Andrew S. Arconti, author's collection.

among them there are not close associations of fathers with mothers. Among maternal kin, then, what is the range of kinship recognition; how far out does maternal recognition of kinship go? To assess this, our best bet is to look at species where females stay together and young males disperse so that there are a number of maternally related individuals in a group. Reviewing recent studies of such primates, Bernard Chapais (2008) concludes that in these groups a female ego could recognize her mother, maternal grandmother, mother's maternal grandmother, maternal siblings, own offspring, daughters' offspring, and granddaughters' offspring. Ego's maternal aunts and sisters' daughters (nieces) are in a "gray zone of kin recognition" (Chapais 2008: 39) and apparently maternal cousins are not distinguished from nonkin.

However kinship recognition occurs, many primates appear not only able to recognize some of their kin but to develop strong emotional attachments to them. This aspect of primate kinship is illustrated in the case study below.

CASE 1: DEATHS IN
THE FAMILIES OF CHIMPS

Takayoshi Kano (1992) studied bonobo chimpanzees in the Democratic Republic of Congo. He gives an account of an adolescent male, Tawashi, and his year-old little sister, Kameko. The young male appeared to be strongly attached to his sister:

> Tawashi often approached his mother, peered into her face, and after looking a while carried Kameko and took her for a walk. Once he made a nest 10 m from Kame [his mother] and, lying on his back, played with Kameko on top of his stomach. He tickled her, held her up by the arms, embraced, and kissed her . . . pressing his large open mouth everywhere on her body. (Kano 1992: 172)

But then Kameko died. Kano writes: "When we found Kameko dead, her small body was being held and carried around by Tawashi. He carried his little sister's body with all four limbs hanging down lifelessly; one of his arms pressed her against his chest; and he walked slowly in the tree apparently in deep thought" (Kano 1992: 172).

Walking with his mother and older brother, Tawashi continued to carry his dead sister, protecting her from his older brother who tried to touch her. In this state, the little family group separated from the other chimps and foraged for food on its own. Kano's observations continued over the next day:

> The following morning, the first to leave his nest and approach the corpse was Tawashi. He lightly touched the corpse. . . . [The] mother, Kame, came later. She lingered near the corpse and stared at it. As the sun rose, flies started to swarm around the corpse. Several times Kame grabbed quickly at the air with her hand as she shooed them. . . . For a while, Kame's family seemed, in general, to live separate from the others. Then the family left together and did not come back to the feeding site. Six days later when we found Kame, she did not have the corpse. (Kano 1992: 173–174)

This account suggests an emotional side to chimpanzee relationships, and one can clearly detect an emotional compassion on the part of the human observer. The observer in this case admits to a bit of "anthropomorphizing this situation" but wishes to make the point that "in chimpanzees, we may have to admit that feelings exist that are similar to those of human beings" (Kano 1992: 174).

Male bonobo chimps often groom their younger siblings and seem quite tolerant of them. Kano (1992: 174) also notes that male siblings continue their associations into adulthood but that the same is not observed among females, who usually disperse from the group at maturity. Adult association among male siblings has also been observed among the common chimpanzees of Gombe National Park in Tanzania—the site of years of research on chimp behavior by Jane Goodall and her coworkers. Goodall (1988) gives one account of a relationship between two male siblings, one that also became emotionally expressed through a death.

This account concerns a chimp whom the Gombe researchers called Mr. Mc-Gregor and his younger brother, Humphrey. Both were adult males. These two traveled together and, often, when other chimps threatened Humphrey, Mr. McGregor would intervene. Then, when Mr. McGregor was an old male, he came down with polio; this occurred at a time when a polio epidemic was afflicting the entire chimpanzee community at Gombe, leaving many animals dead or crippled. The Gombe staff vaccinated themselves and the animals, but it was too late for Mr. McGregor. Goodall writes that she and others discovered Mr. Mc-Gregor's crippled condition when they heard other chimps making "worried calls" around a bush near the camp:

We hurried down to see what was happening. We saw the flies first. . . . As we moved closer, we expected to see some dead creature—but it was Mr. McGregor and he was still alive. He was sitting on the ground reaching for the tiny purple berries that grew on the bush above his head and stuffing them into his mouth. It was not until he wanted to reach another cluster of the fruit that we realized the horror of what had happened. Looking toward the berries the old male seized hold of a low branch and pulled himself along the ground. Both legs trailed uselessly after him. (Goodall 1988: 219)

Over the next ten days the human researchers observed that Mr. McGregor stayed close to the Gombe feeding area. With his paralyzed legs he had trouble making nests and climbing trees. Securing his own food became more and more difficult for him. The researchers tried to help by giving him water and fruit. "He seemed to sense that we were trying to help, and after this he even lay back and allowed me to pour water from a sponge into his open mouth" (Goodall 1988: 220).

What struck Goodall most deeply, and painfully, was the way the other chimps reacted to poor Mr. McGregor. Much of the time they stayed away from him, but occasionally they attacked. One day

the adult males, one after the other, approached [Mr. McGregor] with their hair on end, and after staring began to display around him. Goliath actually attacked the stricken old male, who, powerless to flee or defend himself in any way, could only cower down, his face split by a hideous grin of terror, while Goliath pounded on his back. (Goodall 1988: 221–222)

But it was the social isolation of Mr. McGregor that seemed to affect Goodall the most. She notes one time when the poor animal approached other chimps as they were grooming one another, obviously seeking contact and inclusion in their group. "With a loud grunt of pleasure he reached a hand toward them in greeting" (1988: 222). These chimps quickly moved away and continued their grooming far from Mr. McGregor. Goodall writes: "I watched him sitting there alone, my vision blurred, and when I looked up at the groomers in the tree I came nearer to hating a chimpanzee than I have ever been before or since" (1988: 222).

But there was a singular exception to this social exclusion of Mr. McGregor. His younger maternal brother, Humphrey, stayed close by him. One time, when Goliath attacked Mr. McGregor, Humphrey intervened: "Humphrey, who had always been extremely nervous of Goliath, actually leaped into the tree, displaying wildly at the much higher-ranking male, and for a brief moment attacking him. I could hardly believe it" (Goodall 1988: 223).

Humphrey displayed loyalty to Mr. McGregor up to the time of the older chimp's death. At this point the other chimps in the group, including Humphrey, were moving up the valley. Mr. McGregor tried to follow them, either dragging himself or somersaulting, but he simply could not keep up. The others moved on, but Humphrey came back repeatedly to check on his brother. Eventually Humphrey gave up on following the group and made his nest near Mr. McGregor. Later Mr. McGregor dislocated an arm and was clearly dying. The Gombe researchers kindly put him out of his misery at a time when neither Humphrey nor any of the other chimps were watching. Goodall reports the effect of Mr. McGregor's death on Humphrey:

> For nearly six months he kept returning to the place where Gregor had spent the last days of his life, and would sit up in one tree or another staring around, waiting, listening. During this time he seldom joined the other chimps when they left together for a distant valley; he sometimes went a short way with such a group, but within a few hours he usually came back again and sat staring over the valley, waiting, surely to see old Gregor again, listening for the deep, almost braying voice, so similar to his own, that was silenced forever. (Goodall 1988: 224)

Goodall concludes that "no bond other than that of a family could account for Humphrey's behavior then" (1988: 223). Like Takayoshi Kano, she may be anthropomorphizing her account of Humphrey and Mr. McGregor, yet it would be extremely difficult not to do so. And as in the account by Kano, we are led to contemplate that chimps may have an emotional dimension to their "kinship" links, however formed, that is similar to our own.

KIN SELECTION

Some ideas about the evolution of kinship involve the notion of natural selection, first proposed by Charles Darwin in 1859 and later refined through developments in genetics. Natural selection refers to *differential reproduction,* or the tendency of certain individuals in a particular environment to produce more fertile offspring than other individuals. As mentioned in Chapter 1, those who reproduce the most have the highest fitness (defined as reproductive success), such that their genes are passed on to the next generation with the greatest frequency. Those traits (or, on another level, those genes) that favor fitness in a certain environment will be positively selected. Over time, then, natural selection operates on the basis of genetic variation (brought about by genetic mutation and recombination), ultimately bringing about evolutionary change.

In 1964, W. D. Hamilton considered the problem of altruistic acts among animals in relation to natural selection. If we say that natural selection favors fitness, or reproductive success, then how do we explain individual behavior that enhances others' fitness while simultaneously reducing one's own? Why, for example, do some ground squirrels place themselves at considerable risk to predators by sounding alarm calls so that others can escape? And why do some castes of female wasps forsake reproduction altogether to labor for the wasp colony?

To account for these altruistic behaviors, Hamilton came up with the concept of inclusive fitness, whereby an individual can promote the transmission of his or her genes to the next generation not just through producing children but also through altruistic acts that favor the survival (and eventual reproduction) of others who share at least some of the same genes—namely, close relatives. Thus Hamilton argued that the concept of fitness should include the capacity for altruistic behaviors that favor kin. Today researchers use the term *kin selection* to refer to this process. In essence, kin-selection theory proposes an evolutionary base for kin-favoring behavior.

Primate studies have rather strongly supported kin-selection theory.[2] Researchers have looked closely at primate behaviors such as grooming, food sharing, alliance formation (who regularly comes to the defense of whom), and co-feeding tolerance (which animals feed peacefully side by side). In the context of these and other behaviors, innumerable studies have shown that among primate species there is a strong bias in favor of kin as opposed to nonkin in terms of affiliative behaviors and direct assistance, and that these behaviors are more frequent among close kin than among more distantly related kin (Bernstein 1991; Silk 2002; Boyd and Silk 2012).

Direct support of kin is often highly visible in the primate world. For example, from Gombe, Goodall (1986: 376–377) reported the following:

Goblin once ran 200 meters when he heard the loud screams of his mother, Melissa, who was being attacked by another female. When he arrived, he displayed toward and attacked his mother's aggressor. Adult males often support their younger siblings, especially brothers, during aggressive incidents: thus Faben and Jomeo frequently hurried to help Figan and Sherry, respectively.

PRIMATE KINSHIP

Primates not only recognize certain of their kin, but in many cases kinship forms the backbone of the groups' social structure. This is seen most impressively in the distinct "matrilines" found among multimale-multifemale Old World monkeys, such as common baboons, vervet monkeys, and macaques. These species live in groups consisting of a subunit of females with their young and a subunit of adult males. Mating in these groups is brief and nonexclusive. The males are arranged in a dominance hierarchy among themselves. At the same time, all adult males are dominant over all females. In contrast to chimpanzees, females of these species remain in their natal group and males usually disperse to join new groups at adolescence. The female core groups contain mothers with their young, and in some cases these units extend over a few generations, producing matrilines. Thus, for example, a subunit may contain an old mother, her daughters, and her daughters' infants.

What is more, these different matrilines within the female core group are themselves ranked. For example, all the members of matriline A are higher than those of line B, who in turn are higher than those of line C, and so on. Every female of line A will thus be dominant over any female of line B. Rankings occur within each matriline as well. A mother is dominant over her offspring, and the female offspring assume a rank order based on birth (the most recently born daughter ranks highest). High-ranking mothers give daughters assistance in their rise in dominance over members of lower matrilines, and dominance rank is maintained in general through supportive alliances among females (Chapais 1992). Also interesting is that the rank of the matriline into which a male is born influences his rank among other males in his natal group, at least initially (later his rank may change depending on his own strength and social abilities and still later he will likely migrate out of the group).

These female dominance hierarchies, as they are called, are clear-cut and stable over time. One reason for this stability is that higher rank translates into higher fitness—high-ranking females tend to have more healthy offspring than lower-ranking ones. Thus higher-ranking matrilines tend to grow larger. Members of these will then have more allies to assist them in confrontational encounters with members of other matrilines; this larger size then helps higher-ranking matrilines to maintain their power over time (Silk 2002).

Unfortunately, these primates cannot tell us what their matrilineal hierarchies mean to them. We can only observe that distinct matrilineal units, stable patterns of social hierarchy, and the matrilineal transmission of rank over the generations are present in some nonhuman primate groups. We do not know how or to what extent these primates "think" in terms of generational kinship distinctions but their behavior suggests at least a kind of incipient *recognition of kinship over the generations*, which was undoubtedly important in human evolution. What humans developed beyond this, and what is unknown among contemporary nonhuman primates, is the significant next step: *the notion of descent from a common ancestor*, which, as we saw in the last chapter, is crucial to the formation of human descent groups.

Among primates there is no patrilineal equivalent to these female matrilineal hierarchies found among Old World monkeys. Among chimpanzees, for example, where females disperse at puberty, males left in the group will be patrilineally related to one another, but there is no consistent evidence that chimps recognize paternal kin. We will return to these structures of primate kinship in a later section, but first we will look at some differences between male and female behavior within primate societies.

REPRODUCTION, AGGRESSION, AND DOMINANCE

Male and female primates have very different reproductive strategies, and some of these differences are brought up in discussions of the evolution of human society and gender patterns, as we will later see. To understand these male/female differences, researchers use the concepts of sexual selection and parental investment (Trivers 1972). Sexual selection refers to the process by which one sex (usually male) competes for sexual access to the other. Parental investment refers to the contributions that parents make to the fitness of their offspring (the offspring's fitness by definition benefits the parents' own fitness). Among most primates (and, indeed, most mammals), the female investment is much higher than that of the male. Aside from undergoing pregnancy, female primates spend considerable time and energy nursing, carrying, and otherwise caring for infants. Consequently, females are the relatively scarcer resource for reproduction and males will then compete for access to females. From their high parental investment (or from the great amount of care that their infants need), it also follows that female primates will enhance their own fitness not by getting pregnant as often as possible but by raising fewer offspring with better care. By contrast, males whose parental investment is low or nonexistent enhance their fitness by impregnating as many females as possible.

While lack of male attention to infants characterizes most primates, in some species males do participate significantly in infant care. This is the case with most monogamous species and for the polyandrous tamarins of South America, where all the males mating with one female will assist in infant care to a high degree. Patricia Wright has shown how male care of infants (in defense and protection, food sharing, and carrying) depends on whether infants need male care for survival: "if male aid is not necessary for the survival of the infant, then the male does not invest in parental care" (1993: 136). In addition, males will tend not to care for offspring when, to enhance their own reproductive success, they can easily use their time and resources instead to secure more mating opportunities (Boyd and Silk 2012). Among multimale, multifemale species, males participate somewhat in infant care—a finding that some researchers interpret not as parental investment but as a mating strategy, or a means of gaining sexual access to the mother (Smuts and Gubernick 1992).

Male primates were previously thought to be more aggressive than females, but this assumption has been questioned, at least as far as frequency of aggressive acts is concerned. According to Smuts (1987: 401), there are sex differences in both style and context of aggression. In terms of style, the males of many species are more likely to precede aggression with "ritualized threats" (such as charging displays), whereas females often simply attack without warning. And an example of difference in context is that females are often highly aggressive when offspring protection is at stake, whereas males are highly aggressive when sexual access to females is threatened. However, some female primates also compete over males, and among many monogamous species, females aggressively drive out any female intruder.

There are also other contexts of specifically male aggression. One is territorial defense. Beginning in the 1970s, Jane Goodall's research team reported violent male territorial defense and the gradual killing off of all the males in one group by those of another (Goodall 1986: 503–514). Another situation concerns infanticide by adult males. In certain species—for example, Indian langurs—a male will sometimes kill infants he has not sired. This practice was first brought to scientific attention by Sarah Hrdy (1977, 1981). Indian langurs live in one-male polygynous units. A new male will sometimes enter such a unit, kill the current polygynous male, kill off any infants the females already have, and mate with the females himself. Following Hrdy, this infanticide, which has been also observed in other primate species, has been widely interpreted as a male strategy to promote fitness, or reproductive success, given that females quickly resume estrous after losing nursing infants and so become available for mating.

Another widespread assumption about primates has been that males are typically dominant over females. This idea still holds up in many cases, but our understanding of the overall picture has changed. Until recently both the popular imagination and the media fixed upon a rather extreme version of male dominance in the primate "wild," possibly involving the projection of a masculinity fantasy onto our primate roots. King Kong, after all, not only scaled the Empire State Building with a scantily dressed and vulnerable woman in his grip but also demanded and extracted a virgin every year from his human population back home. Thanks to better field studies, this image has given way to the documentation of greater gender diversity. Seeing male dominance as a social system where males "have feeding priority, spatial priority, and often decide on travel routes," Patricia Wright (1993: 135) concludes that male dominance is a feature of the societies of most Old World monkeys and apes. At the same time she points out that "there are approximately 200 species of primates, and in about 40 percent of them females are dominant or equal in status" (1993: 127). Examples of female-dominant species include squirrel monkeys and some lemurs. Among these species, females lead groups in travel, assume feeding priority over males, and can displace males from a location. In all the female-dominant groups, breeding is strictly seasonal. Among muriqui monkeys, there is equality between the sexes (Strier 1992). Other examples of species in which neither sex is dominant are monogamous species, such as gibbons and tarsiers. And among still other species (for example, some capuchin monkeys), a male is always first in a local linear hierarchy, whereas a female can be second, third, or fourth (Wright 1993: 135).

In another review, Joan Silk (1993: 216) makes the very interesting comment that, despite male dominance in some cases, "in all nonhuman primate species, females maintain considerable autonomy over their own lives." Indeed, although females in male-dominant species may encounter male aggression as well as displacement from males, they actually spend much of their lives on their own with their young or with other females. They exercise considerable choice in mating, they may form coalitions with other females against males, and through either friendly or nonfriendly behavior they can influence the male membership of their groups (Smuts 1987: 407).

In primates, variations in male dominance normally correlate with sexual dimorphism, or the external physical differences between males and females. Sexual dimorphism concerns differences in size and weight, and in features such as larger or sharper canine teeth. For example, among male-dominant species (such as gorillas), males are considerably larger and weigh more than females. Among female-dominant species (for example, lemurs), females are slightly larger. And among monogamous species where neither sex is dominant, the sexes tend to be equal in size. Although humans are more sexually dimorphic than these monogamous species, Silk (1993: 230) maintains that human societies generally exhibit a greater degree of male dominance than primatologists would predict on the basis of sexual dimorphism and mating practices.

THE HUMAN TRANSITION

The transition to human-style kinship occurred during the evolution of our hominid ancestors. The term *hominid* (Family Hominidae) includes modern humans and their extinct ancestors. Most students are probably already familiar with the general outline of hominid evolution. Briefly, hominids diverged from our last common ancestor with chimpanzees some 5 million to 7 million years ago. Remains of an early hominid, *Orrorin tugenensis*, have been discovered in Kenya, dated at 5 million to 6 million years ago. The fossil evidence indicates that Orrorin was bipedal (Galik et al. 2004). Remains of later hominids, the australopithecines, have been found in fossils dating from about 2 million to 4 million years ago or possibly earlier, unearthed at such sites as Laetoli in Tanzania and Hadar, Ethiopia. Among these was *Australopithecus afarensis*, of which the famous Lucy, discovered at Hadar, was one. Analysis of skeletal material, plus amazing footprints preserved in volcanic ash at Laetoli, shows that *A. afarensis* walked bipedally but likely were tree climbers as well. Except for their bipedal gait, these australopithecines probably looked a lot like modern chimps.

It now appears that several different species of australopithecines spanned a period of 2 million years or more in eastern and southern Africa. Experts do not agree on their evolutionary connections, nor do they agree as to which kind of australopithecine was the ancestor of the next important fossil hominid, *Homo habilis* (of the genus *Homo* and the species *habilis*). The latter appeared around 2 million years ago in eastern and southern Africa and lived at the same time as some australopithecines. The brain of *H. habilis* showed a definite increase in size over *Australopithecus*. In addition, *H. habilis* constructed stone tools, some of which were undoubtedly used to butcher meat.

H. habilis is considered ancestral to *Homo erectus*, who appeared in Africa about 1.5 million years ago and then spread to Asia and Europe. *H. erectus* showed a further increase in brain size and left evidence of more advanced tools, hunting of large animals, and use of fire. *H. erectus* lived for about 1 million years, possibly overlapping with archaic *H. sapiens*, who in turn was ancestral to modern *Homo sapiens*. *H. sapiens* first appeared perhaps as early as 200,000 years ago.

What happened, then, to kinship during the last 5–7 million years of hominid evolution? We have seen that extant primates exhibit a great deal in the way of kinship, certainly more than scholars imagined even a few decades ago. They recognize certain of their kin, they recognize each other's kin, they avoid incest with close kin, they generally favor and support close kin in their interactions, and some groups exhibit distinct matrilines that form the basis of their social structure and that transmit rank over the generations. Humans, of course, exhibit much more—for example, notions of descent from a common ancestor, recognition of kin bilaterally through both mothers and fathers, bilateral recognition of "in-laws" (relatives of mates), and the use of mate allocation to forge ties with such "in-laws." What, then, was the ancestral primate base for kinship 5–7 million years ago and how did human kinship evolve from it?

Scholars who have addressed these questions have focused on one distinctive feature of human kinship—reciprocal exogamy. As we saw in Chapter 1, exogamy merely refers to a rule that one must marry outside a specific group—a kin group, a village, a caste, and so on. Reciprocal exogamy is spouse *exchange*. It can be imagined as a process whereby one group gives, say, its women as wives to another group and the other group in turn gives its women as wives to the first group. Or one group gives women to another in return for material goods. Either way, reciprocal exogamy *links* groups, discouraging hostilities between them, as discussed in Chapter 1. This is not only a distinctively human thing to do, it is also considered that this was important in early human adaptations. As nineteenth-century anthropologist Edward Tylor famously remarked, "Again and again in the world's history, savage tribes must have had before them the simple practical alternative between marrying out or being killed out" (1889: 267). How, then, did humans develop reciprocal exogamy?

One set of ideas was put forth nearly forty years ago by anthropologist Robin Fox (1975, 1980). Fox began with the consideration that human kinship, as we also defined it in Chapter 1, consists of the recognition of relationships based on (1) descent and (2) marriage. Fox focused on these two fundamental "building blocks" of human kinship, probing the extent to which either has any basis, however rudimentary, in primate life. His ingenious suggestion was that some species of primates have adopted a rudimentary sort of "marriage" pattern (stable breeding bonds, which he termed "alliance"), whereas other species have adopted a rudimentary "descent" pattern (producing lineal groupings of kin), but that no primate species exhibits both alliance and descent. His idea was that the uniquely human development was merely to put the two elements, alliance and descent, together in one system.

For "alliance" Fox looked at one-male groups, using hamadryas baboons as an example. These baboons live in wooded or steppe areas of countries such as Ethiopia and Sudan. They are organized into polygynous units consisting of one adult male and several females, usually about four, with their young infants. The male mates with these females and "herds" them, keeping them together in a unit, although females do occasionally mate outside these units and may transfer into other units. Young males are driven off at maturity and later use various strategies to secure their own polygynous units. Fox considered that this pattern, with its distinct breeding units and long-term mating arrangements, can be considered as a rudimentary form of what becomes marriage in humans.

Fox then found "descent" among multimale, multifemale species of Old World monkeys, such as vervet monkeys and macaques. As we saw in a previous section here, these species consist of several males, organized in a dominance hierarchy among themselves, and groups of females organized into "matrilines" that may extend over a few generations. Males disperse out at maturity and females stay in the group. Clearly we have here a rudimentary kind of "descent" but since mating in these groups is relatively promiscuous and long-term mating units do not form, we do not have "alliance."

Thus, according to Fox, what our hominid ancestors did at some point was to combine the alliance pattern of the hamadryas baboons with the descent pattern of the multimale, multifemale groups (we will see later what Fox thought may have propelled this combination). Doing so set the basis for what is truly unique to humans, according to Fox and many others before him: descent-group exogamy and the systematic exchange of mates among groups.

Fox was in many ways ahead of his time and his work was largely ignored by sociocultural anthropologists and kinship experts for several decades. Later it received attention from a team of primate researchers (Rodseth, Wrangham, Harrigan, and Smuts 1991) who compared the social organization of a wide range of primates, including humans. They concluded that humans are distinctive among primates in that both sexes maintain lifelong relationships with consanguineal kin—regardless of which sex leaves its natal group or whether both sexes do so. Among other primates, by contrast, only one sex (the one that stays put and does not disperse) maintains these lifelong ties with natal kin. It was, then, this unique development among humans that allowed us to link up and ally with other groups. By maintaining ties with a dispersed son or daughter, humans could forge ties with the group to which the child moved. Thus a uniquely human trait, and one significant to our social organization, is the ability to maintain social relationships with others even when they are absent from us for prolonged periods. This, according to these authors, required the development of human language.[3]

More recent primate research also strongly suggests that Fox was on the right track. Primatologist Bernard Chapais (2008) followed Fox in breaking down human kinship systems into distinct components and searching for evidence of rudimentary forms of these within various primate species. But while Fox dealt with just "alliance" and "descent," Chapais decomposes human kinship into a much longer list of traits (twelve in all) and proposes a sequence in which they likely developed. Among the traits of his scheme are pair-bonding (where a single male and a single female form a stable mating bond), recognition of kinship through both mothers and fathers, and recognition of a mate's relatives ("in-laws").

Chapais suggests that when the human line split from our common ancestor with the chimpanzee, there was likely a chimpanzee-like social structure in place—that is, multimale-multifemale units, promiscuous mating, and dispersal of females.[4] Looking at Figure 2.1, we can see that this pattern produces a patrilineal kinship structure, but among chimpanzees this is not recognized; it lies dormant. What would it take for this patrilineal structure to become activated? Chapais claims that the key to this activation in human evolution was the emergence of stable breeding bonds. In his view these bonds developed (as they do among mammals generally) as a male mate-guarding strategy.

FIGURE 2.1   A Hypothetical Male "Patriline" Among Chimpanzees

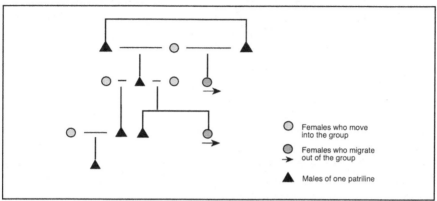

Under certain ecological conditions females will forage in small groups such that a single male can approach them for breeding purposes and fend off other males.[5] However this came about in the hominid line, Chapais (2008, 2011) posits that initially these relatively stable mating bonds were polygynous. In this situation all females are polygynously mated, some males are unmated, and the separate polygynous units occasionally come together, for example, at times of travel, producing a "multiharem" group (like certain baboons today). Later in human evolution, this pattern shifted to general monogamous mating, or pair-bonding (but with a few polygynous units occurring as well) and a resulting "multimonogamous" family structure. Interestingly Chapais proposes a mechanism for this shift in hominid evolution: weapons (or the use of any tool as a weapon). The use of weapons equalized male fighting abilities; larger size or strength would no longer ensure greater success in competition for access to females. The resulting pattern of monogamy meant a more equal distribution of females among males. One further consequence of this arrangement was that it allowed for the reduction in sexual dimorphism in the evolving human line.

With pair-bonding, we have a new social structure consisting of multifamily groups. We also have a new figure in the picture, "father" (mother's relatively stable mate), and potential recognition of father's kin—his father, his mother, and his brothers—through their association with one's father. By the same process, a father could recognize his own offspring (his mates' children). When this is added to the already existing ability to recognize one's own mother and, through her, one's own maternal siblings, kinship recognition is considerably expanded. In addition, some bonds within a family unit are strengthened. Full siblings, for example, are drawn together through associations with two parents, not just the mother.

Looking at the larger picture (and returning to Figure 2.1), we can see that this expanded kin recognition to and through males activates the patrilineal kinship structure. The males in the figure all now recognize one another as kin. We can further imagine that within this structure the different patrilines were ranked and that fathers assisted sons in their assumption of ranks such that rankings persisted over the generations. This would produce a patrilineal equivalent of the matrilineal-dominance hierarchies discussed earlier for some Old World monkeys.

With this pattern of multifamily groups and female dispersal we would also have the beginning of affinal kinship recognition. Thus a female dispersing into a new group would pair-bond with a particular male and recognize certain of his kin through their association with him—his brothers, father, mother, etc. But at this stage the reverse would not be possible—the female's "husband" would not recognize the female's kin (his "affines") since upon dispersal she severs her links to them.

Later, in Chapais's scheme, what changes this situation is the incipient development of the tribe, itself made possible through pair-bonding. As he notes, primates (in contrast to humans) are not organized above the local group. Local groups avoid one another or, if they come into contact, are largely hostile to one another, at least among males. As we have seen among the chimpanzees of Gombe, the intergroup encounter may become violent and lethal.[6] But with pair-bonding a new possibility could gradually emerge. Imagine for a moment two hominid groups, A and B, practicing pair-bonding and female dispersal. A female from A then disperses to group B and pair-bonds with a male. Members of the two groups then have some contact at their common border at a time when the dispersed female still can recognize her close natal kin of A and they can still recognize her. Let's say that in such a between-group encounter, the female, her small infants, her bonded mate, and her father or brother meet. Here the father or brother are unlikely to attack the female they recognize, or her small children who, through her, they now recognize as their kin (niece, nephew, grandchild). They might initially like to attack the female's "husband" but through her presence and possible intervention, open hostilities between the female's father/brother and her "husband" are prevented. In this way, to Chapais, dispersed pair-bonded females could have acted as "appeasing bridges" between specific members of otherwise hostile local groups. Imagine then that several females of group A disperse to group B; with each dispersal, additional appeasing bridges are set up. Then imagine that some females of group B disperse to group A. With this, a number of other appeasing links are established between the groups.

Through this process, we now have a new social situation: intergroup pacification (not yet a real tribe in the human sense). Females who have dispersed out can maintain contacts with their natal kin since peaceful intergroup relations allow them to do so. Before, they moved away from one family (their natal family) and into another (their affinal family), severing ties with the former family. Now they remain a part of both families and link them together. With this, we now have a fuller bilateral recognition of relatives. On the mother's side, children can recognize not only their maternal siblings but also their mother's mother, mother's father, mother's brothers. and so on in addition to their relatives through the father. We also now have bilateral recognition of affinal relatives. The dispersed female's pair-bonded mate can now, through her, recognize her natal kin—her father, brother, sister, etc. Finally, this sets up the potential for what Chapais calls "affinal brotherhoods"—special or preferential bonds (potentially cooperative) between a female's brother and her mate. These two have vested interests in the female—her reproduction will enhance her mate's reproductive success directly and will enhance that of her brother through inclusive fitness—and they are not in sexual competition for the female (the brother is excluded through incest avoidance). At this point an exchange of females is, as Chapais put it, "in the air." Indeed groups A and B are, in terms of behavior if not conscious deliberation, already exchanging females as mates. Sitting down together and arranging the process are but a step away. "Language, along with other cognitive abilities, would eventually do the rest" (Chapais 2008: 306).

Once this system is in place, a number of new opportunities are available for evolving hominids/early human societies. One is the development of a true tribal organization: Not only are between-group relationships pacified, but local groups are actually organized together into higher and higher levels (a multilevel structure). Another new possibility would have been residential diversity: Once there is pacification between local groups, males as well as females could disperse. Over time the resulting local communities would consist of individuals related to one another affinally as well as consanguineally and often with no kin links between them at all. Such local communities would look quite different from the patrilineal/female dispersal structure seen in Figure 2.1.

As we saw, central to Chapais's scheme is pair-bonding. There seems to be agreement on the importance of pair-bonding to human social evolution, but different ideas on when it occurred in relation to other developments and how it came about. Chapais suggests it was a relatively early adaptation and came about as a mate-guarding strategy. A more common view is that pair-bonding emerged as evolving human infants came to require more care and mothers came to need help with infant care. It was then a parental care strategy, drawing males into infant care. In Chapais's (2011) view, pair-bonding occurred before paternal care of infants was needed. It was a preadaptation, already in place before it was actually used for parental purposes.

There are still other ideas concerning the evolution of pair-bonding and its place within human social transformations, some having to do with the evolution of the division of labor by sex. Robin Fox (1980), for example, proposes that the "alliance" half of the evolution of fully human kinship occurred with the development of big-game hunting. He places this hunting transition at around the time that *Australopithecus* was evolving into *H. habilis* and suggests that the transition was well under way by the time of early *H. erectus*. Fox suggests that big-game hunting entailed a new division of labor by sex: males engaged in the hunting of large game while females specialized in the gathering of plant food. Before this time males and females foraged for themselves, with some hunting of small mammals and some food sharing, as among contemporary chimpanzees. But the new hunting/gathering order brought about a trade between men and women—meat for vegetables. This changed forever the relationship between men and women. Before, they interacted sexually and there was male protection of females, but now the sexes depended on each other for food. Fox writes that this meat/vegetable trade between the sexes "is probably at the root of a truly human society" (1980: 143) and as we have seen, for him the first truly human society was one in which local groups exchanged spouses among themselves to form peaceful alliances. In Fox's view, the male/female/meat/vegetable trade brought males into closer association with females and their young in domestic units. Ultimately, with their control over the nutritionally valuable meat protein, males came to have power over the allocation of females as mates (in humans, brides) for other groups of men.

Primatologist Richard Wrangham (2009) hypothesizes that it was not hunting as such but the cooking of food that led our hominid ancestors on the path to distinctively human adaptations and domestic organization. Wrangham places this human transition at a slightly later point than did Fox. For him, the cooking of food brought about the evolution of a branch of *H. habilis* into *H. erectus*. He writes:

> I believe the transformative moment that gave rise to the genus *Homo*, one of the great transitions in the history of life, stemmed from the control of fire and the advent of cooked meals. Cooking increased the value of our food. It changed our bodies, our brains, our use of time, and our social lives. It made us into consumers of external energy and thereby created an organism with a new relationship to nature, dependent on fuel. (2009: 2)

Wrangham demonstrates that compared to raw food, cooked food is energy-rich, safer, and more diverse. He shows how the adaptation to a cooked diet that yields softer, more easily digestible food may have allowed for the development of smaller teeth, smaller mouths, and weaker jaws of *H. erectus* and *H. sapiens* compared to those of other hominids and nonhuman primates. He also shows how energy from cooked food may have been instrumental in the impressive growth of brain size, and accompanying mental capacity, in *erectus* and, later, *sapiens*.

In addition, Wrangham speculates that as men specialized in hunting, women came to do the cooking and that this convenient division of labor brought a new relationship of mutual dependence between the sexes in a way somewhat similar to what Fox had proposed. However, Wrangham's emphasis on female cooking (rather than just gathering of plant food) gives a different slant to his scenario. Men, he suggests, protected their mates from being robbed of their food while cooking, and in turn women prepared their mates' meals. In this way, cooking led to human-style pair-bonded mating within domestic units. In contrast, in Chapais's (2011) scheme, pair-bonding predated both large-scale hunting and cooking and likely served as a preadaptation to both.

All of these ideas on the evolution of kinship and the family suggest shifts in the relationships between men and women in the process. For Fox and Wrangham, a sexual division of labor not only brought about pair-bonding but also made men and women dependent on one another in a way that they were not before. Would this mutual dependence promote gender equality? Maybe, but maybe not for long. For both Fox and Chapais (and before them Claude Lévi-Strauss; see Chapter 6), it was men who came to exchange women. Using evolutionary theory, Chapais (2008: 249) offers a reason females were exchanged: Since females, relative to males, contribute a much greater reproductive effort, they are the scarcer, more valuable reproductive resource.[7] For Fox and Chapai it was not the case that women allocated themselves in marriage, or that women allocated men, or, say, that brothers and sisters allocated each other. It was men who allied themselves (and their respective groups) with one another through the exchange of their natal kinswomen. Females had been dispersing out on their own before, but later they did so under the direction or at the whim of men. Were they mere pawns in a male game of political alliance? And if so, does this suggest that the birth of fully human kinship (reciprocal exogamy) was simultaneously the birth of women's subordination to men? Whichever set of ideas we consider, we see that there are immediate links between kinship and gender in the evolution of human society.

Of course, a host of other ideas have been put forth to address the evolution of human gender inequality (assuming that such inequality has been and is a prevalent factor of human life). One set of ideas comes from Barbara Smuts (1995), who began by noting that (as discussed in Chapter 1) human and nonhuman primates seek to maximize their fitness through different reproductive strategies: Males go for "mate quantity" whereas females pursue "mate quality." To pursue mate quantity, according to Smuts, males are aggressive against females in most primate species. Females can effectively resist this aggression, for example, by forming alliances with other females against males. However, human patrilocality, which developed from an ancestral female dispersal, disadvantaged women, leaving them isolated in their husband's group without the support of female kin and allies. Smuts also mentions that in following their own reproductive interests in mate quality, females themselves may promote male control over female sexuality. Thus in some circumstances women facilitate their own reproductive success not so much by allying with other females as by allying with males and complying with customs that increase paternity certainty (the extent to which a male can assume he is the father of a child).

Another set of intriguing ideas has been put forth by Sarah Hrdy (1981, 1997), whose work on infanticide, as we discussed earlier, influenced her theory on the evolution of patriarchy. Hrdy proposed that females were naturally selected to be sexually assertive and to find a plurality of mates so that many males would presume that they could have fathered her children. This would ensure lack of harm to her offspring (preventing, for example, their being killed by intruding males), which would enhance the fitness of the female and her offspring. Hrdy saw the human female's loss of physical signs of ovulation in this light: Concealed ovulation was naturally selected since it helped decrease paternity certainty. Hrdy argued that paternity uncertainty was an advantage for evolving hominid women but that as human society developed, males devised ways to increase paternity certainty through seclusion of women, chastity belts, and so on, thereby gaining control over female sexuality.

Yet another idea on the evolutionary origin of gender inequality, appealing for its simplicity, has been advanced by Marvin Harris (1993). He argues that hominid male hunting of large game gave men the edge over women not because they brought back valued protein from the hunt (as in Fox's scheme) but because men thereby gained familiarity with and monopoly over the manufacture and use of weapons. Perhaps it was as simple as that.

The reconstruction of the evolution of human social behavior is a work in progress. but such reconstructions are no longer idle speculations, as they clearly were in the nineteenth and early twentieth centuries. Today we have substantially more data on hominids, and even more important, this reconstruction is now a multidisciplinary endeavor, relying on information not only from anthropology or archaeology but also from fields such as genetics, ecology, primatology, and many others. New findings from a variety of fields are able to support or cast doubt upon proposed pieces of the puzzle of human social transformations. For example, a recent study analyzed strontium isotope data from tooth enamel of two australopithecine species from cave sites in South Africa (Copeland et al. 2011). The study shows that most of the larger individuals (presumed to be male) fed primarily near the cave sites, whereas smaller individuals (females) fed in other, more distant locations during tooth mineralization, later moving into the cave site locations as young adults. This study then supports the idea that early hominids (following the split of the human line from our last common ancestor with chimpanzees) practiced female dispersal, as held by Chapais. Also supporting Chapais's evolutionary scheme is a recent study by Kim Hill and colleagues (Hill et al. 2011) that analyzed residence patterns in a worldwide sample of thirty-two current hunter-gatherer populations. This study shows that particular features of the residence patterns of these groups show a remarkable similarity to what Chapais's model predicts for early human societies. Among these features are a multilevel social organization, flexibility in patterns of postmarital residence, and a large number of local group members who are affinally related or have no kin relationship to one another.

THE INCEST TABOO

No discussion of the evolution of kinship would be complete without mention of the human incest taboo, if for no other reason than to show some mistaken thinking about it in the past. The human incest taboo is a ban on sexual relations between primary kin: mother-son, father-daughter, and brother-sister (Fox 1989: 31). Some societies include other relatives in their own category of "incestuous union," but what we find common to nearly all societies is the ban on sex between primary kin. The incest taboo is not, however, absolutely universal among humans. It is well known that royal families of ancient Egypt, Peru (Inca), and Hawaii allowed or encouraged brother-sister marriages (and thus mating), and that in Egypt some father-daughter marriages occurred among both royals and commoners.

Within anthropology there was for a long time some confusion on the relation of the incest taboo to exogamy. The incest taboo has to do with restrictions on sexual relations, whereas exogamy has to do with restrictions on marriage. Fox (1989: 54) was quite right when he wrote: "While every teenager knows these [sex and marriage] are different, many anthropologists get them confused." Some anthropologists tried to explain exogamy by calling it an "extension of the incest taboo"; others tried to explain the incest taboo by saying that it forced people to "marry out" and hence form alliances. But these attempts only muddled the problem further.

For decades anthropologists have been interested in explaining why human societies have an incest taboo, why it is nearly universal, and why people in so many societies regard incest with horror and disgust. In terms of kinship systems the taboo is important because if it did not exist (and if people regularly practiced incest), we wouldn't need kinship systems to regulate human reproduction. Instead, as Fox (1989: 54) puts it, a "mother-children group could settle down to a cozy little inbreeding arrangement and be totally self-sufficient for purposes of reproduction."

Over the past century, many theories sprang up to explain the human incest taboo. The two most popular were those originally proposed by Edward Westermarck (1891) and Sigmund Freud (1918). Westermarck proposed that persons raised together, or persons living closely together from early childhood, develop a natural aversion to having sexual relations with one another. He had brother-sister relations in mind, but the same line of thinking applied to parent-child relations as well, accounting for the aversion to sexual relations between child-rearers and children. Since it is usually the case that parents raise children, and siblings live together in childhood, an incest avoidance results between primary kin. In Westermarck's view, this natural incest aversion is a human instinct that evolved or was naturally selected to prevent the harmful effects of close inbreeding. Only later did a taboo develop to discourage any aberrant tendencies.

According to Freud (who focused more on parent-child incest), humans unconsciously do wish to commit incest, but this desire is repressed. His idea was that repression is triggered by guilt. Ridiculous as it might seem today, what Freud proposed was that at some time in the remote past there existed a human "primal horde" headed by a father who kept, all to himself, a group of women with whom he mated. His sons, wanting access to the females, killed him (not unlike Indian langurs). But then, since they had been raised to respect and obey their father, they felt guilty and so "tabooed" their own access to the women (their mothers and sisters). Humans since then have somehow inherited all this trauma and continue to live it out. Of course, later Freudians found it necessary to dispense with this idea of the "primal horde" as a prehistorical event, but they retained the notions of unconscious desire, guilt, and repression to account for an incest taboo.

These two theories of Westermarck and Freud are at odds. One maintains that humans normally do not want to commit incest, so we need a taboo for the few misfits who do. The other holds that humans really do want to commit incest, but that this impulse immediately triggers guilt and repression, leading to a taboo that expresses and confirms that very human psychofamilial process.

Both theories have been criticized, but of the two, only Westermarck's has held up over time. The idea of an aversion to sex between children raised together received support from studies of the Israeli kibbutzim (communal villages), where male and female infants are detached from their parents and raised together through adolescence. According to these studies, children raised together showed no sexual interest in one another upon reaching adulthood and, though free to do so, did not marry one another (Shepher 1983). Additional support for Westermarck has come from studies of a Chinese custom called "minor marriages," whereby parents adopt a female child to raise as the future bride of their son. The girl and boy are raised together and later are forced to marry. These marriages were found to be considerably less fertile, less happy, and far more prone to divorce than regular, or "major," Chinese marriages (Wolf 1970; Wolf and Huang 1980). In addition, the Westermarck effect has been shown to apply to primates and other animals (Pusey 2002).

A lot of the theorizing about the incest taboo entails the implicit or explicit assumption that close inbreeding is biologically or genetically disadvantageous. But just how detrimental would inbreeding be? On the one hand, within a small group whose gene pool contains largely "good" genes, close inbreeding over time would not be harmful and might even be advantageous. On the other hand, close inbreeding would be disadvantageous to sexually reproducing organisms who live in a changing environment, since loss of genetic variation, and thus loss of flexibility in adaptation, would result. In a population with a high frequency of deleterious mutations, high levels of inbreeding will be over time detrimental to the fitness of individuals in the population. This effect is known as inbreeding depression.

NATURE, CULTURE, AND HUMAN KINSHIP

In Chapter 1 we noted that beginning in the 1970s, many cultural anthropologists emphasized human kinship as a purely cultural construction; that is, the way humans perceive their "kin-like" relationships is not everywhere based on genealogy, or acts of procreation. They pointed out that many peoples around the world construct what may look to outside anthropologists like biological "kinship" relations, but they are actually relationships based on common residence, certain rituals, food sharing, and so on. Genealogical or biogenetic conceptions of kinship, they held, are Western cultural concepts that anthropologists mistakenly imposed on other people. With this, they dismissed biology (particularly reproductive biology) as a relevant factor to the cross-cultural study of kinship and, perhaps needless to say, they were uninterested in attempts to understand human kinship in the context of our primate heritage and our biosocial evolution. They went further to say that ideas about procreation are themselves cultural constructions, varying widely among different cultural groups. Thus in the end there are no biological facts of life on which to build a common understanding of human kinship. This chapter, in contrast, has shown the depths of primate kinship, discussed the obvious parallels with human kinship, and reviewed ideas about the biosocial evolution of human kinship from a primate base. From this perspective, the view of human kinship (or for that matter human fatherhood or marriage) as only a matter of variable cultural constructions would seem difficult to maintain.

At the same time, human kinship *is* cultural construction. Humans do use bases other than biology or procreation to construct their kinship. Humans creatively make kin as well as grow their own, and this is uniquely human. Nonbiological bases of kinship construction exist in all societies and for good reason: Human groups can apply notions of kinship flexibly to link up with and/or incorporate outsiders as well as to organize actual or presumed biological kin. In other words, in the course of their evolution, humans did not need to rely on exogamous marriage alone to forge nonkin interpersonal and intergroup alliances; they could do so through extension of kinship terms to outsiders or through rituals, acts of feeding, and so on, to establish kinship with nonkin or even strangers (Stone and Lurquin 2007: 225; Stone 2012). Among humans there are many ways to create "kinship" with unrelated others, to link up with initial strangers and transform them into close associates. It is not precisely known how or through what mechanisms the earliest humans used kinship in this new, creative way. Nevertheless, in hindsight we can see the innumerable advantages of the human ability to both recognize biological kin and to use kinship ideas to build bonds with others, regardless of a biological connection.

The extension of human kinship beyond biological relationships serves to create networks of cooperative, political alliances across time and space and through levels of social organization beyond what is possible in the world of nonhuman primates (Rodseth and Wrangham 2004). From an evolutionary point of view, the human capacity to create kin is adaptive. Thus, however much we find that biology or procreation is not locally conceived as a basis for human kinship construction, it does not follow that our evolution (and hence biology) was not a factor behind the human construction of kinship in the first place, including its creative cultural constructions and variations.

From the world of primates we have seen that humans are not unique in terms of avoiding incest, outbreeding, making kinship connections a core feature of their social organization and behavior, or even in recognizing kinship over more than one generation. Indeed in terms of behavior only a few aspects of human kinship are not found somewhere in the nonhuman primate world. Exogamy, in the sense of outbreeding, is certainly not unique to humans, but the systematic exchange of mates for the purpose of creating peaceful intergroup relations or cooperative intergroup alliances is unique to human society. For this to occur, another uniquely human development—the recognition of a mate's relatives, or "in-laws"—was needed. It appears very likely that at some point in our evolution, descent group exogamy and systematic exchange of mates between descent groups served as a mechanism by which groups could relate to one another in nonhostile ways. We have also seen that male dominance over females is evident in some, though by no means all, primate groups. Finally, we have noted that female nonhuman primates exhibit an autonomy in their own lives beyond that found in many, if not most, human societies.

Beyond the greater complexity of human kinship over that of other primates, what is apparently unique to our species is the notion of descent from a common ancestor, so crucial to forming human-style descent groups and other features of human kinship systems. Humans not only recognize kin and behave for the most part favorably toward them, they also use ideas of kinship to form bonds among people unrelated biologically. With the work of Robin Fox, Bernard Chapais, and many others, it is now apparent that human kinship did not arise out of the blue or purely as a cultural construction. Human kinship has deep roots in our primate heritage. With the development of language and symbolic capacity, human kinship became complex, rule-bound, and institutionalized. Kinship also came to show considerable cross-cultural variation, as we will see throughout the rest of this book.

We do not know what kinds of kinship organization were in place among the earliest, fully human, hunting-gathering groups. What we do know is that human kinship became important as a framework of social structure and that it became tightly interwoven with economic relationships, politics, and religion. With the advent of pastoralism (livestock herding) and food production, kinship likely became even more complex, since it would have been used to define rights over new kinds of productive property and to transmit these rights to subsequent generations. It was at this stage that the "kinship corporations" discussed in the last chapter became so important. In the next three chapters, we shall examine interrelationships between human kinship systems and gender in societies with patrilineal, matrilineal, and cognatic descent.

DISCUSSION QUESTIONS

1. To what extent do you think kin-selection theory could be applied to human behavior?

2. Contrast the ideas of Barbara Smuts, Sarah Hrdy, and Marvin Harris on the evolutionary origins of human gender relationships. Which argument do you find most convincing and why? Could the ideas of all three scholars be true at the same time?

3. Marriage is a human universal. In the evolving human line, what particular kinship or other social traits had to develop before human-style marriage could have occurred? Would language have been necessary?

SUGGESTED FURTHER READING

De Waal, Frans. 2001. *The Ape and the Sushi Master: Cultural Reflections by a Primatologist*. New York: Basic Books. A delightful, readable, and engaging book about the primate origins of human culture. The author argues convincingly that culture is not unique to our species but is exhibited among other animals, especially our higher primate cousins.

———. 2006. *Our Inner Ape: A Leading Primatologist Explains Why We Are Who We Are*. New York: Riverhead Books. A compelling look at chimpanzees, bonobos, and other primates in terms of what their behavior teaches us about ourselves. Covers power, sex, violence, and kindness.

Baboon Tales. 1998. Produced by Tamarin Productions Inc. in association with the Discovery Channel. Bullfrog Films, Oley, PA. Fifty-two minutes. Based on the long-term fieldwork of primatologist Shirley Strum, this film documents the social life of a troop of Olive baboons in Kenya. It focuses on five infant baboons in their first years of life, emphasizing the importance of kin relations and the establishment of friendships and social networks.

WEBSITES

www.youtube.com/watch?v=VWEU0PqcpZ4&NR=1&feature=endscreen. "Capuchin Monkey Fairness Experiment." An interesting video clip of two capuchin monkeys responding to unequal rewards.

www-personal.umich.edu/~kruger/ep10.html. "Sex Differences and Sex Roles." An essay covering evolutionary perspectives on gender. Daniel J. Kruger, University of Michigan.

NOTES

1. There is, for example, some evidence of paternal kin recognition perhaps through phenotypic matching among rhesus macaques (Widdig 2007).

2. A rigorous test of kin-selection theory presents challenges. Hamilton phrased this theory as a rule (now known as Hamilton's Rule) whereby altruistic behavior will be favored by selection if rb>c, where r = the coefficient of genetic relatedness between the actor and recipients, b = the sum of fitness benefit to recipients, and c = the fitness costs to the actor. The difficulty lies in how to measure fitness costs and benefits to actors and recipients (Silk 2002: 853).

3. Using data from hamadryas baboons, this research team also made a case for Fox's "alliance" and "descent" actually already combined in a primate system. Not only do these baboons exhibit "alliance" in their one-male units, but these units are also loosely organized into "clans" and, above these, "bands" in accordance with common kinship through males.

4. In the context of other issues Chapais (2008: 151) bases this characterization of the beginning of the human line on the fact that the pattern of males staying put and females dispersing occurs among our three closest relatives: chimpanzees, bonobos, and gorillas (although the pattern for gorillas is not as complete [Chapais 2008: 142]).

5. Chapais (2008: 173–175) argues this based on the principle that stable breeding bonds in mammals generally arise and function as mating arrangements. Here he is opposing the idea that pair-bonding in humans arose instead as a parental partnership strategy for enhanced infant care (see also Chapais 2011).

6. Intergroup hostility and violence, clearly seen among chimpanzees, is far less pronounced among bonobos. Indeed Frans de Waal writes that "peaceable mingling of communities seems to be the rule," although he further notes that "friendly overtures are made mostly by females; male-male relations between groups are relatively tense" (2002: 51).

7. Still, this does not explain how women came to comply with a system in which they were exchanged by men.

REFERENCES

Bernstein, Irwin S. 1991. The Correlation Between Kinship and Behavior in Non-Human Primates. In Peter G. Hepper, ed., *Kin Recognition*, pp. 6–29. Cambridge, England: Cambridge University Press.

Boesch, Christophe, and Helwige Boesch. 1990. Tool Use and Tool Making in Wild Chimpanzees. *Folia Primatologica* 54: 86–99.

Boyd, Robert, and Joan B. Silk. 2012. *How Humans Evolved*, 6th ed. New York: W.W. Norton & Company.

Chapais, Bernard. 1992. The Role of Alliances in Social Inheritance of Rank Among Female Primates. In Alexander H. Harcourt and Frans B. M. de Waal, eds., *Coalitions and Alliances in Humans and Other Animals*, pp. 23–59. Oxford: Oxford University Press.

———. 2008. *Primeval Kinship: How Pair-Bonding Gave Birth to Human Society*. Cambridge, MA: Harvard University Press.

———. 2011. The Evolutionary History of Pair-Bonding and Parental Collaboration. In Catherine A. Salmon and Todd K. Shackelford, eds., *The Oxford Handbook of Evolutionary Family Psychology*, pp. 33–50. Oxford: Oxford University Press.

Cheney, Dorothy L., and Robert M. Seyfarth. 1980. Vocal Recognition in Free-Ranging Vervet Monkeys. *Animal Behavior* 28: 362–367.

———. 2004. The Recognition of Other Individuals' Kinship Relationships. In Bernard Chapais and Carol M. Berman, eds., *Kinship and Behavior in Primates*, pp. 347–364. New York: Oxford University Press.

Copeland, Sandi R., Matt Sponheimer, Darryl J. de Ruiter, Julia A. Lee-Thorp, Daryl Codron, Petrus J. le Roux, Vaughan Grimes, and Michael P. Richards. 2011. Strontium Isotope Evidence for Landscape Use by Early Hominins. *Nature* 474(7349): 76–78.

de Waal, Frans B. M. 2002. Apes from Venus: Bonobos and Human Social Evolution. In Frans B. M. de Waal, ed., *Tree of Origin: What Primate Behavior Can Tell Us About Human Social Evolution*, pp. 39–68. Cambridge, MA: Harvard University Press.

———. 2006. Primates and Philosophers: How Morality Evolved. Edited by Stephen Macedo and Josiah Ober. Princeton, NJ: Princeton University Press.

Fox, Robin. 1975. Primate Kin and Human Kinship. In Robin Fox, ed., *Biosocial Anthropology*, pp. 9–35. New York: John Wiley and Sons.

———. 1980. *The Red Lamp of Incest*. New York: E. P. Dutton.

———. 1989 [orig. 1967]. *Kinship and Marriage: An Anthropological Perspective*. Cambridge, England: Cambridge University Press.

Freud, Sigmund. 1918. *Totem and Taboo*. New York: A. A. Brill.

Gagneaux, P., D. S. Woodruff, and C. Boesch. 1997. Furtive Mating in Female Chimpanzees. *Nature* 387: 358–359.

Galik, K., B. Senut, M. Pickford, D. Gommery, J. Treil, A. J. Kuperavage, and R. B. Eckhardt. 2004. External and Internal Morphology of the BAR 1002'00 *Orrorin tugenensis* femur. *Science* 305: 1450–1453.

Goldizen, Anne Wilson. 1987. Tamarins and Marmosets: Communal Care of Offspring. In Barbara B. Smuts, Dorothy L. Cheney, Robert M. Seyfarth, Richard W. Wrangham, and Thomas T. Struhsaker, eds., *Primate Societies*, pp. 34–43. Chicago: University of Chicago Press.

Goodall, Jane. 1986. *The Chimpanzees of Gombe: Patterns of Behavior*. Cambridge, MA: Harvard University Press.

———. 1988. *In the Shadow of Man*. Boston: Houghton Mifflin.

Gouzoules, Sarah, and Harold Gouzoules. 1987. Kinship. In Barbara B. Smuts, Dorothy L. Cheney, Robert M. Seyfarth, Richard W. Wrangham, and Thomas T. Struhsaker, eds., *Primate Societies*, pp. 299–305. Chicago: University of Chicago Press.

Hamilton, W. D. 1964. The Genetical Evolution of Social Behavior. *Journal of Theoretical Biology* 7: 1–51.

Harris, Marvin. 1993. The Evolution of Human Gender Hierarchies: A Trial Formulation. In Barbara Diane Miller, ed., *Sex and Gender Hierarchies*, pp. 57–79. Cambridge, England: Cambridge University Press.

Hill, Kim R., Robert S. Walker, Miran Bozicevic, James Eder, Thomas Headland, Barry Hewlett, A. Magdalena Hurtado, Frank Marlowe, Polly Wiessner, and Brian Wood. 2011. Co-Residence Patterns in Hunter-Gatherer Societies Show Unique Human Social Structure. *Science* 331: 1286–1289.

Hrdy, Sarah Blaffer. 1977. *The Langurs of Abu*. Cambridge, MA: Harvard University Press.

———. 1981. *The Woman That Never Evolved*. Cambridge, MA: Harvard University Press.

———. 1997. Raising Darwin's Consciousness: Female Sexuality and the Prehominid Origins of Patriarchy. *Human Nature* 8(1): 1–49.

Judge, P. 1983. Reconciliation Based on Kinship in a Captive Group of Pigtail Macaques. Abstract. *American Journal of Primatology* 4: 346.

Kano, Takayoshi. 1992. *The Last Ape: Pygmy Chimpanzee Behavior and Ecology*. Stanford, CA: Stanford University Press.

Linsenmair, K. E. 1987. Kin Recognition in Subsocial Arthropods, in Particular in the Desert Isopod Hemilepistus reaumuri. In David J. C. Fletcher and Charles D. Michener, eds., *Kin Recognition in Animals*, pp. 121–208. Chichester, England: John Wiley and Sons.

Morin, Phillip A., and Tony L. Goldberg. 2004. Determination of Genealogical Relationships from Genetic Data: A Review of Methods and Applications. In Bernard Chapais and Carol M. Berman, eds., *Kinship and Behavior in Primates*, p. 45. New York: Oxford University Press.

Morin, Philip A., J. J. Moore, R. Chakraborty, L. Jin, J. Goodall, and D. S. Woodruff. 1994. Kin Selection, Social Structure, Gene Flow, and the Evolution of Chimpanzees. *Science* 265: 1193–1201.

Pusey, Anne E. 2002. Of Genes and Apes: Chimpanzee Social Organization and Reproduction. In Frans B. M. de Waal, ed., *Tree of Origin: What Primate Behavior Can Tell Us About Human Social Evolution*, pp. 9–37. Cambridge, MA: Harvard University Press.

Rodseth, Lars, and Richard Wrangham. 2004. Human Kinship: A Continuation of Politics by Other Means? In Bernard Chapais and Carol M. Berman, eds., *Kin-

ship and Behavior in Primates, pp. 389–419. New York: Oxford University Press.

Rodseth, Lars, Richard W. Wrangham, Alisa M. Harrigan, and Barbara B. Smuts. 1991. The Human Community as a Primate Society. *Current Anthropology* 32(3): 221–241.

Shepher, Joseph. 1983. *Incest: A Biosocial View*. New York: Academic Press.

Silk, Joan B. 1993. Primatological Perspectives on Gender Hierarchies. In Barbara Diane Miller, ed., *Sex and Gender Hierarchies*, pp. 212–235. Cambridge, England: Cambridge University Press.

———. 2001. Ties that Bond: The Role of Kinship in Primate Societies. In Linda Stone, ed., *New Directions in Anthropological Kinship*, pp. 71–92. Lanham, MD: Rowman & Littlefield.

———. 2002. Kin Selection in Primate Groups. *International Journal of Primatology* 23(4): 849–875.

Smuts, Barbara B. 1985. *Sex and Friendship in Baboons*. New York: Aldine.

———. 1987. Gender, Aggression, and Influence. In Barbara B. Smuts, Dorothy L. Cheney, Robert M. Seyfarth, Richard W. Wrangham, and Thomas T. Struhsaker, eds., *Primate Societies*, pp. 400–412. Chicago: University of Chicago Press.

———. 1995. The Evolutionary Origins of Patriarchy. *Human Nature* 6(1): 1–32.

Smuts, Barbara B., and David J. Gubernick. 1992. Male-Infant Relationships in Nonhuman Primates: Parental Investment or Mating Effort? In Barry S. Hewlett, ed., *Father-Child Relations: Cultural and Biosocial Contexts*, pp. 1–30. Hawthorne, NY: Aldine.

Stone, Linda. 2013. Kinship Constructed Us: Implications of Primate Studies for Cultural Anthropology. In Michael Egan, ed., *The Last Anthropologist: Essays in Nature and Society for Robin Fox*. New York: Edwin Mellen Press.

Stone, Linda, and Paul F. Lurquin. 2007. *Genes, Culture, and Human Evolution: A Synthesis*. Malden, MA: Blackwell Publishing.

Strier, Karen B. 1992. *Faces in the Forest: The Endangered Muriqui Monkeys of Brazil*. Cambridge, MA: Harvard University Press.

———. 2002. Beyond the Apes: Reasons to Consider the Entire Primate Order. In Frans B. M. de Waal, ed., *Tree of Origin: What Primate Behavior Can Tell Us About Human Social Evolution*, pp. 69–93. Cambridge, MA: Harvard University Press.

Trivers, Robert L. 1972. Parental Investment and Sexual Selection. In B. Campbell, ed., *Sexual Selection and the Descent of Man*, pp. 136–179. Chicago: Aldine.

Tylor, Edward B. 1889. On a Method of Investigating the Development of Institutions: Applied to Laws of Marriage and Descent. *Journal of the Royal Anthropological Institute* 18: 245–269.

Westermarck, Edward A. 1891. *The History of Human Marriage*. London: Macmillan.

Widdig, Anja. 2007. Patrilineal Kin Discrimination: The Evidence and the Likely Mechanisms. *Biological Review* 82: 319–334.

Wilson, E. O. 1987. Kin Recognition: An Introductory Synopsis. In David J. C. Fletcher and Charles D. Michener, eds., *Kin Recognition in Animals*, pp. 7–18. Chichester, England: John Wiley and Sons.

Wolf, Arthur P. 1970. Childhood Association and Sexual Attraction: A Further Test of the Westermarck Hypothesis. *American Anthropologist* 72: 503–511.

Wolf, Arthur, and C. S. Huang. 1980. *Marriage and Adoption in China, 1845–1945.* Stanford, CA: Stanford University Press.

Woodruff, David S. 2004. Noninvasive Genotyping and Field Studies of Free-Ranging Nonhuman Primates. In Bernard Chapais and Carol M. Berman, eds., *Kinship and Behavior in Primates*, pp. 46–68. New York: Oxford University Press.

Wrangham, Richard. 2009. *Catching Fire: How Cooking Made Us Human.* New York: Basic Books.

Wright, Patricia Chapple. 1993. Variations in Male-Female Dominance and Offspring Care in Non-Human Primates. In Barbara Diane Miller, ed., *Sex and Gender Hierarchies*, pp. 127–145. Cambridge, England: Cambridge University Press.

3

THE POWER OF PATRILINES

In Chapter 1 we saw that one advantage of a mode of descent is that people can apply it to form groups within a society. Here, we will see how this works with patrilineal descent, or descent through the male line only. At the top of Figure 3.1, the dead man, A, is a founding ancestor of a patrilineal group. The shaded symbols represent his patrilineal descendants; together they form a patrilineal descent group.

As shown in this diagram, both males and females are born into the group, but only males can pass on membership. All persons inherit membership in a patriline through their father, but only sons can transmit it to their offspring. Notice that when this principle is operating, it is always quite clear who is and who is not a member of the group, and this clarity persists over the generations.

What about women in this system? Obviously their position is different from that of men: Though born into a patriline like their brothers, they cannot pass on membership to their children. Thus the woman B in Figure 3.1 is a member of the shaded group, but her children belong to the patrilineal group of the man C, who is her husband and their father.

Societies vary in terms of the extent to which women are considered full members of their natal patrilines, and in terms of what happens to their membership when they marry. In some societies, such as the Tallensi of Ghana, women hold full membership in their natal patrilines throughout life and retain specific rights and duties vis-à-vis their natal patrilineal group. In other cases, such as that traditionally found in southern China, a woman at marriage is more fully identified with her husband's patriline and retains very few rights in her natal group. Another example concerns a type of marriage that was practiced in ancient Rome, as we will see later in the chapter.

FIGURE 3.1   A Patrilineal Descent Construct

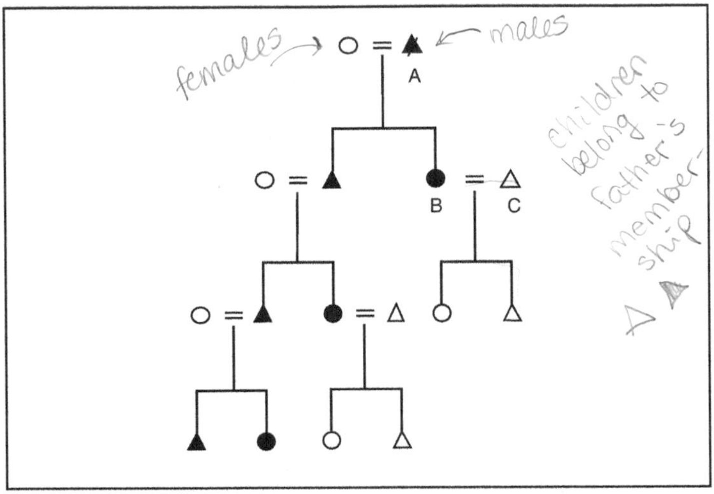

Members sharing patrilineal descent are shaded.

Figure 3.1 illustrates the core definition of patrilineal descent. This construct is important because, for one thing, most of the people of the world follow a mode of patrilineal descent. David Aberle (1961) once calculated that 44 percent of a representative sample of cultures in the world is patrilineal (with 36 percent bilateral or cognatic, 15 percent matrilineal, and 5 percent double). These percentages would look even more impressive if one were to calculate them by population. Patrilineal descent covers large and densely populated regions such as China and India. It is also prevalent in the Middle East and much of Africa. For those of us raised in European or Euro-American societies, then, it is important to grasp the concept of patrilineal descent if only to comprehend the basics of the social worlds around us.

The designation of patrilineal does not mean that the society in question recognizes only kinship on the male side, or through males, or that it ignores kinship to and through the mother. Indeed, virtually all societies exhibit bilateral kinship, whereby individuals consider that they are related to their mothers and fathers and, through them, to other people. Kinship is nearly everywhere recognized through both parents (but see Case 5 in Chapter 4). Kinship is thus normally bilateral, even in societies where descent is unilineal. Why would a society adopt patrilineal descent? As we saw in Chapter 1, by adopting a mode of descent, whether patrilineal, matrilineal, or cognatic, a society has a handy means of forming descent groups, which in turn become fundamental to its social organization. But this fact alone does not explain why some, indeed most, societies adopted patrilineal as opposed to matrilineal or cognatic descent. Many anthropologists have argued that particular modes of descent probably arose out of different patterns of postmarital residence. If, for example, residence is patrilocal, then females born into a group move out at marriage, whereas the males stay put. These males would then be patrilineally related to one another. It thus makes sense that this group would adopt patrilineal descent, since each residential area would already consist of a core of patrilineally related males. As control over resources becomes an important consideration, these males could transmit rights over resources through patrilineal lines. Alternatively, groups with matrilocal residence, in which males leave at marriage to join wives' groups, would adopt matrilineal descent. (Cognatic descent is covered in Chapter 5.)

Some anthropologists have further suggested that different patterns of postmarital residence are, or at least were initially, related to different patterns in the sexual division of labor. Thus, if males make the major contributions to subsistence and if their subsistence activities require close cooperation (as in group hunting or plow agriculture), then it would be convenient to keep closely related males together in a local group. But if a society relies on cooperative groups of women (as in communities that practice hoe agriculture), then matrilocal residence might be a better option (Gough 1961).

It is true that most patrilineal societies are patrilocal. However, residence rules vary among matrilineal societies (Divale 1975). In addition, studies in the 1970s showed no significant correlation between matrilocal residence and a predominance of females in subsistence (Ember and Ember 1971; Divale 1975). But among patrilineal societies, the association with patrilocal residence is strong, and it is possible that whatever fostered patrilocality in human societies simultaneously set up a predominance of patrilineal descent.

In Chapter 2 we saw that chimpanzees display a pattern of female dispersal at maturity—a pattern comparable to patrilocality among humans. Lars Rodseth and his colleagues (1991: 237) suggest that the human pattern may be "derived from a chimpanzee-like pattern." One implication of this idea is that a pattern of female dispersal may have been established among humans even before the institution of marriage developed. Whatever the origin, a pattern of patrilineal descent with patrilocality has persisted in many parts of the globe, surviving even changes in economic and political organization.

We now turn to the question of what patrilineal descent groups do, and why they are important to the societies that have them. In some patrilineal societies, clearly bounded descent groups may own property in common and transmit it through the generations, worship common deities or common ancestors, function as political units, take legal responsibility for the actions of all members, and engender in members a basic and primary identity with the descent group. From the point of view of the individual, the descent group (and not just "the family" in some unspecified sense) may determine how one survives economically as well as when one marries, whom one marries, and, in general, how one lives and what one does throughout his or her entire life. But the specific power a patrilineal descent group has, or the way it functions, must be considered for each society separately.

LINEAGE AND CLAN

A group of people who trace their descent to a common ancestor through known links is called a lineage. If the people do so patrilineally—that is, if they trace their descent to their common ancestor through male links—they are a patrilineage. To see how groups are formed with patrilineal descent, we can look at a hypothetical group of people who have used this principle to form descent groups. Figure 3.2 shows two distinct patrilineages in this hypothetical society. Lineage A consists of all the living descendants of Sam who can trace themselves to him through male links. Lineage B consists of all the patrilineal descendants of Alfred. Lineages A and B can be considered descent groups. We can presume that the members of each recognize their lineage identity and interact with one another in some way. Recalling a distinction made in Chapter 1, we can say that the lineages here are descent groups, but we do not yet know if they are also corporate descent groups. In some societies, lineages are corporate descent groups; in others, they are not. If the members of lineages A and B hold some property and/or have certain rights in common, then each of these lineages is a corporate descent group and, much like a business corporation, can be regarded as a single entity for some purposes.

Another kind of descent group (and one that also may or may not be a corporate group) is called a clan. A clan is like a lineage except that the members do not know all of the genealogical connections among themselves. In Figure 3.3, lineages A and B from our earlier example have been turned into subunits of one larger clan.

Here, the group members consider that they are of the same patrilineal clan because they are all descendants, through male links, of a common ancestor, Snake. They do not know exactly how their own founding lineage ancestors, Sam and Alfred, were related, but they believe that somewhere along the line they link up with two brothers, the sons of Snake. The dotted lines in the diagram indicate uncertainty about genealogical connection. The people of this society may say that since the ancestors' kinship links were formed so many generations ago, no one remembers just how the genealogy goes. But they all know they are of the same clan because they all have the same clan name, Snake, which has been inherited patrilineally. Children always take the clan name of the father. Clans are inevitably given names, and no matter how many generations have passed, everyone knows his or her clan by the patrilineal inheritance of the name.

FIGURE 3.2 Two Patrilineages

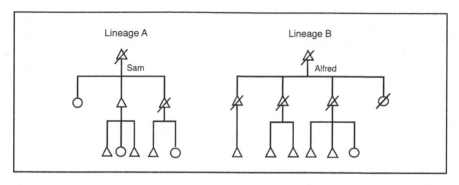

FIGURE 3.3 Two Lineages of One Clan

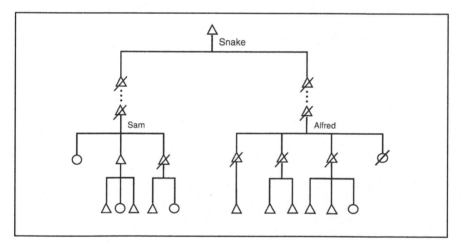

Another difference between a clan and a lineage is that the founding ancestor of a clan is often (though not always) a mythological figure—that is, a god, a plant, an animal, or a special object, rather than an ordinary human being. Many clans have "origin myths" about themselves that involve creation from a mythological being. The clan may be named after this being, as in the case of the Snake clan above. The plant, animal, or whatever has sacred significance to the clan, so clan identity tends to be intermingled with the people's religion and mythology. This identification of a group with a plant, animal, or object is called *totemism*, the totem being the plant, animal, or object with which a group identifies.

It is often the case that a society has both clans and lineages, and, if so, the lineages will be subunits of the clan, as in the hypothetical example given here. In other cases, however, a society will have lineages but no clans (as in Case 3 of this chapter) or clans but no lineages. Either way, lineages and clans represent the descent groupings that people can form using a mode of descent. The difference between them is that lineages are perceived by the people themselves as grounded in known or presumed genealogical connections, whereas clans mark an identity of general relatedness and common descent (Murphy 1986: 107).

One example of patrilineal clan organization is the ancient Roman clan, or *gens.* This organization was discussed by Lewis Henry Morgan, a nineteenth-century American scholar who was himself a founder of the study of kinship. It was Morgan (1964) who first noted organizational similarities among early Roman "tribes" and certain Native American clans in the United States. In this respect he went far beyond previous scholars who had seen the Roman gens as merely a ceremonial institution and not a corporate kinship group based on patrilineal descent (White 1964: xxx–xxxi).

Morgan wrote that early on, before the founding of Rome (around 753 B.C.), there were a number of independent Latin tribes united in a loose confederacy. Tribes were subdivided into *gentes* (clans). The legendary Romulus was said to have united a number of these, and eventually gentes of other groups (such as the Sabines) were added. Over a century, 300 gentes were united at Rome, and the chiefs of these gentes formed a governing council, which became the Roman Senate.

The gens was strictly patrilineal. Morgan (1964: 244) summarized the rights and obligations encompassed by the Roman gens as follows:

I.   Mutual rights of succession to the property of deceased gentiles.
II.   The possession of a common burial place.
III.   Common religious rites; *sacra gentilica.*
IV.   The obligation not to marry in the gens.
V.   The possession of lands in common.
VI.   Reciprocal obligations of help, defense, and redress of injuries.
VII.   The right to bear the gentile name.
VIII. The right to adopt strangers into the gens.
IX.   The right to elect and depose its chiefs.

Morgan elaborated each of these in detail, but even from this summary list it is clear that the gens was a named, exogamous, highly corporate group with land and property rights held in common, and with religious and political significance. Some of the characteristics of the gens influenced later Roman society. For example, regarding the "right to elect and depose its chiefs," Morgan (1964: 255–256) believed the fact that Roman senators were elected, and that the office was nonhereditary, was a direct continuation of the similar democratic element in the determination of the clan chiefs. Regarding

Item II—"possession of a common burial place"—elite Romans also buried their dead in family tombs, as is still done today in parts of Italy.

The corporate nature of the gens faded away fairly early in ancient Rome. According to Morgan, this transition occurred as Roman society developed as a state and as land and other property came into the hands of individuals, ceasing to be communally held by the clan.[1] What eventually emerged among the upper classes in Rome were individual, largely nuclear family units, each in separate control of considerable property. A sense of clan identity continued (and was embodied in the patrilineal family name, or *nomen*), but the clan as such was no longer a corporate group. By this time each clan had come to be named after some illustrious human ancestor, in contrast to earlier clans that had likely taken names from totemic animals or objects (Morgan 1964: 252).

The early upper-class Roman family has been noted for the rather extraordinary powers vested in the male head, or *paterfamilias*. This man held full power over his family property and considerable authority over his children, slaves, and any other dependents attached to his household, often including his wife. Indeed, he wielded the power of life and death over his own children. The authority of the paterfamilias lasted until his death. Thus at the pinnacle of each family unit was the eldest surviving male. A male grew up under the power (*potestas*) of his father (or grandfather or great-grandfather, if still alive) and became legally independent only at this man's death. If at this time he was still a minor, a guardian (usually a father's brother, if available) would be appointed over him until he came of age.

Women, by contrast, were, in a sense, perpetual minors. They had a legal male guardian at all times, regardless of their age (Pomeroy 1975). Legally, this arrangement lasted until the late third century A.D. If a woman married in a union called "free marriage," she remained under the control of her father (or guardian), who not only arranged her marriage but also had the authority to divorce her from her husband and marry her to another man (Treggiari 1991). In "free marriage" a woman retained both her family name (rather than taking that of the husband) and the right to inherit from her father. In another type of marriage, called "marriage with *manus*," the authority over the bride was transferred from the bride's father to her husband; the woman took the name of her husband's gens and acquired the right to inherit a share of his family property. Marriage with manus in ancient Rome was an example of a system whereby a woman at marriage lost many rights in her natal patriline and was largely incorporated into her husband's kin group.

Whether a woman married "free" or "with manus" was up to her father or guardian. Early on, marriage with manus was considered more prestigious, but by the Late Republic (in the first century B.C.) "free" marriage had become the more common form (Corbier 1991).

We will revisit the ancient Romans later in this book. Their case is interesting, first, because ancient Rome provides good illustrations of the manipulation of marriage for the formation of political alliances (Chapter 6) and, second, because Roman patterns of kinship and gender show changes over a long time, some of which are relevant to developments in Euro-American patterns (Chapter 7).

PATRILOCALITY

At this point we must consider once more the question of residence. As we saw in Chapter 1, descent rules and residence rules (or norms) should be considered together in our examination of a given society or culture. What we need to know, first of all, is whether a descent group is also a residence group, or, to put it another way, whether and to what extent descent and residence overlap. If they do overlap, we will know that the descent group is likely to exert a fairly strong influence on the lives of its resident members. We can look at this phenomenon in terms of patrilineal societies. As noted earlier, most patrilineal societies in the world are also patrilocal, such that a couple, at marriage, moves in with or near the groom's kin. For now, let's consider the case of a couple moving right into the groom's parents' household, since this is what often happens. Figure 3.4 shows who would be living with whom in this patrilineal-patrilocal society, in an ideal state (which seldom occurs) where patrilocality continued over the generations and subgroups never split up or hived off from one another.

Here, two different patrilineal groups are illustrated. The members of Descent Group 1 are darkly shaded and those of Descent Group 2 are lightly shaded. Notice that a woman from the former group married a man from

FIGURE 3.4   Patrilocal Residence

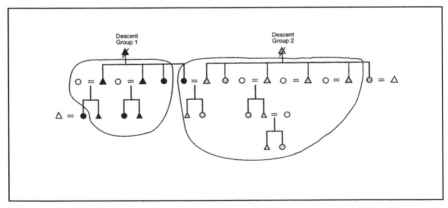

Members of Descent Group 1 are darkly shaded, and members of Descent Group 2 are lightly shaded. The loops surround the people who, following patrilocal residence, will live together.

the latter. The individuals left unshaded are people who belong to assorted other patrilineal groups and who have married members of Descent Group 1 or 2. Loops are drawn around those individuals who all live together in one house. The diagram makes clear that in domestic units the *male patrilineal relatives stay together*. For men, the patrilineal group is literally grounded in residence; these men will inevitably have a lot to do with and be within easy access of one another. If they have to get together to discuss some issue or make some important decision, they're all right there. Since the men are united by both "blood" and residence, the potential for male solidarity is high. So are the potentials for conflict and jealousy, of course. But if these men recognize some lines of authority (for example, that the eldest male acts as "head" and/or that elder males in general have authority over younger ones), an organized social life is possible. By adding another factor such as some valuable property held in common by these men, we can easily see how an important social unit might emerge.

For the moment we must assume that the patrilineal kin groups shown in Figure 3.4 are exogamous; that is, marriage within the patrilineal group is not permitted. Now, the women inside each loop are either unmarried individuals (and bound to leave when they do marry) or married-in "outsiders" coming in from other patrilines. In contrast to the men, their solidarity is likely to be weak. In addition, husbands begin marriage on their own "turf." Thus the burden is on wives rather than husbands to make the major adaptations and adjustments to married life, at least initially.

This diagram depicts an ideal type. In reality, patrilineal-patrilocal groups eventually split up. As discussed in Chapter 1 with respect to "the domestic cycle," residential groups worldwide tend to undergo their own "cycles" of expansion, contraction, and hiving off as marriages, births, and deaths take place and as resources fluctuate (Fortes 1958; Robertson 1991: 6–25). At times other factors also come into play. It may be that in a given society (see, for example, Case 3 in this chapter) the notion of patrilineal males staying together over the generations is a cultural ideal, yet brothers usually split up upon the death of the father and live in separate households. It may be that some of the women marrying into such a group are themselves related, or come from the same community, and so are not initially strangers to one another. Or it may be that, within a given "patrilocal" group, a couple is residing in the town or village of the groom's kin, but not in his parental household. The point is that, whatever its configuration, a patrilineal-patrilocal pattern suggests important, built-in differences in the marital and domestic situations of men and women.

Patrilineal societies tend to be patrilocal, but there are exceptions. For example, the Mundurucú Indians, a group settled on a tributary of the Amazon River in Brazil, are patrilineal with matrilocal residence (Murphy 1986: 78). In this case, men at marriage move to the villages of their wives. Here, they reside not in their wives' dwellings but in a central men's house along with other married-in men and adult but unmarried sons of the village women. In the dwellings surrounding the men's house, sisters live together with their mothers and raise their young children. But these children belong to the descent groups of their fathers. Another example of a patrilineal-matrilocal society is the Yupik Eskimo of southwestern Alaska, whose social organization is very similar to that of the Mundurucú (Ackerman 1992).

Aside from patrilocality, patrilineal societies tend to share two other features. First, relationships traced patrilineally are important and close but are also tinged with a sense of formality and duty. In patrilineal societies this formality is often offset by informal, warm, and affectionate relationships traced through the mother—especially those between a male and his mother's brother (an often special, institutionalized relationship referred to as the *avunculate*). These relationships, which were common in ancient Rome (Bettini 1991: 39–66), will be examined more fully in the case studies in this chapter. Second, although practices vary across societies, patrilineal units tend to have instant and permanent custody of children. In the case of dissolution of a marriage, young children may remain with the mother for a time, but ultimately their fate is in the hands of the patrilineal units to which they belong. Among most patrilineal peoples, children belong not to individuals exclusively but to groups; in the event of divorce, their fate is decided not through a legal battle between individual mothers and fathers but within the principle of patrilineal descent.

LINEAL MASCULINITY

Patrilineal groups share yet another feature, and this one is crucial to gender: To survive, the patriline must acquire male children. Only sons can transmit membership. If only daughters are born, the patrilineal group dies out. Not surprisingly, therefore, patrilineal groups have built within them a whole host of cultural mechanisms that express a "favoring" of male over female children. This does not mean that all patrilineal societies go so far as to disparage the birth of daughters. In fact, as we will see in Case 2, a patrilineal society may have reasons for desiring the birth of daughters as well as that of sons.

Parents in strongly patrilineal societies often say that sons are necessary to "continue the line" (by which they mean the patriline, of course); to serve as heirs; to provide labor or income to a household; to care for parents in old age; and to assist parents spiritually after death. In these societies, the association between sons and the spiritual welfare of parents and other ancestors is strong across cultures. Thus ideas and practices promoting fertility and aiming at the production of sons may be deeply interwoven with religion.

Connections among patrilineal descent, procreation, and gender may be deeper yet. Many, though not all, patrilineal societies exhibit what has been called "lineal masculinity" (King and Stone 2010). Lineal masculinity refers to the idea that males receive from their male ancestors and in their turn transmit to their male descendants a specific, shared masculine quality. In these societies patrilineal descent confers not only membership in a group but also, for men, a larger, time-honored legacy of male being. For men, then, a patriline may also be a mascu-line. Individual males born into a patriline are under some pressure to uphold or, even better, enhance this quality through their behavior and accomplishments in life; they are certainly admonished not to diminish this individual and collective masculine quality through inappropriate behavior or personal failures. One clear way to enhance lineal masculinity is through a man's production of male children, with many better than few. This connection between continuing the patriline, continuing lineal masculinity through strings of fathers and sons, is often connected with ideas of immortality, overcoming death, and allowing a man to "live on."

In particular regions lineal masculinity may be expressed through cultural notions of family/lineage "honor," as seen throughout the Middle East. In one case study in this chapter, as we will see, lineal masculinity is expressed largely through cultural ideas of male spiritual "purity." Lineal masculinity is often celebrated through rituals, especially those that concern male initiation ceremonies or that center on male worship of common patrilineal ancestors or lineage gods.

Lineal masculinity appears to be widespread, occurring throughout China, South Asia, and the Middle East. In some of these areas it is often associated with "patrogenesis," the cultural notion that males, not females, create life, or as Carol Delaney put it, "Males give life, women simply give birth" (1987: 39). In many areas, as mentioned in Chapter 1, male procreation is metaphorically expressed as planting active, life-giving male "seed" into passive female "soil." Women nurture the seed but are not co-creators of life. In these contexts male reproduction is both culturally imperative and perceived as necessarily biological; a man enhances his lineal masculinity by producing his own biological children (especially sons). Women-as-soil are considered to be lineage property, almost as though they were territories or parcels of land that need to be guarded (and need to guard themselves) to avoid a patriline's introducing through them "the wrong seed." Only proper marriage provides a legitimate context for female sexuality. "Woman-as-soil is, by definition, a potential threat to the patrilineage because through a woman's sexual transgressions (sex before marriage or sex after marriage with any man other than her husband), children may be produced, ostensibly for the husband's lineage but by the 'seed' of other men" (King and Stone 2010: 332).

Patrilineal descent carries implications for men and women in their roles as husbands, wives, and parents. Let us now see how this arrangement works inside two very different societies. As we will see, both of these patrilineal groups express lineal masculinity, but in different ways and with different consequences for men and women.

CASE 2: THE NUER

The Nuer were until recently a pastoral, cattle-herding people who inhabited the swamp and savannah areas of southern Sudan. They were studied in the 1930s by British anthropologist Sir E. E. Evans-Pritchard (1990). In the area of his work, there were about 200,000 Nuer. Although some Nuer cultural traditions survived into modern times, much changed as the Nuer were brought under British colonial rule and, later, into the Sudanese state with its devastating civil wars (James 1990: xxi). The description of the Nuer given here refers to their way of life at the time of Evans-Pritchard's now-classic study.

Shortly before Evans-Pritchard embarked on his research, the Nuer were involved both in internal warfare (with some Nuer groups displacing others) and in conquest and displacement of a closely related group, the Dinka (Kelly 1985). The warfare and territorial expansion of the Nuer, halted by British colonial intervention, were important because they undoubtedly influenced some features of Nuer kinship that Evans-Pritchard described as stable, timeless aspects of Nuer culture. In particular, some of the Nuer marriage forms discussed in this chapter may have been promoted, or intensified, as conquering Nuer sought to recruit followings of captive Dinka or other conquered Nuer. The importance of this historical context to Nuer kinship was pointed out by later researchers—most notably, Kathleen Gough (1971). Gough also suggested that much of Evans-Pritchard's discussion of Nuer kinship characterized only a minority, "aristocratic" segment of the population. These points should be kept in mind as we explore Nuer kinship based on Evans-Pritchard's early work.

The largest Nuer political units were what Evans-Pritchard called "tribes," headed by Leopard-Skin chiefs who were sacred persons but had no effective political authority. The real political life of the Nuer was interwoven with their patrilineal kinship structure, organized into lineages and clans. These units regulated blood feuds, warfare, and the settling of disputes (Evans-Pritchard 1940).

Nuer clans were exogamous (marriages were not permitted within them) and subdivided into lineages. The lineages, in turn, were subdivided into segments, the smallest of which were about three to five generations deep. In addition, the lineages were residentially dispersed, so that each village contained homesteads representing different lineages and each such homestead had lineage kin in other villages. Villages were themselves corporate groups, holding the grazing grounds, fishing pools, and plots of land in common. But each village was associated with a main lineage and often called after the name of this lineage.

The Nuer were patrilocal in that wives generally moved into the villages and homesteads of husbands, but various other arrangements were also possible. A woman who had married into another village might have left her husband and returned to her home village, or a man might have decided, for any number of reasons, that he wanted to live and raise a family in the village of his mother's brother rather than that of his own father. In short, along with or in spite of a general pattern of patrilocality, actual residence patterns indicated a great deal of flexibility and individual choice among the Nuer.

Cattle, the economic mainstay of Nuer life, were owned by men. Wives were given certain cows to milk by husbands, but they did not own them and had no rights to dispose of them. The cattle were ultimately considered to be the corporate property of the lineage (Evans-Pritchard 1990: 128). When a man died, his brothers and eventually his sons or other patrilineally related males would inherit them. Men were strongly associated with cattle; aside from owning them, only men could ritually sacrifice them in religious ceremonies or give and receive them as marriage payments.

In many respects, Nuer males and females led contrasting, and often quite separate, lives. For instance, they moved into adulthood in very different ways. The first ceremonial attention a female received took place during her wedding and a female was considered an adult only after the birth of children (Hutchinson 1980). But for males, approaching adulthood meant that their identities would be bound up with warriorhood and strong associations with other males. Between the ages of fourteen and sixteen, young males were initiated into adulthood and warrior status through a painful ritual that involved the incising of six permanent lines (called *gar*) across their foreheads. The gar were seen as the marks of manhood; indeed, the Nuer did not view foreign males, lacking gar, as "men," whatever their ages (Evans-Pritchard 1990: 255). Males who underwent this initiation ritual together formed an age-set, a sort of lifelong club within which members closely associated with one another in a spirit of equality.

Upon initiation, a boy received a spear and an ox from his father, became a warrior, and was henceforth forbidden to milk cows, a task for women. Only after initiation and after serving a warrior stage was a man permitted to marry. For a boy's male elders this was the real meaning of the initiation: Since the boy's marriage and reproduction were now real possibilities, they saw in his initiation the potential for their lineage to continue. In other ways, too, male initiation expressed Nuer lineal masculinity. In receiving and identifying with his new ox at initiation, "a young man necessarily acknowledges a debt to his forefathers, those who have provided him with the means [cattle] for full participation in the masculine domain. In this light manhood may be understood as an ancestral 'gift' passed down from generation to generation through the communal herd" (Hutchinson 1980: 378).

Males and Females in the Web of Kinship

Within villages were homesteads, consisting minimally of a man and his wife (or wives) grouped around a cattle byre, where cattle were sheltered. Wives had separate huts around the byre; the common husband could spend the night in one of the huts, or he could sleep in the byre. Commonly a married man along with his married brothers and, if alive, their father would live together, with their byre and huts grouped in a kind of hamlet.

The byre, considered the heart of a homestead, was seen as a male space (though women could freely enter it): "Very early in life small boys are driven by their father or elder brothers away from their mothers' huts to the byre, the place of the menfolk of the family, where they eat, sleep, and spend the leisure hours of the day" (Evans-Pritchard 1990: 125). The cattle byre was also associated with the patrilineage itself. When a new byre was built, a man would "make a libation of beer to the guardian spirits and ancestral ghosts of the lineage" (Evans-Pritchard 1990: 125). An ancestral shrine was also kept in a byre.

Although they did not own cattle, women were considered to be economically crucial and central to the home because only they (and, technically speaking, young males not yet initiated into adulthood) could milk the cows. Thus, in a sense, men were dependent on women: "However many cattle a man may possess, he is helpless without a wife or mother or sister to milk the cows" (Evans-Pritchard 1990: 130). Indeed, Evans-Pritchard underlined the Nuer cultural view of women as central nodes drawing men together: "In grouping themselves around a herd [the Nuer] also group themselves around the milkmaid who serves the herd" (1990: 131).

Women had very particular roles to play in Nuer patrilineages. First, a married woman reproduced for her husband's lineage, and her children became members of it. But look at the case of the polygynous household illustrated in Figure 3.5. Here, the males of groups A and B are all equal members of lineage X and are patrilineal kin to one another. But those of group A feel a kind of special cohesiveness because they share the same mother and they feel a separateness from group B because their mothers are different persons. The Nuer called all the people of either group (A or B) "brothers of the hut" (*kwi dwiel*). But when referring to paternal half-brothers (A and B together), they called them "brothers

FIGURE 3.5   Nuer Brothers from a Polygynous Marriage

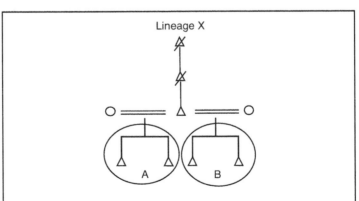

The full brothers of Groups A and B are cohesive, but units A and B feel a distance from one another because their mothers are different persons.

ſ

of the byre" (*kwi luak*). Brothers of the hut were inevitably closer than half-brothers who only shared a byre: "Nuer are not surprised at—they expect—coldness between half brothers, and disagreements and disputes between them" (Evans-Pritchard 1990: 142).

When a polygynous father died, the various sets of half-brothers would likely split into separate groups. Thus there was always potential fission in the group due to the separate loyalties engendered by the separate mothers reproducing the lineage. This idea of the difference that separate mothers can make also affected relationships over the generations; for instance, the Nuer spoke of one's father's paternal half-brother as a kind of "wicked uncle," as someone not to be trusted (Evans-Pritchard 1990: 158).

A second role played by women in this system was to link their children to nonlineage kin (that is, to the children's maternal kin). Recall that earlier in this chapter we distinguished between descent and kinship, observing that in nearly all societies kinship is bilateral (traced through both parents) even where descent is unilineal. Among the Nuer, as with many other patrilineal societies, there was some tension or conflict between lineage-based interests and loyalties on the one hand and kinship-based sentiments on the other. Relationships among close patrilineally related males were rather strained. As Evans-Pritchard elaborated:

> Rights in the herd, duties of blood revenge, and status in the community hold a man to his father's kin, but with these go jealousy about cattle, resentment against authority, and personal rivalries. . . . The paternal ties are stronger, if there is a touch of hardness in them. The maternal ties are weaker and for this reason are tenderer. (1990: 139–140)

The texture of Nuer family life, as discussed so far, can be summarized in terms of the three different kinds of relationships that a male ego would have with three different types of uncle, as illustrated in Figure 3.6. There is a continuum here. With the man A ("wicked uncle"), ego's relationship is tense and problematical. With the man B, the relationship is close and cooperative, but it has that "touch of hardness." With the man C, the relationship is close and highly affective. Notice that the quality of each of these relationships is very much determined by the position of the women in this diagram. Ego has a closer, more relaxed relationship with MB than with FB. But at least with FB, the "linking woman" is fairly close to ego; she is his own FM. With the man A, by contrast, the woman in question (A's M, ego's FFW) is distant from ego.

Looking at the system as a whole, and also remembering women's domestic roles, especially the central role of milking cows, we see that women are affecting the system in three ways: They are continuing the patriline, they are pulling some men together, and as sources of fission they are pulling other men apart. In their role as reproducing wives they both create and destroy. Thus women's roles within the structure of Nuer kinship and descent are related to men's ambivalence toward women as well as to a "latent hostility between the sexes" (Evans-Pritchard 1990: 133). In Nuer mythology, one story tells how women brought mosquitoes to the world; in another, they are bringers of death. Even more telling is the following:

> Nuer men also say that women have bad mouths and that evil comes out of them, and they account for this by a story which relates that the mouths of women used to be, before God changed their position, where their vaginas are now; and they say that women are sensual and fickle, God having at their request, as another story relates, cut their hearts in two so that one half might be added to the male organ to give them greater pleasure in coitus. There are other stories which suggest a deep-lying hostility toward women. (Evans-Pritchard 1950, cited in Beidelman 1966: 457)

This account is interesting in its phrasing of the hostility toward women in such graphic, sexual terms and in the imputation of female sexual greed. But the point I especially wish to stress is that it is within the framework of Nuer kinship that we most clearly see the forces of male ambivalence and hostility toward women. Let us now consider women's and men's roles as they affect reproduction and its consequences.

FIGURE 3.6   A Nuer Male's Relationships with Different Types of Uncle

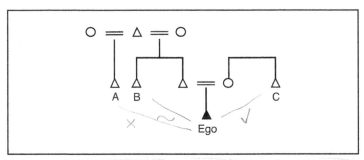

Ego has a close, affective relationship with the man C; he has a more distant relationship with the man B; and he is likely to mistrust the man A.

Marriage and Children

We already know a few things about marriage among the Nuer—for example, that they practiced polygyny. How common it was is not known. Evans-Pritchard mentioned that "monogamous marriage was much commoner," but he adds that polygyny was "frequent enough to have set its stamp, through its association with wealth and social influence, on the lineage system" (1990: 140). Evans-Pritchard also claimed that the Nuer regarded polygyny as the ideal form of family. But we can assume that by this he meant it was ideal in the eyes of men, since elsewhere we learn that the Nuer word for cowife, *nyak*, in its verb form also means "to be jealous" and that jealousy between cowives was likely (1990: 134–135).

Evans-Pritchard was also ambivalent on the subject of the husband-wife relationship. On the one hand, he mentioned (1990: 133) that husbands had unquestioned authority over wives. But he elsewhere referred to wives insulting husbands or, in a quarrel, knocking out a husband's tooth, an act for which the woman's father had to compensate the husband with a cattle payment (di Leonardo 1991: 6).

Along with polygyny, the Nuer practiced a form of the *levirate*, whereby a widow is "inherited" by her dead husband's brother. Among the Nuer the levirate was optional for the woman, and even if she joined the brother he was considered a "pro-husband" and the woman remained the legal wife of the dead husband. The *sororate*, whereby a man marries the sister of his dead wife, was also practiced, but among the Nuer this could happen only if the dead wife had been childless.

In all forms of marriage, a core concern of the Nuer was the acquisition of male heirs for patrilines. And here we see a strong expression of Nuer lineal masculinity. Nuer notions of immortality, for men at least, were tied to the siring of sons: "A man's memorial is not in some monument but in his sons. . . . Every man likes to feel that his name will never be forgotten so long as his lineage endures and that in that sense he will always be a part of the lineage" (Evans-Pritchard 1974: 162).

But where sons were concerned, the Nuer went further than most other patrilineal societies that merely encourage or reward the production of sons; indeed, the Nuer claimed that all males *must* have at least one son. One may wonder how this was possible in cases of male sterility or impotence but, as we shall soon see, the Nuer arranged matters in such a way that any man could eventually have a son.

First, however, we need to delve into Nuer ideas about marriage and paternity. These ideas and their related practices were intimately bound up with cattle, which the Nuer used to pay bridewealth, or the transfer of wealth from the kin of the groom to the kin of the bride. This bridewealth was seen not as a "payment" for the bride but rather as a transfer of wealth that guaranteed the *rights of the husband's patriline to the future children* of this woman. Thus the bridewealth at once legalized the marriage, legitimized the children, and guaranteed the allocation of the children to the husband's patrilineal units.

The practice of bridewealth marriage had an important consequence. To bring in a bride, a Nuer group needed to amass a lot of cattle for bridewealth. Normally the only way this could be done was to first acquire cattle from marrying off a daughter. Thus, among the Nuer, *daughters as well as sons* were necessary and valued. Unlike some other patrilineal groups, the Nuer did not regard the birth of a daughter as unfortunate or sorrowful, for a daughter was a bringer of cattle, a provider of bridewealth for her brothers.

Bridewealth cattle were gradually handed over in stages, and at each stage the two groups of kin would argue about the exact numbers and kinds of cattle. As with the delivery of cattle, so marriage itself was seen by Nuer as a continuum. There was no single "I now pronounce you man and wife" formula that made the marriage real; indeed, if all went well, one simply became more and more married.

Marriages were usually initiated by the young couple and then approved by the two sets of kin. Females married at about seventeen or eighteen to older males of varied ages. Before marriage, both males and females were expected to be sexually active. Young unmarried persons met and conducted their affairs at various nighttime dances, often held at a wedding party for someone else. Apparently courtship and romance occupied a great deal of time and energy among Nuer youth.

Once a proposal was accepted by all concerned, the establishment of the marriage proceeded by stages, and at each stage more cattle were transferred from the groom's kin to those of the bride. The first stage, called *larcieng* (betrothal), signified that both sets of kin provisionally agreed to the union. The next stage, *ngut* (wedding), was held at the bride's home. In one wedding ceremony, the groom's kin and the bride's kin called out the respective clan "spearnames" of the bride and groom as a public affirmation that since the clans were *different*, the marriage was proper (recall that clans were exogamous). At the wedding the ghosts of lineage ancestors were ritually invoked to witness the union. There was also a ritual acknowledgment of the importance of lineage continuity. In one rite, a male relative of the bride, acting as "master of ceremonies," called out that the bride would bear her husband a male child (Evans-Pritchard 1990: 66).

By this stage, many cattle would have been given over to the bride's kin. If any of these cattle died after the transfer, they had to be replaced by the groom's kin. But after the next marriage stage, *mut* (consummation), this replacement was no longer required. During this stage, the bride was taken to the groom's home and put inside a hut. The groom joined her there and the marriage was consummated. With mut, the marriage was starting to get quite serious.

The completion of mut signaled the growing strength of the marriage in ways other than the fact that dead bridewealth cattle no longer had to be replaced. First, after mut, the groom could claim compensation from a man who committed adultery with his wife. The usual fee for this was six cows. Second, after mut, the wife (but not the husband) was no longer permitted to attend nighttime dances. Finally, after mut, the wife's head was shaved, symbolizing her new status as a married woman.

Even after mut the marriage could still be called off, by the bride or groom or a kin group, in which case all the bridewealth cattle would have to be returned to the groom's kin. And at this stage, the husband and wife were still not living together. The next stage, which completed the marriage, was the birth of the first child. Between mut and the birth, the wife remained in her father's home, where she was given her own hut. Here her husband would visit her at night, leaving early in the morning. Later, when the first child was weaned, the wife moved to the husband's home and was given a hut there. Only then would the wife's father begin to disperse the bridewealth cattle among the bride's kin. At this point a divorce could take place, and in this event (or in the event of the wife's death) the bridewealth cattle would be returned to the groom's kin except for six cows that would remain with the bride's group as a guarantee that the one child was the legal child of the husband and a member of the husband's patrilineal groups.

There was one last stage of Nuer marriage: the birth of a second child. With only one child present, the marriage could be ended by divorce. But once a second child was born, divorce was no longer possible because after this point bridewealth cattle could never be returned. Now, at this stage, a woman *could* leave her husband. She could even take up with another man and live with him, a union that Evans-Pritchard termed "concubinage." What the finality of her marriage meant was that (1) she could not remarry, and (2) should she bear other children in the future, begotten by whomever, they were automatically her legal husband's children and members of his lineage/clan. This is the reason all the cattle were given. After two children had been born, the patriline had permanent rights over whatever issued from the woman's womb.

From the foregoing we can see that the production of children for the husband's patriline was a fundamental, core purpose of marriage, and that bridewealth cattle not only established formal marriage but also served as a statement of and guarantee for rights over children of the woman. The whole system of gradual marriage and gradual bridewealth made it easy to break off negotiations or cancel the marriage in the beginning, but once the couple's fertility was verified, this became harder to do, and eventually it was impossible to sever the tie between the husband's patriline and the woman's reproduction.

The Nuer engaged in a number of other interesting marital practices that would seem bewildering if we did not already understand the importance to them of acquiring children (especially sons) as future members of patrilineal groups. We will take a look at these practices and eventually discover how it is possible that all Nuer men could have sons. One clue has already been given. We have seen that if a fully married woman left her husband and gave birth to another man's child, the child would legally be her husband's, even though he and everyone else knew that he was not the biological father. Anthropologists use the term *genitor* for the biological father and *pater* for the legal father. For the Nuer, paterhood was primary; it was what the system had been organized to achieve for all men. The "real" father was a pater who might have been but was not necessarily the genitor.

The Nuer were not unconcerned or uncaring about the role of genitor. Men preferred to beget their own children and, for that matter, acknowledged "social and mystical links" between a child and its genitor (Evans-Pritchard 1990: 120). In addition, in cases where the genitor and the pater of a daughter were different men, the genitor would, upon the marriage of this daughter, receive a "cow of the begetting" from the bridewealth paid for her (Evans-Pritchard 1990: 121).

Still, the pater was primary. Let us now look at male strategies for becoming paters. The first step a man, in collaboration with his kin, could take to have legal children was to get married. His doing so resulted in a simple monogamous union. If the union was fertile, the man, seeking more children and/or possibly having other motives, could add wives to his home.

What happened if the original union was infertile? In this case, the taking of another wife would have been essential and the first wife might or might not have been divorced. Let's say the first wife was not divorced and the man eventually took two more wives but none of the three wives ever became pregnant. We would consider it likely that the man was the one with the fertility problem, and so would the Nuer. At this point there would still have been other options available to him. One would be what I call "blind-eye adultery," whereby the man turned a "blind eye" to an adulterous affair on the part of one or more wives in the hope that someone would get pregnant.[2] He would be the pater of whatever child was produced. Sooner or later this strategy was likely to work. Still, it could happen that a married man died before it did work. Indeed, a man could die before getting married at all, and yet it has been said that all Nuer men (barring those who died before puberty) had to have a male heir. As it turns out, the Nuer system had prepared for even this possibility with the very distinctive option of *ghost marriage*. In this case, a patrilineal kinsman, such as a brother or cousin, would take a wife in the name of a deceased, childless man, and have children by her in the dead man's name, as illustrated in Figure 3.7.

Here, the man A, though considered unmarried in his own right, has ghost-married the woman B to his childless dead brother, C. The woman B refers to C as her dead husband and addresses A as "brother-in-law." The children of this union refer to the man A as the Nuer equivalent of "uncle." Now, why would the man A go to all this trouble? There are two reasons. First, it was his patrilineal duty to do so. Second, the Nuer believed that the soul of a dead childless man hovers about in discontent, eventually attacking its own patrilineal kin and causing illness in one of them or some other misfortune in the group. Arranging a ghost marriage then became a part of the cure for the illness or misfortune (Evans-Pritchard 1990: 109).

Nuer women, like men, were eager to have children, and their identity as women was very much dependent on their fertility (Hutchinson 1980). We have seen that the Nuer system abounded with options and strategies by which males and their patrilines could acquire sons. Some of the same options could of course help women, too. If a married woman failed to have children, "blind-eye adultery" might have alleviated her childless state. But what if the woman herself was barren? In many societies around the world, barrenness is a monumental tragedy for a woman, who may suffer pity and ostracism. The Nuer, however, instituted yet another ingenious marriage form that transformed female barrenness into a kind of reproductive potential. This is the famous institution of *woman-woman marriage*. In this case, a woman presumed to be barren could elect to divorce her husband and remain in her father's home. (Since she had not borne children, she would not have moved to her husband's home.) Then, because of her barrenness, she could "count as a man" among her natal patrilineal kin. A marriage to another woman would be arranged for her, and bridewealth paid, turning the barren woman into a husband. Next, the barren woman would arrange for a man (the choice of the man was hers) to sleep with her wife as a type of surrogate genitor.

FIGURE 3.7 A Nuer Ghost Marriage

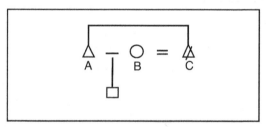

The man A "ghost married" the woman B to his dead brother, C. The children belong to the dead man.

Children of this union were considered members of the woman's natal patrilineal groups, and the woman herself was considered their pater, or legal father. In Figure 3.8, ego is a barren woman who, after divorcing her husband, has entered woman-woman marriage. The shaded symbols represent people who belong to the same patrilineal descent group.

The children of ego's wife would now refer to ego as "father." Woman-woman marriage was not a lesbian relationship, but the barren woman did take on the social role of husband/father. For example, she had a great deal of authority over her wife, just as a male husband would have had. And if the wife independently took a lover (that is, not the genitor chosen by the barren woman) and was discovered to have done so, the barren woman was entitled to claim a fee from the lover as adultery compensation.

As far as her natal patriline was concerned, this barren woman "counted as a man" in every respect and was able to reproduce the patriline, just as would a son. Thus the patriline was able to transform a barren daughter into a mechanism

FIGURE 3.8   A Nuer Woman-Woman Marriage

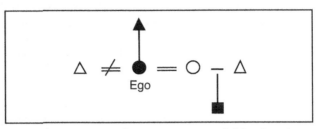

Ego is a barren woman who "counts as a man." After divorcing her husband, she married another woman and arranged for a man to have children with this woman. Ego is the father of the children, and the children are members of Ego's natal patrilineage.

for its own reproduction. Rather than being pitied or scorned, the individual woman became an "honorary male" and was given a socially meaningful role to play. Woman-woman marriage has been also reported in other African societies (Brain 1972: 60; Gluckman 1965: 184; Herskovits 1937).

These forms of marital and nonmarital, but quite acceptable, unions among the Nuer—legal marriage (monogamous and polygynous), concubinage, ghost marriage, and woman-woman marriage—are striking for their sheer variety. But one prominent feature of Nuer marriage forms was the ease with which both men and women could circulate through legitimate sexual and marital unions. Another was the precision and clarity with which children were allocated to husbands' lineages through cattle payments. These different marriage forms can also be seen as available strategies whereby individual Nuer and their lineages could acquire children/sons, even in cases of male or female infertility.

An important consequence followed from this system in which children were allocated according to bridewealth payments: Women had rather autonomous control over their own sexuality (Gough 1971: 111). Premarital sex was not discouraged or punished. Women had a lot to say about whom (or even if) they married. After marriage they were free to leave their husbands (though they would lose whatever children had been born to them). And even adultery was not so serious. Evans-Pritchard (1990: 120) commented that among the Nuer, adultery was illegal but not immoral, adding that he was "struck among the Nuer both by the frequency of adultery and the infrequency of quarrels or even talk about it." A fee was collected from the male offender, but unless the adultery became a persistent problem, in which case a man might divorce a wife (1990: 134), women were not punished for it.

Our next study, Case 3, concerns the Brahman peoples of Nepal, also patrilocal and strongly patrilineal. Here we will see both striking similarities and contrasts with the Nuer.

CASE 3: NEPALESE BRAHMANS

Nepal is a small country in the Himalayas, with a population of around 30 million in 2012. It lies between India to the south and China (Tibet) to the north. Its numerous ethnic groups speak different languages. Many of these groups, especially those classified as Indo-Nepalese speakers, are Hindu. Others follow Buddhist traditions, often mixed with Hindu practices. The Brahmans are an Indo-Nepalese group. Their ancestors came north from India, beginning as early as the twelfth century A.D., when some people in India were fleeing Moslem invasions. In most areas of Nepal, the Indo-Nepalese people became economically and politically dominant. Starting from the eighteenth century, Nepal was a Hindu kingdom, the last one in the world; following a period of political strife over the last two decades, Nepal in 2008 abolished its monarchy and became a republic.

The term *Brahman* is actually a caste designation. Indeed, a few words must be said about the Nepalese caste system, since some of the ideas on which it rests are important to kinship and gender. Castes in Nepal are ranked status groups,[3] with the ranking sanctioned by religion. The whole system is expressed through Hindu religious ideas concerning purity and pollution: Higher castes are considered purer than lower castes. Brahmans are at the very top of the caste hierarchy. And only Brahman males, on account of their higher caste purity, may, if they choose, become Hindu priests. Beneath the Brahmans are a number of other high-ranking castes whose male members, like Brahman males, wear the "sacred thread." This is an actual thread stretched over a shoulder and under an arm, made sacred by the action of Hindu priests and bestowed upon males at the time of their initiation into adulthood and simultaneously into their castes and lineages. Next are a number of mid-ranking castes collectively classed as *matwali*, or "liquor-drinking." This term refers to the fact that it is acceptable for such people to drink liquor, not that they go about drinking excessively. The higher thread-wearing groups, by contrast, are not supposed to consume liquor. Finally, at the bottom are the low untouchable castes, somewhat similar to the untouchables of India. Although other castes interact with them regularly, they are considered impure and physical contact with them is thought to be polluting. If a person accidentally makes physical contact with an untouchable, a ritual of purification is necessary to restore his or her caste purity.

All of these castes have rules covering members' diet and other behavior. In addition, there are rules governing interactions between different castes. The most important one is that higher castes cannot consume boiled rice (*bhat*, the mainstay of Nepalese meals) cooked by lower-caste persons. Conversely, lower castes can and do consume boiled rice prepared by groups they recognize as higher. Thus, for instance, Brahmans may cook boiled rice and serve it to all other groups but can consume only that which has been prepared by fellow Brahmans.

Caste endogamy is both an ideal and a norm in Nepal, and this is especially true for Brahmans. Indeed, the only way Brahman men and women can have caste-pure Brahman children is through a religiously sanctioned caste-endogamous marriage,[4] a matter that I will elaborate on later.

The notions of purity and pollution, so important in the caste system, are also fundamental to kinship and gender among Brahmans. Just as higher castes are considered purer than lower castes, males as a category are considered purer than females. The reason: Women menstruate, and menstrual blood is seen as an extremely polluting substance. During their menstrual periods, women must segregate themselves; they become, like the lowest of castes, untouchable, though in their case this is a temporary state. Afterward they must take a ritual bath to restore a state of relative purity. Contact with menstruating women is thought to be highly polluting for all initiated males.

Nepalese Hindus also perceive other fluctuating states of individual purity/pollution. In daily life and throughout the course of one's life, one will inevitably and necessarily enter a state of personal pollution, after which purificatory acts must be performed. In Brahman culture nearly everything having to do with the body and its functions is considered to be a polluting act or a source of pollution. Thus ingestion of food, bodily eliminations, and sexual activity (however essential they may be to the survival of individuals and groups) are all deemed impure activities that need to be followed by purificatory acts such as washing. For Brahman men, sexual activity is considered to be not only polluting but physically draining and spiritually distracting (Bennett 1983: 126, 220). Not surprisingly, they claim that women need sex more than men and blame women for causing carnal lapses among men that draw them away from more lofty pursuits.

With this background in mind, we can now take a close look at Brahman kinship and gender. Drawing from my own field research (Stone 1978, 1989) and that of Lynn Bennett (1983), I describe the kinship/gender system as it applies to rural Brahman peoples in the hill areas of Nepal, thereby covering a somewhat more orthodox set of beliefs and practices than one would find in Nepalese towns and cities.

In these rural areas Brahmans live in small villages, usually mixed with other caste groups. Households are organized around farming, although some family members may have off-farm jobs that bring cash income. At lower elevations, in the hilly regions of Nepal, the Brahmans' most important crop is wet rice, but other grains are grown as well. Livestock (especially goats and water buffalo) are also kept. Both men and women work the fields (for example, women plant and men plow), but women are primarily responsible for domestic tasks such as carrying water, washing clothes, processing food, cooking, caring for children, and cleaning the house.

Like the Nuer, Brahmans are both patrilineal and patrilocal. But as the reader has probably anticipated, there are striking contrasts between Nepalese Brahmans and the Nuer in the areas of marriage and sex. In particular, the sexual behavior of Brahman women is very strictly controlled. A Brahman woman must be a virgin at marriage; if she is known not to be, a religiously sanctioned wedding

IMAGE 3.1 A wedding in Nepal.

Photo courtesy of Linda Stone.

cannot take place. In the village of my studies, the virginity of brides used to be safeguarded by arranging the marriages of females early (to males a few years older), often before they started menstruating, but pre-puberty marriage of females is now rare, and in rural Nepal generally, the age of marriage has been rising over the past decades.

In her husband's home, where she is probably a stranger, a bride is expected to be shy, demure, and obedient, and her behavior is carefully supervised by her in-laws, especially her mother-in-law. Marriages are arranged by parents. A great deal of time, energy, and expense goes into the search for a groom or a bride and the arranging, negotiating, and carrying out of a marriage union. For a female, marriage is also an initiation into adulthood and into her caste; without marriage a woman is not considered an adult or even a full-caste person. Males experience a separate initiation (at around age eight), through which they assume adulthood and caste membership.

In rural areas Brahman groups seek brides for the labor they can provide as well as for their fertility. Polygyny is permitted, but it is rare and socially approved only if the first wife remains childless. For a man, marriage is an important life transition, but it is a relatively smooth one since he remains home on his turf surrounded by his people, all of whom believe that he and his parents have unquestionable authority over the bride. For females, by contrast, marriage is traumatic, and the adaptations a woman must make are likely to be difficult for a number of years. At the end of a wedding, a particular ceremony (*mukh herne*, or "seeing the face") emphatically underlines the low position of the bride in her new home:

> The bride is seated, always slumped over with downcast eyes, while the women of the family, starting with the groom's mother, lift her veil to look at her face. They must place some money in her lap, and for that they buy the privilege of being as critical as they like in their comments about her. After her mother-in-law has seen her face, the bride must touch her mother-in-law's feet with her forehead (*dhok dine*). The other women of the family also have their feet touched by the bride. And then it is time for the neighbor women to come and see the bride and evaluate the new member of their village (Bennett 1983: 90).

Following a period of "boot camp" existence, during which the bride is given heavy chores, watched, and criticized openly, she begins her rise in the household hierarchy through a demonstration of successful fertility. With the birth of each child, especially sons, she becomes a more trusted family member and is treated more leniently. Eventually her senior in-laws die off, her husband (generally) sets up his own home, and she becomes the most senior woman in the household, where her sons will bring in new brides for her to put through the whole experience again.

The Patriline

Every Brahman belongs to two patrilineal categories: the *thar* and the *gotra*. Males assume the thar and gotra affiliations of their fathers, and women at marriage take the thar and gotra names of their husbands. The thar name is one's last name. Both the thar and the gotra are ideally exogamous. The gotra name, though rarely used in everyday life, is invoked during certain religious rituals and is seen as a kind of religious or spiritual category (Bennett 1983: 17). Thus the thar and the gotra are patrilineal kinship categories, but not actual kinship groups. That is, members of a thar or gotra do not come together for any purpose, own any property in common, or share rights and obligations with one another. Though both are sometimes translated as "clan," neither is a clan in the sense referred to earlier in this chapter. Rather, the thar and gotra are important for personal identification and for specifying those people whom one cannot, or at least should not, marry.

The kinship unit that is a group and has significance in ordinary life is the *kul*, or patrilineage. Women are born into the kuls of their fathers and later affiliate with the kuls of their husbands. Women are best seen as links between kuls rather than as full members of them (Bennett 1983: 165). Kuls may be quite large (five to six generations deep), but they can also be limited to a single family. The essence of the kul is that the members all worship the same set of lineage gods (*kul devta*). This communal worship of lineage gods (the crucial parts from which women are emphatically excluded) is a clear celebration of lineal masculinity.

Beneath the level of the kul is another group, the *pariwar*, or household—the most important patrilineal unit in Brahman society. People of this group live together, work together, and conduct a number of rituals together; in addition, the male members own property jointly. The pariwar is the major unit of both production and consumption throughout Nepal (Bennett 1983: 22). The eldest male of this unit serves as head and exercises considerable authority over the others.

Figure 3.9 illustrates the relationships that exist among the thar, gotra, kul, and pariwar, all by reference to an individual ego (adapted from Bennett 1983: 20). Using the terms developed earlier, we find that the thar and gotra are descent categories, the kul is a descent group, and the pariwar is a corporate descent group. As we can see from the diagram, the thar and gotra are separate categories, but they overlap at the level of the kul. In addition, although ego's kul members share his or her thar and gotra affiliations, other people in ego's thar or gotra are not necessarily relatives of ego.

Nepalese Brahmans believe that, ideally, the pariwar should cover several generations, with sons of one family bringing in their wives to this unit, reproducing children, and staying together until the death of their father or even longer. In actual practice, however, married sons of one family usually split up and separate their property before the common father dies. Even so, most couples start out married life within the husband's household and are well into raising their own children before the group splits. When this split does occur, the brothers divide the family land and property equally. Women do not normally inherit in this system, though a widow can hold land or other property in trust for her sons. Women at marriage are given a dowry of clothing, jewelry, and household utensils.

Using this basic patrilineal framework, we will examine the nature of the Brahman patriline and the ways in which gender relationships are interwoven with it—indeed, inseparable from it. Toward this end we will consider three core

FIGURE 3.9 Ego in Relation to Kinship Categories and Groups Among Nepalese Brahmans

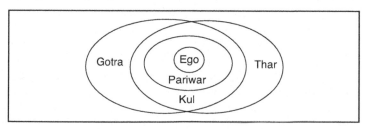

concerns of Brahman society with respect to the patriline (Bennett 1983): (1) The males of a patriline should maintain solidarity; (2) the line should continue (that is, sons should be produced); and (3) the line of descent should be kept "pure." As we will see, wives, or affinal women, are a threat to all three of these core Brahmanical concerns.

1. Male Patrilineal Solidarity.   During my stay in a village of Nepal, a woman with whom I was quite close spoke against her young daughter-in-law, Devi. "She is not shy, that one. When you were photographing the other day, she tried to get into all of the pictures!" She went on in agitation, accusing Devi (who by my own daily observation was quite modest, unobtrusive, and spent most of her time performing the most grueling of household chores) of flirting with village men.

Elsewhere in Nepal, another woman made the following accusation against her sister-in-law: "My elder sister-in-law used *tuna* (black magic) against my brother so that he would separate from mother and father. He had said he wouldn't separate from them until the day he died. So sister-in-law said some spells over some food and gave it to him to eat" (cited in Bennett 1983: 182).

These accusations are typical; over and over again I heard them directed against young women married into a household. The accusations against Devi concerned her presumably immodest behavior, a clear allusion to flagrant sexuality that would bring shame to her family. In the second case, which concerned the presumed use of "black magic," a woman was accused of trying to pull her husband away from his household.

In these and other cases, married-in, or affinal, women are seen as a threat. At stake here is the idea of *male patrilineal solidarity.* We are already familiar with this idea, having encountered it in relation to the Nuer (Case 2). As was true of the Nuer, close patrilineal kin among Nepalese Brahmans in rural areas have a great deal to do with one another. They live with or near one another, stand to inherit each other's land, and in innumerable ways depend upon one another's cooperation and assistance. The lineage (kul) embodies the cultural idea of the importance of male patrilineal solidarity (Bennett 1983: 136).

Why are wives seen as a threat to male patrilineal solidarity? In this respect the Nepalese Brahmans are somewhat different from the patrilineal Nuer, who see women in polygynous marriages as the focus of splits between half-brothers and their descendants. Among Brahmans (for whom polygyny is rare) the idea is not that women will pull half-brothers or their own separate sets of sons apart but, rather, that they will pull apart full brothers, their separate husbands. According to Bennett (1983: 169–170), wives are seen by men, and by other women, too (as we saw in the examples cited earlier), as manifesting this dangerous tendency out of crass self-interest. Recall that a woman enters her husband's household at marriage as a low-status outsider and, usually, as a stranger to all the people among whom she will now live. To promote her own interests, then, she supposedly seeks to lure her husband to her side, encouraging him to split off from his brothers and divide up the property.

The suspicion with which the husband's household regards the new bride is greatest in the early years of her marriage. At this stage, the one person in the household whom the bride might possibly secure as a buffer between herself and her demanding in-laws is her husband. One informant told Bennett (1983: 176) that "if the husband doesn't love you, no one in the household loves you." Yet by trying to pull her husband to her side she is seen by others, and by the society generally, as "pulling him away" from the patrilineal group.

And it gets worse. Bennett reports that "women told me frankly that sex, as the means to have children and as the means to influence their husband in their favor, was the most effective weapon in the battle for security and respect in their husband's house" (1983: 177). But then, the wife's very success in this respect constitutes the image of her as a threat: "A young man's attraction to his wife may be interpreted by his family as a betrayal of them" (1983: 177). Clearly this appears to be a no-win situation for the bride.

One can imagine all sorts of family tensions centering on this very fundamental aspect of Brahman kinship. Perhaps the relationship affected most is that between a woman and her mother-in-law as these two compete over the loyalty of the husband/son. To her mother-in-law a new bride is expected to show great deference and servitude. In the village studied by Bennett, "daughters-in-law are, even now, expected to greet their *sasu* [mother-in-law] by touching their foreheads to her feet. They must also drink the water from washing their sasu's feet before each meal, ask if they may wash her clothes, and rub oil on her feet at night" (1983: 180). Despite these public displays, the mother-in-law feels privately that the daughter-in-law is attempting to seduce her own son away from her.

The most effective way out of the lowly status of outsider-bride is, of course, reproduction—especially reproduction of sons who will continue the husband's patriline. Thus sex serves as a weapon in women's battle for status and respect in the household, not only because it may win the affection of husbands but, even more important, because it may result in pregnancy and birth, the subjects of the next section.

2. *Patriline Continuity.* I believed one older woman in a village of Nepal to be particularly religious, as she was forever performing *puja* (worship) to the gods. When I commented upon her religiosity to one of her kin, her husband's brother's son, he said, "Yes, she does that, but the gods will not accept her offerings." "Why?" I asked, surprised. "Because she is *aputri*" (a woman beyond childbearing age who has never conceived).

Among Nepalese Brahmans there is great concern to have sons: to continue the patriline, to provide heirs, to provide household labor (or income), and to provide parents with caretakers in old age and after their deaths. The ritual role of sons in the funerals of parents, and in their spiritual welfare in the afterlife,

IMAGE 3.2   The author with members of her host family in Nepal.

Photo courtesy of Linda Stone.

entails deeply felt religious beliefs. Brahmans profess that any failure or negligence in the performance of these ceremonies places the departed soul in peril. In particular, if the funeral rituals are performed improperly, or not at all, the departed becomes a "ghost" (*bhut* or *pret*) rather than a proper ancestor. Such ghosts are believed to wander about in painful hunger and inflict harm on the living (Stone 1989: 13).

The pressure to have children, especially sons, falls more heavily upon women than men. For one thing, it is the wife and not the husband who is blamed if a married couple fails to reproduce. This blame is phrased more in spiritual than in physiological terms; it is simply the woman's moral fault, probably on account of sins she committed in her previous lives (Hindus believe in reincarnation). Also, it is older childless women (rather than older childless men) who are pitied and ostracized in the rural community and likely to be suspected of being witches. Finally, if a woman does remain childless, her husband may well take another wife.

In the village of my studies (Stone 1978), Brahmans not only emphasize the importance of reproduction for women but actually make several distinctions that, as illustrated in Figure 3.10, reveal a rather striking hierarchy of values concerning female fertility. Spanning the left side of this diagram are negative categories or conditions. The first three mark categories of women who are considered to be inauspicious as well as unfortunate. A woman who has never even conceived (aputri) is, as we have seen, considered so unworthy that the gods will not accept her offerings. At the next level, among women who have conceived, is a separation between those who have borne live children and those who have experienced only miscarriages or stillbirths. The latter are less inauspicious than the aputri, but they suffer mild ostracism nevertheless. As some Brahman women explained to me, this ostracism was a means of avoiding the contagion of these women's condition (Stone 1978: 8–9).

Regarding women who have given birth, another distinction is drawn between those who bear two or more children and those who bear only one (male or female). An older one-child woman is called a *kaga bandhya*, a word that comes from the name of a crow that, it is said, gives birth to only one offspring in its lifetime. For Hindus this crow, like the lowest of castes, is very impure. The one-child woman does not suffer severe scorn or ostracism, but I was told that orthodox Brahman males should immediately bathe themselves for purification if they spot such a woman upon waking in the morning. At the positive points of this hierarchy (spanning the right side of Figure 3.10) are women with successful fertility. Of course, the luckiest women of all are those whose sons live to reproduce.

Despite all this very real pressure on women and men to bear children, Nepalese Brahmans, in contrast to the Nuer, have very few options by which to acquire children in case of fertility failure. Polygyny might benefit childless or sonless

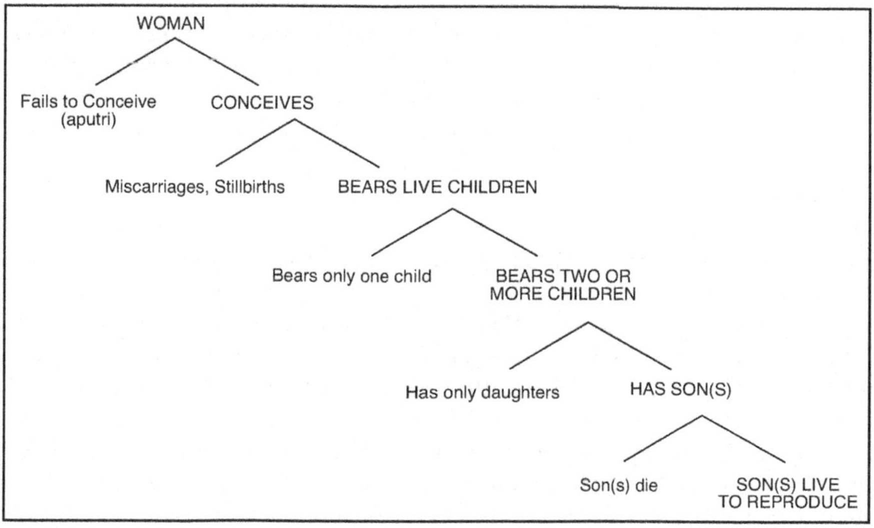

FIGURE 3.10 Nepalese Brahman Distinctions Concerning Female Fertility

men, but it does not help a barren woman. If a woman is fertile but her husband is sterile, she is not free to divorce him and remarry. Brahman society also does not allow for "surrogate genitors," "ghost marriages," or "woman-woman marriages." (Indeed, my village friends in Nepal found my description of Nuer marriage forms and reproductive strategies to be abhorrent.) As we will see in the next section, the complicating issue in rural Nepal is the pressure on couples not only to reproduce children/sons for their lineages and for themselves but also to reproduce pure children. When a Brahman family takes in a bride, they seek from her not just children but Brahman children.

3. *Purity of Descent.*   For a couple to produce caste-pure Brahman children, two things beyond biological parenthood are necessary: First, the man and woman must both themselves be Brahman, and second, they must be united in a religiously sanctioned marriage (*bihaite*) performed by Hindu priests. This type of marriage is also, significantly, called "gift of the virgin" (*kanyadan*) marriage. We will discuss these requirements to see how purity of descent is tied to the sexual behavior of women and, by implication, how women are seen as an ever-present threat to purity of descent.

The first requirement concerns the maintaining of Brahman status by individuals. Caste status can be lost through sexual behavior. For men, the situation is straightforward and simple: A Brahman man loses his Brahman status only if he has sexual relations with a woman of an untouchable caste. In this case he, too, becomes untouchable. But he may have premarital or extramarital relations with any nonuntouchable woman without losing his Brahman rank or his ability to reproduce Brahman children through a Brahman wife. For women, the situation is very different. A Brahman woman becomes a full-caste person only through bihaite marriage to a Brahman male. In terms of sexual behavior, she then maintains this Brahman status if, and only if, her sexual relations are exclusively with this one male, her husband, throughout her entire life, even if her husband should die. Any deviation from these restrictions results in the loss of her Brahman status and her inability thereafter to produce Brahman children. Sex outside the bihaite marriage effectively "pollutes" the woman's womb.

If a married woman's adulterous affair is known, the woman can be sent away, but the problem, of course, is that it may not be known (except to the woman and her lover, who are not telling). This, according to Bennett's analysis, makes Brahman women, in their roles as wives, dangerous. Through any lapse in their sexual behavior, they become a threat to the purity of descent of the patriline: "It is obvious that if a woman's sexuality is not guarded, the offspring of other men, from other lineages and even other castes, may be mistakenly incorporated" (1983: 125).

A Brahman woman may only have one bihaite, "gift of the virgin" marriage union in her lifetime. Widow remarriage in bihaite is not possible. Although a Brahman widow can enter into *lyaite*, a type of elopement marriage, this option is not sanctioned by Hindu religious ritual. And a Brahman widow who enters such a union can no longer be Brahman, so there is this price to pay.

One case from the village of my studies, though it involved the disappearance rather than the death of a husband, illustrates how some women talk about the option of elopement. A Brahman woman was married in bihaite to a Brahman man when she was eight years old. She moved in with his family and began her life as a low-status daughter-in-law, performing all the hardest household chores under the supervision of what she described as a particularly harsh mother-in-law. Then, a few years after marriage, her husband ran away to India and had not been heard from since. When I met this woman and heard her story, she was eighteen. Throughout all those ten years she had remained in her husband's household in her low status, with little hope of any change. I asked her why she didn't run off with some other man in elopement. She reacted as though I had suggested she jump off a bridge, explaining that to do this would mean the loss of her Brahman status and the bringing of shame upon her family. It occurred to me that with this decision, if she stuck to it, the woman was forever forsaking something I had been taught was crucial to all Brahman women. I said, "But then you can never have children," upon which she burst into tears. The decision she made was caste purity over reproduction and motherhood; in her case she could not have both.

Whatever individual choices are made in such circumstances, among Brahmans the idea of a widow is quite negative (Galvin 2005). For one thing, a widow is seen as somehow morally responsible for her husband's death. For another, her husband's patriline can make no further use of her fertility (Bennett 1983: 244). Yet at the same time a widow might be young and therefore potentially sexual. Having no legitimate basis in a marriage, her sexuality can be seen only as a threat to a community's morality. Indeed, the colloquial word for widow—*randi*—also means prostitute (Bennett 1983: 219).

Brahman men may form elopement unions without losing their Brahman status (unless, of course, they take up with an untouchable woman). Still, there is a price to pay for men, too. In these cases of elopement, the man remains Brahman but he cannot produce Brahman children through his eloped wife. Children of these unions are members of his lineage, but since they are beneath the purity of his caste, they are excluded from certain religious rituals regarding his lineage. And a son born of such an elopement union, since he is not a Brahman male, cannot perform the crucial funeral rituals for the father.

Elopement unions among Brahmans are uncommon, but they do occur. The existence in Nepal of a caste called Jaisi testifies to this, for the children of an elopement union between a Brahman man and a Brahman woman become Jaisi in caste. Jaisi is a high, thread-wearing caste, but still, of course, below Brahman. In the village I studied, a multicaste village, 15 percent of all marriage unions were by elopement. Of these (a total of thirty-five), ten involved Brahman individuals.

The Inferiority of Wives

Within the Brahman kinship system affinal women occupy a decidedly inferior status. We have covered three central concerns of the patrilineal system—male patrilineal solidarity, patriline continuity, and purity of descent. In terms of male patrilineal solidarity, affinal women are seen as divisive and threatening. In terms of patriline continuity, they are crucial. But in terms of the third concern, purity of descent, these women are dangerous. Affinal women become a sort of necessary evil.

We have also seen that in terms of patrilineal solidarity, continuity, and purity, it is the sexual aspect of affinal women that is of concern. Thus, in Bennett's account, affinal women are "dangerous" because of their potential as seducers of husbands and polluters of lineages through their illicit sexuality. And as we saw earlier, women are categorically less pure than men because they menstruate.

This concern with female sexuality and its dangers is most vividly represented in *tij-rishi panchami*, an annual women's festival that spans three days. Some rituals are intended to help prolong the life of one's husband, in accordance with the belief among Brahmans that women are responsible for the length of their husband's life. The idea of dangerous female sexuality is clear in this context, since a husband's longevity is considered to depend especially upon his wife's

IMAGE 3.3   A Nepalese Brahman woman conveying a gesture of respect (*dhok dine*) to her husband.

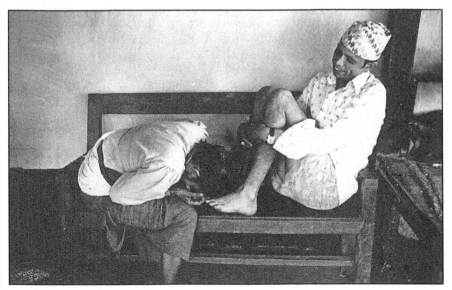

Photo courtesy of Linda Stone.

virtue and chastity, or her sexual fidelity to him. Other rituals are conducted to purify women from the sin of having inadvertently touched a man while menstruating during the previous year, in which case sin accrues to the woman. During the festival, women get together in large groups, go to a river, and undergo purification rituals. These rituals are quite rigorous and involve rubbing mud, oil seed husk, and cow dung on various parts of the woman's body followed by washing (Bennett 1983: 225–226).

Aside from religious ritual, the inferior status of affinal women is also expressed in many ways during everyday life. These often have to do with a woman's relationship to her husband, whom she is expected to see as her "lord" and to whom she must show great deference. Before her daily rice meals, a Brahman woman should bow her forehead down to his feet and, in a quest for her own religious merit, pour water over his feet and drink it. As we saw earlier, a similar act shows deference to her mother-in-law. In both cases, the woman does not gulp down the water, but merely plops a drop or two into her mouth. Still, the symbolic significance of the act is clear.

The Superiority of Daughters

From this description of Brahman life so far, women's inferior position is clear. In so many ways the social and religious strength of the patriline and its concerns with solidarity, continuity, and purity restrict the lives of women and make them subservient to men. However, a major contribution of Bennett's work is to show that this description is "emphatically not the whole picture" (1983: 124).

In all of the foregoing, the impact on women has concerned women in their role as wives—that is, affinal women. But Brahman women, like women in all societies, play more than just this role. To bring out the other dimensions of gender in this society, Bennett distinguishes between the dominant *patrifocal* model of Brahman kinship and the submerged, less visible, but still important *filiafocal* model. By patrifocal (focused on the father) Bennett means the system as seen from the angle of the patriline itself, covering all the ideas, values, and practices discussed in this case study. In this connection, affinal women are important in their roles as reproducers of the lineage, yet they are threatening, dangerous, and inferior to men. But in the same system there is also a filiafocal (focused on the daughter) undercurrent: Here, women are important, not in their roles as wives but in their roles as daughters or sisters. In contrast to affinal women, these consanguineal women are considered sacred to their fathers and brothers (as well as to their mothers and some other kin), and they are literally worshipped by fathers/brothers on certain religious occasions. At these times the males bow down and touch the feet of the daughter/sister. Since a daughter is sacred and religiously superior to her father, he receives religious merit by giving her in marriage to another family. Filiafocal relationships concern not only relations between males and their daughters/sisters but also relatives traced through the daughters/sisters. For example, just as a daughter is sacred and "high" to her father, so too is the man she marries, her father's son-in-law. Thus filiafocal relationships are central to the whole kinship system, a part of the social fabric of Brahman life.

Aside from being religiously sacred, daughters/sisters are generally treated with affection by fathers/brothers and other consanguineal kin. These relationships are important in a woman's life. Even though a woman is under the ultimate authority of her husband and his family, her relationships with her consanguineal kin in her natal home remain strong and serve as "crucial sources of emotional, legal, and sometimes even monetary support" (Bennett 1983: 251). At marriage, women move to a low, decidedly inferior position within the husband's house. But eventually most women, through successful fertility, move away from the position of bride/daughter-in-law to become mothers and, later, mothers-in-law themselves. In contrast to the category "wife," "mother" is associated with purity and regarded with reverence. Bennett (1983: 254–256) shows how motherhood transforms a woman from a low-status and "dangerous" affine into a highly respected and powerful domestic figure that transcends both the patrifocal and filiafocal dimensions of Brahman kinship. In a way, then, motherhood purifies female sexuality.

The case of Nepalese Brahmans shows that patrilineal descent, even in a society that we can characterize as very strongly patrilineal with powerful patrilines, has a more complex relationship with gender than one might at first suppose. It is not simply that patrilineal descent favors males over females. In this case, there are two sides to one system: a dominant one that defines affinal women as dangerous, and a submerged one that defines consanguineal women as sacred. Motherhood, a highly esteemed role, connects and transcends the two and ultimately gives women their most powerful and fulfilling roles. To be sure, the filiafocal dimension of Brahman kinship may not give women much power in the society overall, but it does affect how women and men see themselves and each other, and how gender is dynamically defined and played out over the course of life.

Today Nepalese marriages and the lives of women and men are undergoing change, change now starting to be felt even in the more remote rural areas. Along with a rising age of marriage for women (the average age is now seventeen years), recent decades have seen an increase in female literacy (now 55 percent), education, and income generation. National struggles, in particular the Maoist insurgency (1996–2006), during which Maoists criticized rural inegalitarian gender practices, have had an effect, as have male labor migration and wide exposure to the global media (see McHugh 2004; Sanders and McKay 2012; Bennett, Sijapati, and Thapa n.d.). The extent and depth of the effects of these changes on basic kinship structures and gender values are uncertain but will unfold in the years ahead. For now we see that Nepalese women in rural and urban areas are becoming more active politically, have greater representation in government, and are widely participating in many dynamic women's development groups and initiatives (Bennett, Sijapati, and Thapa n.d.).

PATRILINEAL CONTRASTS

We have taken a close look at two very different societies that trace descent patrilineally. In both societies, patrilineages are important social units, and the cultural ideology that surrounds the solidarity and continuity of these units exerts a powerful influence on both men and women. Also in both societies, the power of patrilines is reinforced with religious beliefs and rituals. In this section we will consider similarities and contrasts among the Nuer and the Nepalese Brahmans in terms of the ways kinship is related to gender.

One of the strongest similarities between the two groups is that, from the perspective of patrilineal interests, women are considered divisive. In both societies they are seen as pulling apart patrilineally related men. Since the Nuer and the Brahman patrilines are strictly exogamous, women from outside are crucial to lineage continuity, yet as outsiders with interests of their own, they are mistrusted and readily accused of causing trouble between men. In the Nuer case, an ambivalence surrounds women because they are seen as both dividing and unifying men—divisive in that they separate half-brothers and unifying in their exclusive roles as milkers of cows who draw men together in a homestead. An ambivalence surrounds Brahman women, too: From a patrifocal standpoint, women as wives are dangerous to the patriline but absolutely necessary for its continuity. Although Nuer women are also necessary to patrilineal continuity, they and their sexuality are not seen as dangerous.

Another similarity between Nuer and Brahmans is that, although patrilineal descent is used in both societies to form important groups, in each case there are also other important sets of relationships based on linkages through women. In both cases, patrilines and a supporting kind of "patrilineal ideology" may be dominant, but in neither case does patrilineal descent and its ramifications provide the complete picture of kinship for the society. In short, among both the Nuer and the Brahmans, linkages through women provide significant countercurrents to the dominant patrilineal structure, and knowledge of these is crucial to an understanding of kinship as well as gender.

Recall that among the Nuer we have seen the formation of matrifocal subunits within patrilines. In this society, where polygynous unions are more common than among the Brahmans, sons of one mother develop their own special solidarity in opposition to their half-brothers, or the sons of the mother's cowife. This matrifocal subunit is important, first, because it is usually along these breakages between half-brothers that patrilineages eventually split. Second, as we have seen, the tensions between sets of half-brothers pass over the generations, so that a man's father's half-brother is seen, culturally, as a "wicked uncle" and the sons of this man are also mistrusted. Among Nepalese Brahmans it is not matrifocal subunits but rather filiafocal ties that bring about what Bennett referred to as the "submerged" aspect of the kinship structure. Filiafocal relationships are those traced to a daughter/sister and, through her, to other relatives as well. In this context we examined some important relationships of affection that could be used by married women as valuable and much-needed sources of emotional and material support. We also saw that a man's consanguineal sister and daughter are sacred to him, and religiously superior to him, so he worships them in religious ritual. In a sense, then, father/daughter and brother/sister relationships are the reverse of that between husband and wife.

There are also sharp differences between the Nuer and the Nepalese Brahmans. Although both societies value female fertility highly and regard the production of sons as necessary, the two groups differ dramatically in terms of the options they provide for acquiring children. Among the Brahmans the options are few. If a couple fails to have children, or sons, it may resort to polygyny, an option that may alleviate the state of childlessness or sonlessness for the man. But that's it. Polygyny does nothing to alleviate the problem for the childless/sonless woman, who will then be stigmatized in the society. At times, polygyny does not work for the man either, in which case he is stuck with his situation and can do nothing more. To acquire children, Brahmans essentially have to "grow their own" and, failing that, must suffer the consequences. Nuer society, by contrast, abounds with options for acquiring children. Aside from polygyny, Nuer society offers strategies ranging from "surrogate genitor" to "blind-eye adultery," and if all else fails there is always "ghost marriage" to ensure that all males will ultimately have sons. Perhaps the most striking contrast with the Brahmans is the Nuer option of "woman-woman" marriage, whereby a barren woman can "count as a man" and, through marriage to another woman and use of a surrogate genitor, acquire children for her father's lineage.

This contrast between the two groups is related to yet another factor: female sexuality. Among the Nuer, as we saw, a woman has rather autonomous control over her own sexuality. Virginity at marriage is not expected, let alone insisted upon. Extramarital affairs might temporarily anger a husband, but the wife is not held to be morally at fault, is unlikely to be divorced, and is certainly not rendered incapable of producing further legitimate children for the husband's lineage. A woman is also relatively free to divorce her husband and to form any number of additional legitimate unions with other men over her lifetime. Among Brahmans, by contrast, there is deep concern with female virginity at marriage and confinement of her sexuality to her husband for her entire life. Any deviation from this restriction results not only in loss of her caste status but also inability to thereafter produce Brahman children.

Thus we can say that among Brahmans the value that a patriline places on a wife's fertility is encompassed by and secondary to the value placed on her sexual purity. Only if she is a virgin at marriage and sexually faithful to her husband can she produce Brahman children for her husband's patriline.

Any case of known adultery would excommunicate the woman from her caste, dispel her from the marriage, and disqualify her from further caste-pure reproduction. But among the Nuer, the rules by which children are allocated to husbands and lineages remain independent from the mother's sexual behavior. In other words, a woman's sexual behavior cannot devalue her fertility. The contrast between Nuer and Brahmans becomes especially clear when we look at the consequences of adultery. To put it somewhat crudely, among Brahmans adultery "pollutes" the woman's fertility; from the patriline's point of view, it is akin to destruction of property. But among the Nuer, again from the standpoint of the patriline, adultery is mere theft, punishable by a fee of six cows.

And what about women's reproductive autonomy? Among both the Nuer and the Brahmans a woman's reproduction is *for* her husband's patrilineage, and the patrilineage has ultimate rights in her children. Should a woman leave her husband, her children will not go with her. In both of these cultures women are also under cultural pressure to reproduce, and especially to produce sons. And in both societies full adulthood for women is contingent on marriage. These issues aside, it would appear that reproductive autonomy is higher for Nuer women than for Nepalese Brahman women. Most notably, an infertile Nuer woman is not punished and may even become an "honorary male" who continues her natal patriline through woman-woman marriage. Nuer women have considerably more say in whom and when (or even if) they marry, compared to Brahman women, who enter arranged unions. Leaving a husband is relatively easy for Nuer women, while Brahman women who leave husbands lose their caste status, and their future children will be of lower caste. Also a Brahman woman's reproduction is crucial to her rise in status within her husband's household. Nuer women are already more domestically autonomous in their separate huts with their separate children.

We have also seen that both the Nuer and the Nepalese Brahmans strongly emphasize lineal masculinity—in their views of the importance of sons, in religious rituals of initiation among the Nuer, and in worship of lineage gods among the Brahmans. But only in the Nepalese case is this concern with male fertility, the production of sons, and the continuity of the patriline connected with sexual restrictions on women. Here is where the Nuer case stands apart. It is a strongly patrilineal society, and it expresses lineal masculinity, but children/sons are ultimately acquired through payments of cattle. Nuer women are seen as the life-giving force, essential for their procreative powers (Hutchinson 1980), but in the end, "from the male perspective, cattle—not women—'produce' children. Bridewealth alone assures a man legitimate offspring" (Hutchinson 1980: 373). Male fertility is extremely important among both groups but fatherhood is far easier to secure for Nuer men.

Many Euro-American readers may find that the sexual restrictions on Brahman women and the consequences to women for violating society's rules are a bit harsh. Yet the Brahman case is in some ways more familiar to Euro-Americans, or closer to their own traditions, than that of the Nuer. Certainly the concept of female sexual "purity" is far from alien to the Western world. We are all familiar with the idea of a woman's reputation being contingent on her sexual behavior. And despite the 1960s sexual revolution, most people would agree that a sexual double standard for men and women still obtains in Euro-American societies. These societies have never gone so far as to categorically devalue a woman's future fertility on account of her past sexuality, but they have very much devalued those women whose sexual "virtue" has supposedly lapsed. Rather, I think, what Euro-Americans would find new and unfamiliar are Nuer arrangements. Nothing in Euro-American traditions compares to woman-woman marriage, for example. And the idea of a married woman's adultery being handled simply by her lover's payment of a fee to the husband goes against Euro-American sentiments.

Why is it that some societies develop a concern with female sexual purity, and why did this concern become a part of Euro-American traditions? We will consider some ideas related to this question in a later chapter. But first, let's take a look at societies with another mode of descent altogether: societies without patrilineages, societies that trace descent directly through women.

DISCUSSION QUESTIONS

1. This chapter discusses the much stronger restrictions on female sexuality among the Nepalese Brahmans than among the Nuer. What other factors do you think might account for the greater autonomy of Nuer women as compared with Nepalese Brahman women?

2. Would you predict that the Nuer system of kinship and marriage would promote higher population growth than that of the Nepalese Brahmans? Why or why not?

3. Using examples from the case studies in this chapter, in what ways does religion reinforce kinship and family practices? How does religion enter into cultural evaluations of men and women among the Nuer and the Nepalese Brahmans?

SUGGESTED FURTHER READING

Galvin, Kathey-Lee. 2005. *Forbidden Red: Widowhood in Urban Nepal.* Pullman: Washington State University Press. This anthropological study vividly portrays the lives, options, choices, and strategies of widows in Nepal. It discusses widowhood in relation to Nepalese kinship and provides interesting case studies.

Holtzman, Jon D. 2000. *Nuer Journeys, Nuer Lives: Sudanese Refugees in Minnesota.* Boston: Allyn and Bacon. This book documents the effect on the Nuer of the Sudanese civil war. As a result of this conflict, several hundred Nuer refugees now live in Minnesota, where the author conducted fieldwork. The book discusses changes in Nuer life since Evans-Pritchard's time. One chapter focuses on gender, kinship, marriage, and the family.

Hutchinson, Sharon E. 1996. *Nuer Dilemmas: Coping with Money, War, and the State*. Berkeley: University of California Press. The book covers the many changes in Nuer life since the 1930s as the Nuer were transformed from an independent pastoral people to an ethnic group within the Sudanese state.

Smith Oboler, Regina. 1992. Is the Female Husband a Man? Woman-Woman Marriage Among the Nandi of Kenya. In William Haviland, ed., *Talking About People: Readings in Contemporary Cultural Anthropology*. Mountain View, CA: Mayfield (reprinted from *Ethnology* 19: 69–88). This article discusses the gender implications of woman-woman marriage among the Nandi.

SUGGESTED CLASSROOM MEDIA

The Nuer. 1971. Produced by Robert Gardner and Hilary Harris, Peabody Museum of Archaeology and Ethnology, Harvard University. Films for the CRM/McGraw-Hill Films, Del Mar, CA. Seventy-five minutes. This now-classic film portrays the earlier, traditional life of the Nuer herders of the Nile basin, focusing on how Nuer life revolved around cattle. Some of the cultural features of Case 2 were still current at the time this film was made.

Saheri's Choice: Arranged Marriage in India. 2002. Films for the Humanities and Sciences, Princeton, NJ. Twenty-seven minutes. Examines contemporary arranged marriage in India by following the story of a girl whose marriage was arranged when she was six years old.

WEBSITES

www.youtube.com/watch?v=6z4nFfc7oJ4. "Naath Nuer Culture: Then and Now." Edited by Bol Jock. A video showing Nuer refugees in Minnesota interspersed with much earlier photos of Nuer in East Africa.

www.johntyman.com/nepal/04.html. "Introduction to Nepal." Beautiful photographs of Nepal with captions that provide information about ethnic groups and cultures of the country.

NOTES

1. It was this aspect of Morgan's work that caught the attention of Karl Marx and Friedrich Engels. They believed that it helped confirm a stage of "primitive communism" in human cultural evolution, an egalitarian stage that ended with the emergence of private property (Engels 1942).

2. Evans-Pritchard reported (1945: 23) that older sonless Nuer men exercised this option, but younger men were still too concerned with their sexual rights in their wives to consider it. A slight variation on this theme, involving the use of a "surrogate genitor," has been reported in other African societies (Barnes 1951: 4; Brain 1972: 162; Gluckman 1965: 188). In this case, a man asked a friend or kinsman to sleep with his wife in the hope that she would conceive.

3. Caste continues to be important in Nepal, especially in the rural areas of the country. There is some regional variation among caste categories and caste rankings. But many Nepalese individuals, including Brahmans, denounce the caste system altogether. And in Nepal, as in India, caste is now illegal in the sense that the government does not recognize discrimination according to caste.

4. In Nepal some castes may marry women upward (into higher castes) in religiously sanctioned unions. However, if Brahman men enter these unions, their children will be of a caste rank lower than Brahman.

REFERENCES

Aberle, David F. 1961. Matrilineal Descent in Cross-Cultural Perspective. In David M. Schneider and Kathleen Gough, eds., *Matrilineal Kinship*, pp. 655–727. Berkeley: University of California Press.

Ackerman, Lillian A. 1992. Yupik Eskimo Residence and Descent in Southwestern Alaska. *Inter-Nord* 19: 253–263.

Barnes, J. A. 1951. *Marriage in a Changing Society* (Rhodes Livingstone Papers, No. 20). London: Oxford University Press.

———. 1968. Some Nuer Notions of Nakedness, Nudity, and Sexuality. *Africa* 38 (2): 1–131.

Bennett, Lynn. 1976. Sex and Motherhood Among the Brahmans and Chetris of East Central Nepal. *Contributions to Nepalese Studies* 3: 1–52.

———. 1983. *Dangerous Wives and Sacred Sisters: Social and Symbolic Roles of High Caste Women in Nepal*. New York: Columbia University Press.

Bennett, Lynn, Bandita Sijapati, and Deepak Thapa. n.d. *Forging Equal Citizenship in a Multicultural Nepal*. Unpublished manuscript.

Bettini, Maurizio. 1991. *Anthropology and Roman Culture: Kinship, Time, Images of the Soul*. Translated by John van Sickle. Baltimore: Johns Hopkins University Press.

Beidelman, T. O. 1966. The Ox and Nuer Sacrifice: Some Freudian Hypotheses About Nuer Symbolism. *Man* 1: 453–467.

Brain, Robert. 1972. *Bangwa Kinship and Marriage*. Cambridge, England: Cambridge University Press.

Corbier, Mireille. 1991. Constructing Kinship in Ancient Rome: Marriage and Divorce, Filiation and Adoption. In David I. Kertzer and Richard P. Sallers, eds., *The Family in Italy: From Antiquity to the Present*, pp. 127–144. New Haven, CT: Yale University Press.

Delaney, Carol. 1987. Seeds of Honor, Fields of Shame. In David Gilmore, ed., *Honor and the Unity of the Mediterranean*. Washington, DC: American Anthropological Association.

di Leonardo, Micaela. 1991. Gender, Culture, and Political Economy: Feminist Anthropology in Historical Perspective. In Micaela di Leonardo, ed., *Gender at the Crossroads of Knowledge: Feminist Anthropology in the Postmodern Era,* pp. 1–48. Berkeley: University of California Press.

Divale, William Tulio. 1975. An Explanation for Matrilocal Residence. In Dana Raphael, ed., *Being Female: Reproduction, Power, and Change,* pp. 99–108. The Hague: Mouton Publishers.

Ember, Melvin, and Carol Ember. 1971. The Conditions Favoring Matrilocal Versus Patrilocal Residence. *American Anthropologist* 73: 571–594.

Engels, Friedrich. 1942 [orig. 1884]. *The Origin of the Family, Private Property, and the State.* New York: International Publishers.

Evans-Pritchard, E. E. 1940. *The Nuer: A Description of the Modes of Livelihood and Political Institutions of a Nilotic People.* Oxford: Clarendon Press.

———. 1945. *Some Aspects of Marriage and the Family Among the Nuer* (Rhodes-Livingstone Papers, No. 11). London: Royal Anthropological Institute of Great Britain and Ireland.

———. 1950. The Nuer Family. *Sudan Notes and Records* 31(1): 21–42.

———. 1974 [orig. 1956]. *Nuer Religion.* New York: Oxford University Press.

———. 1990 [orig. 1951]. *Kinship and Marriage Among the Nuer.* New York: Oxford University Press.

Fortes, Meyer. 1958. Introduction. In Jack Goody, ed., *The Developmental Cycle in Domestic Groups,* pp. 1–14. Cambridge, England: Cambridge University Press.

Galvin, Kathey-Lee. 2005. *Forbidden Red: Widowhood in Urban Nepal.* Pullman: Washington State University Press.

Gluckman, Max. 1965. Kinship and Marriage Among the Lozi of Northern Rhodesia and the Zulu of Natal. In A. R. Radcliffe-Brown and Daryll Forde, eds., *African Systems of Kinship and Marriage,* pp. 166–206. Oxford: Oxford University Press.

Gough, Kathleen. 1961. Variation in Matrilineal Systems: Variation in Residence. In David M. Schneider and Kathleen Gough, eds., *Matrilineal Kinship,* pp. 545–576. Berkeley: University of California Press.

———. 1971. Nuer Kinship: A Reexamination. In T. O. Beidelman, ed., *The Translation of Culture: Essays to E. E. Evans-Pritchard,* pp. 79–121. London: Tavistock Publications.

Herskovits, M. J. 1937. A Note on "Woman Marriage" in Dahomey. *Africa* 10: 335–341.

Hutchinson, Sharon. 1980. Relations Between the Sexes Among the Nuer: 1930. *Africa* 50(4): 371–387.

James, Wendy. 1990. Introduction. In E. E. Evans-Pritchard, ed., *Kinship and Marriage Among the Nuer,* pp. ix–xxii. New York: Oxford University Press.

Kelly, Raymond. 1985. *The Nuer Conquest: The Structure and Development of an Expansionist System.* Ann Arbor: University of Michigan Press.

King, Diane E., and Linda Stone. 2010. Lineal Masculinity: Gendered Memory Within Patriliny. *American Ethnologist* 37(2): 323–336.

McHugh, Ernestine. 2004. Moral Choices and Global Desires: Feminine Identity in a Transnational Realm. *Ethos* 32(4): 575–597.

Morgan, Lewis H. 1964 [orig. 1887]. *Ancient Society.* Cambridge, MA: Harvard University Press.

Murphy, Robert F. 1986. *Cultural and Social Anthropology: An Overture,* 2nd ed. Englewood Cliffs, NJ: Prentice Hall.

Pomeroy, Sarah B. 1975. *Goddesses, Whores, Wives, and Slaves: Women in Classical Antiquity*. New York: Schocken Books.

Robertson, A. F. 1991. *Beyond the Family: The Social Organization of Reproduction*. Berkeley: University of California Press.

Rodseth, Lars, Richard W. Wrangham, Alisa M. Harrigan, and Barbara B. Smuts. 1991. The Human Community as a Primate Society. *Current Anthropology* 32(3): 221–241.

Sacks, Karen. 1979. *Sisters and Wives: The Past and Future of Sexual Equality*. Westport, CT: Greenwood Press.

Sanders, Catherine, and Kimber H. McKay. 2012. Love Is Cheap: Democratic Rise of Love Marriage Among Hindu Maoists in Nepal's Himalayas. *Anthropology News* 4(4): 6–8.

Shelton, Jo-Ann. 1988. *As the Romans Did: A Source Book in Roman Social History*. New York: Oxford University Press.

Stone, Linda. 1978. Cultural Repercussions of Childlessness and Low Fertility in Nepal. *Contributions to Nepalese Studies* 5(2): 7–36.

———. 1989. *Illness Beliefs and Feeding the Dead in Hindu Nepal*. Lewiston, NY: Edwin Mellen Press.

Treggiari, Susan. 1991. Ideals and Practicalities in Matchmaking in Ancient Rome. In David I. Kertzer and Richard P. Saller, eds., *The Family in Italy: From Antiquity to the Present*, pp. 91–108. New Haven, CT: Yale University Press.

White, Leslie A. 1964. Introduction. In Lewis H. Morgan, *Ancient Society*. Cambridge, MA: Harvard University Press.

4

THROUGH THE MOTHER

This chapter explores matrilineal societies—those in which descent is traced through females. Figure 4.1 shows the tracing of matrilineal kin from a common ancestor, with shaded symbols representing persons who share matrilineal descent. Here, females and males are members of their mother's matriline by birth, but, in direct opposition to the case of patrilineal descent, only women can transmit this membership to offspring over the generations. The matrilineal principle, like its patrilineal counterpart, can be used to construct corporate kinship groups such as lineages and clans.

How do matrilineal societies work? Does descent traced through women give females special positions or power in these societies? Do we find cases where the corporate matrilineal property (such as land or livestock) is owned and controlled by women, or cases where women act as heads of the descent groups? When the group is matrilineal and matrilocal, do we find cases where affinal males enter new households as low-status grooms, subservient to their wives and at the beck and call of their fathers-in-law?

As it turns out, matrilineal societies show a great deal of variation. There are indeed cases of female ownership of property. But there are also cases of matrilineal societies in which property is by males, with ownership passing to their sisters' sons. In still other cases, descent-group property is owned by women but *controlled by* their matrilineal male kin. And in matrilocal situations, affinal males may indeed enter their wives' households as newcomers with little authority over their wives, though, to my knowledge, there are no cases where husbands show subservience to wives and in-laws in any way comparable to the patrilocal-patrilineal example of the Nepalese Brahmans discussed in the last chapter. Most commonly, males are heads of matrilineal kinship units, but in some societies, such as the Ashanti of West Africa, females act as heads along with males (see also the Mosuo in Case 5 of this chapter).

FIGURE 4.1   A Matrilineal Descent Construct

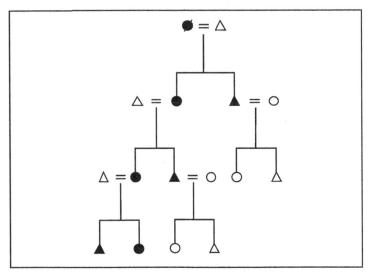

Persons sharing matrilineal descent are shaded.

What sorts of gender relationships occur in societies with matrilineal descent? To address this question, we will first look at how earlier generations of anthropologists viewed matrilineal societies, a discussion that leads directly to the core issue of male dominance.

In the nineteenth century there was some confusion between matrilineal descent and the concept of "matriarchy," or "rule by women." Some scholars, such as Johann Bachofen (1891), believed that the earliest human societies were matriarchal and that matriarchy was an early, and clearly inferior, stage of human cultural evolution. These societies were thought to have been thoroughly controlled by fearsome Amazon-like women. Later, according to this line of thought, a shift to patriarchy occurred as human society became more "civilized." Matrilineal descent was seen as but a part of a larger matriarchal social organization, and the few cases of living matrilineal societies were interpreted as curious remnants of our species' matriarchal past. Other scholars argued against this view at the time, some holding that the earliest human societies were already patriarchal. Eventually the whole idea of distinct stages of human cultural evolution fell out of favor. Still, the association between "matrilineal" and "matriarchal" lingered on in the popular imagination.

Today anthropologists generally agree that cases of true matriarchy do not exist in human society, and that they most probably never have. It's easy enough to find societies in which women play prominent social, religious, or even political roles, where they are clearly influential or powerful in numerous spheres of life. And an argument can be made for the existence of gender equality (Ackerman 1982; Lepowsky 1993) or near-equality (Shostak 1981) in some societies. But convincing cases of female-dominant societies, or societies in which women and not men (or men only rarely or exceptionally) hold the major positions of official authority, have not been found. It is important to emphasize that matrilineal means simply "descent through females." It is not synonymous with matriarchy.

Once this confusion was cleared up, another problem developed. Believing there were no true matriarchies, anthropologists possibly went too far in the other direction and took male authority or general male dominance as a given. Indeed, a few decades ago there was little discussion about why male dominance might be universal or even whether, in what sense, or to what extent it is so. For example, David Schneider (1961: 5), who examined this issue in relation to matrilineal kinship, simply stated that in all unilineal descent groups, whether patrilineal or matrilineal, "women are responsible for the care of children" and "adult men have authority over women and children." In matrilineal systems, according to Schneider, descent is traced through women, but authority is still vested in men.

At this point, matrilineal societies came to be seen, prototypically, as those in which women are primarily under the authority of their brothers and maternal uncles, and men are concerned with exercising control over their sisters and sisters' children. A child's real authority figure would be not his or her own father but his or her mother's brother. Property would be held by males and inherited by their sisters' sons. Seeing matrilineal males in control, some anthropologists, such as Meyer Fortes (1959), went so far as to urge that we see "descent" in matrilineal systems as proceeding not from a mother to her child but, rather, from the mother's brother to the sister's son. Although this argument had some merit (at the very least it moved away from confusing matrilineal descent with matriarchy), it ultimately pushed women too far into the background, where their own kinship roles, interests, strategies, and powers became all too easy to ignore.

Later, Roger Keesing (1975), though critical of the male bias evident in previous studies of kinship, invited students to see male members of a matrilineal group as a kind of "board of directors" of the kinship corporation. Putting it this way had the advantage of specifying that we are here talking about authority within descent groups, and not necessarily about structures of authority in the broader society or, for that matter, about "male dominance" in all spheres of social life.

The hypothetical matriline shown in Figure 4.2 illustrates this view of matrilineal male authority and its transmission. Here, the men A, B, C, and D are currently the senior males of the matriline. They jointly own and control the matriline's property, which passes collectively to their sisters' sons; in

FIGURE 4.2   A Hypothetical Matriline

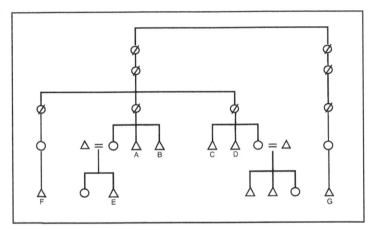

turn, these sons, along with other matrilineal kin of that generation, will be the next generation's "board of directors." Each of the individual men in this system may also pass other property to his respective sisters' son or sons. These senior males meet together to discuss and decide upon the matriline's affairs. Collectively they have authority over women and children who are members of the matriline. Individually they have authority over their respective sisters, nieces, and nephews.

Let's say that the man A is the most senior and, as such, is official head of the matriline. He has authority over all other matriline members. When he dies, his authority passes to the man E, a sister's son. If he has many sisters and those sisters have many sons, there could be a rule that, say, his position goes to the eldest sister's eldest son. Yet even if he has no sister at all, succession could occur, since no doubt there would be someone (an MZDS or MMMZDDDS such as the man F or the man G in the diagram) who would then be head.

THE MATRILINEAL PUZZLE

The earlier anthropologists were rather intrigued by this combination of descent through females with authority vested in males, since it was believed to account for the special tensions in matrilineal societies that were not found in patrilineal ones. Audrey Richards (1950) was the first to coin a phrase for these tensions: "the matrilineal puzzle." This term referred to what Richards saw in matrilineal societies as built-in strains in the relationship between a woman's husband and her brother. Both would want to control her. Also, both would want to control her children, the one man as their father, and

FIGURE 4.3 A Matrilineal, Matrilocal Group

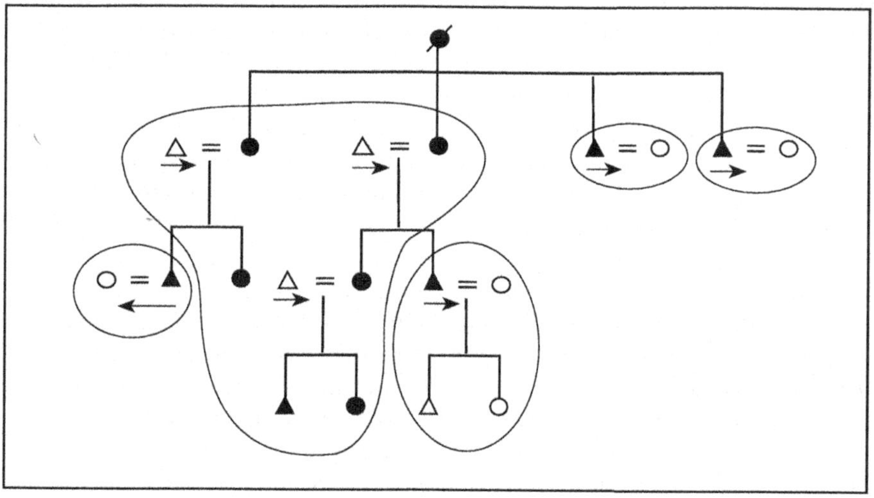

Members of one matriline are shaded. The loops surround those persons who, following matrilocal residence, will live together. The arrows show men moving to the residences of their wives.

the other as their maternal uncle. Naturally this situation would produce some conflict. Schneider (1961: 22) later generalized the brother's control as extending to the "children's matrilineal descent group," since this group as a whole has interests in the woman's children that might run counter to the desires of the husband. The idea of a matrilineal puzzle, then, was based not only on the assumption of male authority over sisters and sisters' children within a matriline but also on the assumption that males, in any society, naturally want to exert some control over their own wives and children. In a sense, male authority comes into conflict with itself.

This image of a "puzzle" focused attention on the question as to how matrilineal societies cope with the combination of authority through men and descent through women. On the basis of this question, anthropologists interpreted certain features of the social structure of matrilineal societies as attempted "solutions" to the matrilineal puzzle. Consider, for example, the case of a matrilineal society that is also matrilocal, as illustrated in Figure 4.3.

In this figure, the symbols representing members of one matriline are shaded. The arrows indicate males moving matrilocally into their wives' residential units at marriage. Loops enclose those people who will stay together. Note that the male members of the shaded matriline are split up upon their marriages, each going off to his own wife's group. In Keesing's (1975: 63) terms, the male "'board of directors' is scattered away from 'corporation headquarters.'" How are these men to run an efficient matriline when they are split up from one another? Not only that, but along with their departure, new men (nonmembers) are moving in with the sisters as their husbands. Won't the affinal husbands be able to exert control over their own wives and children and thus threaten the position of the matriline's male authorities? One partial "solution" here is to have nucleated settlements, with everyone in the society living closely together. Then the brothers can leave their natal households upon marrying, but they don't go very far. They stay close enough to come back together periodically to discuss important matters pertaining to the matriline and to keep an eye on their sisters and their sisters' children.

Another option is to combine matrilineal descent with patrilocal residence. This arrangement keeps male matriline members together, but it also eventually produces another problem, as Figure 4.4 illustrates. Here the males stay together, but this solution works for only one generation. Their sister leaves at marriage and moves in with her husband. So her children, the next generation's male matriline members, are away, growing up elsewhere. Again, this situation invites their own fathers to exercise more control over them. For their mothers' brothers, the problem is, as Keesing (1975: 64) put it, how do they "get back" the children? Nucleated settlements might help in this case, too; another "solution" is avunculocal residence, or residence of a male at marriage with his mother's brother or brothers. This arrangement is illustrated in Figure 4.5, which shows a woman moving patrilocally at marriage. But then her sons, upon their marriages, move back to the place(s) of their mother's brother or brothers. In some matrilineal societies a man in search of a wife must go to the place of his MBs, who then find a local bride and arrange a marriage for him.

Anthropologists saw still another solution to the matrilineal puzzle in the arrangement of the "visiting husband." This arrangement is rare but quite interesting in its own right. Here, brothers and sisters remain together in one domestic unit for life. After marriage neither the wife nor her husband move at all; rather, the husband visits his wife from time to time for purposes of sex, companionship, and procreation. He may spend a night with her from time to time, but he lives with his sister. Meanwhile, the woman's brother or brothers live with her but go off to visit their own wives. Insofar as there really is a matrilineal puzzle, this would seem the ideal solution, since it keeps matrilineal males together over the generations. The "visiting husband" arrangement was found in a few matrilineal societies in times past such as the Nayar (see Case 5 in this chapter). In this case, the people also practiced polyandry and polygyny. Thus, for example, one woman could have many husbands, each of whom visited her on different nights, and a man could have more than one wife to visit. Children, of course, belonged to the matrilines of their mothers, and the issue of which husband was the biological father was not considered important. A child called all of his or her mother's husbands "father."

FIGURE 4.4 A Matrilineal, Patrilocal Group

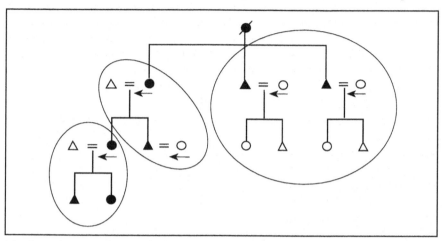

Members of one matriline are shaded. Loops surround those persons who, following patrilocal residence, will live together. Arrows show women moving to the residences of their husbands.

FIGURE 4.5 A Matrilineal, Avunculocal Group

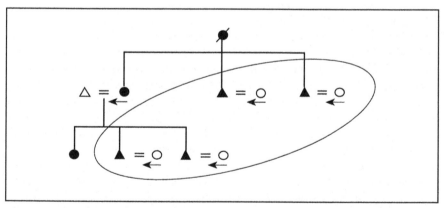

Members of one matriline are shaded. The loop surrounds those persons who, following avunculocal residence, will live together. Arrows show women moving to the residences of their husbands.

All of the so-called solutions to the matrilineal puzzle were seen by anthropologists as only partial. The fact remained that matrilineal societies, however residentially organized, were plagued by tensions. Males and females seemed, at least to these earlier anthropologists, to be pulled in conflicting directions. Consider the case of a married woman. She has a bond with her husband, who has some domestic authority over her and is, after all, generally the father of her children. But first and foremost she must respect the interests of her brother (or maternal uncles, and so forth). If her ties to her husband become too strong, they will threaten the strength of the matrilineal kinship group. The woman also has to take her children into account. Her husband may be their father, but their position in society, their welfare, and most likely their inheritance of property are all bound up with her brother (or with male matrilineal kin in general). Now consider the case of a married man. He may want to have his own children but needs to be more concerned with the fertility of his sister than with that of his wife. If he does have children, he won't have much authority over them anyway, for higher authority will be held by their mother's male matrilineal kin. If his ties to his own wife and children become too strong, they, again, will threaten the strength of the matrilineal kinship group. In the end, it was considered that in matrilineal societies the ties between brothers and sisters must remain stronger than those between husbands and wives. Strong marriage ties would spell the doom of matrilineal descent. So would strong ties between husbands and children. Many matrilineal societies were studied in terms of the ways in which individuals, in their different roles, struggled through these built-in stresses and strains.

Anthropologists writing about the matrilineal puzzle felt that seeing matrilineal descent in this way helped to account for a number of features commonly associated with matrilineal descent. For example, matrilineal societies tend to have high rates of divorce. This finding would be expected since the marriage ties in these societies need to be weak, or at least weaker than brother-sister or niece–maternal uncle ties. If something has to break under the strain of a matrilineal system it should be the marriage. The matrilineal puzzle also accounted for the observation that matrilineal societies are quite rare. And seeing matrilineal descent in this way was consistent with the observation that systems of matrilineal descent are fragile. In the nineteenth and early twentieth centuries, under the impact of colonialism and the advance of world capitalism, most patrilineal societies remained patrilineal, but many matrilineal societies dropped their systems of descent and gradually became patrilineal or bilateral themselves.

Matrilineal systems were thus seen as beset by special strains, as fragile and rare, possibly even doomed to extinction. Early anthropologists became interested in questions such as: How did these systems arise in the first place, and what precisely are the conditions that break them down or, more rarely, keep them going?

These anthropologists were assuming that males would "naturally" be torn between themselves and each other, wishing to control both wives/children and sisters/nephews/nieces. They may have been right to say that clear cases of female-dominant societies or matriarchies do not exist, but were they right in assuming that all matrilineal societies would illustrate the strains and tensions of combining male authority with descent through females? Were they right in assuming, in the first place, that males always have authority over females within descent groups?

Later research on matrilineal societies challenged the monolithic image of male authority implied by the matrilineal puzzle. Without rejecting the premise of universal male authority as such, some anthropologists suggested that the status or power of women tended to be higher in matrilineal societies than in most patrilineal ones, especially if the societies were also matrilocal. Alice Schlegel (1972) granted that in a matrilineal system, matrilineally related males have authority over women within the larger descent group. But her study showed variation in the extent to which a woman's husband or brother held authority over her in the domestic sphere in different matrilineal societies. She concluded that matrilineal societies could be categorized along a continuum ranging from those with strong husband authority and weak brother authority to those with strong brother authority and weak husband authority. Of special interest to her were those societies in the middle of the continuum, showing equal husband and brother authority over a woman. She found that women in matrilineal societies with equal husband and brother authority were more autonomous—in other words, that male domestic authority over women was altogether less in these societies than in the other types of matrilineal societies.

Later anthropologists were even more critical of the concept of the matrilineal puzzle. They argued that matrilineal descent is a perfectly ordinary, reasonable way of forming and operating groups in a society and that it need not be seen as odd or peculiar (Poewe 1981). Why, they asked, should it be viewed as a "puzzle" at all? Without claiming to have found any matrilineal matriarchies, these critics nevertheless called for a reassessment of the whole issue of gender in relation to matrilineal descent. In the process, many of them challenged the idea of universal male dominance, claiming that in at least some matrilineal societies (and in some bilateral societies, too) a case can be made for a kind of gender balance or gender equality.

Meanwhile, the matrilineal puzzle should not be entirely discounted. It did, after all, point up the error of assuming that matrilineal descent indicates matriarchy, or that matrilineal descent is just a "mirror image" of patrilineal descent. In fact, its main virtue is that it drew attention to male roles within matrilineal societies—and clearly these are important. (Better still, of course, would have been a simultaneous focus on the important female roles within patrilineal societies.)

The main limitation of the matrilineal puzzle is its blurry, unfocused vision of women and women's roles in matrilineal societies. In addition, during the "puzzle" era of matrilineal kinship studies, male authority was flatly assumed to be a given. Later researchers brought out the considerable variation that characterizes authority, power, and influence among both males and females in societies with matrilineal descent. Here we will take a look at two very different cases.

CASE 4: THE NAVAJO

During the period from babyhood to adolescence there is little difference in ritualistic treatment of male and female children. At adolescence, however, there is a definite change. The girl . . . becomes a tribal symbol of fecundity at her adolescence ceremony, and from then on a symbol of the power of reproduction.

—*Gladys Reichard (1950)*

These people among whom a girl's first menstruation is a public rejoicing, and among whom women are powerful symbols of life, growth, and rejuvenation, are the Navajo. The largest Native American group, they now number around 200,000.

The ancestors to the Navajo are thought by anthropologists to have been among the last migrants to enter North America from Asia across the Bering Strait more than 12,000 years ago. From homelands in Alaska and western Canada, these people began a migration to the American Southwest. Navajo history places their new settlement in a region now mostly encompassed by northern New Mexico. According to anthropologists, they arrived in this region between 1000 and 1500 A.D., but Navajo tradition asserts that they have always lived in this area. Origins aside, the Navajo of the Southwest were originally hunter-gatherers. It is not clear how far back in time their matrilineal social organization goes.[1]

Early on, the Navajo traded and intermarried with other indigenous peoples, including Paiutes, Utes, and Pueblos in the Southwest; later, after 1540, Spanish settlements began to encroach on native land. From the Pueblos the Navajo adopted agricultural techniques and began to practice a mixed agriculture-hunting economy. From the Spaniards the Navajo acquired the horse in the 1600s, considerably increasing their mobility and their range of contacts with other peoples. Through raids on the Spanish they also acquired sheep and goats, and by the late 1700s sheep herding had become a central feature of their economy. Women's clothing, consisting of a blouse, velvet jacket, and flaring skirt, was also adopted from the Spanish.

With their herding and agriculture, the Navajo adapted to an arid desert region, a harsh land but also beautiful, with deep canyons, grand mountains, and mesas. Within small dispersed settlements they lived in "forked stick" *hogans* (houses) made of earth and wood. Compared with other Native American societies, the Navajo were relatively dispersed, a fact that spared them Spanish domination and decimation from epidemics.

But a far more serious threat lay just ahead. By the mid-1800s, US forces were in the region, determined to put a stop to Navajo raiding. In 1863, under Kit Carson, the US military subdued the Navajo, largely by destroying their homes and crops and taking their livestock. Soon after, about 8,000 Navajo were imprisoned at Fort Sumner, New Mexico. This was a very dark period in Navajo history, often referred to as the "Long Walk" because the Navajo were made to walk the 300 miles to Fort Sumner from the point of their surrender at Fort Defiance, Arizona. Many died or were killed along the way, and at Fort Sumner they endured deplorable conditions.

The Navajo remained incarcerated for four years. In 1868, they were allowed to return home, but "home" was now an Indian reservation, under legal control of the US government. Here, after enduring initial hardships, and despite their pacification and loss of autonomy, the Navajo began to reconstruct their lives around sheep herding and farming, renewing many of their cultural traditions. From this period to the present, the Navajo economy and culture changed dramatically. Wage work and craft production became major sources of income, whereas herding and agriculture declined. Beginning in the 1880s, Anglo influences entered the reservation with the establishment of trading posts, schools, medical facilities, and Christian missions. Along with the loss of many Navajo traditions, recent years have seen a growth in self-government and a strong push for Navajo self-determination.

Since their entry into the Southwest, the Navajo have experienced fairly rapid economic changes, and these undoubtedly had repercussions on gender relationships. As agriculture developed, reliance on male hunting declined. During the same period, male roles in raiding and warfare became important, but these activities were abruptly ended by the US military action in 1863. In early reservation times, agriculture and herding had involved both men and women in important economic activities. Later, wage work was largely available only to males, and women became economically dependent on men. This situation is changing now as more women are becoming employed and pursuing educational opportunities.

The following description of Navajo kinship refers to these people's recent past, roughly from 1940 to the early 1970s. Most of these traditions have not continued, but in some respects the overall character of Navajo kinship and gender is still evident now. As we will see, one aspect of Navajo life that was important in the past and persists today is the centrality of women's social and symbolic roles.

Kinship Traditions

Descent.   Navajo clans (of which more than sixty still exist) were matrilineal, named, exogamous categories. Many of the clan names reflected their origin as place names—for example, Deer Spring, Water-Flows-Together, Coyote Pass, Narrow Gorge, and Yucca-Fruit-Strung-Out-In-a-Line. Navajo clans were not corporate groups in the sense that clan members did not hold property in common or come together for any economic, social, or religious purpose.

Both marriage and sexual relations were forbidden within the clan. Sexual relations between clan members were considered incestuous, and the Navajo believed that those who broke this taboo would become insane, die, or produce deformed children (Aberle 1961: 109). Aside from enforcement of these marriage and sex prohibitions, the main function of the clan was to oblige members to provide one another with hospitality and assistance—particularly assistance with religious, or curing, ceremonies. Clans were residentially dispersed, so that any one area encompassed members of different clans and the members of a specific clan were scattered over a wide region. By the reservation period, the Navajo were not living in highly organized descent groups. Neither clans nor subunits of clans had official leaders or transmitted property.

Some clans had special links to one another, forming what anthropologists call *phratries*, or groupings of clans together into larger units. Among the Navajo some members of linked clans considered themselves to be related. These phratries were exogamous units, so marriages between members of linked clans were forbidden.

Although each Navajo was born into his or her mother's clan, a relationship of descent to the father and the father's matriclan was also acknowledged. The Navajo expressed this distinction by saying that one is "born of" mother's clan but "born for" father's clan. Thus, when asked her identity, a woman might say, "I am Bitter-Water, born for Salt" (Kluckhohn and Leighton 1946: 64). In other words, she recognized a link of descent to and through the father, but it was a link to the father's *matrilineal* clan. Thus Navajo descent tied each person to two matriclans: the one in which the person was a member, through the mother, and the other that he or she was "born for," through the father.

One implication of the "born for" concept was that fatherhood was given importance and seen as complementary to motherhood (Lamphere 1977: 70). Being "born for" father's matriclan also affected other relationships. For example, those who were "born for" the same clan considered themselves to be like siblings and were forbidden to marry. Likewise, a person considered those "born for" his or her own clan to also be like siblings and thus could not marry them. Today, however, in some of the more developed areas of the reservation, these marriage restrictions are breaking down (Miranda Warburton, personal communication).

Another implication of this Navajo concept of descent was that a father was regarded as both an affinal and a consanguineal relative, giving him a kind of dual kinship status (Witherspoon 1975: 31–36). On the one hand, a person's father was an affine because he had married into that person's matriclan. Accordingly, Navajo children sometimes addressed or referred to their fathers as in-laws. On the other hand, the father was seen as a consanguineal relative, a direct ascendant whose clan the person was "born for."[2]

This distinction between consanguineal and affinal relatives was important to the Navajo. In the former sphere, relationships among matrilineally related kin were felt to have a special kind of solidarity, based on ideas of giving and sharing (Witherspoon 1975: 56). The closest and most enduring bond of all was that between mother and child, but the sentiments of closeness, solidarity, giving, and sharing were extended to other consanguineal kin. In contrast to this were affinal relationships, based not on sharing and giving but on exchange and reciprocity. Among affinal relationships, the most important bond was that between husband and wife. Witherspoon (1975: 56–57) elaborated the difference, contrasting the mother-child and husband-wife relationships:

> Navajo mothers do not give life, food, and loving care to their children because they want the same in return. A mother loves and helps her child regardless of whether he is a king or a bum, a worker or an indolent . . . a contributor or a parasite, moral or immoral. . . . [But] when a husband is a bum or an indolent, or immoral, the wife usually gets rid of him. . . . The relationship is supposed to be advantageous to both through mutual obligations of assistance. Where one party falters, the relationship loses its balance and disintegrates.

The Navajo universe of kin was divided into two categories: those with whom the solidarity was mother-child-like—intense, and based on giving and sharing in terms of sheer need—and those with whom the solidarity was husband-wife-like—based on agreement and exchange, with an emphasis on equity in the exchange rather than on another person's need.

Matrilineal descent among the Navajo did not engender tensions between a woman's brother (or other senior matrilineal kin) and her husband, so it did not display this element of the matrilineal puzzle discussed in the previous section. Neither brothers nor husbands appear to have had strong authority over sisters or wives. Among siblings, older ones, regardless of sex, had some authority over younger ones. Nor did Navajo men appear to be pulled in different directions by ties to their sisters' children and their own children. In general, fathers had more authority over their own children than did the children's mother's brothers. The mother's brothers were, however, important figures to children in that they provided instruction and discipline and played an important role in arranging their marriages.

The Navajo case does not show a strain between male authority and descent through women, although Robin Fox (1989: 103) argues that this was the case because the matrilineal clans had few functions. What Navajo matrilineal descent, combined with matrilocal residence, does show with respect to gender are a number of themes pervasive in Navajo culture. One is a complementarity between the sexes. This is expressed in Navajo mythology and religious ritual (Lamphere 1969). One student of Navajo religion summarized as follows: "The ritual teachings stress male and female as a basic form of symbolism; the notion is that only by pairing can any entity be complete" (Reichard 1950: 29). Another theme is the social centrality of women that comes about through their reproductive roles. A third and related theme concerns the dual kinship position of men, as noted earlier, and the tensions that emerge as men move between their roles as sons and husbands of women.

Residence.   The Navajo matrilineal clan was important for identity, marriage and sex prohibitions, hospitality, and cooperation. But the social unit of primary importance in everyday life was the group of people who lived together and placed their sheep into one herd. The camp, as this unit will be called here,[3] consisted of a few hogans, each usually containing a separate married couple, nuclear family, or small extended family group. Camps were quite often far apart from one another and did not link together to form larger communities or villages. The Navajo camp was not a corporate group since members did not collectively own property. However, members did pool their sheep into one herd and did manage many of their resources communally, so the camp functioned as a corporate enterprise (Witherspoon 1975: 73). Along with a sheep herd, members shared food, use of agricultural fields, and other assets and resources.

Camps were organized around women, who played active and forceful roles within them. In his study of the Rough Rock–Black Mountain area, Witherspoon (1975) drew attention to what he called the "head mother," a senior woman around whom a camp would nucleate. All members could trace a tie to her, based upon two rules of residence: (1) Every Navajo had the right to reside with his or her mother, and (2) every Navajo had the right to live with his or her spouse. Individual married couples then worked out their own arrangements (living matrilocally, patrilocally, or neolocally), based on factors such as the relative resources of the camps and personal preference. Matrilocal residence was most often adopted.

In the case of matrilocal residence, the husband was the newcomer. He shared in the resources of his wife's camp but was expected to contribute his share of the labor. Yet, especially in the early years of marriage, the husband retained important ties to his own mother's group, returning there to help with the work. Often the husband would keep his own sheep with his natal group, only gradually moving them over, a few at a time, to his wife's camp as the marriage stabilized.

In his new home, the husband was expected to maintain proper relationships with his wife's kin. Most important was the Navajo practice of mother-in-law avoidance. A respectful restraint in the interaction between a man and his wife's mother is common practice in many societies, but among the Navajo, the two were not to have physical or even eye contact (though this restriction is no longer strictly observed). One consequence was that the two could not share the same hogan. With his wife's married sisters, the husband was also expected to keep his distance to avoid making their husbands jealous, and his sexual relations with them would have constituted adultery. But there were no restrictions on his behavior with his wife's unmarried sisters, whom he later might marry.

Gender Complementarity. Both the husband and wife of the senior generation participated in running the camp and managing its affairs, and within camps, the division of labor by sex was not sharply defined. Men tended to work more in house building, agriculture, and care of cattle and horses, whereas women worked more in care of sheep and goats, weaving, cleaning, cooking, and childrearing. But these divisions were flexible and variable (Lamphere 1989), and many tasks were carried out by men and women together.

Most ceremonial practitioners were male, but women could also become practitioners. As for political roles, which became important on the reservation, they were once held predominantly by men but over the past couple of decades have been taken on by women as well. There are also indications that before the reservation period, some women went to war along with men and that those who were successful warriors became war chiefs (Reichard 1928: 53).

Land was not owned by any one person or group but, instead, camps had rights to use the land they occupied and all resident members shared these rights (Lamphere 1977: 83). Sheep, horses, and other livestock were individually owned, but, as noted, camp members jointly managed livestock. Sheep were the mainstay of the Navajo economy, and there are indications that women owned more sheep than men did, although men owned more of the cattle and horses (Aberle 1961: 142). Parents gave male and female children their own sheep.

Thus among the Navajo both men and women played important economic roles and neither gender had greater access to or control over property. Economically, men and women were complementary. A gender complementarity was also seen in terms of descent that, though matrilineal, incorporated husbands/fathers through the notion that one was "born for" the father's matriclan.

Marriage. In the past, Navajo marriages were usually arranged by parents. Both males and females were considered marriageable after puberty, and it was common to see arrangements for a girl's marriage being made shortly after her puberty ceremony. The bride and groom may not have known each other, but their consent was usually sought. Arranged marriages were customarily accompanied by the payment of bridewealth, consisting of horses and other livestock, from the groom's family to kin of the bride. This bridewealth was believed to ensure the husband's sexual rights to his wife (Aberle 1961: 125; Witherspoon 1975: 24).[4]

It was also possible for a couple to establish a marriage simply by living together, without any public ceremony, parental arrangement, or payment of bridewealth. Many remarriages were enacted in this way. Divorce was frequent and easy for either men or women to instigate: The couple simply split, and no bridewealth was returned.

Polygyny was once permitted among the Navajo, but it is now forbidden. Aberle (1961: 119) estimates that polygynous unions accounted for 5 to 10 percent of all marital unions in the 1930s, but they may have been more common at an earlier time.[5] By far the most common polygynous unions were cases of sororal polygyny, or the marriage of one man to two or more sisters, a situation that sometimes caused conflict and jealousy between sisters (Shepardson and Hammond 1970: 182). Another common practice was the levirate, whereby a woman married her dead husband's brother. Such unions were not mandatory, however. Cases of "stepdaughter marriage," whereby a man is married to one woman and simultaneously to her daughter by a previous union, also occurred (Shepardson and Hammond 1970: 181).

Although adultery occurred among the Navajo, as in all societies, sex was ideally supposed to be confined to marriage, and both husbands and wives expressed sexual jealousy (Leighton and Kluckhohn 1947: 86). Female premarital sex was apparently not considered a serious matter, though some reports indicate that brides were ideally expected to have been virgins (Aberle 1961: 125; Frisbie 1982: 20). Having a child before marriage was "regarded unfavorably" (Aberle 1961: 128), but children born outside of marriage, who would become members of their mother's clan without any problem, were not looked down upon. In addition, no reports indicate concern over premarital male sexual behavior, but "excessive" sexual behavior on the part of either sex was frowned upon and believed to cause illness (Leighton and Kluckhohn 1947: 89).

Women, Men, and Reproduction

According to Navajo religion, there are worlds below and above this one. In the past, Navajo deities, or Holy People, lived in worlds below. At various times, for different reasons, the Holy People climbed up from the lower worlds into higher worlds, reaching the fifth or current world. Once, escaping a flood, they reached the Earth Surface and here, in different ways according to different stories, the Earth Surface People, or Navajo, were brought into being.

By the time they reached this world, the Holy People had lost the power to reproduce, and destructive monsters also inhabited the current world. But then one of the Holy People, First Man, discovered a baby girl and he and First Woman cared for her. She became Changing Woman, a very central and powerful being in Navajo religion. Changing Woman personifies life, reproduction, and motherhood and is considered the creator of the Navajo. She is associated with the Earth itself and is called Changing Woman because, like the Earth with its seasons, she has the power to continually return to her youth after reaching old age. In Navajo tradition, Changing Woman restored the power of generation and, through union with the male Sun, gave birth to twins, Monster Slayer and Child-of-the-Water, who destroyed the monsters threatening the world.

When Changing Woman had her first menstrual period, a great ceremony was held for her. This is the religious referent for the Navajo *Kinaaldá*, or girl's puberty ceremony, that was held upon a girl's first menstruation. During her Kinaaldá, a girl became the symbol of Changing Woman and thus represented the power of reproduction (Frisbie 1967: 373).

The Kinaaldá was a four-day, four-night ceremony through which the young girl was blessed and protected, and during which she received instruction in her life and duties as an adult woman. The Kinaaldá was a highly public ceremony, attended by ceremonial specialists ("singers") who gave songs and prayers. It was a sacred ceremony, a public announcement of the girl's adulthood and eligibility for marriage, and "a time for rejoicing" (Frisbie 1967: 7). There were no puberty rites for males.

During her Kinaaldá the young girl ritually became Changing Woman, and as we saw above, it was Changing Woman who made human reproduction possible. Thus the Kinaaldá ceremony dramatically illustrated the high value placed on human reproduction in Navajo culture, but also the central and overwhelmingly positive position of women as reproducers. Women were associated not just with human reproduction, and their own potential motherhood, but more generally with life-giving forces, renewal, growth, and rejuvenation. As Witherspoon (1975: 16) wrote: "Essential parts, as well as the earth itself, are called mother. Agricultural fields are called mother, corn is called mother, and sheep are called mother. . . . These applications of the concept -*ma* [mother] certainly make it clear that motherhood is defined in terms of the source, sustenance, and reproduction of life."

This ritual focus on women as central symbols of life and reproduction is in striking contrast to Christian mythology in which female fertility is given quite a different role. Here a male God is creator and human reproduction follows from the sin of a woman, Eve. Later, Christ arrives through virgin birth. As different as can be from the female deity of Navajo lore, who continually ages and renews her youth to rejuvenate life, is the composite Christian Eve/Mary figure, an "Unchanging Woman" whose sexuality and fertility are either considered sinful or denied (Moody 1991).

Although menstrual blood was clearly associated with fertility, traditionally it was also seen as dangerous, and there were several restrictions on women at the time of their menstruation. Menstruating women were not to enter ceremonial hogans, nor could they have a "sing" (curing ceremony) performed over them at this time. They were not to milk goats (or the milk would stop), enter crop fields (or the crops would die), carry water, or have contact with children or livestock (Wright 1982a, 1982b; Bailey 1950: 9–11). Contact with adult males was not restricted, and in sharp contrast to the Nepalese Brahmans described in the last chapter, the Navajo did not view menstrual blood as a source of impurity, nor did they connect it in any way with the religious inferiority of women. Wright (1982b) suggests that among the Navajo, menstrual blood was considered dangerous because it signaled temporary infertility and thus was considered threatening to things associated with fertility and creative potential, such as crops, livestock, and children. So, for example, according to Navajo belief, a menstruating woman was not dangerous to an old, infertile horse, but she could harm a young, fertile horse by riding it (Wright 1982b, following Bailey 1950: 9).

In Navajo communities, children have always been highly valued and desired by both women and men. In contrast to the societies discussed in Chapter 3, the Navajo had no religious prescriptions necessitating the bearing of children for the well-being of one's soul after death. Rather, children were economically important and valued for their labor. At young ages they were active in sheep herding, hauling water, and bringing firewood. Parents also wanted children to take care of them in old age. And there was an idea, at least among women, that having children means one will not be lonely (Wright 1982b: 381; Witherspoon 1975: 15).

The Navajo traditionally considered a couple's infertility to be due to sterility in either the man or the woman (Bailey 1950: 20). In cases of failure to have children, divorce would have been an option for both husband and wife. But in contrast to some matrilineal societies, the Navajo did not require the termination of an infertile union, and no censure of childless women, or social punishment such as ostracism, has been reported.[6]

Men and Kinship

This glimpse into Navajo kinship thus far reveals a complementarity between the sexes and a centrality in the position of women, in terms of both their symbolic roles as reproducers and their social roles as transmitters of descent and as "head mothers" in camps. But what about men in this matrilineal-matrilocal system? As noted earlier, Navajo men had a kind of dual kinship status. For one thing, fathers could be seen as either consanguineal or affinal kin. We also saw that this distinction was important, in that consanguineal ties were associated with the strong mother-child bond and the sentiment of "unconditional love," whereas affinal ties were associated with the more fragile husband-wife bond of mutual obligation. Thus "father," in contrast to "mother," held a somewhat ambiguous status, as was reflected in attitudes toward the father: "The father [was] at best a helpful friend, good instructor, and strong disciplinarian, or at worst, an undependable friend, inconsistent helper, or unsure ally" (Witherspoon 1975: 35). In addition, the stability of the father's ties to his children was contingent on the stability and duration of his marriage to their mother. If the marriage broke up, children almost always remained with the mother, and the father had very little to do with his children, particularly if they were young at the time of the divorce and he remarried.

Men had a dual kinship status in another respect, too. In matrilocal situations, it was the husband who bridged two intermarrying families and moved between them. Particularly in the early years of marriage, the husband would divide his time and loyalties between two camps, keeping sheep in both and only gradually becoming a permanent resident in his wife's camp as the marriage stabilized. In the last chapter we saw that affinal women in strongly patrilineal societies were considered divisive and threatening to male patrilineal solidarity. But in the matrilineal Navajo case, we find that matrilocal males, though sometimes blamed for inciting jealousy between sisters, were themselves seen as being pulled apart by women, by wives and mothers. As Witherspoon (1975: 27) wrote:

A Navajo man is virtually tossed between two women, and through them he gets his status and works out his role in the social system. His relationship to these two women involves two kinds of relationship to a womb. One is a kind of extrusion; the other is a kind of intrusion. One is symbolized by birth; the other, by sexual intercourse. One is described as the utmost in security; the other is considered to hold latent danger.

Another important dimension of male-female relationships can be seen by reference to a particular Navajo religious tale. There are many different versions of this story. One relates that, while in a lower world, before his emergence to this one, First Man discovered the adultery of his wife, First Woman, and hit her. First Woman complained of this to her mother, Woman Chief, who scolded First Man and then told him that she, not he, was really master of all things. Soon after, First Man called all the men together and they decided, in retaliation for this affront, to leave the women to themselves and to cross over the water to form their own community. As time went by, the women failed at growing their crops and suffered great hardship. But the men were successful. Both sexes suffered from sexual desire and made inappropriate compensations, but for the women it was much worse. News of their horrible actions got back to one man, who then told the others:

The women, whom you left (for good) four years ago (in order) to cross (over here) are abusing themselves with any old thing. They are fornicating with tapering smooth rocks, fornicating with quills, fornicating with hooked cactus and straight spined cactus (and are) fornicating with the calves of animals. Blue foxes have intercourse with them, and Yellow foxes and badgers, they say. (Haile 1981: 30)

The consequence of such unions was the birth of monsters who plagued this lower world and later the Earth Surface, until they were killed off by Changing Woman's sons. But meanwhile, the men realized they must reunite with the women so that the group could procreate. They then did so.

Like all religious stories, this one can be interpreted in various ways. Karl Luckert (1981: 17, 23) suggested that it developed as the Navajo were switching from hunting and gathering to agriculture. Pointing out that agriculture was originally in the hands of women, Luckert argued that this shift in subsistence deprived males of their primary economic function. Men then took charge of agriculture, and the story represents men's attempt to regain their position as providers.

Others have seen in this tale a theme we have encountered before: the complementarity of the sexes (Reichard 1950: 31; Farella 1984: 134–144). In the version given here, more blame is placed on women than on men for the separation of the sexes (indeed, female adultery is believed to have started all the trouble), and it is women who, with their perverted sexuality, bring forth the monsters. But both sexes suffer from the separation. The women fail completely, but the men realize that they cannot procreate without women. In the end the two sexes come back together, each realizing it needs the other.

CASE 5: THE NAYAR AND THE MOSUO

The Nayar, numbering more than 2 million people, live in the state of Kerala in southwest India. They are presumed to have been a matrilineal hill tribe who moved to the plains and coastal regions of Kerala in the fourth century A.D., possibly fleeing invasions (Gough 1961b: 303). In Kerala they became settled agriculturists, rulers, and warriors in a society based on plow agriculture and organized into kingdoms. This region was a part of South Asian Hindu civilization, with religious practices and a caste system somewhat similar to those of the Nepalese Brahmans described in the last chapter.

The very interesting kinship traditions of the Nayar take us back to a period ranging from the mid-1300s to the late 1700s, before the British conquests in India. These traditions were studied by anthropologist Kathleen Gough (1961b), who used historical records to supplement her own fieldwork among the modern Nayar in the 1940s. By this time many features of the earlier system had disappeared and matrilineal descent was disintegrating, yet some traditions persisted and many earlier practices were remembered, especially by older people.

In these centuries before the British conquests, the people of Kerala were stratified into numerous castes.[7] Below castes of priests and rulers were commoner Nayar castes whose members lived in the rural areas, and it is the kinship traditions of this group that will be discussed here. Below commoner Nayar castes were assorted lower castes (Nayar and non-Nayar), some of them considered highly polluting to all higher groups and physically segregated from other castes. In several of these castes were serfs who worked the land for the commoner Nayars and other, higher castes.

The kingdoms of this period were engaged in a nearly constant state of war, and males of the commoner Nayar group served as soldiers. In earlier centuries this warfare entailed swords, shields, and bows and arrows; later, gunpowder and cannons were introduced and the wars became more destructive. For Nayar males, military training started early (at about age seven) in village gymnasiums, and for much of their young adult lives they were away from their homes and off at war.

Clan and Lineage

Commoner Nayars lived in villages along with people of many other castes. But in these villages they lived in their own neighborhoods among fellow caste persons. They were divided into dispersed matrilineal clans, which were named, exogamous categories. Like the Navajo clans, these were not corporate groups, but members had rights of hospitality in each other's homes. There was one other obligation: All clan members had to be informed of the births or deaths within the clan. Upon receiving the news, all clan members observed a fifteen-day period of birth or death pollution, during which they maintained restrictions on their behavior and diet.

Clans were subdivided into matrilineages. A lineage consisted of all those members of one clan who lived in one neighborhood of a village (Gough 1961b: 324). In any one neighborhood there could be from six to ten lineages representing different clans, but all shared the same caste. Neither clans nor lineages had official leaders.

The lineage was a corporate group. For one thing, if a branch of a lineage died out, the other lineage members became heirs to its property. In addition, whereas clanspeople had only to observe birth and death pollution for all members, the people of a lineage were obliged to attend the funerals of dead members and to visit any house where the birth of a new lineage member had occurred. Lineage members also worshipped a common lineage goddess and felt a moral obligation to avenge the murder of a member or offenses to one another.

The different lineages of a neighborhood, each representing different clans, were linked together in special relationships known as *enangar*. These linkages ensured that an important ceremonial cooperation occurred between the lineages, as I will discuss shortly.

Lineages were further subdivided into property groups, which were also corporate units. Each property group included people who were related within a depth of three to six generations, and there were as many as eight such units within one lineage. Members of a property group normally lived in one household. All members were matrilineally related and jointly owned property, consisting of land, buildings, and serfs. Residence at marriage was natolocal; both husbands and wives stayed where they were, each in their own property group. Children stayed with the mother and her household throughout life. Property groups were headed by the oldest male member, called the *karanavan*. The karanavan rather tightly oversaw and managed all economic activities of the property group and was the legal guardian of all members. This man could inflict corporal punishment on women and children of the group. In his household he was to be shown great respect. The eldest woman of the household directed the activities of the other women and had informal authority over other women and children, but no woman had legal authority over any other.

Each of these matrilineal kin categories and groups was named, and a Nayar person would take these names along with a personal name and the title of "Nayar." "A typical name might therefore be 'Thengiparambil Padikkil Kirakkut-Velappil Govindan Nayar'—Clan of the coconut garden, lineage of the gatehouse, household of the eastern garden, Govindan (personal name) Nayar" (Gough 1961b: 325).

Marriage

The Nayar had one of the most intriguing marriage systems ever found in human societies. Already we have seen that they practiced natolocal residence, which is itself quite rare. Also Nayar females underwent two types of marriages, one known as tali-tying (the tali was a gold ornament) and the other known as *sambandam*, a "joining together" with one or more "visiting husbands."

Here's how it worked. Every ten years or so, each lineage gathered together all of its prepubescent females and on one day, in one grand ritual, married them to the males of its special *enangar* (linked) lineages. A village astrologer paired off grooms and young girls according to their horoscopes. The entire village witnessed the event. The marriage ceremony must have been fairly impressive: In some areas the bridegrooms arrived on elephants, accompanied by musicians (Gough 1955). During the marriage ceremony itself, each groom tied a gold tali around the neck of his bride. With this tali, "a girl was regarded as having attained the status of a mature woman, ready to bear children and perpetuate her lineage" (Gough 1961b: 328). The tali was worn until death.

After the tali-tying, each couple was secluded in a room for three days and three nights. If a girl was nearing puberty, sexual intercourse might take place during the seclusion. On the fourth day the groom departed, and from this day forward, he and the bride did not need to have anything more to do with each other. A woman had to fulfill only one obligation to her tali-tying husband— namely, upon his death, to observe fifteen days of death pollution for him.

After the tali-tying marriage the woman was free to have sexual relations with any man she chose, provided that he was of her own caste or of a higher one. The men with whom she had these acceptable relationships were considered her husbands, even though no religious ceremonies marked the establishment of these "joining together" unions. Either husbands or wives could easily terminate these unions at any time.

There was apparently no limit to the number of "joining together" husbands a woman could have, although most women had only a small number at any one time (Gough 1961b: 358). Since a Nayar woman could have more than one visiting husband at the same time, the society was polyandrous; since a Nayar man could have a number of wives, the society was also polygynous. Marriages were restricted by a rule of clan exogamy and by a rule that women could not marry men of lower castes. In addition, neither a woman nor a man could have two or more spouses from the same lineage. The man who performed the tali-tying marriage with a woman could, if he and she wanted, become one of her husbands, but this outcome was not necessary.

A husband usually visited a wife at night after having dinner in his own household. It was considered impolite to his own mother for a man to visit a wife for many hours during the day, and too much time spent with a wife could arouse jealousy in the man's mother. After spending the night, the husband would leave before breakfast. If two men showed up on the same night to visit the same wife, there was a simple solution: The husband who arrived first would place his weapons outside his wife's door to let any other husbands know that they should come at some other time. Gough (1961b: 359) also notes that "usually a woman's regular husbands knew each other and informally agreed upon their turns." Likewise, cowives apparently did not object to sharing visiting husbands (Fuller 1976: 4).

These arrangements should not be interpreted as reflecting sanctioned casual sex or promiscuity. As we have seen, there were rules governing who could form "joining together" unions with whom. It is true that husbands and wives did not form domestic units and that interactions between them were largely restricted to nighttime visiting, but there was one very crucial obligation that visiting husbands had to wives. When a woman became pregnant, all husbands who might be the father were obliged to acknowledge their possible paternity by giving gifts of cloth to the woman and, after the birth, paying the expenses of the delivery to the midwife. This was a very serious matter, for if no man made these payments, the father of the child was assumed to be a lower-caste male, in which case the woman's male matrilineal relatives could put her and her child to death. Even in more recent times, a sexual union with a lower-caste man has brought punishment: "In an orthodox household today, a girl who becomes pregnant by a low caste man will be either expelled from the house by her male seniors or, at best, will be thrashed and will receive much subsequent harsh treatment" (Gough 1958: 455).

Both the tali-tying and the "joining together" marriages legitimized female reproduction: They regulated sexual relationships and legitimized children. The first tali-tying marriage transformed the female herself into a legitimate childbearer for her property group, lineage, and caste. The tali-tier, who so briefly played a role in the girl's life, was, to Gough, merely a symbolic representative of males of the whole caste—the caste with whose males the woman could legitimately procreate. Whether sexual intercourse actually took place during the ceremony was irrelevant; the seclusion with the male symbolized sex and symbolically conferred potential sexual rights in the woman to males of the caste who were outside the woman's lineage and clan, as all linked-lineage (enangar) males automatically would be. At the same time, according to Gough, the ceremony was a ritual statement indicating that males of the woman's matrilineal kin groups had relinquished their own sexual access to her while retaining their rights over her reproduction. After this rite was performed, a woman and her male matrilineal kin maintained a great deal of distance and formality in their relationship. Indeed, a man was forbidden to touch any junior woman of his property group once her tali-tying ceremony had occurred; after this rite, a man was not even allowed to be alone in a room with his sister's daughter.

Upon completion of the tali-tying ceremony, the girl received a new title of *amma*, or "mother" (Gough 1955: 65). Now that the woman was legitimized as a reproducer, her individual children were further legitimized through the visiting husbands' gifts to the woman and payment to the midwife at each child's birth.

Gough aptly (1961b: 357) describes Nayar marriage as "the slenderest of ties." Neither children nor economic interests, nor common residence, united married couples. Each partner had primary, binding ties with his or her matrilineal kin. Recall from Chapter 2 that in many human societies of the past (as well as some current ones), marriages were enacted to form alliances between groups, and that these alliances were often socially and politically very important. It is clear that the Nayar were not using or benefiting from "joining together" marriages in this way. Yet their system of enangar-linked lineages brought about the same end; indeed, their tali-tying ceremonies could be seen as affirming the intermarriageability of the linked lineages and, hence, as expressing their alliances (Gough 1955: 49). That the tali-tying union had duration and meaning beyond the ceremony itself is suggested by the fact that the tali was worn until death and a woman (as well as her children, by whomsoever begotten) was required to observe death pollution for the tali-tier. She did not, however, observe death pollution for "visiting husbands."

In this system of marriage there was little connection between fathers and children. Husbands neither had rights in a woman's children nor passed property or title to them and, for that matter, often didn't know which of a woman's children were their own. Yet the male role in reproduction was fully recognized, husbands were fond of children they thought might be their own, and children were thought to physically resemble their genitors. But if a husband's relationship to the mother ended, so did all connection with the children who might have been his.

In contrast to father-child and husband-wife ties, the bond between mothers and sons was close and strong. This relationship was based not only on important mutual obligations and expected loyalty but on love as well. Also strong and close, though somewhat less so than the mother-son bond, was that between mothers and daughters. As for authority, children of both sexes quickly learned that it would come not so much from the mother as from her brothers, clearly and directly.

Brother-sister ties were also strong, for which reason the Nayar case was readily used by anthropologists to illustrate the matrilineal puzzle. The Nayar were seen to represent one solution to the problem of how to combine descent through women with authority vested in men. In this case, the solution was to keep matrilineally related males together and the husband-wife bond weak so that brothers could rule over sisters without interference from husbands, who might grow attached to their wives and develop interests in their children.

Indeed, Nayar society does seem to have been organized in such a way that the husband-wife bond was not allowed to flourish or threaten matrilineal solidarity. Aside from natolocal residence and lack of a man's rights in his children, a woman's mother's brother could dismiss any of her visiting husbands if he chose to do so. In addition, we can see in sorcery beliefs both a tension between affinal and consanguineal relatives and a resolution of this tension in favor of matrilineal solidarity. Nayar sorcery was most often practiced by property group members against a wife of their leader, the karanavan. This man, of all the men in a matrilineal property group, was expected to show primary allegiance to the group. He also commanded the group's economic resources. Thus members of his property group did not wish to see him become too attached to a particular wife or to give her valuable gifts or cash that would otherwise be their joint property. If he did so, they might hire low-caste practitioners of sorcery to recite spells to bring illness to this woman or her kin. Whether or not it worked, word of the attempt would get around and hostilities would develop between the two groups. The usual consequence was termination of the "joining together" union (Gough 1961b).

Fertility

The Nayar were very concerned with human reproduction and the fertility of matrilineal women. New births, as we have seen, had to be announced to all clanspeople, and lineage kin were required to visit the houses where new births had occurred. Children may have been desired for any number of reasons but, in contrast to the Navajo case, they were not needed for their labor. Hard agricultural labor was done by serfs. Young boys and girls (before the tali-tying rite) played and went to village schools. When older, the males would serve as warriors and, with distinctions earned in wars, would bring honor to their kin groups. As in other Hindu areas, sons were also needed for religious reasons, since male descendants performed important funeral ceremonies for their departed kin and carried out periodic rituals to assist their well-being after death. In the case of the matrilineal Nayar, the crucial funeral rituals were performed for a woman by her eldest son or next-closest junior male relative; for a man, they were conducted by whatever male was immediately junior to him within the property group, usually a younger brother or a sister's son.

Females, of course, reproduced the group, and concern was expressed for the continuity of the matriline. If a property group had no childbearing women, it would adopt girls from another branch of its lineage. Still, women were blamed for infertility, and childless women were considered most unfortunate. Deborah Neff (1994: 477) writes that this attitude continues today: "Among some Nayars, she [an infertile woman] will be an inauspicious guest at weddings and sacred rituals. Social ostracism serves to increase her suffering and vulnerability, and as a barren woman she is often cut off from networks of sustenance and support."

What also continues today is the idea that a woman's infertility is associated with and brought about by the anger of deities and disharmony in the matrilineage. An infertile woman is a sign of loss of prestige and decreasing fortunes for the whole matrilineage. Women are considered powerful, in a religious sense, because of the greater possession of *sakti*, or divine energy, that accrues to them on account of their ability to reproduce. But in Nayar religion and ritual, this power is most clearly recognized in its negative manifestations. A fertile woman dissipates her sakti for the benefit of the group, but an infertile one accumulates the most sakti, which, upon her death, becomes a source of danger to her matrilineal kin, who in turn may suffer from her frustrated ghost (Neff 1994).

Female fertility was important to matrilineal kin groups but, again in contrast to the Navajo case, the association between women and reproduction was not so much venerated as considered dangerous under conditions of fertility failure. Before the tali-tying ceremony, and at a girl's later first menstruation, lineage members worshipped their lineage goddess, or *dharma devi*, whose propitiation could enhance the fertility of the young girl. In general, it was important to propitiate lineage goddesses since they could inflict miscarriages and sickness in childbirth (Gough 1961b: 342). Snake gods were also worshipped, as they were believed to hold the power of fertility or infertility over women. Each property group household devoted a separate area of its garden to snake gods. If a woman seemed unable to conceive, a special ceremony was held during which the other women of her property group (after purifying themselves through fasting and sexual abstinence) became possessed by the snake gods and danced wildly, some going into a trance. Gough (1961b: 342) suggests that snake gods were phallic symbols, representing the spirits of dead genitors of the matriline "who had been so essential to its perpetuation, yet so firmly excluded from its everyday affairs."

Female sexuality, though allowed rather free rein within certain rules, was also considered a source of social danger. A woman's sexual misconduct brought dishonor to her matrilineal kin groups. Males would sometimes fight duels to avenge the honor of a kinswoman against a charge of her having had sex with a lower-caste man. Another danger was sexual desire between matrilineally related males and females in one household of a property group. We have already seen that interaction was restricted between a woman and her senior matrilineal kin. In addition, the house of a property group was divided sharply into male and female spaces, with separate entryways for women and men. Women's bedrooms, in which they received their visiting husbands, were on a separate upstairs floor, an area hardly ever entered by males of the house.

Most observers have been interested in the polyandrous aspect of Nayar marriage, partly because polyandry is so rare. Looking at it from the standpoint of a matriline, we can see that Nayar polyandry would have helped to maximize fertility for each matrilineal group, in the sense that no one woman, if herself fertile, would be kept childless because of her union with an infertile male. In addition, many observers have drawn a connection between Nayar polyandry and the fact that Nayar males, especially young, virile ones, were specialized in military service and thus sporadically away from their villages for many months at a time. In the context of monogamy (or even polygyny, for that matter) this would have meant that an individual woman would be without a husband (impregnator) for long periods. With polyandry, however, we have a situation where if one husband is gone, so be it, as other husbands may be around. Indeed polyandry began to die out when Nayar soldiering was stopped, around 1810, even though the matrilineal lineage system was maintained for much longer (Gough 1955: 47).

Today very little is left of the Nayar marriage system (Fuller 1976). The major changes that resulted in the termination of polyandry and visiting husbands came about with British rule (Gough 1961a: 646–647). As the British took over politically and militarily in the 1800s, Nayar armies were disbanded. Many Nayar males, now left without a military role, eventually took new occupations and often left their homes in search of work. With the development of a new capitalist economy, land became private property rather than remaining under the ownership of descent groups.

Today the tali-tying rite is no longer performed, marriage is monogamous, and matrilineality has been shifting toward patrilineality (Menon 1996: 141). Husbands now have rights in and obligations to their children, and most couples live in nuclear family units. A shift to patrilineal descent may be a long-term trend, but even today matrilineal kin are considered ideally unified and responsible to one another. They continue to worship the family goddess of fertility and to be concerned with the reproduction of matrilineal women. Over time Nayar gender relationships have tended to follow the pattern of the broader Indian society such that, along with arranged marriages, there have been trends toward social concern for female virginity at marriage, marital fidelity, and authority of husbands over wives. These trends led one observer to remark: "The autonomy of Nayar women has declined; their status and position has relatively worsened, although it remains, of course, considerably higher than that of the majority of Indian women" (Fuller 1976: 149).

A CASE FROM CHINA: THE MOSUO

A case of "visiting" practices very similar to that of the Nayar occurs among the Mosuo of southwest China. The Mosuo (also called Na, Naze, and Moso) number around 40,000 people settled along the border of Yunnan and Sichuan provinces. They are rural agriculturalists who grow crops such as corn, wheat, and vegetables and also raise pigs and other livestock. They speak a Tibeto-Burman language and they follow a form of Tibetan Buddhism. Although the Mosuo case is ongoing in many respects, it has been changing rapidly under Chinese government policies and, more recently, tourism (Walsh 2005; Mattison 2010).

Like the Nayar, the Mosuo are matrilineal and natolocal, with brothers, sisters, and sisters' children residing together. They are organized into matrilineal lineages and clans, but the important corporate unit is the household that owns common property (land, livestock, and money) that is collectively transmitted from one generation to the next. Ideally descendants of one household will stay together over many generations, but households will split when they grow too large or when the harmony of the household is disrupted. Each household typically has both a female and a male head (usually the eldest male and female members), with the male head taking care of external affairs and the female head supervising the internal, domestic affairs of the household (Cai Hua 2008). Or a male or a female alone may serve as household head (Shih 2010: 220).

The Mosuo practice a visiting relationship called *tisese* ("walking back and forth" [Shih 2010: 75] or what some observers have called "walking marriages"). There are two somewhat different forms of this practice. In one, which Cai Hua (2008) has called "the furtive visit," a male visits a female at her house late at night and leaves early the next morning, "before the first crow of the rooster" (Cai Hua 2008: 186), so that the woman's matrilineal kin are not made explicitly aware of the relationship. It is particularly important for the visiting male not to encounter the male matrilineal kin of the female during visits. A man and a woman in this union refer to each other as *acia* (lover). The relationship may last anywhere from one night to several years and may be initiated or broken off at any time by either partner. These relationships are emphatically nonexclusive; indeed sexual jealousy in them is considered shameful. Typically women and men have a number of lovers at the same time (an average of five for females and more than six for males, according to Cai Hua's study).

Another form of visiting is what Cai Hua has called the "conspicuous visit" where, following initial visits, a couple decides to be more open about their relationship with the woman's matrikin. This arrangement is marked with a ritual meal in the woman's home and a gift exchange, after which the restrictions on the man encountering the woman's male matrikin are relaxed. This type of visiting relationship tends to be more durable; usually a person will have only one such relationship at a time although he or she may also continue to have other "furtive" relationships alongside it. The one restriction on all tisese unions is that they cannot take place between matrilineal kin. In addition (and very similar to the Nayar), there are strong restrictions on the interactions among matrilineal kin of the opposite sex; any discussion of or allusion to sexual matters among these kin also is strictly forbidden.

Among the Mosuo, cohabitation is, and was earlier, also possible. For example, a woman's lover may move into her household if the household needs male labor. And finally, actual marriage is, and was in earlier times, an option. Here a man and a woman enter into a legally binding union that is celebrated with a wedding ritual; the couple will reside together and create affinal ties between their respective natal families (Shih 2010). In the past, marriages were sometimes arranged when a man's household had no female heir; a wife was then brought in to produce such heirs for the household. But until recently marriages were rare. Shih (2010) reports that as late as 1989 only about 14 percent of adults in the villages of his study were married (about 57 percent were practicing tisese and nearly 30 percent were uninvolved in any union).

The Mosuo have a saying: "If the rain does not fall from the sky, the grass will not grow on the ground" (Cai Hua 2008: 119), which expresses a cultural view of human reproduction. A woman carries a seed of life within her that, to grow, must be watered by a man. Men see themselves as merely waterers. They express their "watering" as a charitable contribution to the woman's household, an act that continues the woman's lineage. As with the Nayar "visiting husband," the Mosuo visiting males have no rights in or obligations to their biological children. People may recognize that a particular child physically resembles one of its mother's lovers, but men show little interest in having children or in knowing which children may be their own.

The Mosuo place great emphasis on harmonious relationships among matrilineal kin within the household and connect the practice of visiting relationships to this core cultural value. Marriages, conjugal units, and in-law relationships are seen as potentially disruptive to this harmony. "Sustainable harmony can be realized only in a household formed by matrilineal blood relatives" (Shih 2010: 262).

The similarities between the Nayar and Mosuo cases are strong and obvious, but there are important differences as well. For one thing, the Nayar visiting arrangement can be seen as "marriage" since it serves to legitimize children. By contrast, the Mosuo tisese cannot be considered "marriage" since it entails no binding obligations of any kind and is not used to legitimize children. Mosuo society does, however, have actual marriage as an option.[8] A second sharp difference is that in contrast to the Nayar, where women were so clearly under the authority of senior male matrilineal kin, Mosuo women are relatively independent and apparently equal with men in domestic authority and control over resources. Women are as likely, if not more so, as men to serve as household heads; men and women share agricultural work and household tasks, including cooking and child care (Shih 2010: 233).

Mosuo kinship and gender have been considerably affected by the views and actions of outside groups. In the 1950s the Chinese government officials considered the Mosuo to be sexually licentious and their mating arrangements backward. In line with the ideas of Marx and Engels, Chinese officials depicted the matrilineal Mosuo as "living fossils" of an earlier stage of human social evolution, a stage of "primitive matriarchy." Early Communist work teams sought to help the Mosuo develop out of their primitive state of matrilineal households and sexual looseness.

For three decades the government attempted (through various laws, policies, incentives, and disincentives) to encourage legal monogamous unions and to end "walking marriages." These attempts, especially intensive during the Cultural Revolution, were largely unsuccessful (Cai Hua 2008). By the 1990s the government had shifted to a position of accepting, even celebrating, ethnic diversity but by this time the region of the Mosuo had opened up to explosive ethnic tourism. In some cases a small village of around 500 people grew to lodge over 3,000 tourists at one time (Walsh 2005). Over the years media accounts and tourist agencies sensationalized the Mosuo "matriarchy" and sexual relations outside of marriage. Tens of thousands of tourists (mostly urban Han Chinese but also international travelers) thronged into the region annually, lured by the promise of either witnessing a feminist matriarchal society or, largely for men, seeing and even participating in the "free love" of Mosuo nighttime sexual visits. "Tourists came by the busload to see Mosuo culture, to experience a 'land where women rule' and in some cases to give zouhun [visiting] a try" (Walsh 2005: 449). Sex workers (dressed in Mosuo costume) were soon seen strolling around the tourist sites, and red-light districts sprang up. Mosuo culture and particularly Mosuo gender (or outsiders' fantasies of Mosuo gender) became commodified. As a result of this tourism, the Mosuo replay their "traditional" customs to meet tourists' expectations but at the same time are heavily exposed to new ways of life, new judgments of their culture, and new money. In particular, tourism has meant expanded economic opportunities for men, which may trigger a shift toward bilateral inheritance and more stable male/female unions (Mattison 2010). Today relationships based on tisese are more stable and exist alongside increasing legal monogamous marriages, within which other sexual visiting is not acceptable (Walsh 2005).

THE MATRIFOCAL FAMILY

Another kind of grouping based on women, but that does not necessarily involve matrilineal descent, is the matrifocal family. The matrifocal family has been defined in slightly different ways but basically it refers to a household where women form the stable core. Men are only loosely attached to the household. Their residence is often temporary or sporadic and their economic contributions are absent or minimal. A matrifocal household may, for example, consist of a mother, her adult daughters, and the daughters' young children as the core residents. Men—as either visiting lovers, husbands or male partners, adult sons, or brothers of these women—may be present for longer or shorter periods of time but they do not assume authority within these units. Relationships between households are also traced through ties of kinship and friendship among women who provide economic and social support to one another.

Matrifocal households are very common in the Caribbean region. Here, matrifocal families are often found in contexts where, among working-class people, employment options are far more limited for men than for women. Women are able to secure income through marketing produce, operating small businesses, or providing domestic service, whereas male employment is irregular or seasonal at best. Areas with predominantly matrifocal households tend to express a particular gender ideology: "Women in matrifocal households are used to fending for themselves in cooperation with their female kin. These consanguineal ties are seen as lasting in comparison to the often transient nature of the conjugal bond. Men are important for sexuality and reproduction, but their support cannot be relied upon" (Safa 2005: 333).

Studies of matrifocality have shown a bias (similar to what we saw in the "matrilineal puzzle"): Matrifocal families were sometimes seen in relationship to a background model of male-headed, nuclear families based on a heterosexual married man and woman with their children. This model was seen as somehow "normal," making matrifocal or woman-headed families appear deviant or less than desirable (Blackwood 2005), described as cases of family breakdown or unfortunate adaptations to poverty. Today these families are approached with greater awareness of the cross-cultural variety of domestic units and are seen as viable alternatives to other family forms.

A new perspective on matrifocality has been developed by anthropologist Robert Quinlan (2006), who approached the topic through evolutionary theory. Based on his study of a village on the Caribbean island of Dominica, Quinlan looked at matrifocal families in terms of parental investment, which, as we recall from Chapter 1, refers to the contributions parents make (in resources, time, attention, etc.) to their offspring. In evolutionary theory, parental investment is geared toward maximizing parents' own long-term fitness, or genetic representation in future generations. In the cultural and economic context of the Dominican village, investing in sons is a relatively risky proposition: No matter what parents do, sons are more likely to end up poor and to develop alcoholism (in this village 50 percent of males showed signs of alcoholism by age fifty). Hence parents bias their investments toward daughters who have better economic and social prospects. This favoring of daughters promotes strong bonds of reciprocity between mothers and daughters and the marginalization of boys. From this study, Quinlan suggests that Caribbean matrifocality may be a response to the fact that daughters provide a more certain return on parental investment.

MATRILINEAL CONTRASTS

In this chapter we have taken a look inside three very different matrilineal societies. Economic differences among the groups had varying effects on the lives of women and men. Among the Navajo and Mosuo, both males and females played important economic roles and neither sex appears to have had greater access to or control over crucial resources. Among the Nayar, neither males nor females played direct roles in subsistence, for they had serfs who engaged in agricultural and other labor for them, but males controlled the matrilineal group's productive property and economically managed the group's estate.

In all of these societies, descent was traced through the mother and important descent categories were formed on this basis. But in the case of the Navajo, descent through the mother was not the sole means of determining descent identity, for the Navajo also identified each person with the father's matriclan and held that one was "born for" the father's clan. Somewhat like the patrilineal Nuer with their "matrifocal subunits" (see Chapter 3), the Navajo illustrate that a dominant unilineal mode of descent does not always provide the whole picture of kinship within one society. Fatherhood was important to individual Navajo and, in many respects, complemented motherhood. Among the Nayar and Mosuo, by contrast, individual fatherhood was barely recognized and descent through the father was not used to identify a person with any kinship category or group.

Although all three groups were matrilineal, this principle of descent through the mother was related to gender in different ways. Most striking is the contrast in the connection between matrilineal descent and authority within residence groups. For the natolocal Nayar, residence groups consisted exclusively of kin who were matrilineally related. In these groups, the eldest male was the official and legal head of the group, and no woman could assume this position. Mothers' brothers held authority over sisters' children. Older women had informal authority over younger ones, and over their own young children, but all women and children were legal minors. By contrast, among the Mosuo, who also resided in large natolocal households, a senior male and female shared domestic authority or a man or a woman alone could function as a household head. Similarly among the Navajo, domestic authority was shared among women and men. Nothing comparable to the Nayar karanavan, or head of the property group, existed in the Navajo camp. Here, women exercised a great deal of power, and it was around "head women" that camps were organized. While the Nayar saw female reproduction in opposition to the world of male leadership, among the Navajo, men and women were seen as complementary in terms of both reproduction and leadership.

Both Navajo and Nayar women had culturally valued status because of their reproductive and transmission-of-descent capabilities, but the two societies differed widely in terms of the nature and implications of this valuation. In both societies reproduction and children were considered very important. But here the similarity ends, and at this point, we must ask the question: reproduction *for whom*? The Navajo apparently expressed no strong concern with "continuing the line." They also had no religious ideas about the necessity of bearing children. Ancestors were not worshiped, nor did people's fate in the afterlife depend on the ministrations of their descendants. There is no indication that Navajo women were under pressure to reproduce for their matriline. In the end, reproduction seems to have been largely a matter for the married couple—perhaps for women in particular, as they generally had a stronger bond with their children. All of these factors may be related to the fact that the Navajo, unlike the Nayar, did not use matrilineal descent to develop highly organized descent groups in control of transmittable property. At the same time, Navajo women were symbolically associated with reproduction and life itself, an association that was venerated and given public, religious expression at a girl's puberty ceremony. It is possible that the positive symbolic role of women as life-givers in this matrilineal society was connected to the absence of well-defined matrilineal descent groups with strong interests in the actual reproduction of real-life women. Significantly, Navajo women were not ostracized or socially punished for infertility.

A very different situation obtained among the Nayar. Here were well-defined descent groups with property, interests in a woman's reproduction, and concern for continuity. A woman's reproduction, however personally rewarding it may have been, was also a vital issue for these groups. Female children were needed to continue them; male children were needed to lead them and to worship their departed members. The Nayar religious rituals that linked women and reproduction largely expressed anxiety over real women's actual reproduction; hence their propitiation of lineage goddesses and snake gods who could enhance or hamper a woman's fertility. A lineage goddess was herself a manifestation of Bhagavadi, a major Nayar deity who was a goddess of war and "more concerned with men than with women" (Gough 1958: 456). This female image is certainly quite different from the life-giving, rejuvenating Changing Woman of the Navajo.

In terms of reproduction and its consequences, however, there are some basic similarities among these three matrilineal societies. In these cases, and in contrast to the patrilineal societies discussed in the last chapter, the placement of a woman's children in kin categories and groups was relatively easy and straightforward. Children belonged to their mothers' categories and groups. Paternity, whether social or biological, was less important than in the patrilineal cases. There was no need for, say, cattle payments to govern the allocation of a woman's children to individuals and groups, as among the Nuer; there was also no need to tie a woman permanently in marriage to a man, as among the Nepalese Brahmans. As with matrilineal groups generally,

Navajo, Nayar, and Mosuo women were free to enter and leave marital unions. In terms of fertility, this arrangement meant that infertile unions could be terminated.

Among the Navajo, Nayar, and Mosuo, women had fairly autonomous control over their sexuality and its consequences, with one major difference: For Nayar women, sexual relations with a lower-caste man were forbidden. If they were discovered, the woman was subjected to severe punishment, her fertility was henceforth devalued, and she and any presumed child of this union were expelled from the group. In addition, a Nayar woman had to have a tali-tying marriage before she was permitted any husbands; otherwise, she was expelled. These rules safeguarded the honor and caste standing of the group in ways similar to the case of the Nepalese Brahmans described in Chapter 3.

Another contrast between the Nayar and Mosuo on the one hand and the Navajo on the other concerns the relationship between female sexuality and female fertility. Aside from the restrictions already noted, Nayar and Mosuo women were allowed any number of sexual partners. From the standpoint of the kin group, female sexuality was given free rein in the service of fertility, somewhat comparable to the situation among the Nuer, who had many options to maximize a kin group's reproduction. But among the Navajo, the sexuality of both males and females was ideally restricted to one partner in marriage (or more, in cases of polygyny), and it was within these individual marriages that reproduction assumed its greatest meaning. For the Navajo, then, as revealed in their religious stories, sexual desire (both male and female) was considered necessary for procreation in general, even though it was known to bring about friction (jealousy, adultery) between women and men. Sexuality and fertility, with all their attendant blessings and problems, were centered on the marital relationship.

The most interesting comparison among the three matrilineal societies reviewed here concerns women's reproductive autonomy. Here we find the Mosuo system to be distinctive. Mosuo women have been characterized as enjoying "virtually unlimited reproductive autonomy" (Shih and Jenike 2002: 22). Back in the heyday of their "walking marriages," not only were Mosuo women free to engage in (or not) sexual activity with any number of partners, they were apparently not under strong cultural or interpersonal pressure to reproduce many offspring. One reason was that Mosuo culture entailed a very high value on harmony within the matrilineal household, achieved by reproducing roughly equal numbers of male and female children in each generation for household labor requirements to be met and for lineages to continue. But once these goals were reached, further reproduction was not encouraged, and was even discouraged since "at that point further household population growth might lead to an increase in internal household tension which in turn could result in household division" (Shih and Jenike 2002: 25).

In addition, the Mosuo perceived the reproductive needs of households to be met not by individual women but by sets of sisters. "For the Mosuo it is the number and gender of the entire group of children born to coresident sisters that is significant, not the size and configuration of any individual woman's offspring set" (Shih and Jenike 2002: 24). To the extent that one sister reproduced sons and daughters, the other sisters were under less pressure to do so or may have been discouraged from doing so.

It may come as a surprise to hear that despite the relatively unrestricted sexual life of Mosuo men and women, the Mosuo consistently have shown patterns of lower fertility than surrounding groups in China. For a particular period (the 1940s to the late 1950s) this was partly due to the spread of sexually transmitted disease in the area, likely brought in by Yi and Tibetan traders, but then treated in 1958 by a Chinese government medical team. In other time periods Mosuo women also showed a considerably later age of first birth, longer interbirth intervals, and lower fertility than women in other nearby populations. Shih and Jenike (2002) attribute this in part to the distinctive Mosuo family system and the reproductive autonomy this system afforded women. Although Mosuo women became sexually active as early as seventeen years of age, these observers note that "unlike spouses in a marital relationship who live together and are usually obliged to answer each other's (more often the husband's) sexual advance, a Mosuo girl enjoys total autonomy over her sexuality. She is under no obligation to provide sexual service to anyone. . . . She is under no obligation to bear children for her sexual partner(s)" (2002: 3–38). In the same way, Shih and Jenike suggest that women's relatively high interbirth intervals have been related to the absence of marriage, the restricted reproductive goals of matrilineal households, and women's ability to themselves decide when they will have sex.

In contrast with this distinctive Mosuo system, Navajo women's sexuality ideally took place within marriages, which were often arranged unions. And Nayar women, nearly as sexually autonomous as the Mosuo, were under cultural pressure to bear many children, especially sons. They were also culturally and socially punished for infertility, a condition not seen among either the Mosuo or the Navajo.

Through these three cases we have seen that matrilineal descent does not produce matriarchies and that different societies vary considerably in terms of the ways that matrilineal descent is related to gender. But perhaps one thing is true of almost all matrilineal societies, at least in contrast to many strongly patrilineal ones: The men who have the most authority over a woman (brothers and mothers' brothers) are not the ones who have legitimate sexual access to her. By contrast, in the two patrilineal societies discussed in the last chapter, it was husbands who had both authority over wives and sexual rights to them. Personally, I would have thought that women in matrilineal societies would feel more independent, or less constrained, when men with authority over them were not also their sexual partners. Interestingly, exactly the opposite idea was expressed by a contemporary Nayar woman in her conversation with anthropologist Shanti Menon (1996: 140): "It is easier to talk with and persuade a husband, rather than a brother. I think most women have some degree of power over men in a situation where they are sexually involved, and that is not the case with brothers. There is always a distance and it is impossible to talk with them beyond a point."

DISCUSSION QUESTIONS

1. Contrast the roles of men in Navajo, Nayar, and Mosuo societies. Along with the many differences, what do men in these societies have in common with each other and with men in matrilineal societies generally?
2. Discuss the various residential solutions to the "matrilineal puzzle." Why did anthropologists see all of these solutions as only partial? Based on the case studies in this chapter, would you agree with their view?

SUGGESTED FURTHER READING

Simonelli, Jeanne M., and Charles D. Winters. 1997. *Crossing Between Worlds: The Navajos of Canyon de Chelly*. School of American Research Press. Based on an anthropologist's personal experiences, this book gives an intimate view of Navajo family life.

SUGGESTED CLASSROOM MEDIA

Navajo Moon. 1983. Films for the Humanities & Sciences. Twenty-four minutes. The film is a documentary story of Navajo life on a reservation in New Mexico that focuses on the lives of three children.

Seasons of the Navajo. 1983. KAET-TV. Peace River Films. Producer/director: John Borden. Fifty-six minutes. This film follows a year in the life of a Navajo family in Canyon de Chelly, Arizona.

Kingdom of Women: The Matriarchal Mosuo of China. 2007. Educational Training Videos, Films for the Humanities & Sciences. Fifty-four minutes. Covers Mosuo way of life, including "walking marriages."

WEBSITES

www.ashiwi.org. Official site of the Zuni tribe in the southwestern United States. Click on "About us," then "Culture" for a description of Zuni matrilineal clans.

http://bryteyedgemini.hubpages.com/hub/NAYAR-CULTURE. An overview of the Nayar people, covering the life cycle of men and women.

Notes

1. Some anthropologists believe that the Navajo adopted matrilineal descent from the Pueblo Indians, but others have suggested that the Navajo were already matrilineal when they entered the southwest (see Levy, Henderson, and Andrews 1989).

2. Witherspoon (1975: 45–46) used this idea of a father being both an affinal and a consanguineal relative to address a controversy in Navajo kinship studies over whether a marriage into one's own father's clan was permitted. According to him, local attitudes toward marriage into the father's clan depended on whether the individual Navajo wished to emphasize either the affinal aspect of the relationship to the father, in which case the marriage would be condoned, or the consanguineal aspect of the relationship, in which case the marriage would be disfavored.

3. Other terms in the literature include "subsistence residential unit" (Witherspoon 1975: 71), "homestead group" (Downs 1972: 31), and "extended family" (Shepardson and Hammond 1970: 45).

4. Witherspoon (1975: 24) further suggested that the bridewealth payment conferred the woman's reproductive rights to the husband, and that if a wife failed to bear children a husband could leave her and ask for the return of the bridewealth. But these arrangements seem unlikely. Shepardson and Hammond (1970: 173–174) wrote that bridewealth cannot be regarded as progeny price since with matrilineal descent the children would automatically have become members of the mother's clan. And Aberle (1961: 125) held that there was no evidence to suggest that bridewealth was paid in return for paternal rights.

5. Polygyny may have been more common earlier due to a shortage of men. In pre-reservation days, many men were killed in raiding and hunting (Shepardson and Hammond 1970: 179).

6. One possible exception was reported by Kluckhohn (1944: 15). He refers to a study of witchcraft in which "some informants insisted that only childless women could be witches." The same study found that, in general, accusations of witchcraft were far more commonly directed at men than at women. In addition, Ginsburg and Rapp (1991: 319), using material from Wright (1982b), argue that Navajo women's menstrual taboos "subtly point out and punish women who do not become pregnant." I, however, do not draw this conclusion from Wright's study.

7. At the top were Nambuduri Brahmans, themselves subdivided into higher and lower orders, who served as priests and religious leaders over a wide region, collectively operating somewhat like the Catholic Church in medieval Europe (Gough 1961b: 306). Below them were Nayar rulers, consisting of members of royal matrilineages that ruled kingdoms; below these were chiefdoms controlled by chiefly Nayar matrilineages. Chiefdoms were divided into villages, and in some of these were Nayar village headmen whose matrilineages owned the village land through appointment by chiefs or kings.

8. According to Cai Hua (2008), actual marriage was imposed on the upper levels of the Mosuo, particularly on the family of the Mosuo chief, by the Chinese Qing Dynasty beginning in 1644. If this is the case, then prior to 1644 the Mosuo would have been a culture without marriage and thus an exception to the universality of marriage in human societies.

REFERENCES

Aberle, David F. 1961. Navajo. In David M. Schneider and Kathleen Gough, eds., *Matrilineal Kinship*, pp. 96–201. Berkeley: University of California Press.

———. 1981a. A Century of Navajo Kinship Change. *Canadian Journal of Anthropology* 2(2): 21–36.

———. 1981b. Navajo Coresidential Kin Groups and Lineages. *Journal of Anthropological Research* 37(1): 1–7.

Ackerman, Lillian A. 1982. *Sexual Equality in the Plateau Culture Area*. Ph.D. dissertation, Washington State University, Pullman.

Adams, William Y. 1983. Once More to the Fray: Further Reflections on Navajo Kinship and Residence. *Journal of Anthropological Research* 39(4): 393–414.

Bachofen, Johann J. 1891 [orig. 1861]. *Das Mutterrecht* (The Motherright). Basel, Switzerland: Benno Schwabe.

Bailey, Flora L. 1950. *Some Sex Beliefs and Practices in a Navajo Community*, vol. 40, no. 2. Papers of the Peabody Museum of American Archaeology and Ethnology, Harvard University.

Blackwood, Evelyn. 2005. Wedding Bell Blues: Marriage, Missing Men, and Matrifocal Follies. *American Ethnologist* 32(1): 3–19.

Cai Hua. 2008. *A Society Without Husbands or Fathers: The Na of China*. Translated by Asti Hustvedt. New York: Zone Books.

Downs, James F. 1972. *The Navajo*. New York: Holt, Rinehart, and Winston.

Farella, John R. 1984. *The Main Stalk: A Synthesis of Navajo Philosophy*. Tucson: University of Arizona Press.

Fortes, M. 1959. Primitive Kinship. *Scientific American* 200(6): 146–157.

Fox, Robin. 1989 [orig. 1967]. *Kinship and Marriage*. Cambridge, England: Cambridge University Press.

Frisbie, Charlotte Johnson. 1967. *Kinaaldá: A Study of the Navajo Girl's Puberty Ceremony*. Middletown, CT: Wesleyan University Press.

———. 1982. Traditional Navajo Women: Ethnographic and Life History Portrayals. *American Indian Quarterly* 6(1, 2): 11–33.

Fuller, C. J. 1976. *The Nayars Today*. Cambridge, England: Cambridge University Press.

Ginsburg, Faye, and Rayna Rapp. 1991. The Politics of Reproduction. *Annual Review of Anthropology* 20: 311–324.

Gough, Kathleen. 1955. Female Initiation Rites on the Malabar Coast. *Journal of the Royal Anthropological Institute* 85: 45–80.

———. 1958. Cults of the Dead Among the Nayars. *Journal of American Folklore* 71(281): 447–478.

———. 1961a. The Modern Disintegration of Matrilineal Descent Groups. In David M. Schneider and Kathleen Gough, eds., *Matrilineal Kinship*, pp. 631–652. Berkeley: University of California Press.

———. 1961b. Nayar: Central Kerala. In David M. Schneider and Kathleen Gough, eds., *Matrilineal Kinship*, pp. 298–384. Berkeley: University of California Press.

Haile, Father Berard, O.F.M. 1981. *Women Versus Men: A Conflict of Navajo Emergence* (The Curly Tó Aheedlíinii Version). Edited by Karl W. Luckert. Lincoln: University of Nebraska Press.

Keesing, Roger M. 1975. *Kin Groups and Social Structure*. Fort Worth, TX: Holt, Rinehart, and Winston.

Kelley, Klara B. 1982. Yet Another Reanalysis of the Navajo Outfit: New Evidence from Historical Documents. *Journal of Anthropological Research* 38(4): 363–381.

Kluckhohn, Clyde. 1944. *Navajo Witchcraft*, vol. 22, no. 2. Papers of the Peabody Museum of American Archaeology and Ethnology, Harvard University.

Kluckhohn, Clyde, and Dorothea Leighton. 1946. *The Navajo*. Cambridge, MA: Harvard University Press.

Lamphere, Louise. 1969. Symbolic Elements in Navajo Ritual. *Southwestern Journal of Anthropology* 25: 279–305.

———. 1970. Ceremonial Cooperation and Networks: A Reanalysis of the Navajo Outfit. *Man* 5(1): 39–59.

———. 1977. *To Run After Them: Cultural and Social Bases of Cooperation in a Navajo Community*. Tucson: University of Arizona Press.

———. 1989. Historical and Regional Variability in Navajo Women's Roles. *Journal of Anthropological Research* 45(4): 431–456.

Leighton, Dorothea, and Clyde Kluckhohn. 1947. *Children of the People: The Navaho Individual and His Development*. Cambridge, MA: Harvard University Press.

Lepowsky, Maria. 1993. *Fruit of the Motherland: Gender in an Egalitarian Society*. New York: Columbia University Press.

Levy, Jerrold E., Eric B. Henderson, and Tracy J. Andrews. 1989. The Effects of Regional Variation and Temporal Change on Matrilineal Elements of Navajo Social Organization. *Journal of Anthropological Research* 45(4): 351–377.

Luckert, Karl W. 1981. Editor's note, paragraphs 20 and 31. In Father Berard Haile, O.F.M., *Women Versus Men: A Conflict of Navajo Emergence* (The Curly Tó Aheedlíinii Version). Edited by Karl W. Luckert. Lincoln: University of Nebraska Press.

Mattison, Siobhán M. 2010. Economic Impacts of Tourism and Erosion of the Visiting System Among the Mosuo of Luga Lake. *Asia Pacific Journal of Anthropology* 11(2): 159–176.

Menon, Shanti. 1996. Male Authority and Female Autonomy: A Study of the Matrilineal Nayars of Kerala, South India. In Mary Jo Maynes, Ann Waltner, Birgitte Soland, and Ulrike Strasser, eds., *Gender, Kinship, Power: A Comparative and Interdisciplinary History*, pp. 131–146. New York: Routledge.

Moody, Gail. 1991. *Mythological and Kinship Roles of Women in Navajo and Euro-American Cultures*. Unpublished manuscript.

Neff, Deborah L. 1994. The Social Construction of Infertility: The Case of the Matrilineal Nayars in South India. *Social Science and Medicine* 39(4): 475–485.

Poewe, Karla O. 1981. *Matrilineal Ideology: Male-Female Dynamics in Luapula, Zambia*. London: Academic Press.

Quinlan, Robert. 2006. Gender and Risk in a Matrifocal Caribbean Community: A View from Behavioral Ecology. *American Anthropologist* 108(3): 464–479.

Reichard, Gladys A. 1928. *Social Life of the Navajo Indians, with Some Attention to Minor Ceremonies*. New York: Columbia University Press.

———. 1950. *Navajo Religion: A Study of Symbolism*, vol. 1. New York: Pantheon Books.

Richards, A. I. 1950. Some Types of Family Structure Amongst the Central Bantu. In A. R. Radcliffe-Brown and D. Forde, eds., *African Systems of Kinship and Marriage*, pp. 207–251. Oxford: Oxford University Press.

Safa, Helen. 2005. The Matrifocal Family and Patriarchal Ideology in Cuba and the Caribbean. *Journal of Latin American Anthropology* 10(2): 314–338.

Schlegel, Alice. 1972. *Male Dominance and Female Autonomy: Domestic Authority in Matrilineal Societies*. New Haven, CT: Human Relations Area Files Press.

Schneider, David M. 1961. The Distinctive Features of Matrilineal Descent Groups. In David M. Schneider and Kathleen Gough, eds., *Matrilineal Kinship*, pp. 1–29. Berkeley: University of California Press.

Shepardson, Mary. 1982. The Status of Navajo Women. *American Indian Quarterly* 6(1, 2): 149–169.

Shepardson, Mary, and Blodwen Hammond. 1970. *The Navajo Mountain Community: Social Organization and Kinship Terminology*. Berkeley: University of California Press.

Shih, Chuan-kang. 2010. *Quest for Harmony: The Moso Tradition of Sexual Union and Family Life*. Stanford, CA: Stanford University Press.

Shih, Chuan-kang, and Mark R. Jenike. 2002. A Cultural-Historical Perspective on the Depressed Fertility Among the Matrilineal Moso in Southwest China. *Human Ecology* 30(1): 21–47.

Shostak, Marjorie. 1981. *Nisa: The Life and Words of a !Kung Woman*. New York: Random House.

Walsh, Eileen Rose. 2005. From Nü Guo to Nü er Guo: Negotiating Desire in the Land of the Mosuo. *Modern China* 31(4): 448–486.

Witherspoon, Gary. 1975. *Navajo Kinship and Marriage*. Chicago: University of Chicago Press.

Wright, Anne. 1982a. An Ethnography of the Navajo Reproductive Cycle. *American Indian Quarterly* 6(1, 2): 52–70.

———. 1982b. Attitudes Toward Childbearing and Menstruation Among the Navajo. In Margarita Artschwager Kay, ed., *Anthropology of Human Birth*, pp. 377–394. Philadelphia: F. A. Davis Company.

Wright, Anne, Mark Bauer, Clarina Clark, Frank Morgan, and Kenneth Begishe. 1993. Cultural Interpretations and Intracultural Variability in Navajo Beliefs About Breastfeeding. *American Ethnologist* 20(4): 781–796.

5

DOUBLE, BILATERAL, AND COGNATIC DESCENT

This chapter introduces two other types of descent and shows the different ways in which they interrelate with systems of gender. In the last two chapters we saw that patrilineal and matrilineal systems of descent are quite distinct from each other in terms of structure. But in this chapter, after going through the remaining modes of descent, we will see that there is sometimes only a fine line between forms of descent that are called by different names. The first one we will examine is the rare form known as double descent.

DOUBLE DESCENT

A society whose kinship patterns are traced on the basis of double descent contains both matrilineal and patrilineal groups at the same time. Accordingly, each person in that society simultaneously belongs to two groups, one traced through the mother and one traced through the father. Figure 5.1 shows the structure of double descent.

Here we see two groups, one traced by matrilineal descent and the other by patrilineal descent. Ego belongs to both—that is, to both his or her mother's *matri*lineage and his or her father's *patri*lineage. Both descent groups are corporate groups. The key to double descent systems is that the two descent groups always have quite different functions, or are important in very different contexts. Otherwise there would be clashes. For example, if matrilineal groups sought to transmit land or houses matrilineally while patrilineal groups were seeking to transmit them patrilineally, then each man's own sons and sisters' sons would be at odds over the inheritance of the man's land and house. The following case study shows how in one society matrilineal and patrilineal groups coexist yet are kept distinct, and why maintaining a distinction between them is seen as important to the people themselves.

FIGURE 5.1   A Double Descent Construct

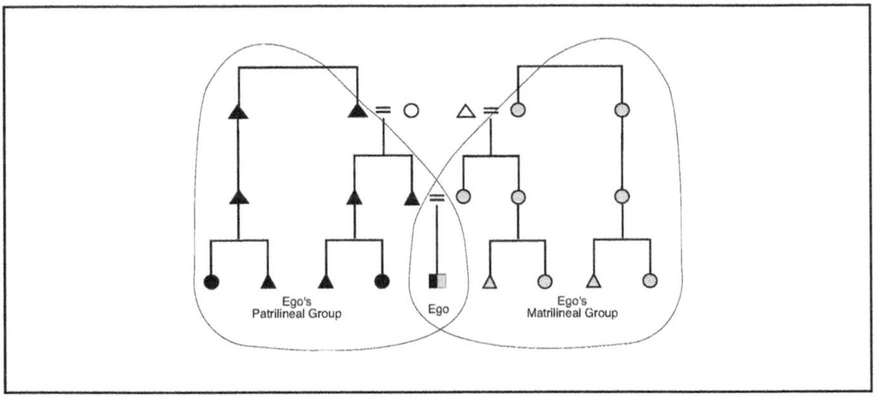

Ego belongs to two descent groups, one patrilineal (the members of this one are darkly shaded) and one matrilineal (the members of this one are lightly shaded).

CASE 6: THE BENG

The Beng are an African group living in Côte d'Ivoire (Ivory Coast). At the time that anthropologist Alma Gottlieb lived with the Beng in the late 1970s and early 1980s, they numbered around 10,000. Before the colonial era and French domination of this region, Beng subsistence had been based on hunting, gathering, and horticulture. The Beng also carried out extensive trade with neighboring groups, largely through their production of valued kola nuts. When the French introduced cash cropping, especially of coffee and cocoa, male hunting declined and male labor became important in agriculture. Today women also work in agriculture and continue to gather.

Politically the Beng are divided into two regions, each with its own king and queen. (These regional leaders are, of course, under the higher authority of the Republic of Côte d'Ivoire.) The kings are publicly more prominent than the queens, but the queens are powerful and the kings consult them on major matters (Gottlieb 1989b: 247). In both regions there are several villages, each of which is presided over by a male and a female chief. These chiefs are seen as co-rulers and must come from the same matriclan, as do the king and queen of each region.

By now many Beng have converted to Islam and a few are Catholic. Still, an older, traditional religion coexists with the new religions. Traditional Beng religion focuses on a cult of the Earth, a major (male) deity. Each village has shrines to the Earth, with priests (called "Masters of the Earth") who offer sacrifices to these shrines. The Earth is believed to have great powers, including control over human fertility and fertility of crops (Gottlieb 1988: 66).

IMAGE 5.1 Beng relatives.

A Beng woman (second from left) is seated with her son (far left); to the right are her daughter and her matrilateral cross cousin. Photo courtesy of Alma Gottlieb.

The Beng recognize double descent, with both matriclans and patriclans. Both the matriclans and the patriclans are corporate groups, and both subdivide into lineages. The patriclans are strictly exogamous. Aside from this marriage restriction, patriclans are important in several ways (Gottlieb 1992: 62–69). It is from one's patriclan that one inherits a number of food taboos, or a list of particular foods that one is forbidden to eat. The Beng believe that if a person violates a patriclan food taboo, he or she will become ill and must seek a healer who is a patriclan member. Each patriclan has rights to its own local medical knowledge concerning the treatment of food taboo violations. This is regarded as secret clan knowledge. One's patriclan also becomes important at death. Patriclans carry out ritual treatment of the corpse of a dead member and determine the burial spot of the deceased. Finally, patriclan members are believed to inherit certain talents and personality types.

In some ways the matriclans are more prominent than the patriclans in Beng society and culture. For one thing, agricultural land is inherited matrilineally, from mothers' brothers to sisters' sons. Second, as noted, political leaders must be members of specific matriclans. Third, and perhaps most important, one's personal identity is enmeshed in the matriclan. The Beng say that the soul is inherited from the mother and, "when asked to characterize matrikin, Beng typically explain . . . 'we are all one'" (Gottlieb 1986: 700). Matrikin, who are seen as "close" and "caring," provide one another with cooperation and emotional support. Yet in another sense Beng matrikin see themselves as "too close," saying, for example, that they are too close to be friends, whereas patrikin can be friends (Gottlieb 1989a: 70).

On the negative side, witchcraft power is believed to be inherited matrilineally and witchcraft is believed to be effective only against a witch's matrikin. Thus the relationships among matrikin, though "close" in one respect, are also tinged with mistrust. Interestingly, one may not only inherit witchcraft power but also "buy" it from other witches, either by paying with money or by giving up a part of oneself—say, the use of an arm. For women, another means of "buying" witchcraft is by "selling" one's menstrual cycle and breasts (Gottlieb 1989b: 253). In this case, the woman who is "purchasing" witchcraft power never develops breasts or menstruates and is, of course, infertile. Harm to the matriclan is in-decided opposition to the function of reproducing it; as a parallel to many other societies, an infertile Beng woman is likely to be suspected of witchcraft.

Unlike the patriclans, the matriclans are not exogamous. Indeed, a preferred form of marriage is one in which a man marries a matrilateral "second cousin"—say, an MMZDD. The Beng say an advantage of this form of marriage is that, should a couple quarrel, the matriclan members will intervene to put pressure on the couple to resolve their differences (Gottlieb 1986: 700).

Marriages are arranged by parents, with both bride and groom having little say in the matter (Gottlieb 1986: 699). Residence is patrilocal. Polygyny is permitted and considered an ideal by men. Particular co-wives may get along, but Beng women generally disfavor polygyny (Gottlieb 1988: 57). Females, but not males, are supposed to be virgins until their engagement or marriage. Many years ago, a child born to a woman before her engagement or marriage was killed (Gottlieb 1989a: 67).

Gottlieb (1989a) provides an interesting analysis of how double descent among the Beng is interwoven with relationships between the sexes as well as with major religious beliefs and practices concerning men, women, and sexuality. She points out that the Beng see their two types of descent groupings as complementary and jointly responsible for the social structure. But the Beng say that these two types of descent, these two different types of clans, should be kept distinct; they should have complementary but different spheres of activity. As we have seen, this di-vision of the functions of matrilineal and patrilineal descent groups is the key to understanding how double descent systems work. For the Beng, the sex act, which intimately joins male and female, becomes a symbol of the mixing together of types of clans. Since this mixing is seen as dangerous, the sex act itself is regarded as a potential threat and must be subjected to certain controls: "The sex act is a symbolic means of 'straddling a fence,' separating two discrete realms. To (metaphorically) straddle this fence through sex is to combine metaphorically the two types of clans, which should not be combined; hence the sex act, as metaphor, must be strictly regulated in order to control and contain the meaning for which the . . . act stands" (Gottlieb 1989a: 72).

One way in which the sex act is regulated concerns an important Beng religious taboo: Sexual intercourse should not, under any circumstances, take place in the forest or fields. These natural areas (in contrast to the village, where sexual intercourse is permitted) are the special province of the Earth, the aforementioned Beng male deity who is regularly worshipped by elders of the various matriclans. The Beng go to some trouble to mark off the boundary between things of the village and things of the forest and fields—specifically, by ritually planting a kapok tree in each village, "which serves to make sexual activity in that village acceptable" (Gottlieb 1988: 62). Human copulation in the areas of the Earth is believed to pollute the Earth. The seriousness with which Beng regard the taboo against copulation in the forest is evident from the punishment meted out for its violation:

> As punishment, the couple are led to the spot where they committed their act. They are accompanied by old and middle-aged men of their own and some surrounding villages. A Master of the Earth (a ritual leader who offers sacrifices to the Earth) oversees the ritual punishment: the couple is made to repeat the sex act while jeered on by the angry crowd, who beat them and burn them with switches and firebrands. . . . The punishment over, a cow is sacrificed to the Earth by way of apology for having been polluted. (Gottlieb 1989a: 70)

One suspects that a Beng, once caught, is unlikely to try copulating in the forest again. Under the circumstances, it seems unlikely that a couple would try it even one time, but Gottlieb (1988: 63) reports that, "in fact, such illicit acts seem to be common: an informant of about thirty-three years recalled at least five cases as having occurred within her recent memory for three Beng villages." She also reports that this punishment was given to an errant couple during her stay among the Beng. Some cases of forest sex are cases of rape, and these may be blamed on madness caused by witchcraft: "In one case I recorded a well-known healer was bewitched and attempted to rape his wife in the forest. She escaped, and when he 'came out of it' within a few hours, he hanged himself in the forest for shame" (Gottlieb 1988: 63).

Even after undergoing public punishment for their act, a man and woman who have had sex in the forest or fields are considered to be permanently polluted, or "dirty," and to bring bad luck to others. For this reason, if unmarried, this man or woman will have difficulty finding a spouse or will have to marry someone else who is permanently "polluted" (Gottlieb 1989a: 71).

There are other punishments for sex in the forest. Perhaps the anger of the Earth will bring a difficult childbirth to the woman offender, or stop the rains and so harm the crops. The latter outcome is one from which everyone suffers;

thus a couple violating this taboo "jeopardize the lives of the entire Beng people: a general drought will ensue that, if the Earth is not properly propitiated in time, will result in the ruin of the entire year's crop and, ultimately, the starvation of all the Beng" (Gottlieb 1988: 62).

Significantly, both punishments—difficult childbirth and drought—represent "aborted fertility in, respectively, the village (human) and the farm (crop) spheres" (Gottlieb 1989a: 70). Gottlieb argues that in Beng thought, human and forest/field fertility are related and seen as parallel, but that the point is to keep these fertility realms separate. Human sex in the forest violates the boundaries between things of the village and things of the forest, angers the Earth, and brings destruction to both human and crop fertility. But if these realms are kept properly separated, the Earth can enhance both crop and human fertility. A ritual connection between the Earth and human fertility can be seen in the following rite: "During his wife's pregnancy a husband should contribute an egg to the Master of the Earth to ask that his wife's childbirth go well and she deliver the baby successfully. After the delivery the husband will sacrifice a chicken with which to thank the Earth" (Gottlieb 1988: 66).

A number of other Beng rules deal with human sexuality out of its proper place, seen as offensive to the Earth and thus harmful to fertility. One is that all Beng adults are to bathe in the morning to "wash off sex" before going to the fields or entering the forest. In fact, they must do so regardless of whether they actually had sex the previous night. Another Beng rule is that a menstruating married woman (a symbol of human fertility) must not go into the forest or fields. If she violates this rule, her next childbirth will be difficult and the crops in the field will die. Gottlieb (1988: 60–61) provides an example:

About a year ago a menstruating woman was in the forest to work in her husband's yam field. Two days later, all the leaves of the yam plants in that part of the field fell off and the yams died. In addition, she herself developed bad stomach cramps. She consulted a diviner to discover the cause of her stomach cramps and he accused her of having been in the forest while menstruating. She confessed but explained that her period had come while she was in the fields and she didn't want to return to the village right away. However, as a result of her misjudgment the whole year's yam crop . . . in that field was destroyed and the Earth was polluted. . . . To rectify the latter condition, the woman's husband was required to sacrifice a female hairy goat.

There are other menstrual taboos among the Beng but, significantly, these are all means of keeping human fertility in its place or ways to protect the woman herself from danger. Thus, Gottlieb (1989a: 72–73) points out that among the Beng, and in contrast to many patrilineal societies, menstruating women are not seen as polluting in and of themselves or as dangerous to men; rather, menstruation is seen as a symbol of human fertility, so to protect successful fertility in both humans and crops, menstruating women must be kept from the realm of the forest and fields. Gottlieb also points out that punishments for violating the taboo on human sex in the forest are equal for men and women.

Other examples of equivalent status for males and females in Beng society can be seen in the marriage relationship. First, when it comes to arranging the marriage of a daughter, the Beng follow a principle whereby all of a couple's odd-numbered daughters (by birth order) are considered to "belong" to the father, who can marry them off as he likes; all of the even-numbered daughters belong to the mother, for her to marry off at will (Gottlieb 1986: 712). Second, husbands and wives are expected to show respect to each other, and the social judgment that results from failure to do so is equal for men and women. For the Beng, the gravest insult to a spouse is to throw a live chicken at him or her during the heat of an argument. When either the husband or the wife commits this act, the marriage is considered irreparably ended. But Gottlieb (1986: 702) also points out one slight advantage of women over men in marriage: "Women's hearts are said to be 'hard' . . . in contrast to men's hearts, which are seen as 'soft' . . . [thus] women are quicker than men to anger, and after an argument, women remain bitter but men forget quickly. Because of this constellation of perceived gender-linked differences, in case of any conjugal dispute, it is the duty of the husband to apologize to his wife, regardless of whether he thought himself in the wrong."

Why some societies develop double descent is not precisely known. The most popular explanation has been that double descent societies are transitional, inasmuch as they represent societies that were once matrilineal but later incorporated patrilineal descent principles as well (Fox 1989: 132). Most, if not all, double descent societies are patrilocal, whereby patrilineally related men stay together and bring their wives into the group.

BILATERAL SOCIETIES

A bilateral society is one that traces kin connections over the generations through both males and females, but without the formation of corporate descent groups. Thus the descent idea is the same in bilateral societies as in cognatic ones, but the latter use this idea to form descent groups, whereas bilateral societies do not.[1]

Euro-American societies are bilateral, but there are also many other bilateral groups elsewhere in the world. One example is the Rungus of Malaysia (G. Appell 1976; L. Appell 1988). These people cultivate rice, maize, and other crops, and raise chickens, pigs, and water buffalo. They live in longhouses, and their postmarital residence is normally matrilocal. A husband moves to the bride's house, and bride and groom live with her parents for about one agricultural season. Then the husband builds a separate family apartment attached to the longhouse and the couple resides there. Longhouses may contain anywhere from two to thirty-two separate apartments, each accommodating a married couple along with any children they may have (G. Appell 1976: 79). The longhouse is not a corporate group; it does not hold common property. Rather, it is best seen as an aggregate of separate nuclear families. Each family constitutes a separate unit of production and consumption.

Each Rungus village, which comprises between one and five longhouses, is led by a headman. Villages can be seen as corporate units since they control land-use rights. But rights to village membership are not based on descent. A person has a right to reside in a village and use its land if he or she was born in the village or married someone there or, failing these connections, can make an application for membership to the headman, which can be accepted or rejected. Once in, each family farms a piece of land separately, using the surplus to acquire other goods from the market.

Inheritance of family property (excluding land, which is not privately owned by families) is essentially bilateral. For the marriage of their son, parents provide the bridewealth, consisting of brassware, ceramic ware, and other items, and this becomes the joint property of the bride's parents and their unmarried children. Some of it may be used to pay the bridewealth for sons. When a daughter marries, her parents may give her and her husband some movable property. Any items not given by the time a couple is old and unable to farm usually go to the youngest child who stays with the couple.

The most important unit in Rungus society is the nuclear family. Although families aggregate in longhouses and cooperate with one another, there are no corporate descent groups among the Rungus. In other words, married couples (with children, if they exist) and villages are corporate units, but there are no groupings of descendants of a common ancestor that are corporate.

Laura Appell (1988) describes the Rungus as a case of "gender symmetry." The generally egalitarian relationships between the sexes appear unrelated to the fact that the society is bilateral. Instead, the relative gender symmetry might be related to matrilocality, to the economic roles of males and females, and to certain Rungus religious beliefs. Males are involved in the political sphere and act as informal heads of families, but in the domestic sphere female contributions are valued and considered complementary to those of males. Women also have specialized roles as spirit mediums. Another striking feature is the central Rungus premise that illicit sexual relations (defined as any sexual relations outside marriage) are dangerous to the whole society: "Any illicit sexual relationship causes 'heat' to radiate outward from the offending couple. This heat angers the spirits, who then cause illness and crop failure. Thus the act of fornication or adultery will affect the health of the offending couple, the families, the longhouse members, the village, and the world at large" (L. Appell 1988: 100). Not only are males and females equally cautioned to avoid illicit sex, but the consequences of failing to do so are the same for both sexes. Interestingly, this society is also one in which there are no menstrual restrictions whatsoever.

COGNATIC DESCENT

A descent group can be formed through the tracing of an ancestor's descendants through both male and female links. This is a case of cognatic descent, whereby both males and females may reproduce the group. Figure 5.2 shows a cognatic descent construct. All of the people in this diagram are the cognatic descendants of the founding ancestor. Notice that person A is connected to the ancestor through two female links; person B is connected through a male and a female; and person C is connected through two males. Indeed, purely "matrilineal" or "patrilineal" links between an individual and the founding ancestor are possible, as is any combination of male and female linkages.

The cognatic descent construct reflects the way that most Euro-Americans perceive their connections to their ancestors and descendants. However, most Euro-American societies are not cognatic because they do not form corporate groups based on descent. There have been some exceptions; for example, the Scottish clan was a true cognatic descent group (Fox 1989).

FIGURE 5.2   A Cognatic Descent Construct

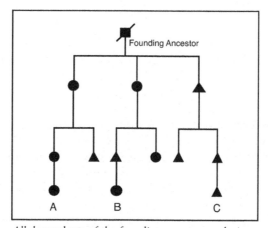

All descendants of the founding ancestor can be included in the descent group.

It may be helpful at this point to emphasize the difference between cognatic descent and double descent. In Figure 5.3, double descent is illustrated by the diagram on the left, and cognatic descent by the diagram on the right. In the case of double descent, two loops enclose ego along with his or her separate matrilineal and patrilineal groups. Notice that ego does not share any group membership with two of the four grandparents (his or her FM and MF).

But in the right-hand diagram, loops enclose ego with all of his or her ancestors. Ego can trace descent equally from all ancestors through any male and/or female links.

FIGURE 5.3   The Difference Between Double Descent and Cognatic Descent

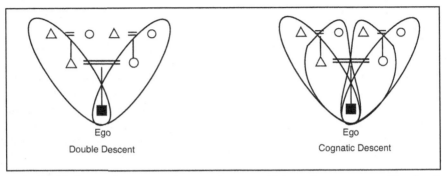

In the double descent diagram, two loops enclose ego with his or her separate patrilineal and matrilineal groups. In the cognatic descent diagram, four loops enclose ego with all of his or her ancestors.

To see how cognatic descent works, recall our encounter in Chapter 1 with a hypothetical woman, Z, who formed groups in her society based on descent from a common ancestor. Also recall the man F, who became a member of a descent group separate from that of Z. Figure 5.4 illustrates these two descent groups in this hypothetical society. Thus far, Z's group, A, and F's group, B, are discrete groups. If we apply the concept of "descent from a common ancestor," there is no question of which individuals belong to which group. But look what happens in Figure 5.5 when a member of group A marries a member of group B. Here, using a cognatic principle, we see that the children of this union, the individuals x and y, belong to both descent groups. The same would be true for the children, grandchildren, and so on, of any persons who married with members of other groups. By extension, the number of groups to which individuals can belong would increase over the generations. Thus, in the case of intermarriage between groups, cognatic descent results in descent groups with overlapping membership. These are quite different from the neat, discrete unilineal descent groups formed through matrilineal or patrilineal descent. This overlap is not a problem in and of itself. It is possible for people in this system to belong to a plurality of groups at the same time. After all, in cases of double descent, a person belongs to two descent groups simultaneously, as we have seen.

In fact, cognatic societies do form discrete groups, and they do so simply by using some mechanism other than descent to pare down the large group of all possible members to a smaller group of "real" or "active" members. One mechanism often employed is parental residence (Keesing 1975: 92). For example, a cognatic society can have a rule that all the descendants of an ancestor are potentially members of a group. But in that event, whenever two people from two different descent groups marry, they must decide with which group they will live. Their children will then become "real" members

FIGURE 5.4 Descent Groups A and B in Z's Society

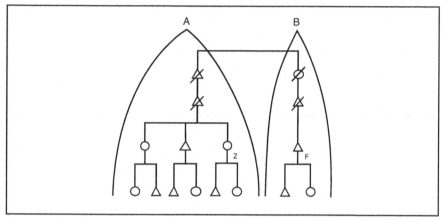

Ogives enclose the separate descent groups.

FIGURE 5.5 Overlapping Cognatic Descent-Group Membership

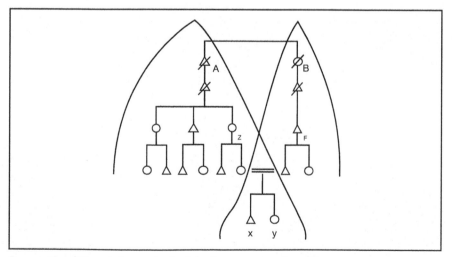

Persons X and Y can belong to both of the descent groups A and B.

of that group. Thus the children, potentially members of two descent groups, become active members of one through their parents' residence choice. In Figure 5.6, we can see that the children of the husband (X) and wife (Y) will become members of group A should the couple reside with the husband's people, or members of group B should the couple reside with the wife's people.

This is not to say that once the parental choice is made the children necessarily lose all rights in the other group; rather, the point is that, for now, their primary affiliations (or "primary rights," as Keesing [1975: 92] termed them) are set with one group. In some cases the situation may be quite fluid, with people switching memberships through life, becoming a part of one group now and affiliating, through residence, with another group later.

In light of such factors as membership in descent groups based on parental residence and the possibilities for shifting memberships, many anthropologists came to view cognatic descent systems as simply more "flexible" than unilineal ones and speculated that these systems might be found in areas characterized by a precarious relationship between resources (such as land) and people. Thus, for example, if the territory of one descent group becomes too crowded, individuals can use their cognatic ties to join other groups (Fox 1989: 153). Or in cases where postmarital residence is an open choice, couples can go to whichever group had more resources to offer at the moment. Some ecological forces may be at work behind the formation of descent systems, but there are also many exceptions to the outcomes that these ecological considerations would predict (Keesing 1975: 139).

FIGURE 5.6   Residence Choice and Descent-Group Membership in a Cognatic System

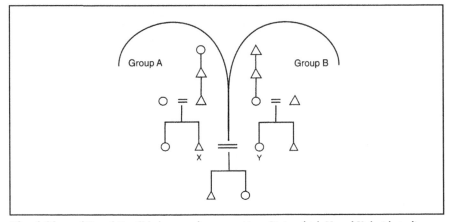

The children of X and Y will belong to the group (A or B) in which X and Y decide to live.

Another way in which a cognatic society can get around, or at least reduce, overlaps among memberships in descent groups would be to follow descent-group endogamy, or to encourage marriage within the group (for example, between cousins). Whenever two people born into the same group marry, their children will, through both parents, belong to one group. Of course, they can be linked by descent to yet other groups through their grandparents, who were not cousins, and so on, but each case of descent-group in-marriage will cut down on the number of possibilities.

A feature common to many, though not all, groups with cognatic descent is that they have a built-in "patrilineal bias." In other words, the group members may express a strong preference to reside patrilocally, or patrilineal descendants might be given preference to a group's land and resources. Regarding the latter case, Keesing (1975: 92) argues that both a principle of cognatic descent and a principle of patrilineal descent would be at work in the society: Patrilineal descendants would be given preference for residence and land rights, but if there were enough land to go around, other, cognatically related kin can also come in, though it would take their descendants a few generations to become accepted as full members of the group.

When a cognatic society exhibits a "patrilineal bias," there is really very little difference between such a cognatic society and an ordinary patrilineal society such as the Nuer (Case 2) who, though strongly patrilineal and basically patrilocal, also allow nonpatrilineal kin to join their residence groups. Over time, the descendants of these people come to be considered real patrilineal members and are treated accordingly. There is no point in quibbling over whether a particular society is best described as "cognatic with a patrilineal bias," "cognatic but also with a patrilineal principle," or "patrilineal and patrilocal but with allowance for some cognatic kin to move in." If a terminological distinction needs to be made, the best course is to follow what the people themselves say about their own system. If they say that all the descendants of an ancestor have rights to membership in the group, they can be considered cognatic.[2]

Cognatic descent interrelates with gender in some important ways. One way applies to societies in which affiliation with a descent group depends on postmarital residence choices. In these cases each descent group will have somewhat uncertain control over female fertility, or its own reproduction. Thus, if a woman is born into descent group A, and if she and her husband decide to affiliate with A, her fertility belongs to that group and through her fertility the group is perpetuated. But if the couple decides to affiliate with her husband's descent group, B, then A loses this opportunity. Similarly, a son of descent group A may bring in a wife patrilocally and through her fertility the group is perpetuated, or the couple may decide otherwise and A loses this opportunity for reproduction.

An example of how this type of descent interrelates with gender comes from the cognatic Maori of New Zealand. Before British colonial rule, the Maori were a highly stratified society organized into chiefdoms. In this society one's social rank was very important and could supersede considerations of gender. Thus, although women were inferior to men of their own rank, a higher-ranking woman was superior to a lower-ranking male. Traditionally the Maori were organized into cognatic descent groups called *hapu*. These in turn were internally stratified. The highest-ranking member of a hapu was the chief, and normally this was a man who descended through a pure line of patrilineal descent and primogeniture (succession of eldest sons) from the founding ancestor. Within the hapu, all senior lines of descent (those genealogically closer to the main, chiefly line) were superior to junior lines. Within families, the sons were ranked by age, with elder brothers superior to younger, and the descendants of elder brothers were also superior to the descendants of younger brothers. Most males affiliated with the father's hapu and lived patrilocally. But in some cases, a man would have more to gain if he affiliated with the descent group of his mother or his wife (that line might be more senior in another hapu than his father's line in the father's hapu). Or a man who was a younger brother might want to leave his hapu to avoid the older brother's domination and superiority. Patrilineal affiliation and patrilocality were considered ideals, but these ideals were not always achieved.

Officially, older brothers were superior to younger ones, but in many cases the younger brothers, through sheer creativity and ability, managed to wrest power and prestige away from older ones. This happened frequently enough that younger brothers constituted a threat to the system and were viewed, in some aspects of Maori culture, with fear and mistrust. Karen Sinclair (2001) suggests that among the upper levels of society, the position of women was similar to that of younger brothers. Though officially not very powerful, they, too, challenged the system with their "creativity" (in this case, their fertility): The children that a woman produced could be destined for her husband's hapu, and such was the cultural ideal. But given the element of choice and flexibility in this system, they could wind up in her hapu instead. Thus, unlike patrilineal-patrilocal groups, the upper-ranking Maori hapu lacked control over female fertility. Sinclair shows how Maori mythology depicts both younger brothers and women as threatening entities and how women in particular are seen as both givers and takers of life.

Another way in which cognatic descent may carry implications for gender concerns those societies in which cognatic descent and options for residence result in groups with fluid and shifting membership. To see how this system ties in with the roles of men and women, we will briefly look at two cases from Melanesia, an island group in the southwest Pacific.

CASE 7: THE KWAIO

The Kwaio, who number around 7,000, live on Malaita Island of the Solomon Islands in Melanesia. Roger Keesing (1970, 1982, 1987) studied their kinship traditions. Along with other groups of the region, the Kwaio have been subjected to Christian missionary activity, colonization, and Westernization. Keesing (1987: 34) writes that despite these influences, in the central mountains of Malaita some 3,000 Kwaio speakers remain "defiantly committed to their ancestral religion and customs. These traditionalists preserve a numerically thinned but substantially intact social structure."

Like many other Melanesian groups, the Kwaio subsist on pig-raising and horticulture. In the past, they had informal leaders and engaged in blood feuds and wars. The informal leaders were characteristic of a type of political leaders once found throughout Melanesia called "big men." Melanesian "big men" had no formal authority but led factions and competed with one another for power and dominance. Their success depended on their ability to enhance their prestige by operating as central points in the exchanges of goods between local groups.

The Kwaio region is divided into territories controlled by different descent groups. Each territory is associated with a set of founding ancestors. To follow the Kwaio system, Keesing (1970) distinguishes between the "primary" and "secondary" rights that one can obtain in these territories. By secondary rights Keesing means the rights to live in the ancestors' territory, garden the land, and participate in some of the descent group's religious rituals. Primary rights are a little stronger: A person exercising them participates more extensively in the affairs of the descent group, takes a larger role in its rituals, and becomes similar to a "voting member with full rights" in the landowning corporation of the descent group (Keesing 1975: 93). Primary rights in the descent group territories, called *fanua*, are transmitted to the groups' patrilineal descendants. Each fanua consists primarily of scattered settlements of male patrilineal kin, along with their in-marrying wives from other groups.

So far the Kwaio may seem to be a standard patrilineal-patrilocal group. But in addition to this structure, any person has secondary rights to other fanua— not fanua to which his descent link is purely patrilineal but rather those to which he traces a link through female ancestors or through a combination of male and female ancestors. Thus a man has primary rights to the fanua of his father, but he may, for whatever reason, decide to suspend these rights and reside, say, in the fanua of his mother's father, activating his secondary rights in this fanua. There he brings his wife and raises his children and, after a prolonged residence, he acquires full primary rights in this fanua.

This system is quite fluid: Over the course of his life, a man may live in and activate secondary rights in several different fanua to which he has cognatic links. However, since most men stay in their fathers' fanua, and since postmarital

IMAGE 5.2   Melanesian women in Irian Jaya (Indonesia), Dani tribe.

Photo courtesy of Linda Stone.

residence is usually patrilocal, it turns out that these cognatic descent groups consist mostly of patrilineally related males and their wives, and basically look very much like a patrilineal-patrilocal society. This feature, along with the fact that the strongest rights (the primary rights) are transmitted patrilineally, gives the Kwaio system a definite "patrilineal" twist. At the same time, the Kwaio themselves emphasize that all descendants of a founding ancestor (descendants traced through both male and female links) have rights to live and garden in the ancestor's fanua.

Each fanua is associated with ancestral shrines, and ritual worship of the ancestors is the major focus of Kwaio religion. Indeed, the ancestors are so important to the Kwaio that they are considered "unseen members of the community." As Keesing notes:

A substantial portion of the conversations that take place in a Kwaio settlement are not between living humans but between the living and the dead. . . . Almost every day . . . [a particular woman] . . . will converse silently with her mother and father, long dead, and her grandfather; and through them to more remote ancestors. . . . [The ancestors] . . . are part of the daily social life of Kwaio communities. (1982: 112–113)

Ancestors, like humans, desire pork, and so are offered pigs as sacrifice. Sacrifices are made to please the ancestors, who, if pleased, may protect their descendants or, if displeased, may harm them. Nearly every illness or misfortune is attributed to the wrath of ancestors. In this way the ancestors serve as powerful sanctions on human behavior; fear of their anger discourages disobedience to the many rules governing proper behavior in Kwaio culture.

Although any given fanua may appear to be largely patrilineal-patrilocal based on its composition, the relationship between the Kwaio and their ancestors is fully cognatic. Ancestors are worshipped by their cognatic descendants. When a woman marries and lives in her husband's fanua, she raises pigs to be sacrificed to her own ancestors along with the pigs she raises for her husband and his ancestors. It is thus from both of their parents that children "inherit" ancestors to worship. In addition, each descent group has a priest who propitiates ancestors, and when this priest dies, the group holds a great ritual that draws in his cognatic descendants and includes them all in a temporary ritual seclusion.

Women and men play very different roles and have very different relationships to the Kwaio cult of the ancestors. For one thing, direct propitiation of the ancestors is a strictly male affair. And, as is the case throughout Melanesia generally, women are considered sources of "menstrual pollution," which is seen as dangerous to men and to sacred phenomena.

The different roles of men and women are best seen in relation to male/female spaces in a Kwaio settlement. At the center of this settlement is a dwelling. Both men and women may occupy it, though there are separate male and female spaces within. In addition to occupying this space, the males of a household may sleep or eat in a separate men's house located on higher ground. Beside that is a sacred area where ancestral shrines are kept and worshipped. No woman may ever go to either the men's house or the sacred area. But below the central dwelling are exclusive women's spaces—menstrual huts and, below these, a separate area for giving birth. During menstruation, a woman must go to a menstrual hut for seclusion. Any vegetables she eats can be taken only from special "menstrual gardens" located there. Her very young children can accompany her in menstrual seclusion, but at about the age of one and a half, a male child can no longer do so. To give birth, a woman goes lower still, to a place where she has built a "childbirth hut." Here she will remain for fifteen days after the birth, out of the sight of men.

Aside from these sharp spatial divisions, there are innumerable behavioral restrictions ensuring that the world of men and ancestors is kept apart from the world of women and reproduction. Keesing (1982) points out that in Kwaio cosmological thought, women with their reproductive powers are indeed opposed to men and the power of the ancestors. He describes how the rituals surrounding a woman giving birth are the opposite of the rituals of a man "creating an ancestor" at the death of a priest. Yet in the end the two realms connect, since women, by giving birth, are producing future ancestors. And senior or respected women, though never allowed near sacred ancestral shrines during their lifetimes, may be buried there in death.

From this standpoint we see that women's reproductive powers define their religious roles, that their reproduction separates them from the male realm of ancestral powers, and that their menstruation and childbirth are "polluting" to men and to the ancestors. Yet Kwaio women themselves do not view their menstrual seclusion as oppressive. As Keesing (1982: 221–222) notes, "In addition to giving women dangerous weapons, it [menstrual pollution] establishes a separate base for women's power. Women in the menstrual hut or clustered in support of a mother in childbirth have a solidarity . . . which they do not have in everyday domestic life. . . . They are free from both male domination and from the heavy work burdens of everyday life." This example reminds us that menstrual taboos, as such, cannot always be interpreted cross-culturally as indications of female oppression (Buckley and Gottlieb 1988). Among the Beng, too, as we saw in the previous section, menstruation is a powerful symbol of fertility, and the restrictions on menstruating women are aimed at protecting human and crop fertility.

Keesing (1987) reports that although Kwaio women do not challenge men's rights and claims, they have their own distinctive visions of themselves in relation to Kwaio culture. They see themselves not only as important agents in maintaining virtue and order in society but also as primarily responsible for cultural transmission and continuity over the generations. Moreover, whereas men view women as sexually passive and vulnerable, and thus in need of male control, women view themselves as in control over their own sexuality.

Keesing also points out that Kwaio women play important ritual and religious roles, even though the sphere of their activity is kept separate from male/ancestor religious spaces. In addition, he notes that in Kwaio culture, emissions from men (for example, vomit and urine) are deemed polluting and that Kwaio women, though potentially polluting on account of their menstruation, are not themselves considered polluted (Keesing 1982: 70).

These cultural ideas about the pollution of female menstruation, and about the danger of women generally, are widespread throughout Melanesia. In Keesing's assessment, however, the situation among the Kwaio is far milder than what has been reported from nearby highland New Guinea, where most of the groups are patrilineal. Many attempts have been made to explain these Melanesian expressions of the dangers of sexual contact with women, and especially the dangers of menstrual pollution. Before returning to this issue, let's take a brief look at one of these New Guinea groups—in this case, a group, like the Kwaio, with cognatic descent.

CASE 8: THE HULI

The Huli live in the southern highlands of New Guinea. Early studies by Robert Glasse (1965, 1968) were undertaken in the 1950s, at which time the Huli numbered about 30,000. Since Glasse's work, the Huli way of life has been and continues to be radically altered due to the influence of Christian missionaries, government officials, and major economic changes.

Like the Kwaio the Huli raised pigs, practiced horticulture, had "big men" informal leaders, and were involved in constant internal warfare. Also like the Kwaio they had a system of cognatic descent, holding that all descendants of a founding ancestor were eligible for membership in the group that controlled that ancestor's territory. The rights of the patrilineal descendants of the ancestor were regarded as superior to the rights of other cognatic descendants. In contrast to Kwaio residence, however, Huli residence was extremely fluid, and most of the males in one local area were not patrilineally related.

Glasse called the Huli local group a "parish." Parish members owned territory in common, and rights to membership could be acquired through cognatic descent. But membership in the parish was not based on residence. Instead, for males, membership was activated and maintained by fulfilling obligations to the group. There were basically three such obligations: (1) defense of the group in war, (2) contributions to the group's war debts, and (3) participation in certain of the group's religious rituals (many of these were fertility rites). Any cognatic descendant of a founder who kept up these obligations was a parish member, whether or not he also lived in the parish. Failure to keep them up resulted in suspension or termination of membership.

Not just cognatic descendants of founders but also affinal relatives and even friends of members could come to reside in a parish, and if they fulfilled the three obligations mentioned above, they could acquire membership. In addition, many males had multiple memberships and multiple residences in the various parishes to whose founding ancestors they were cognatically related. Some men kept two or more households in different parishes and rotated between them. And finally, people could change residences, abandoning old ones and taking up residence in new parishes. In short, although the parish was a geographically bounded and named unit, its resident membership was in constant flux.

Warfare was a central preoccupation among the Huli. Wars arose out of interpersonal grievances, which were as likely to start within one parish as between two parishes. Conflicts spread, men took sides, and the whole thing could be easily perpetuated since people needed to avenge the deaths of those killed in battle. Peace could be made by one party's payment of compensation for a death. Glasse (1968: 107) maintained that Huli cognatic descent fostered conflict precisely because membership in Huli groups was "nonexclusive." Members of groups had divided loyalties. At the same time, the Huli system offered outlets: To escape conflict one could always leave and join another parish.

Women (although they did not participate in warfare obligations) also had memberships, based on cognatic linkages, in different parishes. It was possible for them to have multiple residences as well—in part, because husbands and wives did not live together in the same household. At marriage a woman usually moved to a parish in which her husband was a resident member, but there she would live in a separate house, perhaps with her mother-in-law, while her husband lived in another house. The houses of a husband and a wife could be a few yards or a couple of miles apart. At a later stage in her life, a woman might reside part of the year elsewhere, with other relatives. Meanwhile, since polygyny was practiced, a man might have different wives in different parishes.

The Huli had some beliefs about sex and about relations between women and men that were roughly similar to those of many other highland New Guinea groups. Young males were taught that contact with women, especially sexual contact, was dangerous. They were taught that sex would hamper their health and bring premature aging. Menstruating women were considered especially dangerous: "If a man should be seen by one his skin will shrivel and his hair will turn gray. Copulating with an unclean woman injures a man internally, even fatally. To avoid these hazards men restrict contact with women" (Glasse 1965: 29). In fact, menstruating women were believed to emit a kind of poison. There were several menstrual taboos that women were to follow in order not to harm men, and among men a leading reason for divorce was that a wife had failed to observe these taboos.

To help avoid contact with women, young males, after initiation at about age seven or eight, left their mothers' houses and joined those of their fathers. From about age thirteen, boys were forbidden to eat food cooked or handled by women. Thus married men not only lived apart from their wives but cooked for themselves. Even plots of garden land were divided into male and female portions!

In their late teens, about half of all male youths voluntarily joined a "bachelor society" in their parish. Here they remained for a couple of years while observing strict avoidance of women. If one member failed in this avoidance, the act was believed to bring misfortune to the whole group. As a safeguard against any inadvertent exposure to women, the bachelors performed monthly purificatory rituals such as "washing their eyes under a waterfall to remove the stigma of the female image" (Glasse 1965: 43).

After learning all about the dangers of women and sex, young men eventually married. On average, they married at age twenty-five to women of about age fifteen. Understandably, the young male approached sexual relations with some trepidation, but fortunately the Huli made available to married men a magical preparation that would help fight off the dangers of sexual intercourse. Even so, another practice no doubt dampened sexual enthusiasm in a young male: "Before copulating for this first time, the husband pours foul-smelling tree oil on his wife's vulva, for the genitals of a virgin are 'hot' and may damage his penis" (Glasse 1968: 59).

Eventually, of course, life went on and men and women reproduced. Many men later took additional wives; Glasse (1968: 48) estimated that married Huli men had an average of 1.5 wives. An opportunity for acquiring secondary wives was available to married men through "courting parties," which involved the sacrifice of pigs to ghosts. Married women and unmarried men were rigorously excluded from these parties, but older, married men were provided an opportunity to meet unmarried women and widows (Glasse 1968: 53).

Sexual intercourse between husband and wife was carefully timed around the wife's menstrual cycle. During her period, of course, a woman kept great distance from her husband. Afterward, however,

> a wife sends a leaf to her husband to signify that she is no longer dangerous. The next day she emerges from seclusion, but still must avoid her husband. The following day she may speak to him from a distance, but they should not look at each other. As each day passes, more intimate relations are permitted, until they resume copulating. As the wife's period approaches again, the couple once more restrict their action. (Glasse 1968: 60)

Thus, husband and wife may not have been having intercourse frequently, but they were free to indulge around the time of the wife's ovulation. And, indeed, a wife was desired for the children she would produce. A husband's rights in children were superior to those of the mother; in cases of divorce, children would normally remain with the husband.

To a certain extent, childbirth lessened a woman's dangerousness. Before a child was born she was considered an especially potent menstrual polluter, but afterward she was regarded as safer (Glasse 1968: 60). Another reward for fertility was that a woman who had borne many children was believed to have won the favor of certain deities (Glasse 1965: 47).

Husbands were considered to have exclusive sexual access to wives. In cases of adultery, the male offender, and the natal kin of the wife, paid compensation (in pigs) to the husband. A wife could be punished for adultery by having stinging insects placed up her vagina, or "her husband may tie her to a tree and light a fire under her genitals. He may shoot an arrow into her buttocks, or he may merely beat her severely" (Glasse 1968: 72).

According to Glasse (1965: 48), Huli "women are inherently evil owing to their menstrual role, and their wickedness persists in the afterlife." Male ancestral ghosts were protective, whereas female ancestral ghosts (except for the ghost of one's own mother) were harmful and dangerous. In particular, they were believed to cause barrenness in women and pigs.

Nevertheless, Glasse (1968: 76) noted, "by comparison with women from other [New Guinea] Highland societies, Huli women enjoy a fairly high status." He pointed out that Huli women could own pigs and that they could initiate marriages and divorces on their own. Yet another factor accounting for the relatively better position of Huli women was the Huli form of cognatic descent. In the same way that warring men could seek refuge in other parishes through their cognatic connections, women could abandon unhappy marriages and turn to other groups in which they had cognatic ties. Thus, according to Glasse, although the Huli system of cognatic descent stirred up trouble between men, it also provided an escape from difficulty for both men and women.

A study undertaken in 2004 has shown that, despite all the socioeconomic changes in the region since Glasse's time, the Huli remain very aware of their traditional cultural beliefs and practices concerning female pollution, marriage, and sex (Wardlow 2008). The Huli have broken with these patterns in some respects but still uphold them in other ways, at least to some degree. Now most married couples live together in one house but they usually sleep in separate rooms and occupy separate house spaces. A husband also likely will leave the common house (going temporarily to a separate men's house) during his wife's menstrual period. In this study most men reported that their marriages were more intimate and affectionate than those of times past. And many younger men saw the earlier strong avoidance of women as "backward." On the other hand, some men feared that certain breaks with tradition—for example, showing strong emotional attachments to a wife, being open about sex with a spouse, and, especially, openly expressing sexual pleasure to a wife—would undermine male dominance in the marriage. Such behavior would place a man in a weak position and wives would be quick to take advantage of the situation. As one man said of his wife, "I married her to have my children and take care of my pigs. My secrets are my secrets. That's my law for myself. I don't tell her my secrets. If I told her everything, she would use this knowledge to dominate me. That's the way women are" (Wardlow 2008: 203–204). Indeed some Huli men were considering going back to the practice of living apart from their wives to reestablish the emotional distance that would enable a smoothly functioning marriage. Finally, many men emphasized that marriage should be focused on reproduction and that long-term, close contact with a wife leaves men vulnerable to weakness, illness, and aging.

Since Glasse's time, more recent investigations of highland New Guinea societies have challenged the older descriptions of menstrual pollution and exclusions of women among peoples such as the Huli. Researchers have observed that in certain groups, men express hostility to women in some contexts but envy of female reproductive powers in others. They have also found that the "pollution" of women, though negative and harmful in some settings, was positive and health-enhancing in other settings.[3]

Clearly, then, the earlier reports provided only a partial picture. One of the best accounts to balance this limited view was Anna Meigs's (1984) study of the Hua, whose concerns about women, pollution, and sex are similar to those reported for the Huli. Meigs shows that alongside these ideas are others that express a completely different gender ideology. One idea concerns the Hua concept of *nu*, a "vital essence" located especially in the fluids of the body. To the Hua, women by nature have greater nu than men, allowing them to grow faster and to stay healthier longer. Also, in sex, men deplete their nu through loss of semen, whereas women gain nu by the same process. Hua men acknowledge that women's greater nu accounts for their superiority, which is all for the good since women need this greater nu to carry out their life-giving functions of reproduction.

To be sure, female nu is polluting to men, but in the larger scheme of things, many individuals, both men and women, must avoid contact with the nu of another. Thus males as well as females can be sources of pollution. Over their lives, men and women fluctuate in terms of their pollution and their vulnerability to pollution. Children start out fairly high in pollution due to their recent contact with the mother in childbirth. Male children increasingly shed this pollution; then, when they become young men, they strive for a height of "purity" attained by avoiding contact with women and observing a number of taboos. Later in life, through marriage and contact with women, men increasingly absorb pollution from women; however, they also become less vulnerable to pollution in the process. By the time they are old, they no longer need to observe the many taboos designed to keep males "pure." At this point, the Hua say, they become "like women." For women the process is different. Their maximum pollution period occurs between menarche and menopause, but over time they lose some of this pollution, expelling it through menstruation and childbirth. Eventually a woman past menopause, who has borne three or more children, becomes largely free of her own pollution, is allowed into the men's house, and can participate in otherwise secret male knowledge and rituals. At this point, however, she is most vulnerable to pollution by others and must submit to many of the same restrictions that young men observe to keep themselves "pure." The Hua say such a woman has become "like a man."

Another more balanced view of gender relationships in highland New Guinea comes from the work of Pamela Stewart and Andrew Strathern (2002). As these authors note, earlier ethnographies had created a stereotype of the region that emphasized male dominance bolstered by cultural ideas about female menstrual pollution. They write, "Particularly with regard to notions of pollution, the stereotype also includes the supposed denigration of sexual activity and patterns of avoidance, separation and antagonism between men and women" (2002: 1). While not discounting these patterns, Stewart and Strathern's work uncovers another, far more positive side to gender relationships in the highlands. Their focus is on cultural expressions through, for example, courting songs, folk tales, ballads, and body decoration. Their analysis of these expressions reveals what was hidden before: namely, cultural sentiments of sexual longing and desire, closeness between men and women, and associations of menstrual blood with fertility (and not just female pollution).

DESCENT, RESIDENCE, AND FEMALE POLLUTION

We may never find a fully satisfactory explanation of all the ideas about female pollution and general aversion to women that were and still are expressed, at least in some contexts and by some men at a certain stage of their lives, in so many societies of Melanesia. But several ideas have been both interesting and pertinent to our discussion of gender, descent, and reproduction. One very tempting theory was that all the ways and means by which women and sex with women are culturally denigrated are really mechanisms of population control, or cultural birth-control devices (Lindenbaum 1972). Males were taught to fear and avoid women, and sex was surrounded with restrictions to reduce actual rates of intercourse, pregnancy, and ultimately fertility. Some evidence supports this theory, but it is also weakened on many grounds. For one thing, we saw in the Huli case that despite all the fears and restrictions directed at sex, it was most permitted within marriage during a wife's ovulation. Moreover, throughout the New Guinea highlands, it was young, unmarried males who were exhorted to fear and avoid women; older, married men evidently experienced far less concern over the "dangers" of women and themselves showed interest in procreation (Gelber 1986: 117). As we also saw among the Huli, married men attended "courting parties" from which unmarried men and married women were excluded.

Another theory was one we might call the "gerontocracy argument." It suggested that in many areas of Melanesia, older males had and vigorously sought to maintain dominance over women and junior males (Gelber 1986). These older males competed with one another to become socially prominent members of society or "big men" (informal leaders). Their success depended on the prestige they gained through displays of lavish feasting and the ability to participate in trade and ritual exchanges of pigs and other valued commodities. Since women raised pigs, men's control over women and their labor was a vital resource in the competition with other men. In many Melanesian societies men also gained from bridewealth transactions and, hence, sought to maintain control over the marriages of females. In addition, according to this argument, older men wanted sexual access to women and so reduced competition from younger men by training them to fear and avoid women. Thus older men seem to have considerably eased their own fears of women and sex at the same time that they were socializing younger males to fear and dread intercourse.

Keesing (1982) supported the gerontocracy argument in his analysis of gender in Kwaio society. According to him, the Kwaio beliefs and rituals associated with the powerful ancestors served to strengthen the privileged social status of adult males, who controlled the ancestral cult: "The physical strength of mature adulthood sustained the power of adult men. . . . But so, too, did power of the *adalo* [ancestors]. . . . This control of ancestral knowledge and power gave seniors a political power in the community far beyond their sheer physical strength" (1982: 227).

As for female pollution, Keesing (1982: 227–228) suggested that "it is the dominance of men over women that is most directly sustained by the ideology of pollution, and the myriad rules that bind women's lives." Keesing (1982: 141) also noted that women, not men, do the labor of raising the pigs for human consumption and sacrifice to the ancestors. But after ritual sacrifice, the pork is almost exclusively consumed by men.

Keesing offered an interesting argument that ties in Kwaio gender relationships with its system of descent. In speculating that the Kwaio descent system grew out of an earlier matrilineal base, he noted that the closest linguistic relatives of the Kwaio all had matrilineal systems and, significantly, "none, apparently, had similar ideologies about isolating the dangers of menstruation and childbirth" (Keesing 1982: 228). In his view, the emergence of patrilineal and cognatic principles in Kwaio society "and the emergence of the polluting powers of women were probably closely connected" (Keesing 1982: 229).

According to Marilyn Gelber (1986), another factor helped account for the antagonism directed against women in the New Guinea highlands, and this one, too, relates to the issues of descent and residence. In her view, New Guinea highland corporate kin groups, the cores of social organization, were highly unstable given their fluid, shifting memberships. This, she said, was true both of societies with cognatic descent (such as the Huli) and of the patrilineal societies in New Guinea. The latter were ideologically patrilineal: Their members said that rights to membership in the group were transmitted patrilineally, but in fact many cognatic kin joined these groups and, after a few generations, their descendants were similar to real, patrilineally related members. Thus these New Guinea groups functioned very much like the cognatic societies we have reviewed. As corporate groups they may have benefited ecologically from shifting, fluid memberships, but one problem was that they were engaged in active warfare. For purposes of defense, the males of these groups needed to come together and cooperate; yet fluid group membership divided their loyalties. To reunite for purposes of defense, males deflected their antagonism onto women and sought cohesion in opposition to women.[4] As Gelber (1986: 55–56) put it:

> I would suggest that the exclusion of women from ritual, the explicit devaluation of women's worth and the concomitant emphasis on the value of being a man . . . and the view of women as a mysterious and dangerous unknown quantity, may be explained in part by the significant contribution of these attitudes to a feeling of sameness, cohesiveness, and fellowship among men. . . . By seeing women as outsiders, the men of a local group make themselves "insiders" with respect to one another.

DOUBLE AND COGNATIC CONCERNS

Recall that among the Beng, the group that recognizes double descent, it is heterosexuality and not female sexuality that is regarded as potentially dangerous and thus must be regulated. Female fertility is clearly valued in this society. Both the matriclan and the patriclan have interests in each new birth, but the two groups, each with their separate activities and functions, are not threatened by each other and do not compete over women's fertility. The Beng require that different types of clans be kept separate, yet they view heterosexual intercourse as, metaphorically, a mixing of these clans. Hence sex is potentially dangerous and regulated by certain taboos. Any improper sexual activity (especially sex in the forest) threatens both female fertility and crop fertility. Moreover, the dangerousness of sex applies as much to males as to females; after violating sexual taboos, men are as polluted, and as subject to punishment, as women.

The Beng case is thus quite different from the cognatic societies considered here, in which female sexuality is expressed as dangerous and polluting to men. Of course, cognatic descent and beliefs about female pollution are not invariably linked. There are cognatic societies in the world that do not express these beliefs and, as we saw above, there are patrilineal societies in New Guinea that do express them. Still, I suggest that a connection does exist between cognatic descent and cultural visions of women as dangerous and polluting. This contention, at least as it applies to the groups covered here, is supported by evidence indicating that cognatic descent and flexible rules of residence give kin groups uncertain control over female fertility, or over their own reproduction.

Melanesian beliefs and practices concerning female pollution may seem extreme and, indeed, we may find it difficult to view them as anything other than forms of female subordination. Yet this is not the whole picture. For one thing, the other side of dangerous pollution is power. Recall Keesing's (1982: 221) observation that the Kwaio belief in women's menstrual pollution gives women "dangerous weapons" and "establishes a separate base for women's power." Also note Meigs's (1984) caution with respect to the interpretation of female pollution beliefs. According to her study, in the Hua society both men and women are sources of pollution, and relationships among men, women, and pollution change over the life course.

With this chapter we end our discussion of gender in relation to different modes of descent. The next chapter covers marriage, the institution through which new kin relationships are formed and perpetuated.

DISCUSSION QUESTIONS

1. Contrast female-pollution beliefs in the societies covered in this chapter. In which societies, if any, and in what ways do you think that these beliefs are detrimental to women?

2. What different theories have been put forth to help explain cultural beliefs about female pollution in Melanesia? Which one do you find most persuasive, and why?

SUGGESTED FURTHER READING

Lepowsky, Maria. 1993. *Fruit of the Motherland: Gender in an Egalitarian Society*. New York: Columbia University Press. An ethnography of Vanatinai, a small island of New Guinea. Lepowsky presents this island society as a case of gender equality. Set aside the classic accounts of male dominance among peoples in the interior of New Guinea, this book testifies to the diversity of gender relationships in the region.

SUGGESTED CLASSROOM MEDIA

Bridewealth for a Goddess. 2000. A film by Chris Owen with anthropologist Andrew Strathern. Ronin Films. Seventy-two minutes. This film covers the Kawelka people in the western highlands of New Guinea. It focuses on an elaborate religious ritual where men seek marriage with a powerful goddess who, among other blessings, gives them protection from the menstrual pollution of their wives.

Advertising Missionaries. 1996. Chris Hilton and Gauthier Flauder. Aspire Films, Ellipse Programme and the Australian Film Finance Corporation, New York. Fifty-three minutes. This film portrays the earlier, traditional culture of the Huli of Papua New Guinea and covers how this culture is changing radically as the Huli are impacted by global capitalism and, especially, advertising.

WEBSITES

http://content.cdlib.org/ark:/20775/bb2355939j. Photos of anthropologist Roger Keesing with the Kwaio people.

www.gabelomas.org/huli/htms/huli1.htm. This site gives a good, general description of the Huli today and includes great photos.

NOTES

1. Anthropologists use the terms cognatic and bilateral in different ways. Some refer to them interchangeably. Others consider bilateral to be a subtype of cognatic, saying that bilateral societies form kin groups on the basis of kindred rather than descent. Keesing (1975) distinguishes cognatic societies from societies with "bilateral kinship" and reserves the term *descent* for specifically those societies that form descent groups based on descent from a common ancestor. Finally, Fox (1989) categorizes societies according to both their method of recruitment to groups and their system of "focus" (that is, whether the system was ego-focused or ancestor-focused).

2. Attempts have been made to deal with these somewhat problematic issues of descent and residence by adopting for some cases the concept of "house societies" developed by Lévi-Strauss (1987). House societies contain corporate estates (houses) that perpetuate themselves over time by transmitting their names, privileges, and property through patrilineal, matrilineal, or both lines of descent, real or imagined. People in these societies perceive their own identity in terms of membership in their houses. Membership in houses can simultaneously follow a plurality of different paths—through descent, marriage, adoption, and fictive kinship (see Carsten and Hugh-Jones 1995).The emphasis here is on houses as core units of social organization with less importance attached to principles of descent or norms of postmarital residence. House societies are considered to be prominent in Southeast Asia, Melanesia, and many other areas.

3. An example of the latter was found among the Huli (Glasse 1965: 43). In the bachelor's cult, each member cultivated a bog iris that, according to Glasse, originated in ground saturated with menstrual blood. These irises, along with a tube containing a female ancestor's blood kept by the cult, were believed by the Huli to protect the health of the young men.

4. L. L. Langness (1967) expressed a similar idea about males opposing women to promote the male solidarity needed in highland New Guinea warfare. And M. J. Meggitt (1964) suggested that male antagonism toward women would tend to be found in those New Guinea societies where marriage took place between hostile, warring groups. In such cases, affinal women would presumably have been associated with the "enemy."

REFERENCES

Appell, G. N. 1976. The Rungus: Social Structure in a Cognatic Society and Its Ritual Symbolization. In G. N. Appell, ed., *The Societies of Borneo: Explorations in the Theory of Cognatic Social Structure*, No. 6. A Special Publication of the American Anthropological Association. Washington, DC: American Anthropological Association.

Appell, Laura W. R. 1988. Menstruation Among the Rungus of Borneo: An Unmarked Category. In Thomas Buckley and Alma Gottlieb, eds., *Blood Magic: The Anthropology of Menstruation*, pp. 94–112. Berkeley: University of California Press.

Buckley, Thomas, and Alma Gottlieb. 1988. A Critical Appraisal of Theories of Menstrual Symbolism. In Thomas Buckley and Alma Gottlieb, eds., *Blood Magic: The Anthropology of Menstruation*, pp. 1–50. Berkeley: University of California Press.

Carsten, Janet, and Steven Hugh-Jones, eds. 1995. *About the House: Lévi-Strauss and Beyond*. Cambridge, England: Cambridge University Press.

Fox, Robin. 1989 [orig. 1967]. *Kinship and Marriage: An Anthropological Perspective*. Cambridge, England: Cambridge University Press.

Gelber, Marilyn G. 1986. *Gender and Society in the New Guinea Highlands: An Anthropological Perspective on Antagonism Toward Women*. Boulder, CO: Westview Press.

Glasse, Robert M. 1965. The Huli of the Southern Highlands. In P. Lawrence and M. J. Meggitt, eds., *Gods, Ghosts and Men in Melanesia: Some Religions of*

Australian New Guinea and the New Hebrides, pp. 27–49. London: Oxford University Press.

———. 1968. *Huli of Papua: A Cognatic Descent System*. Paris/The Hague: Mouton and Co.

Gottlieb, Alma. 1986. Cousin Marriage, Birth Order, and Gender: Alliance Models Among the Beng of Ivory Coast. *Man* 21: 697–722.

———. 1988. Menstrual Cosmology Among the Beng of Ivory Coast. In Thomas Buckley and Alma Gottlieb, eds., *Blood Magic: The Anthropology of Menstruation*, pp. 55–74. Berkeley: University of California Press.

———. 1989a. Rethinking Female Pollution: The Beng of Côte d'Ivoire. *Dialectical Anthropology* 14: 65–79.

———. 1989b. Witches, Kings, and the Sacrifice of Identity, or The Power of Paradox and the Paradox of Power Among the Beng of Ivory Coast. In W. Arens and Ivan Karp, eds., *Creativity of Power: Cosmology and Action in African Societies*, pp. 245–272. Washington, DC: Smithsonian Institution Press.

———. 1992. *Under the Kapok Tree: Identity and Difference in Beng Thought*. Bloomington: Indiana University Press.

Keesing, Roger M. 1970. Shrines, Ancestors, and Cognatic Descent: The Kwaio and Tallensi. *American Anthropologist* 72: 755–775.

———. 1975. *Kin Groups and Social Structure*. Fort Worth, TX: Holt, Rinehart, and Winston.

———. 1982. *Kwaio Religion: The Living and the Dead in Solomon Island Society*. New York: Columbia University Press.

———. 1987. Ta'a Geni: Women's Perspectives on Kwaio Society. In Marilyn Strathern, ed., *Dealing with Inequality: Analysing Gender Relations in Melanesia and Beyond*, pp. 33–62. Cambridge, England: Cambridge University Press.

Langness, L. L. 1967. Sexual Antagonism in the New Guinea Highlands: A Bena Bena Example. *Oceania* 37: 161–177.

Lévi-Strauss, Claude. 1987. *Anthropology and Myth: Lectures 1951–1982*. Oxford: Blackwell.

Lindenbaum, Shirley. 1972. Sorcerers, Ghosts, and Polluting Women: An Analysis of Religious Belief and Population Control. *Ethnology* 11: 241–253.

Meggitt, M. J. 1964. Male-Female Relationships in the Highlands of Australian New Guinea. *American Anthropologist* 66: 204–224.

Meigs, Anna S. 1984. *Food, Sex and Pollution: A New Guinea Religion*. New Brunswick, NJ: Rutgers University Press.

Sinclair, Karen. 2001. Mischief on the Margins: Gender, Primogeniture, and Cognatic Descent Among the Maori. In Linda Stone, ed. *New Directions in Anthropological Kinship*, pp. 156–174. Lanham, MD: Rowman & Littlefield.

Stewart, Pamela J., and Andrew Strathern. 2002. *Gender, Song, and Sensibility: Folktales and Folksongs in the Highlands of New Guinea*. Westport, CT: Praeger.

Wardlow, Holly. 2008. "She Liked It Best When She Was on Top": Intimacies and Estrangements in Huli Men's Marital and Extramarital Relationships. In William R. Jankowiak, ed., *Intimacies: Love and Sex Across Cultures*. New York: Columbia University Press.

6

MARRIAGE

Every society in the world has something we might recognize as marriage. But beyond this, little can be said of marriage that holds cross-culturally. We may think of marriages as uniting males and females, yet we have already seen that Nuer woman-woman marriage is an exception to this, as are modern marriages of homosexual couples. We might expect that sex is universally permitted within marriage, only to discover that certain early Christian cults practiced celibate marriage. Usually marriage is enacted with some kind of ceremony, often religious in nature, but there are plenty of cases where this is not done or at least is not obligatory. Often marriage is associated with the legitimizing of children, or the allocation of rights over children. But this would not apply to the Navajo, for whom a child born out of wedlock still acquires full rights in his or her mother's clan, suffering no disadvantages. And we have already seen that marriage does not always involve participants in a common domestic unit or common residence. In short, perhaps the only generalization one can make about marriage is that everywhere it entails intimate, if not emotionally charged, relationships between spouses, and everywhere it creates in-laws.

In this chapter we explore two dimensions of marriage: first, relationships between spouses in terms of differences in marriage forms (monogamy, polygyny, and polyandry) and, second, the creation of in-laws, or the nature of marriage as a mechanism for alliance. This investigation will return us to the questions raised in Chapter 2 concerning the origin of gender inequality.

MONOGAMY, POLYGYNY, AND POLYANDRY

Human societies feature three types of marital unions: monogamy, or the union of two persons, usually one man and one woman; polygyny, a union between one man and two or more women at the same time; and polyandry, the marriage of one woman with two or more men. Monogamous groups, such as Euro-American societies, do not legally permit the other types of unions. Societies characterized as "polygynous" permit polygyny along with monogamy. In many polygynous societies most of the marital unions are in fact monogamous. The religion of Islam permits a man to take up to four wives, but the incidence of polygyny is low in many Islamic areas. Some African societies show relatively high rates of polygyny (up to or even exceeding 30 percent of all marital unions). Many groups in Asia also permit polygyny, but here, in contrast to Africa, it occurs at significantly lower rates. Finally, polyandry is very rare. In the few societies where it is permitted, polygyny and monogamy are usually also practiced (Levine and Sangree 1980).

We have already seen examples of polygyny and polyandry in previous case studies—for example, polygyny among the Nuer and, more rarely, the Nepalese Brahmans, and polyandry-polygyny among the Nayar. From these case studies it should now be clear that even the same types of unions work differently in different societies. Among the Nepalese Brahmans, polygyny is usually arranged only when a first wife is childless. Women view it negatively, as a kind of punishment for their childlessness. Among the Nuer, polygyny was not only more common but also apparently preferred by men as a sign of wealth or prestige. (What women thought about it is less clear.) It was also used by Nuer men as a strategy to acquire children or increase the number of their children. By contrast, among the matrilineal Nayar a man's ability to have and visit several wives was not considered a strategy to increase the number of his legal children.

Plural unions inevitably raise questions about sexual jealousy. Most Euro-American women simply could not imagine, let alone tolerate, taking on a co-wife. Of course, Euro-American marriages are not arranged by kin and are ideologically rooted in the tradition of romantic love. But ethnographic studies show that, among societies with relatively high rates of polygynous unions, there is considerable individual and group variation in women's responses to these unions. Co-wife jealousy and mutual accusations of witchcraft occur alongside reports of peaceful cooperation among co-wives, or even of co-wives happily ganging up on a husband to secure their own ends. And of course in some polygynous societies, women cooperate with husbands for reproduction and domestic concerns but then have their own lovers on the side.

The effects of a predominant or prevalent type of marriage union on gender must be considered within the particular cultural context of each group. Euro-American women may feel that a co-wife would be dreadful, but not so many years ago many women of this culture felt it was perfectly appropriate for wives to be economically dependent on their husbands and for a double sexual standard to exist in their society. In some West African polygynous societies, women are and always have been economically independent, a circumstance that gives them considerable freedom to develop their own social lives and pursue their own interests apart from their marriages.

And what about polyandry? This form of marriage has fascinated anthropologists perhaps more than any other, one reason being that it is so rare. As we have seen, the Nayar of South India practiced it, but it also occurs (or has occurred) among some Tibetan peoples, some groups in northern Nepal, some hill tribes in India, and the Shoshoni Indians of Nevada, as well as on the Marquesas Islands (Polynesia) and in a few other places in South Asia, Africa, and the Americas. Polyandry can take a variety of forms, one of which is fraternal polyandry, whereby a set of brothers shares a wife. Another, as exemplified by the Nayar, is nonfraternal polyandry, whereby the husbands are not brothers; indeed, among the Nayar, brothers could not be the visiting husbands of the same woman. There are many other variations in terms of residence patterns, property rights, and sexual arrangements in polyandrous societies.

In earlier years the study of polyandry was clouded by male biases. Some male observers were so upset about these unions that they branded them as perverted or decided they did not constitute marriage at all. Later there were more serious and objective studies of polyandry (for example, Aziz 1978; Goldstein 1976; Schuler 1987; Levine 1988). Nancy Levine (1988: 4), whose work constitutes the next case study, pinpoints the problem behind these previous male biases in the study of polyandry: Some observers found it simply inconceivable that males would willingly give up their exclusive sexual and reproductive rights to their wives. And when they did not find sexual jealousy among polyandrous husbands, they simply assumed that the jealousy was being "repressed" (Aiyappan 1937). Levine (1988: 170) raises a good question: "Why do we assume that sharing a spouse is impossible for men, but not for polygynous women?" As Levine notes, these reactions to polyandry tell us more about our own culture's ideas about gender than about how polyandry actually works.

The following study is a case of fraternal polyandry. But first we should note one important effect that fraternal polyandry may have—namely, low population growth. It's easy to see how this consequence comes about. Let's say a set of three brothers acquires one wife. She can produce only so many children in her lifetime; let's say she produces three. If the three brothers had each taken equally fertile wives, they would have together produced a total of nine children. By the same reckoning, polyandry will mean that there are fewer married women than men in the population. Indeed, some anthropologists (for example, Goldstein 1976) argued that polyandry develops in part as a device for population control, given that it often exists in areas with scarce or precarious environmental resources. It keeps the population down and so maintains a balance between humans and the natural environment. Although Levine's study of the polyandrous Nyinba describes this phenomenon, it also suggests that population control by itself is insufficient to account for polyandry.

CASE 9: NYINBA POLYANDRY

When anthropologist Nancy Levine first entered a Nyinba village, she was struck by its relative wealth:

> I will never forget my first journey there and the impoverished villages I passed along the way. . . . It was springtime, people were hungry and, lacking food for themselves, had none for sale. . . . When I finally reached . . . the first Nyinba village on the main road, there was a dramatic change of scene. The road suddenly widened; it was better maintained, lined by fruit trees in bloom, and bordered by broad, carefully terraced fields. . . . The houses seemed large and the village well planned. . . . This extraordinary wealth in a difficult environment owes much to the system of polyandry, as I was to find out. (Levine 1988: xiv)

The polyandrous Nyinba are a small group of Tibetan people, numbering just over 1,300. Their ancestors came from Tibet but, like the Brahmans discussed in an earlier chapter (Case 3), the Nyinba now live in the country of Nepal. Culturally, however, they are quite different from the Nepalese Brahmans. The Nyinba speak a dialect of Western Tibetan, follow the religion of Buddhism, and have their own distinctive way of life based on herding and long-distance trade as well as agriculture.

The Nyinba reside in four villages in the far northwest of Nepal, a particularly remote and rugged region. This environmental factor is important: Since resources here are limited and difficult to manage, population expansion would put considerable pressure on these resources, resulting in increased poverty and environmental degradation (as has happened elsewhere in the country). But as noted, polyandry can support low population growth, and this is partly why the polyandrous Nyinba have been successful in the region and, indeed, why their relatively wealthy villages so impressed Levine. In addition, polyandry is central to a particular domestic economy that the Nyinba have developed and that has helped them sustain relative prosperity.

Many Nyinba males are away from their villages for long periods of time. Following particular routes, they simultaneously herd their goats and sheep and trade in salt, grain, and other items, moving all the way from Tibet to northern India. When in their villages, men also engage in agricultural activities, but the routine tasks of agriculture are largely women's work. Women clear fields, apply compost, weed, and do the husking, drying, winnowing, and storing of grain. They also weave, fetch water, wash clothes, cook and serve food, and take care of children—all tasks that keep them close to home inside their villages. The Nyinba highly value male labor, especially trading. Women's work is relatively devalued, even though its contribution to subsistence is substantial. The work of women is also seen as dull and simple, whereas men's work is seen as more diverse and requiring skill.

In times past, Nyinba society was divided into slaves and masters. Slaves lived in small houses adjacent to large master households and performed agricultural and domestic labor. They could be bought, sold, and inherited by masters. Slavery was abolished in Nepal in 1929, but after emancipation most of the former Nyinba slaves remained in their villages. Some stayed on as dependent freedmen of their former masters, continuing to labor for the large household in exchange for food, shelter, and the right to grow crops on small plots of land. Others broke away, acquired land of their own, and became economically independent and wealthier than the dependent freedmen group.

There remains a sharp status distinction between the descendants of former slaves and the descendants of former masters. The latter are the larger group, constituting about 87 percent of the population. In slave times, the two groups did not intermarry. More recently, the freedmen group that acquired land and became economically independent has gradually sought to raise its status over the generations through intermarriage with the former master group.

The Nyinba are patrilineal and largely patrilocal. It sometimes happens that parents have a daughter but no sons, and in this case they may bring in a husband to live matrilocally with them and inherit their estate. But this arrangement is not the ideal. The parents-in-law tend to distrust the incoming husband as an outsider. Although they need the new husband, they are also suspicious of him because he is a person willing to leave his own father and brothers.

The Nyinba are organized into patrilineal clans, which are descent categories, not corporate groups. The clans are exogamous, and sexual relations are also forbidden and considered incestuous between clan members. Clans do have religious significance inasmuch as members of one clan worship a set of common clan gods.

In slave times, the slaves themselves were, of course, a group apart and had no connection with the patrilineal clans of the master group. Interestingly, whereas the master group was polyandrous and patrilocal, the slaves were monogamous and matrilocal. It was the slave owners "who decided to keep slave women at home and bring them husbands from other slave households" (Levine 1988: 73). One result of this arrangement was that slave households became female-centered and slave women played a dominant role within them. At the same time, the master group considered monogamy and matrilocality to be signs of slave inferiority. Today dependent freedmen continue these domestic patterns; the independent, landholding group, meanwhile, has been adopting polyandry and patrilocality.

Along with patrilineal descent, the Nyinba recognize important relationships traced through women. These are best seen in relation to Nyinba notions of heredity. The Nyinba say that fathers contribute their "bone" to a child, passing it on through their sperm, and that mothers contribute "blood." But the father's contribution is more important in the sense that males are believed to contribute more to a child's character and physical appearance. Also, when a woman produces a child, she passes on something of the "bone" of her father, which within her has become transformed into "blood." In this way a child has a hereditary link to his or her mother's patrilineal clan. Note, too, that the children of two sisters are considered closely related by "blood" through their mothers. Being so related, the children of sisters, though of different clans, cannot marry.

Kinship based on patrilineal descent as well as on relationships through women is very important to the Nyinba, who say that one can only really trust one's kin. This sentiment is expressed clearly, as we shall see, in their polyandrous marriages.

For Nyinba, an important group is the *trongba*. Trongbas are corporate, land-holding households. Each trongba has a special name that, along with a personal name, is used to identify individuals. Trongba members own land, houses, domestic animals, and other property in common. Each trongba also has a shrine to its own gods who protect the household. The shrine consists of arrows (a symbol of male continuity), with one arrow added every New Year. When a bride moves into a trongba, her hand is tied to the arrows with a thread that remains a part of the shrine.

Sons of the trongba will jointly inherit the estate and are to remain together for life. Ideally, the trongba should not split up or partition its property. But sometimes a trongba grows too large or its members come into conflict, in which case a partition takes place. Thus, although partition is generally discouraged in a village, it is occasionally seen as necessary. The Nyinba prefer to maintain a stable village size, which for them means a stable number of village households. If at times a number of households die out, then village growth by partition of other trongbas is needed.

At the core of Nyinba culture, interwoven with many aspects of daily life, is polyandry. The Nyinba practice fraternal polyandry, the marriage of a set of brothers to one common wife. Virtually all males who have brothers marry polyandrously. All brothers are equally husbands to their wife; they all have sexual and procreative rights to this woman. Even if another brother is born after the marriage of his older brothers, he will, when mature, automatically acquire sexual and procreative rights to her. Ideally, a woman is expected to treat all her husbands equally, without sexually excluding any of them. It is all right if she feels or shows more affection for one over others so long as she does not deny any brother roughly equal sexual time and equal chance to father her children. In real life, of course, not all marriages conform to this ideal; however, sexual jealousy among brothers is rare.

Regarding the actual arranging of sex, Levine (1988: 164) writes that "for most couples, the problem of sexual equity is handled by having the wife spend an entire night with one husband at a time and with all husbands in more or less equal measure." The planning of sex is open and flexible, and the wife participates in the process along with her husbands: "Plans may be made early in the day, through glances, an exchange of words, and so on. At night, some women go to their husband's beds; others think this is too forward and let their husbands come to them" (Levine 1988: 164).

IMAGE 6.1 A Nyinba woman with her children.

Photo courtesy of Nancy E. Levine.

When the brothers are still quite young and under the authority of their parents, it may be the parents who decide the matter, "literally assigning people to various beds in the house" (Levine 1988: 164). With parental regulation, a precedent for sexual equity can be set early in the marriage. In addition, decisions about sex may occasionally be simplified when some brothers are away trading. And there is a general rule that when a brother returns from a long trading trip, he should have precedence to spend the night with the wife.

Sexual relations are not confined to marriage for either men or women. Indeed, Levine (1988: 148) reports that "virtually all women engage in extra-marital affairs, most frequently in the early years of their marriage." Men accept this situation, without necessarily approving of it, but if the affair becomes public, the woman's lover can be fined and a man might beat his wife for adultery. There is little that wives can do to prevent or stop the affairs of husbands; a woman may be motivated, however, to try to curtail the adulterous behavior of a favorite among her husbands.

Other forms of marriage are also permitted and practiced by the Nyinba, as is generally true of all polyandrous societies. Among the Nyinba, monogamy may come about naturally—for example, with the marriage of a man who has no brothers. Or it may result when a woman marries two brothers and one of them dies. But such outcomes are related to particular circumstances and changes over time; they do not represent options or preferences. In fact, among the Nyinba "there is no notion of monogamy as opposed to polyandry" (Levine 1988: 157). Marriage is simply perceived polyandrously: Brothers have rights in a common wife. But given all the fluctuations in individual cases, only slightly more than half of all Nyinba marriages turn out to be polyandrous.

Polygyny, though not common, is also practiced. It is acceptable when a first wife is childless. In this event, the brothers will add another wife to the marriage but still maintain the first one. Childless women are pitied, but childlessness by itself is not considered a sufficient reason for divorce. Levine (1988: 144) reports that in 1983, 1.3 percent of Nyinba marriages were cases of "polygynous polyandry." Nonpolyandrous polygyny can also occur. For example, a sonless couple may bring in a single husband for a daughter, in which case this man will inherit the estate. Although the arrangement starts out as simple monogamy, the bride's sisters may later join the marriage.

Yet another possibility is what Levine calls "conjoint marriage." Here, one or more brothers in a polyandrous union become dissatisfied in the marriage and then seek to bring in another wife. This may happen for any number of reasons. Perhaps there are many brothers involved (say, four or more) and it becomes too difficult for one woman to cook, serve, do laundry for, and have sex with all of them. Or it may be that one or more brothers is much younger than the common wife, originally brought in by an older brother. Levine (1988: 166) writes of one youngest brother who, "in his early teens, felt that the wife treated him like a small boy or ignored him."

When a new woman joins a household in conjoint marriage, theoretically all the brothers will have sexual and procreative rights to her as well as to their first wife. But in these cases of multiple husbands and wives, distinct "subcouples" may end up forming more exclusive sexual relationships. Partition is often the result, with the groups later splitting along the lines of the subcouples into separate households. Conjoint marriages are discouraged because they so readily establish lines for partition. These marriages are rare, accounting for only 5 percent of all polyandrous marriages.

Reproduction, especially of sons, is important to the Nyinba. Sons will jointly inherit and carry on the management of the trongba estate, and they will patri-lineally carry on the name of the ancestors. They are also expected to care for parents in old age. Daughters may be valued for the alliances with other house-holds that their marriages will bring, but female children are not otherwise seen as long-term assets; as adults they will leave the household, contributing their la-bor and reproduction to another.

Wives, not husbands, are blamed for childlessness. As Levine (1988: 148) writes: "Discovering this, I asked several people if there were no sterile men. The response was that there might be, but no one knew of any cases." Of course, given polyandry and the fact that many women have extramarital affairs, any fertile woman is likely to become pregnant (Levine 1988: 149).

One might suppose that with polyandry there would be little interest among brothers in identifying individual paternity. Interestingly, just the opposite is the case. Nyinba men are very concerned about siring their own biological children, and about determining which of a woman's children are theirs. In some cases the latter is easy to do, since women keep track of their periods and sexual activity over each month, and it may be that not all brothers are home at the same time. Or, for a few years during a marriage, the eldest husband's brothers may be too young for sexual activity. But "inevitably there are pregnancies where the father could be any of several husbands. Then the parents wait for the birth of the child and compare its appearance to the men to make an assignment of paternity" (Levine 1988: 167).

Wives are primarily responsible for assigning paternity and this gives them some power in the household:

> Women may use paternity designations for political purposes: to please a husband who feels himself neglected, to insure that all her children are fathered by the man or men with whom she is likely to partition, and for other pragmatic reasons. . . . Both men and women say that wives can use their rights of paternity designation to mask illegitimacies. (Levine 1988: 167)

Once designated, the relation between a father and his child becomes a close one, and children are told who their "real" father is. A son must have a designated father to gain full membership in the trongba and rights of inheritance in it, and a daughter must have a designated father to receive a dowry upon marriage. Men seek to have their own sons in part because these offspring are considered a more secure source of support in old age.

The key to Nyinba polyandry and inseparable from it is the corporate household, or trongba, and its management. The ideal trongba is a large group consisting mostly of males, spanning a few generations. It is considered best to have only one fertile wife for each set of brothers in each generation, and best for each woman to have sons. Brothers should stay together in strong solidarity and keep the trongba land and other property undivided. The Nyinba point out that polyandry supports fraternal solidarity and keeps brothers together: If they all had separate wives, their interests would be divided and the brothers would split.

Women also say that they prefer polyandry because having more than one husband brings them greater economic security (Levine 1981: 113). But this arrangement may also bring about a shortage of female labor in a household. Although female labor is not highly valued, it is recognized as essential to agriculture and, hence, to subsistence. In the past, slavery filled the gap caused by this labor shortage, since slaves did "women's work"—routine agricultural tasks and domestic labor. Thus slavery facilitated polyandry. In the process it carried implications for gender, too. Slaves were associated with "females" and female roles, masters with "males" and male roles. Both slaves and women were economically and politically dependent on nonslave males. Today some of this same labor need is filled by a trongba's dependent freedmen or hired laborers.[1]

An important consequence of polyandry is that it fosters low population growth: The marriage of one woman to multiple brothers produces fewer children per household than there would be if each brother took a separate wife. In addition, marriageable women are not a scarce commodity, since only one is needed for each set of brothers rather than one for each adult male. Given the strong favoring of sons over daughters, sons are better treated and cared for. As a result, more sons than daughters live to adulthood. The sex ratio among adult Nyinba living in trongba households is 118 men to 100 women, whereas worldwide, the average sex ratio among adults is 95 men to 102 women (Levine 1988: 74).

The Nyinba have a proverb: "As you change the sole of your shoe, so can you change your daughter-in-law or wife." The women of the household, as opposed to the men, are seen as substitutable. Each household needs adult women for labor and reproduction, but the males, related to one another as fathers, sons, and brothers, are really the core. Indeed, the Nyinba system, of which polyandry is a central part, supports a large, solid group of closely related males who jointly own, control, and pass on property. Women do not share in the inheritance of this property. At marriage a woman takes a dowry, but this consists of household utensils and jewelry and is not considered to be particularly valuable. In her husband's home, a woman has rights of maintenance, for as long as she lives or until divorce, and her sons will be coparceners of this family property.

A woman may initiate divorce, but if she leaves her husband or husbands and returns to her natal family, she may soon wear out her welcome. Her position there is also somewhat disadvantaged since she lacks the right to inherit natal family property. If she has children, they remain with or eventually return to her ex-husband(s). And other women will be suspicious that she is after their husbands.

Among the Nyinba, female sexuality is subject to little constraint. In many situations married women not only have multiple husbands but also engage in extramarital affairs. At the same time, care is taken that her children are allocated to individual husbands. In this connection, Levine and Sangree (1980: 406) note that "it appears to be virtually universal for polyandry to entail a jural separation of a woman's sexual and procreative attributes." In other words, her sexuality can be shared by many men, but each of her children is allocated to a particular husband. This separation between the sexual and reproductive attributes of women recalls the situation of the Nuer (Case 2), in which female sexuality is effectively given free rein but legal paternity is secured through bridewealth cattle payments.

Although Nyinba women are seen as substitutable, they do have some sources of power. As we have seen, they can use the right to designate the paternity of their children to their own advantage. In addition, each household includes the position of headwoman as a counterpart to the male household head. Still, the male head has formal authority in the household and receives deference from others. This authority is shown by the fact that he "has first rights to occupy the seat directly beneath the main beam and pillar of the hearth room" (Levine 1988: 119). The position of male household head normally passes from father to eldest son, whereas the position of headwoman is generally filled by the senior woman of the household (usually the wife of the household head) and passes at her old age or death to her daughter-in-law. The headwoman supervises women's work. She also has a special seating place beside the hearth. It is here that she cooks "with household members surrounding her, and this facilitates her domination over mealtime conversations. Since she serves the meals as well, she can regulate the portions to reward her allies with better or more food" (Levine 1988: 120).

The Nyinba seek sons for a set of brothers through one wife and the result is low population growth.[2] Many anthropologists have tried to explain the existence of polyandry in Nepal, Tibet, and elsewhere, in terms of its role in population control. They point out that polyandry tends to occur in areas, such as that inhabited by the Nyinba, where population growth would place considerable stress on already scarce environmental resources. In Levine's (1988) view, however, population control—though clearly related to polyandry—cannot be given as its sole cause or foundation. She points out that many ethnic groups other than the Nyinba live in the same hilly, rugged Nepalese environment but do not practice polyandry. Rather, her work has shown that polyandry among the Nyinba has complex and pervasive connections with the domestic economy, kinship values, household structure, gender, and other cultural traditions of these people.

MARRIAGE AND ALLIANCE

The use of marriage as a mechanism for alliance between groups may have been a brilliant human invention, but arranging a marriage between groups is no easy task. In the last three chapters, and in Case 9 especially, we have seen how notions of common descent are frequently associated with kin-group solidarity and members' mutual feelings of "oneness." Getting two such kin groups to come together and agree to entrust their members in marriage to each other is another matter. In fact, in-law individuals and groups often mistrust one another. Possibly this is why many societies practice various forms of in-law avoidance—as we saw, for example, among the Navajo. The mother-in-law jokes told in Euro-American society may similarly both reflect and defuse in-law tensions. In many societies a great deal of time, energy, negotiating, and bickering goes into the arranging of a marriage. And in many societies divorce is frequent enough to indicate a fragility of affinal ties.

Euro-American society remains somewhat distinctive in regarding marriage as a means of securing happiness for individuals and in imbuing marriage with notions of romantic love and sexual exclusivity. Throughout most of the rest of the world, especially in the past, marriages have been arranged by kin groups with a view toward their own social, economic, and political interests. Yet in all cultures, Euro-American and otherwise, there is, I think, a basic tension between marriage as a social, political, or economic strategy and marriage as an institution involving individuals in intimate interpersonal relations.

The issue under discussion in this section, marriage as alliance, returns us to the concept of exogamy (marriage outside a certain category or group). Later we will also examine endogamy as a political and economic marriage strategy. But for now, in the context of marriage as alliance, let us concentrate on descent-group exogamy, with special attention to a new piece of kinship jargon: the distinction between cross cousins and parallel cousins.

EXOGAMY AND CROSS-COUSIN MARRIAGE

Cross cousins are the children of two opposite-sex siblings. *Parallel cousins* are the children of two same-sex siblings. Figure 6.1 illustrates both in relation to an ego. The importance of this distinction will be clearer if we confine the discussion to unilineal descent groups (that is, groups that are either matrilineal or patrilineal). Accordingly, Figure 6.2 shows an ego's cross and parallel cousins in relation to the broader picture of unilineal descent. To illustrate both the matrilineal and patrilineal cases in this diagram, the darkly shaded symbols represent ego's patrilineal kin and the lightly shaded ones represent ego's matrilineal kin. The diagram shows that for either mode of unilineal descent, ego's cross cousins *are always excluded as members of ego's own unilineal descent group*. Hence, with descent-group exogamy, cross cousins may be marriageable. Among ego's parallel cousins, in contrast, the MZC will be members of ego's group if the group is matrilineal and the FBC will be members of ego's group if the group is patrilineal.

In some societies, only one type of cross cousin (FZC or MBC) is permitted as a spouse; in others, both types are permitted. Cross-cousin marriage does not necessarily mean that ego is marrying a first cousin, or that the people involved are systematically practicing first-cousin marriage. It may be that ego is marrying, say, a second or third cross cousin or, for that matter, any person who is linguistically classified as a cross cousin.

With Figure 6.2, then, it is easy to see that cross cousins may be permissible spouses in societies that have exogamous descent groups. But why would some societies prescribe or generally prefer cross-cousin marriage? In the next section we will see how cross-cousin marriage has been related to certain types of marital exchanges between groups.

FIGURE 6.1   Ego's Cross and Parallel Cousins

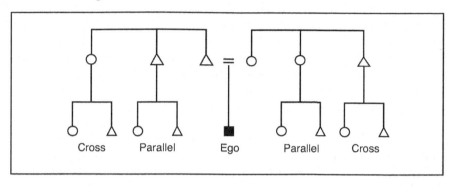

FIGURE 6.2   Cross Cousins and Unilineal Descent

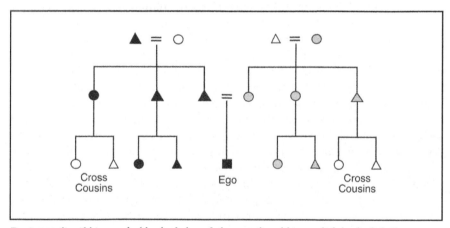

Ego's patrilineal kin are darkly shaded, and the matrilineal kin are lightly shaded. Cross cousins will always be excluded as members of ego's unilineal descent groups.

EXOGAMY AND EXCHANGE: MANIPULATING WOMEN?

In Chapter 1 we examined the idea that rules of exogamy would force groups to look beyond themselves for spouses and develop alliances with other groups. Exogamy would thus help promote peaceful relations, or at least prevent groups from forming only hostile relationships and killing each other off.

Anthropologist Claude Lévi-Strauss (1969) took this line of thinking further. First, for societies practicing descent-group exogamy, he distinguished between those with "complex" marriage systems and those with "elementary" marriage systems. In the former, there is just a rule that one must marry outside the descent group. Most societies that practice descent-group exogamy are of this type. In the latter, there is not only a rule of descent-group exogamy specifying whom one cannot marry but also rules specifying whom, or into what groups, one *should* marry. Lévi-Strauss then said that early human groups were of this "elementary" type. These groups were not just marrying out, they were systematically intermarrying with other groups; they were not just practicing descent-group exogamy, they were exchanging women. By exchanging women over the generations, these early groups were essentially setting up forms of enduring and perpetual alliances.

The gender implications of this view will be discussed later, but first we need to look at how systematic exchange of spouses works on paper. The simplest way to start is to imagine two sets of brother-sister pairs who intermarry. As illustrated in Figure 6.3, these pairs represent two descent groups, A and B. Let's also assume that the two groups are patrilineal. To clarify who belongs to which descent group, the circle and triangle symbolizing the members of patrilineal descent group A are shaded. Here, a man of A is marrying a woman of B and a man of B is marrying a woman of A.

This exchange may be kept up over the generations, such that the children of these first two unions intermarry, their children also intermarry, and so on. Figure 6.4 shows what happens over time. In short, every male ego is marrying an FZD who is also an MBD—in other words, a double cross cousin. Likewise, every female ego is marrying an MBS who is also an FZS. Thus cross-cousin marriage (or in this case, double cross-cousin marriage) is a systematic way of perpetuating the alliance between groups A and B over the generations. Another way to put this is to say that if A and B decide to systematically exchange spouses in each generation, the result will be a case of systematic double cross-cousin marriage.

Figure 6.4 is highly idealized. What it shows, in the simplest way possible, is that two unilineal descent groups could practice exogamy, link up through marriage, and perpetuate their alliance over and over. Real societies, of course, deal with much larger numbers of people and greater numbers of descent groups. It may help to look again at this diagram and imagine that the triangles and circles represent not individuals but whole lineages or clans. It is sometimes the case that a group of people is divided up into clans, which in turn are clustered into two *moieties*, or halves; the marriage rule is then that one must marry into a clan of the moiety opposite one's own.

These types of exchange marriages are no longer common on a world scale, but they have been found, with many variations, among some hunting and gathering peoples. For example, Australian aborigines developed highly complex forms of spouse exchange (sometimes called "section systems") that are variations of the idealized model in Figure 6.4. Lévi-Strauss (1969) interpreted all these versions of spouse exchange as evidence of similar kinds of marriage exchange among early humans.

FIGURE 6.3 Spouse Exchange Between Groups A and B

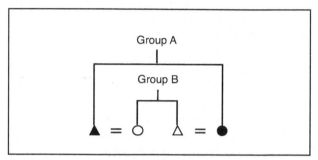

Members of Group A are shaded.

FIGURE 6.4 Systematic Spouse Exchange Between Groups A and B over the Generations

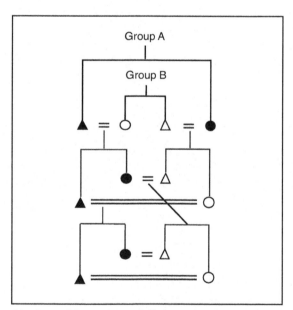

Members of Group A are shaded.

Other ways of arranging marital exchanges between groups are also possible. For example, Group A could give women systematically and in each generation to Group B, which in turn could give its women to Group C, which could then give its women to Group A. A simplified version of this type of exchange is illustrated in Figure 6.5; in real life, of course, many more groups would be involved, and the situation would be far more complex. The diagram focuses on the circulation of women, but a circulation of men could just as easily be represented. Note that the broken circles represent the women of C who are marrying the men of A.

In this type of system, every ego winds up marrying only one type of cross cousin. A male ego marries his MBD and a female ego marries an FZS. An example of a society that practices this form of marriage is the Purum, a tribal group in India (Keesing 1975: 85–88).

I could go much further in this vein, showing all sorts of spouse-exchange marriages that entail different kinds of cross-cousin marriage. These systems have preoccupied anthropologists and provoked many arguments. Thus far, in fact, there is no consensus as to exactly how these systems work, or what precisely they mean to the groups that practice them, or what they should mean to the outsiders who study them. Most theorists who attempt to account for cross-cousin marriage focus on social structure and discuss the implications of this type of marriage in terms of the maintenance of marital alliances

FIGURE 6.5   Systematic Marriages Among Three Groups

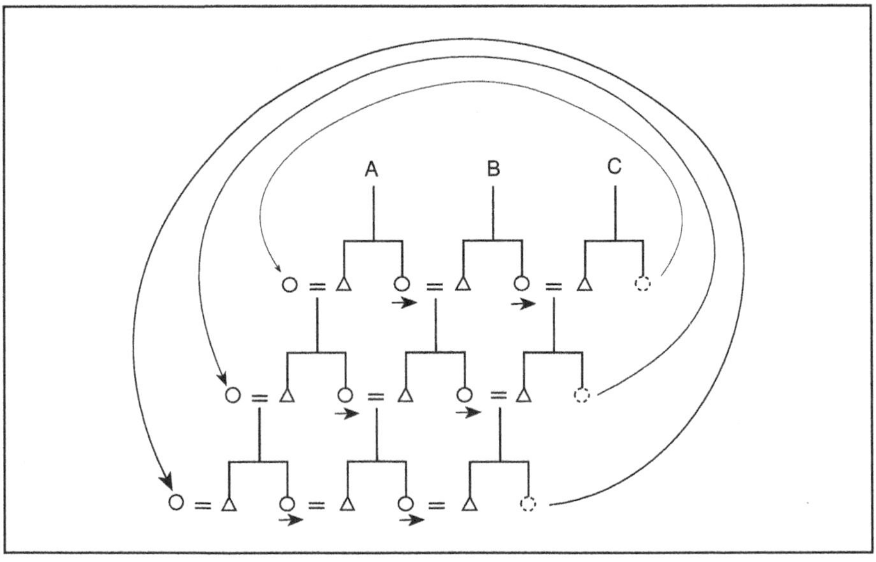

Women of A marry men of B; women of B marry men of C; and women of C (shown in broken circles) marry men of A. Arrows indicate the circulation of the women.

between groups of people. Against this approach, however, Margaret Trawick (1990) offers a novel interpretation of cross-cousin marriage among the Tamil people of South India. She suggests that cross-cousin marriage in this society is in part related to the culturally patterned emotional dynamics between certain kin. In particular, she points out the highly affective bond between brothers and sisters in Tamil culture. A sibling, then, "may become like a desired but forbidden mate" (Trawick 1990: 183). A kind of "longing" between brother and sister cannot be directly fulfilled, but it can be indirectly expressed through the marriages of their children to one another. What makes Trawick's approach interesting is that she discusses marriage practices not as abstractions of social structure but in terms of the emotional lives and cultural experiences of real people.

This having been said, we can now return to Lévi-Strauss's ideas about exogamy and the origin of spouse exchange. Even more important than what Lévi-Strauss said about marital exchanges is the way in which he phrased his original proposition: Early human groups exchanged women. Needless to say, for those interested in exploring the origins of female subordination, this was a very powerful idea, the implications of which were drawn out by Gayle Rubin (1975). It suggested that very early in human adaptation, women became subordinated to men because they were, in a sense, the first items of trade between men of different groups. In other words, males were playing a political game with women as the pawns; they were in control of allocating female sexuality and reproductive capacity, whereas women were merely the allocated. This idea concurs with Fox's (1980) view, discussed in Chapter 2, that males (with their control over valuable meat from hunting) maintained power over the allocation of females to others and used it to recruit other males as allies. Fox (1989: 179) also suggested that the custom of bridewealth emerged when men, in order to acquire wives, started offering goods instead of their own sisters and daughters as exchange.

If women appear somewhat passive in Lévi-Strauss's scheme, it is certainly not because he intended that they be seen as lacking in value. On the contrary, he saw a woman as the "total gift" between men. At some point, he said, human men emerged from a state of primitive promiscuity and incest. They renounced sexual access to their own women to trade with one another and so become allies. They bonded together precisely because their items of exchange, live women, were valuable. Thus was alliance born between men—and thus was marriage born, too. But according to Lévi-Strauss, marriage was primarily a relationship between men and only secondarily involved a union between a man and a woman. Women were valuable, but valuable in the world of men as items of exchange between them.

Is any of this true? It's hard to say, because so little is known about the actual behavior of Paleolithic hunter-gatherers. We saw in Chapter 2 that Lévi-Strauss's original idea of men exchanging women was supported by

primatologist Bernard Chapais (2008) in his construction of the evolution
of human kinship. Chapais argued from evolutionary theory that since females, relative to males, contribute a much greater reproductive effort, they
are the scarcer, more valuable reproductive resource. As for modern human
groups, some anthropologists have criticized the idea that males exchanged
women (in elementary systems) or merely farmed them out to form alliances
(in complex systems) to play their own political games. Karen Sacks (1979:
114–115) wrote that marriage exchanges in hunting-gathering societies generally do not involve male-controlled exchanges of women, who in these societies are economically and socially equal to men. And Diane Bell (1980)
showed that, among one group of Australian aborigines, although spouse
exchange was ceremonially in the hands of men, women had also directly
participated in the selections before the ceremony. We have seen, too, that
among the Beng (Case 6), a group with double descent, husbands arrange
the marriages of the odd-numbered daughters, and wives, the marriages of
their even-numbered daughters. My own study has shown that among
Nepalese Brahmans (Case 3), women actively work to arrange marriages for
their daughters to men in the villages of their own brothers to secure some
social support for the new brides. In all these cases, marriages are definitely
"political" in that they establish alliances between groups, but matchmaking
appears to be a game that both women and men can play. And finally, there
are cases of matrilineal groups (such as the Minangkabau of West Sumatra,
Indonesia) that clearly exchange men in marriage and where it is primarily
women who conduct, control, and benefit from these exchanges (Peletz 1987;
Krier 2000; Godelier 2011). But still, even with all of this, it is possible that
among early human groups, males indeed exchanged females as mates, subordinated women in the process, and set a precedent for later human cultural
patterns. French anthropologist Françoise Héritier (1981, 1999) has revived
Lévi-Strauss's ideas on marriage exchange along with the proposition that
among early humans men were exchanging women. In her view, evolving
humans were distinctly aware of male/female biological differences and the
fact that only women give birth. Men, perceiving themselves as fundamentally disadvantaged in this respect, sought control over this mysterious power
of women.

Whether men were exchanging women, women were exchanging men, or
some combination thereof, what is important here is that with this kind of
human/cultural mate assignment, both women and men enter a whole new
world of social, not just biological, reproduction. Both lose reproductive autonomy in that they are no longer mating on their own, with whatever consequence and through whatever strategies, but are now reproducing *for* larger
groups—families, lineages, clans, even ancestral spirits—and with new goals,
such as forming intergroup alliances. Later, even-larger groupings—states,
religious institutions—develop interests in individuals' reproduction and place

pressures upon them to conform to those interests. In this process, by the simple fact that women experience pregnancy, birth, and lactation, their position and their behavior come under greater control than that of their male partners by whatever groups harbor interests in human reproduction.

Marriage alliances may have helped early humans to develop cooperative intergroup relationships, but they did not (and still do not) always work to maintain peace between groups. It is probably true that if two descent groups systematically intermarried over the generations (as illustrated in Figure 6.5), they would be unlikely to attack each other, since each group would encompass the other's sisters, daughters, and grandchildren. But in any looser arrangement, marriage bonds are not enough to prevent war. In some groups, such as the Huli (Case 8), much warfare took place between male affines, and there was the saying that "we fight where we marry." In addition, alliances can be terminated through acts of divorce when need be.

ENDOGAMY

Now, what about descent-group endogamy or, more specifically, endogamy within a unilineal lineage? We presume that few Paleolithic hunter-gatherer groups practiced descent-group endogamy, inasmuch as we know that few, if any, modern hunter-gatherers have done so. But descent-group endogamy is found among some other groups. Arab societies with patrilineal lineages are one example. Here a man is permitted to marry his parallel cousin, an FBD (though she need not be a first cousin; she could, for example, be an FFBSD). In some areas of the Arab world (or in regions that have converted to Islam and adopted many Arabic customs), a man's marriage to an FBD is preferred and widely practiced, though not mandatory.

In the case of lineage endogamy, the descent group cannot use marriage to forge or maintain alliances with other descent groups, but it acquires other advantages. One is that the descent group retains its rights in the reproduction of its female members; it does not need to rely on cooperation with other descent groups to reproduce itself. Another advantage is that in situations where females as well as males inherit lineage property, this property will stay in the lineage. Otherwise, with lineage exogamy, women at marriage might take property out of the lineage (say, in the form of a dowry). This latter advantage is the one most frequently mentioned by people practicing this form of endogamy. Along with material property, valued but more abstract assets such as power, prestige, and social status can be kept within a group through endogamy. A third advantage falls to women. Since a woman is marrying into her own descent group, she is not moving into a new group where her natal kin have no influence and where she will be left to fend for herself. If she has trouble in her married life, she can rely on her F, Bs, and many others to exert influence on her husband, who is their own (and her) lineage kinsman.

The contrast in the strategic use of kin-group exogamous marriage and the use of kin-group endogamous ones is very well illustrated in the history of ancient Rome. The period of interest here is roughly 100 B.C. to A.D. 100; this span of time encompasses the Late Republic and Early Empire. By the Late Republic the Roman *gens* (clan) that we discussed in Chapter 3 had ceased to be a corporate group, and Romans were well along the path of their long-term shift away from patrilineal descent and toward becoming a bilateral society. During this brief historical period, Roman society went from being a republic to becoming the great Roman Empire that went on to influence the course of Western civilization for several centuries. In the process of this transformation, the political class, those seeking to gain and sustain power, shifted its marriage forms and strategies.

There were two phases to this transformation. The first part, which entailed the use of kin-group exogamy to create alliances, is clearly seen in the career of Julius Caesar (100 B.C.–44 B.C.). Indeed, Caesar's matchmaking was as important as his military campaigns in his rise to power. Caesar's first marriage aligned him solidly with an important political faction in Rome. Sixteen years later this wife died (having given Caesar his only legitimate child, Julia). Caesar then arranged a marriage to a second wife, Pompeia, allying him to a very powerful family and signaling a temporary truce with an opposing political faction. This wife was divorced seven years later;[3] three years after that Caesar arranged a marriage to his last wife, Calpurnia, daughter of an important man (Piso) who helped Caesar secure command of the province of Gaul. This enabled him to achieve stunning military victories and add substantial territory to the Roman state, all of which was decisive in his political rise to the top.

In addition to his own marriages, Caesar carefully arranged the marriages of others to promote his political ambitions. The most famous of these maneuverings was his arrangement of the marriage of his daughter, Julia, to his political rival, Pompey. This marriage sealed the historically significant alliance known as the First Triumvirate (allying Caesar and Pompey with another man, Crassus). The political payoffs were great: Through this alliance, Caesar received the Roman consulship and became established as a very serious political figure in Rome. A rift nevertheless grew between Caesar and Pompey, a rift greatly widened by Julia's death. Indeed when Julia died, civil war broke out, as many Romans had feared. Then in 45 B.C. Caesar's forces defeated those of Pompey, and Caesar became the Roman dictator for life. That life, however, lasted only one more year, as Caesar was murdered in 44 B.C.

Next to assume power in Rome and to become its first emperor was Augustus (63 B.C.–A.D. 14), Caesar's designated heir. Augustus had nothing much going for him other than the fact that his mother's father had married Caesar's sister. Caesar himself had no legitimate son and his only daughter had died childless, making Augustus his next-best choice for a male heir. In

44 B.C., nineteen-year-old Augustus came to Rome to claim his place in history. In the beginning Augustus, like Caesar before him, arranged a number of kin-group exogamous marriages to bolster his power. For example, his early alliance with Mark Antony (in the Second Triumvirate) was sealed with an arranged marriage: Antony, whose previous wife, Fulvia, had conveniently died, married Augustus's sister, Octavia. Further cementing this alliance, Augustus became betrothed to Mark Antony's stepdaughter. However, Augustus broke this engagement to secure even more advantageous political connections through marriage to a woman related to the Pompey family. Later he divorced this woman (on the very day she bore him a daughter, Julia) to marry his last wife, Livia, a member of the powerful, aristocratic Claudian family.[4]

Not long after this marriage Augustus's power in Rome was solid and supreme. It is at this point that he and his family members shifted their marital strategies into the second phase: They began to marry endogamously within their kin group, which was by now a bilateral group known as the Julio-Claudians. One very important such marriage was that between Tiberius (Augustus's stepson, Livia's son by her previous marriage) and Augustus's own daughter, Julia (then a widow). Augustus ordered Tiberius and Julia to marry; for this to happen, Tiberius needed to divorce his beloved and currently pregnant wife, which he did only with great reluctance. For the Roman history buff Figure 6.6 shows the genealogy of the Julio-Claudians. One can see that the pattern of kin-group endogamous marriages that Augustus initiated continued through the Julio-Claudian line and the reigns of Rome's earliest emperors. After Tiberius, the Julio-Claudians split into two kinship factions that occasionally murdered each other's members. This imperial period also saw plenty of intrigue, love affairs, forced marriages, divorces, and so on, continuing the patterns set earlier.

With the Romans we have seen, then, how exogamous marriages reach outward; they have the advantage of connecting individuals and families to new, useful groups. This was the pattern for all of Caesar's own marriages and his arranging of others' marriages. Kin-group endogamous marriage, by contrast, focuses on consolidating power and wealth inward, within the family group. Once secure in power, Augustus made great and repeated use of this strategy. Another advantage of endogamous marriages for emperors and royal families generally is that royal blood does not, as it were, seep out of the family, allowing others to use it as a claim to power. In the case of the Julio-Claudians, occasionally outsiders tried to move into this bloc of power through love affairs or marriage proposals, but the Julio-Claudians managed to keep them out by sticking to their endogamy. In the end the lesson of Roman history seems to be: Use descent-group exogamy for your rise to the top; once there, use endogamy to preserve and transmit your superior power and wealth.

FIGURE 6.6　A Genealogy of the Julio-Claudians

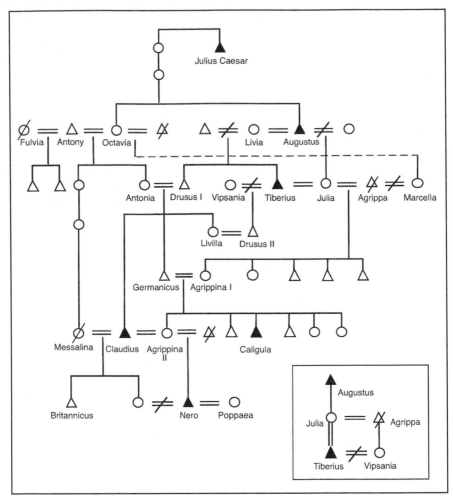

Julius Caesar and the emperors are shaded. Some deaths and divorces are shown to indicate the sequence of marriages. The box at the lower right shows the complex relationships between Julia, Agrippa, Tiberius, and Vipsania.

MARRIAGE AND FERTILITY

In Chapter 4 we saw that the Mosuo of China showed a lower fertility than did other nearby populations and that the greater reproductive autonomy of women entailed in their "visiting" arrangement may have been an important factor behind this pattern. In this chapter we have seen that Nyinba polyandry controls village and household size, allowing the Nyinba to adapt to their rugged, precarious environment and scarce resources. In this case women's reproductive autonomy is not as high as among the Mosuo: Women are allowed a number of sexual partners (automatically in cases of fraternal polyandry, but also women have affairs outside marriage) and they can divorce their husband(s), but they are under significant cultural pressure to reproduce, to reproduce sons, and to provide more than one husband with children. Among the Nyinba, polyandry did not lower the fertility of individual women but did limit the reproduction of each household, or each male sibling set.

In ancient Rome, too, there were some distinctive fertility patterns but here the issue was controversial. During the period covered in this chapter, upper-class Romans were lowering their fertility, but some, notably the Emperor Augustus and his close followers, were alarmed at this trend and sought to reverse it. To understand the Roman case, we need to look more closely at gender and transformations in gender in ancient Rome; in the process we will see other links between marriage, gender, and reproduction.

Ancient Rome shows us an enduring image of the ideal woman as chaste and virtuous. In the early periods of the Republic, brides were to be virgins (women were married young, often at the legal minimum age of twelve [Rawson 1986: 21]), and wives were to be absolutely faithful to husbands. Husbands, by contrast, had automatic sexual rights not only to their wives but also to their female slaves, and their relations with prostitutes or lower-class women were their own affair. Marriage was explicitly believed to serve the purpose of providing legitimate children for the husband, in whose legal power they would be placed and with whom they would stay in the event of divorce.

There was great emphasis on women's sexual purity. Culturally, this emphasis was expressed in the cult of the Vestal Virgins, which survived for more than 1,000 years, until A.D. 394. These virgins (always a total of six) were selected before their first menstruation from upper-class families. For a period of thirty years they were to tend the sacred fire in the temple to the Goddess Vesta (Goddess of the Hearth), making sure it never went out. They took a vow of virginity for the period of their service; if this vow was violated, which fortunately happened only very infrequently, they were punished by being buried alive. In times of great national strife, the chastity of the Vestal Virgins was surrounded with suspicion (Beard 1980: 16). On another social plane, ordinary Roman women tended the household hearth, and it

IMAGE 6.2   Statue of a Vestal Virgin in the
Roman Forum (Rome).

Photo courtesy of J. Thomas Bradley.

was likewise on their virtue that the honor of the family rested (Cohen 1991).
The Vestal Virgins and the fire of Vesta were symbols of the unity, continuity,
and honor of the Roman state. The cult itself also symbolized fertility; the virgins' rituals were carried out to promote the fertility of the Roman people, a
cause for which their own fertility was sacrificed (Fantham et al. 1994: 235).

In the period before the Late Republic and the rise of Julius Caesar, most
upper-class Romans arranged a type of marriage called "marriage with
manus," meaning that the power (*potestas*) a father held over a daughter was
transferred, at marriage, to her husband. Legally speaking, a woman in this
type of marriage was in many respects like a daughter to her husband. A
woman married with manus could not initiate divorce. But her husband could
divorce her or, in consultation with her consanguineal relatives, put her to
death for particular offenses such as committing adultery or drinking wine.
Upper-class Romans seem to have had a problem with women drinking
wine. Wine was believed, at least by men, to inflame women's passions and

induce "sexual aberration" (Baldson 1963: 213). A husband could also divorce a wife for counterfeiting his keys, some of which might unlock the wine cellar. This exercise of male control over female sexuality, played out in reference to wine, also involved a woman's male consanguineal kin: "Women were customarily kissed on the mouth by their male blood relations in order to determine if they had alcohol on their breath" (Pomeroy 1975: 153).

This clearly patriarchal state of affairs had changed in many respects by the time of the Late Republic, at least among the upper classes. For one thing, by the Late Republic marriage "with manus" had declined and most unions were now "free marriages," whereby a woman remained under the legal power of her father after marriage and retained his *gens* (clan) name. Divorce, undoubtedly rare before, was now both frequent and easy to obtain. Wives (or their fathers, who had legal power over them) could initiate divorce as easily as men. So by the Late Republic, husbands did not have the great power over wives that they had had before.[5]

In "free" marriage a woman brought a dowry, but in the event of divorce, the dowry had to be returned to the woman's father, or, if he were dead, it became her property. Property also fell into the independent coffers of women through another route. During the expansion of the Republic, many Roman husbands died or were away for long periods on military campaigns, leaving wives and widows to fend for themselves and to manage estates in their husbands' absence. These wars also brought back new wealth. As women were by now more financially autonomous and adept, some of this wealth found its way into their hands (Pomeroy 1975).

For women these changes in marriage and property were significant and led to their increasing autonomy and independence. A woman in a "free" marriage was still under the authority of her father (or eldest male ascendant of that family). If her father died, she was then given a legal guardian (usually a brother of the father or someone the father appointed before his death), but the powers of guardians were weak compared to those of the father. Guardians were appointed primarily to ensure that women did not foolishly lose property that devolved upon them. Even though these guardians officially had authority over a woman's property, many ways and means were found around them, and by the Late Republic, women's legal guardians were largely a formality (Crook 1986: 85).

By the Late Republic adultery seemed to have increased substantially, or at least it was more open and tolerated. Previously, as we saw, men could have relations with women outside marriage, but they were not to have sex with married upper-class women. Yet this is what was happening now: Men were having affairs with elite married women, and upper-class married women were taking lovers. Julius Caesar, for example, had a number of affairs with upper-class married women, among them Mucia, Pompey's own wife, and Servilia, mother of Brutus, one of the men who murdered Caesar.

Some historians have referred to this occurrence as a kind of sexual "liberation" of women and have described the Late Republic as seeing the emergence of a "new woman" (Fantham et al. 1994), one now assertive, willful, and in command, if not of the official rules and values of her society, then of her own sexuality and its consequences.

It was not the case that all the old ideals regarding women and sex had changed, or that all women were committing adultery. Female virtue was still praised, and sexual indiscretion, though more common during this period, was still frowned upon. But now "the Roman woman had choices" (Pomeroy 1975: 188); she could select from among a greater variety of socially tolerated lifestyles.

Many Romans were alarmed at this state of affairs, especially the Emperor Augustus himself, who set about reforming the sexual behavior of the Roman upper class. Once secure in power, Augustus launched a strong campaign for what we would now call "family values." He sought a return to the Rome of the Early Republic, when women were virtuous and men were valiant protectors of that virtue. He also focused new attention on children and sought to promote female fertility and motherhood. His famous Altar of Peace in Rome shows an early representation of children in Western art. Augustus's own family came to epitomize the new moral order, with his wife, Livia, and his sister, Octavia, serving as exemplary models of virtuous women. Fantham et al. (1994: 313) describe what this family meant to the Roman people:

> First, the Imperial family was a family and its continuity under a dignified and protective father and a noble and fertile mother guaranteed the health and happiness of the Roman people, its children. Second, this notion of family was disseminated throughout the empire on works of art, coins, and domestic shrines, in the patronage of buildings and the inscriptions that marked them, and [in] the ceremonies and choreographed public appearances of members of the court.

In addition, Augustus enacted laws (in 18 B.C. and A.D. 9) that made adultery illegal in the eyes of the state. As was the case before, for a married woman, sexual relations with any man other than her husband constituted adultery. For a man, adultery meant only sexual relations with a married upper-class woman. If caught in the act, a woman could be killed by her father. Under certain conditions her husband could kill her lover, though he could not kill his wife (Cohen 1991: 111).

These laws of Augustus also attempted to promote fertility. Divorced or widowed women were required to remarry within a specified time. Unmarried adults could not claim their inheritances; those who were married but childless had to forfeit some of their inheritance. And there were rewards for high fer-

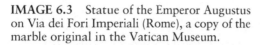

IMAGE 6.3   Statue of the Emperor Augustus on Via dei Fori Imperiali (Rome), a copy of the marble original in the Vatican Museum.

Photo courtesy of J. Thomas Bradley.

tility: If a freeborn woman had borne three children (for a freedwoman, or ex-slave, the number was four children), she no longer had to have a legal guardian (Cohen 1991: 124).

Augustus's efforts to curb Roman adultery failed miserably. A severe blow came with the case of his own daughter, Julia. Augustus had arranged marriages for her, and she had pleased Augustus by bearing many children. But then, in 2 B.C., Augustus was notified that Julia had not only committed adultery but was leading a rather sexually licentious life. Augustus was told that she had had dozens of lovers and that she roamed about at night having sexual adventures in the Forum. Mortified, Augustus banished her to an island where she was expressly forbidden both men and wine. One of her recent lovers (who was, incidentally, a son of Mark Antony and Fulvia) was ordered to kill himself, and others were exiled.

Augustus's attempts to increase Roman upper-class fertility were also in-
effective. The Roman upper class, like the lower classes, lived in a context
of low average life expectancy (at birth, it was only about twenty-five years),
high infant mortality (about half of all children born died before age ten
[Garnsey 1991: 52]), and frequent deaths of women in childbirth. Still, it appears that fertility among upper-class people decreased with time and was
significantly lower than that among other groups. It is possible that these
people, concerned with wealth and the status it maintained, sought to limit
the number of their children in order to limit the division of their property
(Saller 1991: 26). Some historians have speculated that a voluntary low fertility or infertility of the upper classes came about as family life disintegrated—
that is, as sex moved outside marriage and into adultery, where it became
entwined with romantic love (Hunt 1994: 88–89). It is also possible in my
view that fertility declined as women became more autonomous, and in particular, as they became less under the power of husbands.

Certainly Roman society was familiar with techniques to reduce fertility,
such as infanticide, abortion, and contraception. Augustus's wayward daughter, Julia, though quite fertile herself, allegedly claimed that in order to ensure
that her children belonged to her husband, she took lovers only when she
was already pregnant. One Roman writer, Macrobius, satirizes Roman morality of this period by attributing to Julia this remark: "I never take on a pas-
senger unless the boat is full" (Macrobius 2.5.9, cited in Richlin 1992: 72).
Some Roman contraceptive techniques may have been effective, such as the
use of goat bladders for condoms or oils and wool as blocking agents. But
other common techniques—for example, having a woman hold her breath
during the man's ejaculation, or wearing amulets containing cat liver
(Pomeroy 1975: 167)—were no doubt disappointing.

In the next chapter we will trace historical developments in the patterns
of European and American kinship and gender within which, to this day, we
can hear the echoes of ancient Rome. With regard to reproduction, later on
in Europe fertility rates were also relatively low, but this was in part because
of something quite new: a relatively late age of marriage for women.

Discussion Questions

1. How does systematic cross-cousin marriage perpetuate alliances between
or among descent groups?

2. Looking at Nyinba culture and its practice of polyandry, what factors
do you think may account for the general lack of jealousy among brothers
who share a wife?

3. In terms of gaining and maintaining a descent group's power, status,
and wealth, what are the advantages and disadvantages of descent-group exogamy and endogamy?

Suggested Classroom Media

Strange Relations. 1992. A coproduction of Biniman Productions Ltd. PBS Video, Alexandria, VA. Narrated by anthropologist David Maybury-Lewis. Sixty minutes. This film covers and contrasts marriage practices in Nepal, Niger, and Canada. The portion on Nepal focuses exclusively on polyandry among the Nyinba.

I, Claudius. 2000 [orig. 1976]. A BBC production in association with London Film Production, Ltd., Twentieth Century Fox Home Entertainment, Beverly Hills, CA. This excellent production is based on Robert Graves's novel *I, Claudius.* It covers the Roman Empire from Augustus to Claudius as told by Claudius. The whole production, which includes many episodes and takes 669 minutes, is too long for classroom use. I recommend Episode 3, which covers Augustus's banishment of his daughter, Julia.

Websites

www.youtube.com/watch?v=u7HKmu3eMEk. "Brothers Share One Wife—Fraternal Polyandry." Video of polyandry in India.

www.historylink101.com/ancient_rome/ancient_rome_daily_life.htm. "Daily Life of Ancient Rome." Click on "Roman Family" for excellent descriptions of kinship, gender, and family in ancient Rome.

Notes

1. The trongba generally hires as laborers either poor freedmen or poor people from other ethnic groups in the region.

2. Population growth among the Nyinba occurs at a rate of 1 to 1.5 percent per year, compared to more than 2.6 percent per year in Nepal overall (Levine 1988: 241–242).

3. This divorce followed a scandal. Pompeia was evidently being pursued by Publius Clodius, a debauched playboy. At Caesar's house, where an all-female religious ceremony was taking place (the Festival of Bona Dea), Clodius attended the festival by dressing up as a woman to gain entrance to the house and make love with Pompeia. The deception was uncovered by Caesar's enraged mother.

4. This was an unusual match. At the time Livia was already married, the mother of one child, and pregnant with another. For whatever reasons of his own, Livia's husband, Nero, not only agreed to the match, he also attended the wedding, gave the bride away, and provided Livia with a dowry. Her two sons by him (one born after the wedding) remained with Nero, but Nero willed that upon his death Augustus should adopt them. Nero died five years later.

5. This shift to "free" marriages may have been related to the fact that upper-class Romans were becoming wealthier and more concerned with wealth (Pomeroy 1975: 155). Large dowries could be used to attract good husbands for one's daughters (and, thereby, to secure political alliances), but at the same time, a father did not wish to

see all that wealth pass out of his family and into another. "Free" marriage of a daughter allowed him much greater control over this wealth.

REFERENCES

Aiyappan, A. 1937. Polyandry and Sexual Jealousy. *Man* 37: 104.

Aziz, Barbara Nimri. 1978. *Tibetan Frontier Families: Reflections of Three Generations from D'ing-ri*. Durham, NC: Carolina Academic Press.

Baldson, J. P. V. D. 1963. *Roman Women: Their History and Habits*. New York: John Day Company.

Beard, Mary. 1980. The Sexual Status of Vestal Virgins. *Journal of Roman Studies* 70: 12–27.

Bell, Diane. 1980. Desert Politics: Choices in the Marriage Market. In Mona Etienne and Eleanor Leacock, eds., *Women and Colonization: Anthropological Perspectives*, pp. 239–269. New York: Praeger.

Chapais, Bernard. 2008. *Primeval Kinship: How Pair-Bonding Gave Birth to Human Society*. Cambridge, MA: Harvard University Press.

Cohen, David. 1991. The Augustan Law on Adultery: The Social and Cultural Context. In David I. Kertzer and Richard P. Saller, eds., *The Family in Italy from Antiquity to the Present*, pp. 109–126. New Haven, CT: Yale University Press.

Crook, J. A. 1986. Feminine Inadequacy and the *Senatusconsultum Velleianum*. In Beryl Rawson, ed., *The Family in Ancient Rome: New Perspectives*, pp. 83–92. Ithaca, NY: Cornell University Press.

Fantham, Elaine, Helene Peet Foley, Natalie Boymel Kampen, Sarah B. Pomeroy, and H. Alan Shapiro. 1994. *Women in the Classical World*. New York: Oxford University Press.

Fox, Robin. 1980. *The Red Lamp of Incest*. New York: E. P. Dutton.

———. 1989 [orig. 1967]. *Kinship and Marriage: An Anthropological Perspective*. Cambridge, England: Cambridge University Press.

Garnsey, Peter. 1991. Child Rearing in Ancient Italy. In David I. Kertzer and Richard P. Saller, eds., *The Family in Italy from Antiquity to the Present*, pp. 48–65. New Haven, CT: Yale University Press.

Godelier, Maurice. 2011. *The Metamorphoses of Kinship*. Translated by Nora Scott. London: Verso.

Goldstein, Melvyn C. 1976. Fraternal Polyandry and Fertility in a High Himalayan Valley in Northwest Nepal. *Human Ecology* 4: 223–233.

Héritier, Françoise. 1981. *L'Exercise de la Parenté*. Paris: Hautes Études/Gallimard Le Seuil.

———. 1999. *Two Sisters and Their Mother: The Anthropology of Incest*. Translated by Jeanine Herman. New York: Zone Books.

Hunt, Morton. 1994. *The Natural History of Love*. New York: Anchor Books/Doubleday.

Keesing, Roger M. 1975. *Kin Groups and Social Structure*. Fort Worth, TX: Holt, Rinehart, and Winston.

Krier, Jennifer. 2000. The Marital Project: Beyond the Exchange of Men in Minangkabau Marriage. *American Ethnologist* 27(4): 877–897.

Levine, Nancy. 1981. Perspectives on Love: Morality and Affect in Nyinba Interpersonal Relationships. In Adrian C. Mayer, ed., *Culture and Morality*, pp. 106–125. Oxford: Oxford University Press.

———. 1988. *The Dynamics of Polyandry: Kinship, Domesticity, and Population on the Tibetan Border*. Chicago: University of Chicago Press.

Levine, Nancy, and Walter H. Sangree. 1980. Conclusion: Asian and African Systems of Polyandry. *Journal of Comparative Family Studies* 11(3): 385–410.

Lévi-Strauss, Claude. 1969 [orig. 1949]. *The Elementary Structures of Kinship*. Translated by James Harle Bell, John Richard von Sturmer, and Rodney Needham; edited by Rodney Needham. Boston: Beacon Press.

Peletz, Michael. 1987. The Exchange of Men in Nineteenth-Century Negeri Sembilan (Malaya). *American Ethnologist* 14(3): 449–469.

Pomeroy, Sarah B. 1975. *Goddesses, Whores, Wives, and Slaves: Women in Classical Antiquity*. New York: Schocken Books.

Rawson, Beryl. 1986. The Roman Family. In Beryl Rawson, ed., *The Family in Ancient Rome: New Perspectives*, pp. 1–57. Ithaca, NY: Cornell University Press.

Richlin, A. 1992. Julia's Jokes, Galla Placida, and the Roman Use of Women as Political Icons. In Barbara Garlick, Susanne Dixon, and Pauline Allen, eds., *Stereotypes of Women in Power: Historical Perspectives and Revisionist Views*, pp. 65–191. Westport, CT: Greenwood Press.

Rubin, Gayle. 1975. The Traffic in Women: Notes on the "Political Economy" of Sex. In Rayna Reiter, ed., *Toward an Anthropology of Women*, pp. 157–210. New York: Monthly Review Press.

Sacks, Karen. 1979. *Sisters and Wives: The Past and Future of Sexual Equality*. Westport, CT: Greenwood Press.

Saller, Richard P. 1991. Roman Heirship Strategies in Principle and in Practice. In David I. Kertzer and Richard P. Saller, eds., *The Family in Italy from Antiquity to the Present*, pp. 26–47. New Haven, CT: Yale University Press.

Schuler, Sidney Ruth. 1987. *The Other Side of Polyandry*. Boulder, CO: Westview Press.

Trawick, Margaret. 1990. *Notes on Love in a Tamil Family*. Berkeley: University of California Press.

Weiner, Annette B. 1976. *Women of Value, Men of Renown*. Austin: University of Texas Press.

7

A History of Euro-American Kinship and Gender

What characterizes Euro-American traditions in terms of kinship and gender? One central feature, first found in northwest Europe far back in time, is the idea that each marriage will establish a new independent economic unit and a neolocal residence. Regarding northwest Europe from 1350 to 1800, Beatrice Gottlieb (1993: 14) writes: "Every marriage there was regarded as an occasion for establishing a new household. It was assumed that nobody would get married until there was a place for the couple to live and a way for them to have a livelihood." This is quite different from the many other societies we have examined, where new wives or husbands are simply brought into larger economic units in which their labor is considered an asset.

Possibly this pattern is related to another distinctive feature of Europe, as compared to the rest of the world—namely, a relatively late age at marriage, especially for women (Hajnal 1965). Between 1350 and 1800 the average age of marriage was around twenty-five, though women were often a little younger and men usually a little older (Gottlieb 1993: 60). In Europe, dowries needed to be secured for daughters and land or a livelihood needed to be arranged for sons before a new viable economic unit could be set up. Age at marriage varied in time, by region, and by social class. Aristocrats tended to marry at younger ages; in eastern and southern Europe and in the colonial New World, age at marriage was lower than in northwest Europe; and in North America it remained lower until the twentieth century (Gottlieb 1993: 59). But for northwest Europe the later age had some important consequences: Women had fewer children, and couples entered marriage as mature adults.

Another frequently mentioned distinction, possibly related to these others, is that in the Western tradition, love becomes a fundamental part of marriage. Today, Euro-American marriages are not arranged by parents, and they are supposed to be based on mutual attraction, affection, and emotional com-mitment. Normally the purpose of these marriages is not to create political or social alliances, or to continue lines of descent, but to make individuals happy and fulfilled. If children are part of the picture, their purpose, too, is to make parents happy and fulfilled.

My own opinion is that this distinction has been somewhat overempha-sized, not in terms of the importance of love in Euro-American marriages but, rather, in terms of its alleged lack in other parts of the world. To be sure, in most of the cases we have seen so far, the inclinations of brides and grooms are subordinated to the interests of larger kin groups. But this is not to say that sexual attraction plays no role in marriage initiation, since it clearly did so among the Nuer and the Navajo, or that some kind of affection and com-patibility is not expected or at least hoped for in arranged marriage, as it is among the Nepalese Brahmans. What I have found is that in many cultural traditions there is some tension between the practical or sociopolitical di-mensions of marriage and its emotional dimensions. One problem with this issue—having specifically to do with the question of deciding just when love entered marriage in Europe—is that no one is quite sure what "love" should mean. Are we talking about "consensual union," as opposed to arranged marriage? Or are we referring to what some have called "companionate mar-riage"? Or does "love" necessarily imply passion and romance, exclusiveness and sexual jealousy? As we will see in this chapter, the Euro-American tra-dition has developed a strong ideal of marital love, but the nature and mean-ing of that love is not always easy to interpret.

Other features covered in this chapter concern the relatively restricted ties of kinship and lack of corporate descent groups in Euro-American soci-eties. Historians and anthropologists have offered varying ideas about the origins and implications of this pattern.

Finally, the chapter will show that in some respects, the Euro-American tradition of kinship and gender is not unique; in fact, it has shared many im-portant features with the Asian tradition (Goody 1993). One such feature is the differential evaluation of male and female sexual behavior, which I refer to simply as the "double sexual standard." Why in so many areas of Europe and Asia has there been such a concern with female premarital virginity (which must have been a particular challenge in Europe, given the late age at marriage for women)? Why in so many of these areas has the sexual be-havior of women reflected on the honor of male kin? Why has female sexu-ality, and not male sexuality, been seen in so many contexts as negative? Because the double sexual standard has been such a vital part of gender in Euro-American history and lingers on to the present day, this chapter begins with a discussion of ideas about how and why it may have developed. Specifi-cally, we will start with the work of anthropologist Jack Goody, who draws several links between European and Asian patterns of marriage.

DOWRY AND THE DOUBLE STANDARD

Goody (1973, 1976, 1993) has noted some general contrasts between the societies of sub-Saharan Africa and those of Europe and Asia (referred to collectively as "Eurasia"). In both cases he is talking about older, pre-industrial societies, rather than about practices in the early twenty-first century, although many of these traditions remain in some areas. Prominent among these contrasts was the widespread use of bridewealth in Africa and dowry in Eurasia. Recall that bridewealth is a marriage payment that passes from the kin of the groom to the kin of the bride. Eurasian dowry is wealth that parents bestow upon a daughter at her marriage. It is wealth that devolves (to use Goody's term) upon the bride, but its ultimate purpose is to serve as an economic resource for the new couple and, beyond that, to support and be inherited by the couple's children. Dowry, together with the property that a groom will bring into the marriage in the form of his inheritance, becomes what Goody calls a "conjugal fund." Seen in this way, bridewealth and dowry are not mirror opposites. The former ends up with the kin of the bride, and the latter ends up in a conjugal fund. However, the whole of a dowry need not be a conjugal fund. In some Eurasian societies, for example, certain dowry items (clothing, jewelry) are regarded as the bride's personal property, and other parts of a dowry may enrich not the bride or the couple but the groom's kin.

Other Eurasian societies practice a form of marriage payment whereby the groom's family gives goods or property to the bride (or it gives goods to her father, who then gives most of these to the bride). Some writers have referred to these goods as bridewealth or "brideprice," but Goody calls them "indirect dowry," since, like the type of dowry discussed above (which Goody calls "direct dowry"), the goods come to the marriage with the bride and become a part of the conjugal fund.

Goody then links this contrast between African bridewealth and Eurasian dowry (direct or indirect) to broad differences in agricultural practices and inheritance patterns between Africa and Eurasia. In Africa (at least before the economic changes caused by colonialism in the nineteenth century), agriculture was largely a matter of shifting cultivation, carried out with a hoe or digging stick. Women were active in this type of agricultural production, which was oriented toward subsistence (Boserup 1970). Land was relatively plentiful and was corporately controlled and used by kinship or residential groups. Perpetuating this economy over time was an African pattern of inheritance that Goody calls "homogeneous": Males inherited from males and females from females. Productive property was generally held by and transmitted between males. It may help at this point to think in terms of a patrilineal-patrilocal society where males of a patriline inherit corporate rights to land, which they prepare for cultivation. Females marry into these units and plant, weed, and so on. From their mothers, these women will inherit personal possessions. Productive property is in the hands of males, who are organized into corporate kin groups, but women play essential roles in production.

This kind of production and inheritance system has been found in, and is compatible with, societies that are not stratified into socioeconomic classes. Imagine a society like the Nuer (Case 2) that pays bridewealth in cattle. If one family or kin group produces a lot of daughters, it may become temporarily wealthy because it will receive cattle upon the marriages of the daughters. But who knows, in the next generation there may be a lot of sons, such that all this wealth moves out upon their marriages. With bridewealth, the cattle circulate, but they do not accumulate in one group. Hence bridewealth, tied as it is to the vagaries of the production of male and female children, works against the formation of true socioeconomic classes.

Goody sees the systems of production and bridewealth in the African situation as closely intertwined with African marriage forms. For one thing, he said, bridewealth facilitates polygyny. In cases where it takes some time for a family to amass enough wealth to pay out upon their sons' marriages, the males will marry relatively late. But the same family will be eager to marry its daughters, because doing so will bring in wealth that can then be used to pay the bridewealth of the sons. Thus the females will marry relatively early. It follows that husbands will tend to be older than wives. As people die off over time, older age cohorts will have fewer numbers than younger ones. In short, with this male/female difference in age at marriage, the surplus of marriageable women is built in: There will always be more females (in younger age cohorts) of marriage age than males (in older age cohorts), allowing at least some males to have multiple wives without depriving other males of a wife.

Goody thus links up such African features as hoe agriculture, lack of socioeconomic classes, bridewealth, and polygyny. Let us now take a look at the Eurasian dowry situation along similar dimensions. Here the economy was quite different, in that it was predominantly based on plow agriculture. This form of agriculture increased productivity; fostered population growth; made land a more important but, with greater population density, a less abundant commodity; and ultimately promoted the rise of the state and the formation of socioeconomic classes. Some groups grew powerful and leisured while others became dependent workers. Thus, as plow agriculture was adopted in different regions, Eurasian societies became class-stratified. Control of land (a scarce resource) became a primary basis of status. Differences between families or status groups were rooted in differences in landholding. "Consequently it became a strategy of utmost importance to preserve those differences for one's offspring, lest the family and its fortunes decline over time" (Goody 1973: 25). The upper classes now had property and wealth to protect and pass on. These class divisions and the wealth within the upper classes were maintained by the practice of class endogamy, or what Goody calls "status group endogamy." The wealthy and privileged carefully arranged marriages within their own ranks to ensure that their children would enjoy the same or better status and wealth in the next generation.

How did this Eurasian system work? Goody claims that it worked through the development of what he calls "diverging devolution," an inheritance pattern whereby property or wealth goes to both males and females—say, from one estate to both daughters and sons. Sons receive their portions (usually land) by becoming direct heirs; daughters receive their portions (usually movable property and cash) in the form of dowries at marriage. To maintain class endogamy, parents need only look for a match between a prospective bride's dowry and a prospective groom's inheritance. Indeed, it is this match of property or wealth that lies behind the English expression of marriage "as a 'match,' a word that implies the pairing of like to like" (Goody 1976: 14).

Class endogamy does not mean that everyone marries an exact equal. In Europe, for example, parents were only too pleased to marry a son or daughter into a slightly wealthier or higher-status family, seeing this achievement as enhancing their own status. "Marriage into another social group was, in fact, the recognized path of social mobility in this rigidly stratified world" (Gottlieb 1993: 58). Moreover, in areas of India, hypergamy, or marriage of a woman upward into a higher group, was the norm. Hypergamous marriages have also been a theme of European myth and folklore, as in the story of Cinderella. But throughout Eurasia a general class endogamy was maintained, and wide gaps in the status of husband and wife were rare and usually denounced.

Thus dowry marriage became an instrument of class endogamy. And further, according to Goody, just as bridewealth promoted polygyny, so dowry promoted monogamy. Today monogamy is the primary form of marriage throughout Eurasia, even though some Asian societies permit polygyny. Dowry promotes monogamy because, along with the groom's inheritance, it establishes a "conjugal fund" that will ultimately go to the couple's children. It would be difficult and complicated to merge additional wives' dowries into the fund and to sort out the inheritance rights of the separate sets of children of these women. When the conjugal fund is combined with monogamy, the husband-wife bond becomes strengthened and the relationship more solid and intimate. This arrangement contrasts with the African bridewealth-polygyny pattern, whereby husbands and wives are more independent of each other.

The Eurasian type of economy, based on plow agriculture, also brought a profound change in sexual divisions of labor. Essentially, women's roles in production decreased whereas male labor became vital to agriculture. Ester Boserup (1970: 51) had early on made the point that under hoe agriculture women were valued as workers and as child bearers, whereas in systems of plow agriculture they were valued only as mothers. Of course, in the upper classes, everyone was withdrawn from production since agricultural labor, depending on the period in question, was performed by slaves, serfs, or hired laborers. But upper-class men had important economic roles as landowners and managers, whereas upper-class women, with some exceptions in certain times and places, did not.

With this understanding of plow agriculture, social classes, and Eurasian marriages, Goody's analysis moves us deeper into the issue of gender. A key point, following Goody's thinking, is that perpetuation of the class system through class endogamy requires that property devolve upon women. Specifically, dowry must be given to a daughter to attract a husband of appropriate rank; the dowry is used to "match" what the prospective groom stands to inherit from his family. With a dowry, then, a woman is not merely inheriting personal items from her mother; she is now dowered, and can take a chunk of family wealth with her to her marriage. One might suppose that this arrangement was advantageous to women, or that it was gender equalizing, since both males and females would have brought wealth to a marriage. But in fact women did not benefit.

Since family property was at stake in Eurasian dowry marriages, parents carefully arranged the unions of their offspring. We may presume that, since males were usually a little older at marriage than females and were seen as more responsible, they had more say in arranging their own marriages. But regarding Eurasian women in this system, Goody (1973: 21) writes that "it is a commentary on their lot that where they are more propertied they are initially less free as far as marital arrangements go." This statement, which sounds a bit indifferent to women's plight, covers only a part of the difference between men and women in dowry systems. Later in his work Goody hints at what I think is really at stake—namely, a difference between men and women in terms of not only marital but also sexual freedom.

Goody writes that, just as it became important to control marriages to perpetuate status-group endogamy, so it became important to control the premarital activities of offspring as well—hence the use of chaperones and the many restrictions on young people's behavior to ensure that marriageable children did not form inappropriate attachments on their own. As Goody (1976: 17) further notes, one way to prevent inappropriate attachments from forming was to "place a high positive value on premarital virginity, for sex before marriage could diminish a girl's honor, and reduce her marriage chances." But why was just the girl's honor diminished and just her marriage chances reduced?

Alice Schlegel (1991: 345) raises similar questions about Goody's statement, saying that we can accept it at face value only if we assume an innate male preference for virgins; otherwise, the statement takes for granted precisely what we need to explain. Schlegel then goes on to posit her own answer to the question of why it is *female* premarital virginity that is guarded, valued, or insisted upon, at least among the upper classes in Eurasian dowry systems. She argues that a girl's virginity had to be protected to prevent her from being impregnated by a lower-class man, a man who, claiming to be the father of her child, might demand a right to her (and hence her property) in marriage. Premarital sex for males, then, for the simple reason that males do not get pregnant or give birth, was not nearly as great a threat to the system. It is interesting to note that, in Schlegel's argument, the social concern is not that a daughter will produce children out of wedlock, or that she will produce illegitimate children as such, but rather that her premarital sexuality could open a way for an undesirable (lower-class) male to stake a claim to her family's property.

The work of both Goody and Schlegel provides an insight into that most important element of Eurasian gender, one very familiar to all of us as it lingers on in Euro-American society: the double sexual standard. It's a little grim to think that, throughout all these centuries, Eurasian women themselves complied with, or even enforced, the double standard, only to wind up as the tools by which the privileged perpetuated the class system and socioeconomic inequality.

Possibly the whole complex of Eurasian cultural values centering on female "purity," including the notion that the honor of kin groups rests on the sexual purity of its women, is related to the institution of dowry as an instrument for preserving and perpetuating socioeconomic classes. Indeed, Schlegel (1991) holds that the value placed on female premarital virginity acquired "secondary meanings" in Eurasia, culminating in an emphasis on female marital chastity, discouragement of widow remarriage, and the view that celibacy is spiritually higher than marital sex—all factors we will encounter in the next section as we look at European traditions.

Others, too, criticize Goody's work on Eurasian dowry. Some point out that in certain cases, such as in India, dowry is not considered female property, or property devolving on women, since women have no control over the use and distribution of their dowries (Stone and James 1995). Others contend that it is oversimplifying to treat societies as though they have only one type of marriage transaction when in fact many societies have multiple kinds of such transactions (Huber, Danaher, and Breedlove 2011). Caroline Brettell (1991) shows that there is a great variation in actual marriage payments and inheritance practices in Mediterranean Europe, challenging the broad pattern that Goody tries to draw. She also observes that dowry may be determined not by inheritance interests but by cultural ideas about gender, such as the cultural notion that men are under obligation to provide for women.

Other explanations of the double sexual standard have been offered as well. Sherry Ortner (1978), for example, discussed what she termed the "female purity ethic," the cultural idea that the honor of a social group rests on the purity of its women—that is, on female virginity and chastity. Unlike Goody, she emphasized not changes in agricultural production but the rise of the state, which was based on those changes. The rise of the state was interwoven with class stratification and led to changes in the division of labor, religious thought, family structure, and marriage patterns. Ortner outlined the ways in which all these developments may have contributed to the female purity ethic, but she gave most weight to changes in marriage patterns, focusing in particular on the factor of hypergamy, or marriage of a woman into a higher-status group. She based her argument on the assumption that hypergamy is an ideal, if not an actuality, in premodern state societies.

Ortner noted that families in class-stratified societies seek to marry their daughters "up" to enhance their own status through this link by marriage. Even when and where hypergamy was not easily achieved or at all common, it was a social ideal. But for daughters to be married upward, their value needed to be enhanced. This, Ortner wrote, is why dowry developed: to enhance the value of daughters so as to make them worthy of marriage to higher-status spouses. Similarly, a daughter's virginity enhanced her value "because virginity is a symbol of exclusiveness and inaccessibility. . . . A virgin is an elite female among females, withheld, untouched, exclusive" (Ortner 1978: 32). Women themselves are drawn into the whole hypergamy ideal. They want to marry up as Cinderella did; their culture encourages them to fantasize that "someday my prince will come" (Ortner 1978: 32).

In Ortner's view, it is not just that a daughter's virginity guards the honor of the kin group; indeed, females in this system also come to represent the higher classes. They represent what everyone wants and at the same time hates others for having: higher status. This, Ortner (1978: 32) said, may account for the "anger toward women expressed in these purity patterns."

Ortner's ideas are compelling but her argument breaks down precisely where, according to Schlegel, Goody's analysis falls down. The idea that a daughter's virginity enhances her value is considered a given by both Ortner and Goody; it once again assumes some "innate preference" for virgins. (As noted, Schlegel argues that it takes for granted exactly what we want to explain.) In saying that a virgin is "withheld, untouched, exclusive," Ortner merely restates the issue. Why would males necessarily prefer brides who are "withheld, untouched, exclusive"? Why doesn't a little sexual experience enhance the value of brides instead? And why is it that virgin brides are seen as "enhanced" in some stateless societies as well as within states?[1]

At least in Ortner's scheme, female compliance with the double standard is a little more understandable. Goody held that dowry promotes status-group endogamy and so maintains the class system; Schlegel's idea was that female virginity protects the family estate from seductive lower-class fortune hunters. In these models, women—who themselves uphold and cater to the double standard, or the female purity ethic—emerge as mere tools by which the upper classes maintain and transmit their hegemony. But in Ortner's analysis, women uphold the purity ethic for another reason. They want to marry hypergamously; after all, it is by this means that they and their children will rise in status and enjoy a higher standard of living. In Ortner's model, women may be crass materialists and status seekers, but at least it is their own motives and interests that play a role in maintaining the status quo.

Despite their different approaches and the occasional flaws in their arguments, Goody, Schlegel, and Ortner have all drawn a connection between the widespread double sexual standard and the equally widespread concern with social status. The emphasis on female premarital chastity (at least among the upper ranks) and the notion that the honor of a family or kin group depends on the sexual purity of its women are, according to these three authors, interrelated with issues of maintaining and transmitting status and wealth. Their work, especially that of Goody (1993), draws attention to what Euro-American cultures share with those of Asia in terms of kinship and gender. Whether we assume an "innate preference for virgins" or agree with Schlegel that the female purity ethic was connected to avoiding lower-class fortune hunters, the fact remains that Eurasian societies placed new burdens on men and women to monitor and control women's sexual behavior. Eurasian women had important connections to property, but they lost sexual autonomy and their behavior was subjected to a different standard than that applied to men. Thus the work of Goody and Schlegel addresses a question raised in Chapter 3 relating to a comparison between the Nuer and the Nepalese Brahmans—namely, why do some societies develop concerns for female sexual purity? The ideas of Goody and Schlegel place this issue in a broad regional and historical perspective and draw out the important interrelationships between gender and class inequalities.

From its Eurasian roots, the Euro-American system took some new turns of its own. In the following sections we will trace these changes as they occurred, first in Europe and then in North America.

FROM THE MIDDLE AGES TO MODERN TIMES

We saw in the last chapter that Roman society had become largely bilateral by the fall of the Roman Empire. So, too, had many Germanic tribes that invaded Rome; some groups were already Christian as well. However, some of the Germanic tribes may have been patrilineal. As we know, these groups settled in the former Western Empire and developed a new culture that drew from Roman, Christian, and Germanic influences. Later in some parts of Europe, and among the aristocracy, patrilineal descent groups developed and persisted for a time, but the vast majority of Europe's people experienced a weakening of kinship groups altogether.

There may have been different forms of marriage payments (bridewealth, indirect dowry) early on in the region, but gradually a shift to full direct dowry took place throughout Europe (McNamara and Wemple 1988; Hughes

1978). As for marriage, the Germanic practice of polygyny persisted through the early Middle Ages among peoples such as the Anglo-Saxons and, at least among the ruling classes, the Franks (Wemple 1981). For example, Merovingian and Carolingian kings were polygynous. And even after the Christian church managed to impose monogamy on Europe's monarchs, the keeping of mistresses and concubines continued, often quite openly, among royalty and nobility. Among the Germanic peoples, husbands, but not wives, also had relatively easy access to divorce (Herlihy 1985: 51)—a situation that persisted until the eleventh century, when the church managed to make marriage indissoluble.

Bilateral societies, strict monogamy, and dowry characterized Europe, and later the European New World, for many centuries. Only in the past two centuries has one of these features, dowry, declined in importance and practice. But what was kinship like for these European peoples? How were their views and practices regarding kinship interrelated with gender? And in what ways did kinship and gender change over time?

Some readers may be surprised to learn that in certain respects, and for most classes of people, there has been very little change at all. During much of the Middle Ages and up to the 1800s, most men and women of Europe married in their middle to late twenties, raised only a few children, and lived in small nuclear families (though their households may have contained servants and other nonkin). The variation in family forms in Europe has occurred not so much over time as between classes and regions. For example, it was only among the small upper classes that large extended families lived in one household.

It is a myth that the small, nuclear family either helped to precipitate or was itself fostered by the Industrial Revolution; in fact, it was a well-established norm long before the 1800s.[2] Moreover, as Gottlieb (1993: 13) notes, "The outstanding fact about the nuclear family households is that all through the past in the Western world, no matter where we look or how far back we go in time, they were extremely common."

Yet, other aspects of family life and gender did undergo transformations in Europe. Undoubtedly an important force in shaping European kinship and gender was the Christian church. For one thing, Christianity presented a revolutionary new message: Sex, for both men and women, is equally unspiritual and, outside marriage, equally sinful. The view of the early church was that lifelong celibacy among both men and women was the highest state. Marital sex was accepted, but only because it helped to avoid fornication. Many early Christians responded to this message by entering celibate religious orders; others attempted "continent marriage," whereby man and wife would live together but resist the temptations of the flesh. Of course, such an arrangement, if successfully practiced, would deny them children, but this was an age of religious fervor in which St. Augustine had proclaimed that the Second

Coming of Christ would not be served by procreation, and in which it was popularly felt that the world was already worn out, overcrowded, and straining its resources (Herlihy 1985: 24).

Another interesting response to the Christian glorification of celibacy was "spiritual marriage," whereby unmarried virgins (called *agapetae*) lived with male clergy as the spiritual wives of these men. Not surprisingly, this arrangement, widely practiced between A.D. 100 and 500, came under suspicion of church leaders and was later pronounced heretical. The official Christian ideas about sexuality ultimately held firm. Celibacy, praised for all, was mandatory for clergy. Marital sex was permissible (indeed, sex came to be defined as a marital duty), but human lust was bad, both for men and women, and both outside and inside marriage.

Christian theology may have downgraded sex, but at least it did so equally for men and women. And yet the double standard lived on. In fact, as far as the law was concerned, it grew, reaching a peak around 1800 (Gottlieb 1993: 100). Throughout the Middle Ages and into the modern period, a wife could be repudiated by her husband for adultery, or punished in court. But confronted with her husband's infidelities, she was expected to look the other way and had no legal recourse against him. Thus Christian Europe retained the attitudes of pagan Rome regarding adultery (Clark 1993: 39), and it likewise retained the association between the honor of a family and the chastity of its daughters and wives (Gottlieb 1993: 100).

There were other ideas at work here, too—ideas that bolstered the double sexual standard. These concern the ambivalent male images of women that have come down to us in the art and literature of the period. On the one hand, women were feared and blamed as sexual temptresses. Because the unholy but powerful force of human sexuality was believed to reside in women, they were seen as sexually charged and out of control. This comes very close to the view of women as inherently more sexual than men, and as having very little control over their own impulses, that we saw among the Nepalese Brahmans, discussed in Chapter 3. In Europe this image of women was attached to the biblical Eve, who tempted Adam away from God's command. On the other hand, women were idolized as good and pure and so were identified with the Virgin Mary. Mary was the ideal woman. But of course no mortal woman could actually be like Mary, who encompassed both virginity and motherhood. A married, and thus nonvirgin, woman was particularly vulnerable to these ambivalent male views. As Gottlieb (1993: 100–101) comments, "The awful thing about married women was that, once they had sexual experience, the floodgates might open and the potential Eve in every woman might emerge. Men seem to have been both repelled and fascinated by this possibility."

Although Christianity opposed the double sexual standard, Christian teaching affirmed the subordination of wives to husbands. We may recall what the Apostle Paul wrote:

Wives, be subject to your husbands, as to the Lord. For the husband is the head
of the wife as Christ is head of the church. . . . As the church is subject to Christ,
so let wives also be subject in everything to their husbands. . . . A man shall leave
his father and mother, and shall be joined to his wife, and the two shall become
one. . . . Let each one of you love his wife as himself, and let the wife see that
she respects her husband. (Ephesians 5:22–33)

Thus husbands were to love wives, and spouses were to be "one," but
within this unity the divinely sanctioned authority of the husband is clear.
Gottlieb (1993: 91) refers to the proper attitude of European husbands as
one of "loving despotism." This attitude was supported by the social and
legal fact that "when a woman married, her identity was swallowed up in
her husband's." Disobedient wives were disparaged as "shrews," and "there
were laws all over Europe giving men the right to beat their wives" (Gottlieb
1993: 92).

Just as official Christian teaching lost out to a double sexual standard as
it filtered through real society, medieval women apparently lost ground on
other fronts as well. In the early and high Middle Ages, the absence of males
(who had gone off to wars and the Crusades) left upper-class women to manage estates on their own, perhaps giving them an independence similar to
that of Roman women during the Punic Wars. But later, in most of Europe,
changes in law and inheritance practice considerably restricted women's ability to accumulate property (Herlihy 1985: 100).

Women's role in medicine was likewise restricted. Women had been active
in healing, particularly in midwifery, but this potential could not develop because medical training moved into the universities, from which women were
excluded (Williams and Echols 1994: 43). Moreover, in the medieval towns
where a class of rich merchants grew, women initially played active economic
roles. But later the merchant guilds excluded women, and by the 1400s they
predominated in the lower-paying, less prestigious jobs, much as they did
throughout the twentieth century and beyond.

In an early study, Herlihy (1971) noted the effects on women of the Gregorian reform (1073–1085) that banned marriage of the Catholic clergy. Before this reform was enacted, marriage of the clergy was common, though
long officially discouraged by the Church. Also common were monasteries
containing both men and women, and, as noted earlier, the virgin agapetae
were "spiritually married" to clergy. But all of these practices disappeared
after the reform. Men continued in their religious roles, albeit more celibately,
but what effect did the reform have on women? As Herlihy (1971: 9–10) described it:

The Gregorian reform of the medieval Church . . . seems to have lowered the
status of women, by virtually excluding them from one of the most powerful

elite groups in society. . . . In the battle for clerical celibacy, the leaders of the reformed Church nurtured an exaggerated fear of women. . . . This hostility towards women went on to influence other institutions of society, most notably the schools and the new universities. With some notable exceptions, the world of formal scholarship in the Middle Ages was a bastion of male chauvinism, and this particular tradition has been slow in dying.

Although European society was bilateral, there was a patrilineal twist in the system that emerged in several contexts. When the use of last names became common (around the mid-1300s), they were transmitted from fathers to children, and wives adopted the last names of husbands. Women received dowries, but inheritance otherwise favored sons. (In the absence of sons, however, a daughter might have inherited property.) In most regions the dowry was under the husband's control for the duration of the marriage. A woman could not ordinarily sell or alienate either this dowry or property she inherited from a deceased husband, as both were destined to be inherited by her children.

Above all, at least in the upper classes, there was a patrilineal ideology— a widely expressed feeling that sons, and not daughters, carried on the "line" by continuing the family name and serving as its heirs. For this reason the birth of sons was often favored over that of daughters. Indeed, this was always the case where royal succession was concerned. Daughters may have been particularly unwelcome during the period of dowry inflation, in the thirteenth century. The transition from indirect dowry to direct dowry shifted the "burden of matrimony" from the groom's family to the bride's family (Herlihy 1985: 98). But the burden grew until

> poets and preachers protested the rising costs of marriage, which the bride and her family were forced to meet. In the early fourteenth century Dante remarked in *The Divine Comedy* that the size of dowries was exceeding all reasonable measure, and he harkened back to better days, in the eleventh and twelfth centuries, when the birth of a daughter did not strike terror in her father's heart. (Herlihy 1985: 99)

This situation became a major social problem. Many females were unable to marry at all for lack of adequate dowry. Convents were able to absorb some of them, but even this remedy had its limits, and in any case, convents also required dowries (albeit lesser ones) from the girls they took. Providing dowries for otherwise unmarriageable girls became a major focus of Christian charity during this period (Herlihy 1985: 99).

Part of the problem behind dowry inflation was precisely that dowries were used to express the social status of the brides' families. In short, the momentum was driven by the status-seeking of the brides' families, not by the quest of the grooms' families to enrich themselves (Gottlieb 1993: 222).

Along with preserving or enhancing their status through the marriage of daughters, Europeans of the propertied classes were concerned with transmitting their property and status over the generations. There were many different patterns of inheritance, but the central issue was: How can estates be transmitted intact over time, given that each generation may produce a number of sons? One solution was primogeniture, or inheritance by only the eldest son. This arrangement was used in parts of northern Europe and was particularly favored by England. Primogeniture preserved an estate intact, but it did not address the problem of what to do with younger sons. Not being heirs, they were obviously poor marriage prospects. Some went off to religious orders or to fight in the Crusades; others went off to become fortune hunters in search of an heiress with no brothers. Still others simply remained behind to work on their older brother's estate.

In the southern part of Europe it was more common to divide estates equally among sons, but a drawback, of course, was that estates would be fragmented. One way to guard against this outcome, or to lessen its effects over time, was to adopt a practice we encountered in the last chapter: kin-group endogamy. In this case, two brothers, as equal heirs, could split an estate in one generation, but if the daughter of one married the son of the other, the property would come back to the original estate in the next generation. In a similar way, occasional marriages between second cousins, third cousins, and so on could help keep property consolidated within a kin group.

In parts of Italy, where property was usually divided equally among sons, yet another development occurred. Brothers sometimes kept their property together in a system of communal ownership. Over time, this system encompassed true corporate patrilineal descent groups. Some of these Italian *consorteria*, as they were called, developed a solid patrilineal solidarity, expressed by adopting a lineage name and a coat of arms, as well as by offering prayers for their ancestors in the groups' own corporately owned family chapels. Others became powerful merchant groups in cities. By legal contract they admitted some nondescent members into their corporations and went on to found banks and commercial companies that ultimately played a great role in the economic transformation of Italy during the Middle Ages.

Elsewhere in Europe, nobility formed patrilineal descent groups that likewise developed names and coats of arms. But none of these latter groups persisted for very long or set the pace for the modern age. Europe embarked instead on another path, leading away from descent groups or large kin groups of any kind. Indeed, the overall thrust of European history was toward a breaking down of the wider ties of kinship, a paring back until only ego-centric kindreds and restricted sets of relatives remained. This was a distinct trend, one that clearly established the first patterns of kinship and gender among Europeans in North America. But how and why did such patterns come about?

THE RISE OF THE CHRISTIAN CHURCH

Anthropologists have tried to answer this question in different ways. Robin Fox (1993: 143–144) suggests that the wider ties of European kinship were broken down with the rise of the modern state. The state, in turn, works through bureaucracy and binding contracts, not through ties of "blood" or alliances made through marriage. And since it requires the loyalty of its citizens, it would be threatened by a people's higher loyalties to powerful kin groups. According to Fox, the state can and does tolerate small families, but this is as far as it will go.

A more intriguing, though also more controversial, answer to the same question comes from Goody (1983), whose work on dowry we have already reviewed. Goody claims that the real force behind the breakdown of wider ties of kinship in Europe was the Christian church. As Christianity rose in Europe, moving from its status as a minor sect to that of a fully organized and eventually very powerful church, kinship groups declined, having failed to develop and flourish as corporate units. The reason, according to Goody, is that the church sought to acquire property and wealth. The success of its quest is, of course, well documented. But in the beginning the church had no wealth and needed funds to establish itself and to conduct its ecclesiastical and charitable activities. How did it achieve this end, and what connection existed between church wealth and European kinship? Goody argues that to encourage bequests and other donations from its followers, the church sought to sever the hold that kin groups had on property. To this end it instituted "reforms" in marriage and other practices that ultimately broke down kin groups and ties between kin in Europe.

Starting in the fourth century, the church explicitly introduced a number of changes in the lives of its members. Specifically, it attempted to ban such practices as polygyny, clerical marriage, cousin marriage, adoption, the levirate, divorce, and concubinage, to name just the major ones. A ban on close-cousin marriage began in the fourth century; by the eleventh century, the prohibition had been extended to cover all persons related consanguineally within seven generations.[3] The church successfully discouraged adoption until the Reformation. It also banned the levirate in the fourth century; indeed, it banned marriage to the widow or widower of any close kin, as well as marriage to a dead spouse's sibling. Finally, the church strongly discouraged men from taking concubines.

All of these banned or discouraged practices, says Goody, had one thing in common: They were *strategies of heirship*. All of them involved the passing of property from one generation to the next, and most of them involved ways of doing this *within the kinship group*. In earlier chapters we saw how a man can use polygyny, for example, to increase the number of his heirs or, if a first wife is infertile, to produce an heir. We also saw that divorce, with remarriage, can be used by childless married men and women to test their fertility in other unions and so potentially acquire children and heirs. The Nuer, as noted in Chapter 3, made use of both of these strategies. And the levirate, another option among the Nuer, can be used to keep a woman's fertility (her ability to produce heirs) in her husband's kinship group. In this chapter and the last one, we also saw how parallel-cousin marriage, or endogamy within a kin group, works to keep property intact and under the control of the kin group as it moves over the generations.

What the church did, then, was to ban or discourage such practices to lessen the use of these handy means of promoting the production of heirs. Thus, in situations where people had property but no heir, they could be persuaded to give the property to the church. If a married man found his union to be childless, well, instead of trying polygyny, adoption, or divorce and remarriage, he could stay childless and bequeath his property to the church upon his death.

Similarly, the church not only banned the levirate but discouraged the remarriage of widows to anyone. Widows reclaimed control of their dowries; if they were childless, they could also gain control of their husband's property. If they remarried, their property would go into another marriage. But if they did not, it could be given to the church. Indeed, the church readily took widows (with their property) into nunneries, cared for them, and made them caretakers of others, such as orphans. It is also true that a significant proportion of the early converts to Christianity were women and that women were the largest donors of property to the church (Herlihy 1962).

When viewed in this way, many of the church's policies make a new kind of sense, one in keeping with the motive of property acquisition. Goody claims, for example, that the ban on clerical marriage, though it did not bring in property, nevertheless prevented church property from seeping out, since the celibate clergy would not have been tempted to use church wealth to provision their own wives and children.

According to Goody, some of the church's moves, such as its ban on polygyny and divorce, were aimed at increasing heirlessness—by reducing the number of people who had claims, by kinship, to property. The church's policies on concubines would have had this effect, too. Earlier a man could name his children by a concubine as his heirs; now, as decreed by the church, these claims were taken away. In Goody's (1983: 77) words, "under Christianity, the concubine became the mistress and her children bastards."

Other of the church's moves appear to have been aimed not at increasing heirlessness as such but at loosening the hold of kin groups on property—that is, by finding ways to prevent property from staying within kin groups over the generations. Of course, whatever the church could do to place a wedge between kin groups and property, it did to its own material advantage, since any such loosened property could more easily wind up in church coffers.

Goody (1983: 45) puts it best: "If they [the church's prohibitions] inhibited the possibilities of a family retaining its property, then they would also facilitate its alienation." In essence, the church wanted persuadable *individuals*, not powerful *corporate kin groups*, to have control over property and to make uncontested decisions about its ultimate destination. Marriage between cousins or between certain degrees of consanguineal kin was banned, then, precisely because such marriages promoted the consolidation of estates and their undivided inheritance within kinship groups.

With the ban on cousin marriage, the church seemed to win out on two fronts. First, the ban gradually helped break up property. Second, for centuries to come, people (especially those in the upper classes) were able to marry their cousins anyway, simply by paying for dispensations from the church, which further increased church wealth (Goody 1983: 146).

The church fought for and eventually gained control over marriages in general. It won its battles against kin-group endogamy and divorce, and increasingly influenced the marriage ceremony. More and more it came to define not only who could or could not marry whom but what marriage itself should mean. In 1439, marriage became the seventh Sacrament.

In this process the church came to define marriage as based on the consent of the partners rather than on the arrangement of the parents. Thus a consensual union made in defiance of parents was still valid in the eyes of the church.[4] Again, this position was in the material interests of the church since it eroded kin groups' control over property transmission, as exercised by the older generation through its arrangement of the younger generation's marriages. This point is significant because it suggests how a particular Western idea—that love should be a basis for marriage—may have been promoted. Goody claims that another distinctive feature of the modern Western family—its "child-oriented" nature—was also linked to the church (1983: 153). The church did encourage a strong mother-child bond—for example, by discouraging wet-nursing and glorifying the Madonna and Child in art.

In Goody's view, the church fought against and conquered many "strategies of heirship" that were previously prominent in Europe. This action of the church then fostered the very set of traits (such as monogamy, love matches, and lack of corporate kin groups) that came to distinguish the European pattern of kinship and marriage from the pattern that remained in Asia. Indeed, Goody groups these traits within a single frame, one grounded in a single cause: the material acquisitiveness of the Christian church. In support of this claim, he presents a wealth of historical evidence.

Some critics, uncomfortable with this image of the church as a single-minded pursuer of property, question whether the church leaders could have been so consistently farsighted and cunning over so many centuries or, for that matter, so materialistic and manipulative in the first place (Verdery 1988;

IMAGE 7.1   The strong mother-child bond became a theme often represented in art in the Western tradition.

Le Berceau ("The Cradle," 1872) was painted by a French woman impressionist, Berthe Morisot. Plate courtesy of the Musée d'Orsay, Paris.

Herlihy 1985: 13). Goody (1983: 57) does point out that the church leaders never couched their policies in such terms; instead they gave moral or practical explanations for their position. For example, marriage within a range of consanguineal kin was prohibited not in the name of breaking up property but for the moral reason that consanguineal kin should be respectful of one another and not intimate, or for the practical reason that marrying more distantly would widen the social net of alliances.

But then we must ask: Did the church leaders even know what they were up to? On this point, Goody (1983: 215) himself seems not entirely sure:

It may seem that I have allocated the Church a rather calculating role in the development of kinship. But when I refer to the Church acting in its own interest, I do not necessarily mean that the whole Church was monolithically engaged in consciously promoting those interests. . . . [Rather] I am talking about the means by which ends are achieved, whether or not those means are aspects of the actor's intention. . . . But in the long run I do assume some kind of relationship between actions and interests.

However the church's rulings on marriage came about, Goody also points out how the church fostered notions of a new "spiritual kinship," almost as though it realized that it needed to give back to its people something of what it had ripped away from them. God was the Father, and priests became "fathers"; members became "brothers" and "sisters"; and so on. On top of this, the church created a new, special category of fictive kin called "godparents" that created new ties between people. These ties did not involve property and, in the absence of adoption, which was discouraged, they provided some security to children in the event that they were orphaned.

Another critic of Goody's ideas is historian Richard Saller (1991), who points out that some of what Goody considers to have been new marriage practices urged by the Christian church were not really new at all; for example, Roman society also was strictly monogamous and did not practice the levirate.

An even more challenging criticism has come from Michel Verdon (1988), who essentially turns Goody's argument on its head. His thesis is that European kinship, far from being the result of church acquisitiveness, came about as "a strategy of female emancipation!" (1988: 488). He notes, as did Goody, that many of the early Christian converts were women and that many of the bequests to the church over the early centuries were made by women. But Verdon (1988: 500) then charges that Goody's thesis characterizes women as powerless victims, as "people who are acted upon instead of people who are capable of deciding for themselves, capable of understanding their own interests and acting accordingly."

Next, Verdon takes up the question of the development of European kinship. He asks not why and how the church pursued women's property but, rather, why women wanted to give their property to the church. His answer is that what women saw in Christianity was *freedom*—namely, freedom from marriage and reproduction. This was what the new religion of Christianity offered, and what no other major religion had offered before: the freedom to choose to marry or not. Some religions, he notes, prescribed celibacy for a priesthood, "but no church openly stated that the ideal life was a *life outside marriage*, not for a chosen few, but for everyone" (1988: 493; original emphasis).

The church freed women through its praise of lifelong celibacy as the highest state and, for weaker people, through its praise of chastity; in other words, it took the core position that, where possible, "the less sex the better" (1988: 496). As we saw before, the early church deemed sex to be decidedly unspiritual: It was best to choose lifelong celibacy, but since many ordinary people could not, they should at least marry to avoid fornication. Indeed, as the Apostle Paul had written, "But if they cannot exercise self-control they should marry. For it is better to marry than to be aflame with passion" (1 Corinthians 7:9). Even within marriage, sex was excusable only as a means for reproduction. Carnal desire—again, even within marriage—was bad. And celibacy and chastity, like conversion to Christianity itself, were matters that had to be freely chosen by individuals. In effect, Christianity promoted individual free choice over both religion and sex.

From this core position on sex followed many of the church's new policies on marriage. For example, as noted, the church came to define marriage as based on the consent of the partners rather than on the arrangement or permission of the parents. And the free choice of partners, Verdon argues, logically followed from the free choice to marry or not. In the same way, both the ban on marriages between close kin and the ban on the levirate can be interpreted as means of freeing women from social pressure to marry—that is, as means of freeing them from being pressured by their kin into unions they did not want.

Why did women find liberation in the choice to marry or not? Verdon (1988: 503) provides an answer:

> In circumstances where reproduction is not controlled and women do not have equal access to labour opportunities, to wealth and means of production, women remain above all child-bearers and child-carers. This is precisely where Christianity struck, and why it had such appeal for women. It offered women an ideal life free of child-bearing and child-caring, and free of their subordination to reproduction and, indirectly, to men. . . . Freedom from men could only come from freedom from reproduction; and freedom from reproduction, from freedom from sex. . . . If the Church saw its profit in women's property, women saw their own profit in virginity and church-assisted widowhood.

Thus, many women saw in Christianity a sanctioned alternative to the reproductive roles that were otherwise imposed upon them and immersed them in subordination to men. In this way, Verdon draws close ties among European kinship, gender, and religion. These ties are strengthened in his discussion of adoption, which, he points out, was not so much banned by the church as discouraged. Adoption largely disappeared as a European practice over the centuries, and the reason it did so, according to Verdon, is that, with the conversion to Christianity, the ancestral cult disappeared. In earlier Roman society, he notes, "the spiritual salvation of any man . . . depended entirely on his leaving descendants to perform this cult . . . since . . . the soul left without anyone to look after it is condemned to eternal damnation" (1988: 497). Thus men without male descendants to perform the ancestral rites adopted other men as heirs, leaving their property in return for this service. But when Christianity took hold, adoption was no longer necessary; now that salvation was a matter of the individual soul, it no longer depended on reproduction. It was this change that allowed Christianity to assert a new equality between the sexes: "Christianity established an absolute equality between the sexes from the spiritual point of view since spiritual salvation no longer rested on the ability to produce a line of sons" (1988: 498).

In valuing neither marriage nor reproduction, early Christianity was liberating to women, but what about men? What was in it for them? Verdon writes that the church offered men, as husbands, domination over wives: "Once women chose marriage, the Church then advocated submission to their husbands. There was thus enough in it for men" (1988: 504).

Historians and anthropologists may disagree about how the European pattern of kinship and gender emerged, but many, including both Goody and Verdon, trace it to and through the Christian church. Goody holds that material conditions (namely, the economic interests of the church) were the prime movers, whereas Verdon holds that Christian ideology and its appeal to women paved the way. In Goody's view, male clergy were in command and women remained fairly passive, perhaps guilelessly losing their money, whereas in Verdon's scheme women were assertive, self-interested actors. It is also possible that parts of both views are true. But in opposition to Verdon we should note that if women used Christianity for their own liberation, it was a strategy that ultimately did not work. Most women ended up married, with children and dominating husbands, in a society that stressed the double standard. Those who opted for a life of celibacy were secluded from society.

In the end, what did emerge was a European pattern that saw the breakdown of kin groups and stressed monogamy, marital permanence, and marital love. Concomitant developments included class endogamy, dowry, and a relatively late age of marriage. What happened, then, when this pattern was transferred to the shores of North America?

THE NORTH AMERICAN EXPERIENCE

Just as Gottlieb (1993) and others assert that families of the European past were in some ways not so different from modern ones, Stephanie Coontz (1992) makes a similar point regarding North American families. Coontz argues that people in the United States nostalgically look back to a past that never was, that we have created an image of stable, happy families of the past that is largely mythical. In doing so, she says, we blur our vision of the troubled present, rife with family "breakdown," domestic violence, teenage pregnancies, and alienated youth. Today 20 percent of American children live in poverty, but in 1900 the same percentage lived in orphanages because their parents could not afford to raise them (Coontz 1992: 4). And marriages of the past did not last longer than modern ones because they were likely to be terminated by the death of a partner. Thus, about the same proportion of children were raised in single-parent households in 1900 as at present. Divorce rates have risen since the 1960s, but some studies have shown that marital satisfaction was greater in the late 1970s than in the late 1950s (Coontz 1992: 16). As for teenage pregnancy rates, they reached a peak in 1957, not during the 1990s (Coontz 1992: 39). All these comparisons with the past, and many others, suggest extreme caution in interpreting the country's problems as stemming from a breakdown of "family values" or the movement away from the "traditional" American family.

But what did happen? And how did the organization of kinship and family in the United States, whatever it was, affect ideas about gender and relations between the sexes? Of course, these questions are complicated by the fact that the United States has long been a land of ethnic and class diversity. The history of working-class families has been quite different from that of the middle class. The experience of black families has contrasted with those of white families (Gutman 1984; Stack 1974). And immigrant groups have had varying experiences in this country (Yanagisako 1987; di Leonardo 1984). Moreover, even within one ethnic group, people's experiences with kinship and gender relationships vary by region and by class. Bearing all this diversity in mind, we will briefly explore some major shifts in North American kinship and gender from the colonial period to the present with a focus on the white middle class.

The early European settlers in the New World brought with them some key features of their European tradition—namely, attachment to the state, notions of private property, and socioeconomic class stratification. But one thing the colonists did not bring with them were large descent groups; nor, with few exceptions, did these ever develop among their descendants or the new European immigrants.

The colonists lived in households, each typically consisting of a nuclear family; wealthier households contained servants as well. In addition, many less wealthy families sent their children to wealthier households to work as servants or to learn a trade, a practice also common in Europe. Some people had come to the New World as indentured servants, agreeing to serve a master's household in return for the cost of passage out of Europe. Thus many households contained large numbers of people who were not kin. It was these households, rather than their own "biological" families as such, that were important in people's daily lives (Coontz 1988: 83–85). Biological children were treated much like servants, especially if they were of similar age.

The households themselves did not contain separate, private spaces for married couples or for parents and their children. As Coontz (1988: 85) writes:

> The central room or hall was where work, meals, play, religious instruction, and often sleep took place. . . . Even genteel families put several people to a room and several people to a bed. Most household members sat together on benches for meals and prayers, rather than in separate chairs. There was thus little concept of a private family set apart from the world of work, servants, and neighbors.

Households were closely linked and highly interdependent on one another for cooperation and economic exchanges. People freely intruded into other households, and all people's affairs were carefully monitored and regulated by village and church officials. What we would consider very private business today was then considered the business of neighbors and the whole community. This point is strikingly illustrated by Coontz (1988: 85–86), who cites a study by Cott (1976):

> The assumption that household affairs were the business of all community members is seen in Nancy Cott's study of divorce records, which show that neighbors nonchalantly entered what modern people would consider the most private areas of life. Mary Angel and Abigail Galloway, for example, testified that they had caught sight through an open window of Adam Air "in the Act of Copulation" with Pamela Brichford. They walked into the house "and after observing them some time . . . asked him if he was not Ashamed to act so when he had a Wife at home."

The contrast to the private, bounded nuclear family of later American life could not be more striking. The family of colonial times was not separated out, nor was "the home" seen as a retreat from the strain of the outside world. Indeed, since the colonial household was a center of economic production (in terms of, for example, agriculture and farm management, cloth production, and trade), there was little division between the public and domestic spheres of life. In the household, both women and men played active roles in production. Aside from food processing and preparation, wives wove cloth, traded with neighbors, managed servants, and helped to keep accounts (Coontz 1988: 93).

Each household was under the authority of its male property owner. Wives were under the authority of husbands, but so were children, servants, apprentices, and anyone else attached to the man's household. In fact, colonial society itself was altogether hierarchical, such that lower males were as subservient to higher ones as wives were to husbands. Women "did not need to grapple with reasons for their lack of equal status, since equal status was not even a social value for men" (Coontz 1988: 97). This was a society that viewed its parts as interdependent and so required a hierarchy for its organization. Women were clearly subordinate, but "a colonial woman's subordination was viewed as a social necessity—one of many unequal relations required by society—not as a unique female condition caused by her biology" (Coontz 1988: 97).

Many of us associate colonial society with rather strict rules governing sex. And, indeed, there were laws against fornication and adultery in all the colonies (though these laws seem to have reverted to the Roman definition of adultery as involving sex between a man and a married woman, excluding sex between a married man and an unmarried woman). Adultery was often severely punished, with public flogging or even death. Dancing and certain forms of dress were also widely forbidden. Still, sex was frankly discussed, offenses were openly described and punished, and sexual matters were not hidden away from children (Coontz 1988: 89). Moreover, wives were expected to be affective companions to husbands (Hunt 1994: 236).

Initially, marriages followed the general European pattern of dowry (both direct and indirect) and parental control. In some places, such as the South (United States) and New France (Quebec) (Molloy 1990: 8), cousin marriage was practiced to consolidate land and transmit wealth in family lines. Thus, as in Europe, the dowry and endogamy promoted the solidification of classes.

The patriarchal colonial family faded away as population expansion, migration, new waves of immigrants, urbanization, and other economic and political changes occurred in the United States. In general terms there was a trend toward increasing *privacy* of the nuclear family. However, this trend took hold much more slowly in rural and working-class families (Hareven 1977). Also, families maintained important ties with wider kin for support and help, especially during periods of war, economic disruption, and urbanization over the next few centuries.

Important changes in family life and gender came with industrialization in the late eighteenth and early nineteenth centuries. New industries needed workers and managers, often at work sites away from the home. Whereas the household had formerly been a unit of production and consumption, it was now a unit of consumption only. Hence the split between the home (private, domestic) and the workplace (public, productive) was born. Among poor and working-class people, both women and men went out to work, though women were pushed into lower-paying jobs with less hope of advancement—as is still generally true for women in the United States today. Among the middle and upper classes, industrialization meant the withdrawal of women from production. Their roles became confined to the home, to childrearing, to domesticity. Indeed, among the middle classes, a nonworking wife was important for the social image and self-esteem of males, who believed it was their duty to provide for and protect wives and children. It was with a sense of shame that a middle-class married woman went to work because she had to, owing to widowhood, sudden unemployment of the husband, or some other financial difficulty.

This shift of production from the home to the workplace had an impact on family life and gender that cannot be overstated. Many writers draw attention to the links between the industrial capitalist economy that prevailed at the time and the perpetuation of patriarchal social relations in the United States and Europe. Removed from production, wives become economically dependent on husbands and in this condition are easily subordinated to them. Males, now expected to support wives and children, "become bound to their work and often endure difficult conditions out of fear of losing their jobs and falling short of their society's and their own expectations" (Bonvillain 1995: 171). Thus, in a capitalist patriarchy, workers are subordinate to employers, and women are subordinate to men. Women are also useful to capitalism because in their domestic roles they sustain and reproduce the workers (Zaretsky 1973). In addition, when and where women have to work, their labor is available at less cost to the capitalists.

Between the period of early industrialization and the present, important shifts occurred in men's and women's roles, masculine and feminine ideals, and the ideals and realities of family life and kinship. A cornerstone on which these changes have turned, and one that may be unique to the United States, is that notions of female sexuality appear to have been perpetually at odds with ideas about female fertility. Sheila Rothman (1978) discussed the transitions in American ideas about "woman's proper place" that took place between the end of the 1800s and the 1960s. These ideas passed sequentially through stages she labeled "virtuous womanhood," "educated motherhood," "wife-companion," and finally "woman as person." These terms refer to ideals of womanhood, and they apply largely to middle-class women, but they shaped the lives of women of all classes and have permeated American popular culture. We will take a look at these stages and examine the tension in each between female sexuality and fertility.

"Virtuous womanhood" appeared after the Civil War in the closing decades of the nineteenth century. At that time, women considered themselves and were considered by men to be innately more pure, more virtuous, than men. Of course, bad, unvirtuous women existed as well, but the idea was that women had a natural capacity for higher virtue and that this higher virtue could benefit men and society. Women were supposed to encompass and foster this "inherently feminine kind of morality, chastity, and sensibility in their families and throughout the society" (Rothman 1978: 5). The virtuous woman was also perceived to be frail and, indeed, quite vulnerable to periodic mental breakdowns. Doctors and others urged that great care be taken to ensure her well-being, which entailed restrictions on all kinds of physical and mental activities.

The virtuous woman was particularly needed in the home, especially in her role as mother. Children were now seen as creatures in great need of the care and love that only a mother could give. Wives were supposed to be care-giving "mothers" to their husbands as well. With their virtue, they were to tame their husbands who, after all, were otherwise "savage beasts" (Rothman 1978: 82). These nurturing and caretaking aspects of women, which stemmed from their childbearing capacities (that is, fertility), were opposed to women's other dimension, their sexuality.

This dichotomy was seen not only in ideas about proper female chastity and sexual restraint but, even more so, in attitudes toward contraception. The virtuous woman condemned contraception. It was believed to draw attention to female sexuality and thus to work against the taming of men through virtue: "Contraceptive practices were so reprehensible precisely because they separated sexual activity from procreation, thus enabling the male to indulge all his lusts while free of the responsibility of rearing children. . . . Contraception would turn woman into a 'slave to her husband's desires'" (Rothman 1978: 82). In short, the sexual dimension of woman was at odds with her fertility dimension and, indeed, female sexuality could be justified only in terms of motherhood. We can trace this antagonism between female sexuality and fertility back to the Christian Mary/Eve problem in which, as we saw earlier, Eve was depicted as the sexual temptress in contrast to Mary, the Virgin Mother.

The idea of the virtuous woman encompassed what has elsewhere been referred to as the "cult of domesticity" for this period (Bonvillain 1995: 154–155). According to this "cult," men and women were innately different and so properly performed very different activities in different spheres, with men outside at work and women inside at home. Women as nurturing care-takers were needed to balance the competitive, aggressive, stressful world of male providers. Husbands needed the home, with a wife inside it, as a retreat from this stressful outside world. These two separate worlds—one male, individualistic, and competitive, the other female, caring, and altruistic— were to be "bridged by love" (Coontz 1992: 59). Yet Coontz sees this love as tainted, given that wives in the late nineteenth century were, after all, economically dependent on husbands. Thus, she says, a wife's "giving" nature was suspect, which had a rather dismal impact on husband-wife relationships: "Men were uneasily aware of the material considerations that contaminated a wife's gift giving and altruism; that is why men's greatest veneration of female self-sacrifice was often reserved for mothers and why deference to mothers has historically been compatible with contempt for other women" (Coontz 1992: 55).

While women's proper place was in the home, the virtuous woman was not actually confined to it. On the contrary, she was expected to take her virtue outside to society and so reform it (Rothman 1978: 63). Indeed, middle-class women of this period were active in reform-minded social clubs and temperance movements. And within these they built strong female friendships and solidarities.

Gradually, according to Rothman (1978), the ideal of the virtuous woman shifted to include a notion of "educated motherhood." Benevolent child-rearing came to be seen as too important to be left to a woman untrained for it. Thus the way was opened not only to innumerable books and manuals on childrearing but also to something truly new and potentially transformative: the value of a college education for women. Women's colleges opened and were justified on the basis not of freeing women from domesticity or preparing them for careers but of enhancing their capabilities as mothers. Needless to say, though women in 1900 may have been studying art, music, and home economics in these colleges, the seeds of more fundamental change were planted.

Later, around the 1920s, there was another and more radical shift to the "wife-companion." According to this ideal, a woman's tie to her husband was her most important relationship. But instead of the virtuous nurturer she had been in the past, she was now to be a romantic, sexual partner. As Rothman (1978: 177) puts it, women "moved from the nursery to the bedroom." As for premarital sex, a minor sexual revolution was involved since women were now encouraged to loosen their sexual restraints (without going all the way to sexual intercourse) to attract a husband. Rothman notes that these new ideas and ideals grew among young people on college campuses, many of which had become coeducational. Moreover, according to Rothman, sociologists were encouraging the shift toward the wife-companion ideal, claiming that in the United States the family was in crisis because it had lost its solidarity with the demise of home-based production and the rise of industrialization. The way to bring the family back together was romantic love and marital sexuality. This solution was considerably advanced by campus sororities, which became training grounds for wife-companions and offered courtship opportunities as well.

Women were now supposed to be beautiful and exciting and to maintain these characteristics not only in courtship but throughout marriage. The cosmetics industry boomed, and the advertising industry put out a new message: "Advertisements that once had presented full-bosomed mothers holding their babies and proclaiming the sanitary marvels of a particular soap gave way to pictures of slim and attractive young girls praising deodorizing qualities of the product" (Rothman 1978: 185).

As women's sexual dimension came to the fore, their fertility dimension receded, as seen not only in advertisements but also in the dramatic shift in attitudes toward birth control. Birth control was embraced as a device to liberate marital sexuality and to prevent pregnancy and children from interfering in the romantic love of the husband and wife. Women were now focused on securing and keeping the man in their lives, and their concerns with both motherhood and their female friendships were sacrificed to this end.

The wife-companion ideal was set aside in the emergencies of the Depression and World War II, only to reemerge and flourish in the 1950s. During the war many women had entered the workforce while men were away on military duty. But upon the men's return, women left or were pushed out of the workplace and the ideal of the wife-companion began anew. The relatively relaxed restrictions on women's premarital sexual behavior also continued into the postwar period. Romantic love was now the basis for marriage, and parental control over spouse selection had become a thing of the past. Young people found one another, engaged in courtship, and got married.

It was also during these postwar years that a curious and distinctively American precourtship ritual developed (or, more precisely, was revived from the 1920s). This phenomenon, best seen from an outsider's perspective, was described by British anthropologist Geoffrey Gorer. Upon visiting the United States, he reported on an odd media program:

> Pairs of young service men, chosen from the audience, had to compete . . . for the favors of invisible models, the model making her choice on the basis of a couple minutes' . . . conversation, herself saying just enough to keep the conversation going. The winners spent an evening together at the Stork Club at the sponsor's expense. . . . The exhibitionist fervor with which the competitors put over their "lines," with a considerable part of the United States listening in, was extremely revealing. (Gorer 1948: 118)

This was not the televised *Dating Game* of later decades; the year was 1943, and Gorer was listening to a radio program called *Blind Date*. He had discovered the peculiar institution of dating, about which he made a number of interesting observations. For openers, he was quite correct in observing that "no other society has been recorded which has developed a similar institutionalized type of behavior for its young people" (1948: 110).

The point of dating, as Gorer noted, was not to provide opportunities for premarital sexual experimentation. Rather, in dating, "sensual and sexual satisfactions may play a part (though this is by no means necessary) as counters in the game, but they are not the object of the exercise; the object of the exercise is enhanced self-esteem, assurance that one is lovable and therefore a success" (1948: 110). Indeed, Gorer saw dating as comparable to a game. In this game, a male "scores" when "he is able to get more favors from the girl than his rivals, real or supposed, would be able to do" (Gorer 1948: 116). But it is not his intention to attempt seduction; an "easy lay" would be disappointing, "too easy a victory," and definitely not a good date.

Both males and females reaped their real rewards not so much during the date as after it, in intense discussions about the date with their respective same-sex peers. Here their self-esteem was truly on the line. The male sought to prove to his peers that he was able to secure a date with a popular girl and to extract more favors from her than others had managed. The female wished to show her peers that she was popular and worthy of attention from males (as measured, for example, by the number of requests for dates she received and the amount of money males spent on her), but without being an "easy lay."

Over time the rituals of the dating game changed, and sexual restrictions became, if anything, more relaxed. Nevertheless, as late as the 1990s Dorothy Holland and Margaret Eisenhart found that many women college students were still falling into a consuming "culture of romance" that in the end lowered their career ambitions. On the two campuses of their study, the prestige of men came from their attractiveness to women and their success in other areas of life, but "women's prestige and correlated attractiveness comes *only* from the attention they receive from men" (Holland and Eisenhart 1990: 104, original emphasis).

In Gorer's time, participants in the dating game went on to marriages based on romantic love, within which women strove to become the ideal wife-companions discussed by Rothman. Some look back to this postwar period as the Golden Age of the American family, a time when what Coontz (1992) refers to as the 1950s *Leave It to Beaver* family prevailed. A thoroughly middle-class phenomenon, this was a nuclear family that had moved to the suburbs, where it eventually owned its own home. The father-husband went off to work and functioned as the breadwinner. The full-time wife-mother stayed at home, absorbed in domestic efficiency, wife-companionship, and childrearing. According to this particular ideal, the father, though busy at work, had an active family life, too. The family was very private, and its members spent quality time together; all were happy and had a lot of good, clean middle-class fun.

But Coontz suggests that this 1950s family is largely a myth; it represents nostalgia for a re-created past, not a solid cultural tradition. For one thing, she contends, this ideal family was never a reality for the majority of people in the United States and certainly not for groups such as blacks and the poor. Some families maintained a facade of this ideal on the outside, but inside were wracked by alcoholic parents and abusive relationships. And women of this time were excluded from so many fields and suffered so many financial restrictions (such as not being allowed to take out credit cards in their own names) that "there were not many permissible alternatives to baking brownies [or] experimenting with new canned soups" (Coontz 1992: 32).

Many women were not happy with their isolated, domestic roles or their full economic dependence on their husbands. Of the same period Rothman

(1978) writes that the wife-companion became lonely in suburbia and saw that her identity was encompassed by that of her husband and children. Everything she did was for others, not herself.

Even for those few people in the United States who had anything like the ideal 1950s family, this family form, according to Coontz, was a historical fluke.[5] It is true that, with the end of the war and relief at its end, the age of marriage dropped, fertility rose, divorce declined, and the middle class moved to the suburbs. But the 1950s family with its nonworking wives and affordable homes emerged only because of the United States' brief postwar prosperity. Within a short span of time "the American dream" was no longer affordable and so middle-class women went out to work.

Indeed, women's participation in the labor force increased then and has been increasing ever since. Today a majority of working-age women and of women with young children are in the workforce. This increase among working women was as much a function of economic necessity as a response to the doldrums of housework. But once begun, it may have played a role in inciting the feminist movements of the 1960s and 1970s. Rothman (1978: 231) describes this development in terms of the shift from the wife-companion ideal to that of the "woman as person":

> This was a view of woman as autonomous, energetic, and competent. Woman was not to be defined by her household role, by her responsibilities as wife or mother; she was in no way to be limited by any special gender characteristics. This new definition of womanhood emphasized the similarities between the sexes, not the differences. It rendered the notion of special protection outmoded and irrelevant. In brief, woman-as-person was fully capable of defining and acting in her own best interest.

But no sooner had the "woman as person" emerged to lead another sexual revolution and to battle sexual discrimination of all kinds than a new problem developed. Whereas female fertility (motherhood) had previously been at odds with female sexuality, it was now at odds with female personhood. This dichotomy was expressed in innumerable debates and discussions about the conflict between women as autonomous persons in the workforce and women as mothers. Many people felt that women working outside the home were harming their children; others fiercely defended women's rights to work and to equal pay. Once again, the different dimensions of American womanhood were split up and at war with one another, leaving many women at war with themselves (McKee and Stone 2007). Today it looks like women are in the workforce to stay and there is evidence that their earnings are increasing. The next case study looks at shifts in gender and marriage that are occurring as a result.

CASE 10: BREADWINNING WOMEN

In this chapter we have traced the cultural images of women as wives in the United States from colonial times to the present; we have seen wives move through the phases of virtuous womanhood, the wife-companion, and the "woman as person." But in all of these transformations, one factor has remained generally constant: Women as wives have been largely financially dependent on husbands. Now, what would happen if women gained substantially in economic power, or if they came, on average, to out-earn men? Apparently this is in fact happening in the United States (as well as in some countries in Europe and elsewhere). Journalist Liza Mundy discusses the consequences of this dramatic trend in her book *The Richer Sex* (2012).

A handful of statistics from *The Richer Sex* shows us where we are in the United States and where we are headed. Currently nearly 40 percent of married women earn more than their husbands, up from 24 percent in 1967. In part this is due to the fact that a postindustrial economy has given women an edge, decreasing employment in male-dominated sectors, such as heavy industry, and favoring jobs in a global information economy. There has also been a decrease in sexual discrimination at the workplace. And women continue to dominate in economic sectors that are more likely to grow over the next decades (for example, health care). In addition, today's higher-paying jobs require more education and today women are more educated than men in the United States: They outnumber men on college campuses, accounting for about 60 percent of undergraduate students; they earn 57 percent of all bachelor's degrees; they cover 60 percent of graduate school enrollment; and they receive 52 percent of doctoral degrees (Mundy 2012: 42). The gender wage gap remains but is narrowing (for full-time work, women now earn about 81 percent of what men earn; in 1979 it was 62 percent [Mundy 2012: 56–57]). Meanwhile, marriage has declined and today 40 percent of children are born to unmarried mothers (Mundy 2012: 39), up from 5 percent in 1960.

If present trends continue (and there is every indication that they will), more families will be supported by women, and women, not men, may become the primary breadwinners. What will this trend mean in terms of gender roles, marriage, and the family? Will women breadwinners assume more power in their relationships with men? Will men take on a greater share of domestic tasks and child care? Will marriage come to be seen as optional? So far, the answer to all of these questions is "very likely."

Women's increased earnings are giving them more power. Married women who earn more than their husbands report that they do make substantially more decisions than their husbands regarding household finances. They may make some of these decisions unilaterally, without consulting their husbands. Breadwinning women are self-confident and assertive; they are very unlikely to remain in unhappy marriages or partnerships. Today considerably more divorces are initiated by wives than by husbands.

Married men are also taking on more domestic tasks—housework, cooking, and child care. Indeed by 2010 men in the United States nearly tripled their labor contributions in these domestic spheres. Some men are making greater domestic contributions while they continue to work outside the home but more men are assuming the position of "house husband," where they are the children's primary caretakers. Here we see some interesting gender-role reversals. One woman told Mundy, "At the end of the school year [the children] came home with their art projects. . . . I'm going through them and I'm devastated. All the art projects did not have mom in them. It was all the two boys and dad. I'm like—'Where am I?'" (Mundy 2012: 132). And Mundy reports of another woman, "One foreign correspondent I spoke with reflected that when she is away on travels, her husband sometimes invoked her as the authoritarian. They have an adolescent son, and to discipline him, her husband will use the wait-till-your-mother-gets-home scenario" (2012: 132). Breadwinning women, writes Mundy, must, like men before them, figure out how to fit themselves into a domestic family sphere that largely operates without them.

Many breadwinning women regret their lack of time with their children, or worry about how their absence will affect them, but also report that they enjoy seeing their husbands or partners interacting with the children for sustained periods of time. Here, too, we see some expressions of a gender-role or gender-attitude reversal. One woman, while praising her husband's child-care activities, speaks in a patronizing, almost demeaning way about her husband's domestic efforts: "He's been working at potty training—he's been sitting and singing potty songs. . . . He's really good with her. I thought it was kind of special. They had a lot of good times—they would have their little things. It's so funny to hear him say, 'It's her naptime' or 'She hasn't eaten yet.' He knows the whole routine" (Mundy 2012: 130). Are breadwinning women becoming as insensitive as were breadwinning men?

As for marriage, it has declined in the United States. Today slightly over half of all people age eighteen and over are married (Mundy 2012: 191), whereas the figure was 72 percent in 1960. Much of this decline is due to the fact that men and women are marrying at later ages than before. In addition, more people are cohabitating without marriage or are opting to remain single, not living with a partner. These nonmarital alternatives are facilitated through women's increased earnings.

Men, according to Mundy, show a variety of reactions to women's increased earnings, or to the fact that their wives make more than they do. Most adjust quite well, saying that they are relieved not to carry sole responsibility for breadwinning. Some express that they really want to have more leisure time or spend more time with their children. Others are clearly uncomfortable with this new state of affairs and retaliate, often in subtle ways:

A man could make his wife feel bad about herself by ignoring her accomplishments or by telling her she has gained weight and isn't sexually attractive. . . . He could become distant and uncooperative. He could refuse to attend office parties or help her advance. He could say niggling little things in public. He could provoke fights the night before she has to leave on a business trip. He could complain when she takes business calls during dinner. He could refuse to move for her career. (Mundy 2012: 101)

But what emerges most prominently from Mundy's book is that overall men are expressing a great deal of ambivalence about wives/partners as primary breadwinners. They can be both supportive and undermining. They may be proud of their high-earning wives and at the same time threatened by them. They may develop a love/hate relationship to their wives' money. Mundy writes, "It's possible to send all sorts of mixed messages. 'He loved the gold credit card,' one New England businesswoman I talked to reflected. . . . 'And he resented me for it'" (2012: 103).

Breadwinning women are expressing ambivalence as well. On the one hand, high-earning women are proud of their success and happy with their financial independence. On the other hand, many single women worry that their success will repel potential male partners and they may go to some lengths to hide or downplay their achievements. One woman Mundy interviewed, a university vice president, tells men she is dating that she works "in administration." Another, a software consultant, tells male prospects that she teaches music. Some women also spend considerable energy trying to bolster the egos of unemployed or low-earning partners or husbands, praising them abundantly for whatever they do at home, stressing the importance of whatever they contribute to the household resources or upkeep.

Many breadwinning women feel anxious about their own possessive attitudes toward their income, especially given that previous cohorts of women criticized men for their proprietary feelings toward their income, or their disregard for the vital but unpaid labor of housewives. For example, one woman who earns twice as much as her husband was upset when her husband, without consulting her, authorized an expensive veterinary treatment for their cat: "I did kind of feel like— you just spent a bunch of my money without telling me" (Mundy 2012: 126). Another high-earning woman with a relatively low-earning husband expressed the tension she felt over her own possessive attitude toward her earned income:

I have friends where it's the man who's earning more money, and the woman says to me, "He really gets upset when I want to redecorate the kitchen," and I'm supposed to be very sympathetic to the woman because I'm a woman. . . . But I also understand the territorialness—the territoriality of: I did earn the money. I understand the husband's point of view much better than I would like to. I understand the feeling that "I've earned it." (Mundy 2012: 126–127)

These trends in the United States—higher educational levels attained by women compared to those by men, a surge in women's earnings, and a decline in marriage—are also occurring in other countries, in some cases more dramatically than in the United States. In some Asian countries, such as Japan, South Korea, and Taiwan, growing proportions of women are remaining single and the proportions are higher than among US women. For example, in Taiwan 37 percent of women ages thirty to thirty-four are unmarried (Mundy 2012: 211). A main reason is not that the women choose to remain single but that men in these Asian regions are highly reluctant (more so than in the United States) to marry women who are more educated than they are and/or who earn more than they do. In the context of these countries, the decline in marriage also means a drop in reproduction since in many Asian countries reproduction outside marriage is socially and culturally unacceptable. In many European countries, by contrast, marriage has declined, but couples are cohabiting and reproducing in these unions without incurring negative social stigmas. In Sweden now, over half of all births are to unmarried women.

One result of these trends in Asia is the rise of a new global "foreign bride" industry (Mundy 2012: 218). Agencies have sprung up to provide males of developed Asian countries with less-educated, poorer, and predictably subservient women from nearby less-developed countries. "For example, women from rural Vietnam might be brought into Taiwan, South Korea, or Japan to make up the dearth of [acceptable] homegrown mates" (Mundy 2012: 218). A similar process is taking place in Europe, although not through commercialized agencies. For example, many Spanish men are marrying "more traditional" immigrant Latin American women while many Spanish women are marrying northern European men, who are more accepting of their higher education and financial independence.

The Richer Sex captures some interesting consequences of new economic trends at a very early stage in their development. But it is difficult to predict at this stage what the future will hold. Will the rise in women's income result in earnings that are roughly equal to men's? Or will women indeed come to generally *out*-earn men and become *primary* breadwinners for a clear majority of families? If the latter, I would predict that we will see more in the way of matrifocal households (discussed in Chapter 4), where women (mothers, daughters, and sisters) form the residential and economic core. Grandmothers or older maternal aunts will become primary childrearers; men will be loosely attached to households, becoming temporary residents or visiting lovers even as they are fathers of household children.

DISCUSSION QUESTIONS

1. Critically evaluate how Jack Goody, Alice Schlegel, and Sherry Ortner each connect the double sexual standard with class stratification.

2. In what ways may Christianity have historically shaped kinship and gender in the Western world? To what extent and how do you think Christianity, broadly defined, still impacts gender in Euro-American societies?

3. On what basis does Stephanie Coontz claim that the 1950s *Leave It to Beaver* family in the United States was largely a myth? To what extent do you think this family form remains an ideal in the United States today?

4. Looking at the broad sweep of the history of gender in the United Sates, where are we now? Would you say that the United States has consistently moved toward greater gender equality? What gender issues, or conflicts, are currently being expressed?

SUGGESTED FURTHER READING

The following books by Stephanie Coontz cover the entire history of the family, marriage, and gender in the United States from 1600 to the present. All the books are engaging and highly informative.

1988. *The Social Origins of Private Life: A History of American Families 1600–1900*. New York: Verso.

1992. *The Way We Never Were: American Families and the Nostalgia Trap*. New York: Basic Books.

1997. *The Way We Really Are: Coming to Terms with America's Changing Families*. New York: Basic Books.

2006. *Marriage, a History: How Love Conquered Marriage*. New York: Penguin Books.

SUGGESTED CLASSROOM MEDIA

Medieval Women. 1987. Produced by Extended Degree Program, University of Wisconsin, Green Bay. International Film Bureau, Chicago. Twenty-four minutes. This film covers the lives and status of women in the Middle Ages (500–1500) in Europe, using beautiful illustrations from books and manuscripts of the period. It is well narrated by historian Joyce Salisbury.

Gender War/Gender Peace. 2005. Films for the Humanities & Sciences. Thirty minutes. Covers issues of gender and communication in North America.

The Motherhood Manifesto. 2006. Bullfrog Films. Fifty-eight minutes. Looks at obstacles challenging working mothers and their families and what changes are needed to restore work/life balance.

WEBSITE

www.wic.org/misc/history.htm. "Women's History in America." Provided by Women's International Center. The site covers the history of American women in legal status, work, political life, and other categories.

NOTES

1. In a later publication Ortner (1981) addressed this question, but by this time she had modified her views on female virginity. Here she claims that the female purity ethic arises not in state societies but in "hierarchical" societies, regardless of whether they are also part of state systems. This observation is intended to accommodate her finding that female premarital chastity was emphasized in Polynesia before the advent of the state.

2. It may be another popular misconception that the small, nuclear family is unique to Western civilization. Indeed, Goody (1972) demonstrated that, throughout the world, the rural "farm family" (a single unit of production, reproduction, and consumption) is typically nuclear and small-sized and varies only within very narrow limits, even in areas where joint or extended households mark a temporary phase in household development.

3. Following Germanic custom, the generations were counted as "degrees." The number of degrees between ego and another relative covered the number of generations between their common ancestor and the person furthest removed from the common ancestor. Thus, for example, ego's FBSS would be a relative in the third degree. The church's restrictions on marriage were gradually reduced to relatives in the fourth degree.

4. This ruling was made official by the Council of Trent in the mid-sixteenth century.

5. Coontz (2006) later changed her views about this type of postwar family. Rather than seeing it as a historical fluke, she came to see it as a phase in a much broader evolution of love-based marriage.

REFERENCES

Bonvillain, Nancy. 1995. *Women and Men: Cultural Constructions of Gender*. Englewood Cliffs, NJ: Prentice Hall.

Boserup, Ester. 1970. *Women's Role in Economic Development*. New York: St. Martin's.

Brettell, Caroline B. 1991. Property, Kinship, and Gender: A Mediterranean Perspective. In David I. Kertzer and Richard P. Saller, eds., *The Family in Italy from Antiquity to the Present*, pp. 340–353. New Haven, CT: Yale University Press.

Clark, Gillian. 1993. *Women in Late Antiquity: Pagan and Christian Lifestyles*. Oxford, England: Clarendon Press.

Coontz, Stephanie. 1988. *The Social Origins of Private Life: A History of American Families 1600–1900*. New York: Verso.

———. 1992. *The Way We Never Were: American Families and the Nostalgia Trap*. New York: Basic Books.

———. 2006. *Marriage, a History: How Love Conquered Marriage*. New York: Penguin Books.

Cott, Nancy F. 1976. Eighteenth-Century Family and Social Life Revealed in Massachusetts Divorce Records. *Journal of Social History* 10(1): 20–43.

di Leonardo, Micaela. 1984. *The Varieties of Ethnic Experience: Kinship, Class, and Gender Among California Italian-Americans*. Ithaca, NY: Cornell University Press.

Fox, Robin. 1993. *Reproduction and Succession: Studies in Anthropology, Law, and Society*. New Brunswick, NJ: Transaction Publishers.

Goody, Jack. 1972. The Evolution of the Family. In Peter Laslett and Richard Wall, eds., *Household and Family in Past Time*, pp. 103–124. Cambridge, England: Cambridge University Press.

———. 1973. Bridewealth and Dowry in Africa and Eurasia. In Jack Goody and S. J. Tambiah, *Bridewealth and Dowry*, pp. 1–58. Cambridge, England: Cambridge University Press.

———. 1976. *Production and Reproduction: A Comparative Study of the Domestic Domain*. Cambridge, England: Cambridge University Press.

———. 1983. *The Development of the Family and Marriage in Europe*. Cambridge, England: Cambridge University Press.

———. 1993. *The Oriental, the Ancient, and the Primitive: Systems of Marriage and the Family in the Pre-industrial Societies of Eurasia*. Cambridge, England: Cambridge University Press.

Gorer, Geoffrey. 1948. *The American People: A Study in National Character*. New York: W. W. Norton.

Gottlieb, Beatrice. 1993. *The Family in the Western World from the Black Death to the Industrial Age*. New York: Oxford University Press.

Gutman, Herbert G. 1984. Afro-American Kinship Before and After Emancipation in North America. In Hans Medick and David Warren Sabean, eds., *Interest and Emotion*. Cambridge, England: Cambridge University Press.

Hajnal, J. 1965. European Marriage Patterns in Perspective. In D. V. Glass and D. E. C. Eversley, eds., *Population in History: Essays in Historical Demography*, pp. 101–143. London: Edward Arnold Publishers.

Hareven, Tamara K. 1977. Introduction. In Tamara K. Hareven, ed., *Family and Kin in Urban Communities, 1700–1930*, pp. 1–15. New York: New Viewpoints.

Herlihy, David. 1962. Land, Family, and Women in Continental Europe, 710–1200. *Traditio* 18: 89–120.

———. 1971. *Women in Medieval Society*. Smith History Lecture, University of St. Thomas, Houston.

———. 1985. *Medieval Households*. Cambridge, MA: Harvard University Press.

Holland, Dorothy C., and Margaret A. Eisenhart. 1990. *Educated in Romance: Women, Achievement, and College Culture*. Chicago: University of Chicago Press.

Huber, Brad R., William F. Danaher, and William L. Breedlove. 2011. New Cross-Cultural Perspectives on Marriage Transactions. *Cross-Cultural Research* 45: 339–375.

Hughes, Diane Owen. 1978. From Brideprice to Dowry in Mediterranean Europe. *Journal of Family History* 3: 262–296.

Hunt, Morton. 1994. *The Natural History of Love*. New York: Anchor Books/Doubleday.

McKee, Nancy P., and Linda Stone. 2007. *Gender and Culture in America*, 3rd ed. Cornwall-on-Hudson, NY: Sloan Publishing.

McNamara, Jo Ann, and Suzanne Wemple. 1988. The Power of Women Through the Family in Medieval Europe, 500–1100. In Mary Erler and Maryanne Kowaleski, eds., *Women and Power in the Middle Ages*, pp. 83–101. Athens: University of Georgia Press.

Molloy, Maureen. 1990. Considered Affinity: Kinship, Marriage, and Social Class in New France, 1640–1729. *Social Science History* 14(1): 2–26.

Mundy, Liza. 2012. *The Richer Sex*. New York: Simon & Schuster.

Ortner, Sherry B. 1978. The Virgin and the State. *Feminist Studies* 4(3): 19–35.

———. 1981. Gender and Sexuality in Hierarchical Societies: The Case of Polynesia and Some Comparative Implications. In Sherry B. Ortner and Harriett White-head, eds., *Sexual Meanings: The Cultural Construction of Gender and Sexuality*, pp. 359–409. Cambridge, England: Cambridge University Press.

Rothman, Sheila M. 1978. *Woman's Proper Place: A History of Changing Ideas and Practices, 1870 to the Present*. New York: Basic Books.

Saller, Richard P. 1991. European Family History and Roman Law. *Continuity and Change* 6(3): 335–346.

Schlegel, Alice. 1991. Status, Property, and the Value on Virginity. *American Ethnologist* 18(4): 735–750.

Stack, Carol B. 1974. *All Our Kin: Strategies for Survival in a Black Community*. New York: Harper & Row.

Stone, Linda, and Caroline James. 1995. Dowry, Bride-Burning, and Female Power in India. *Women's Studies International Forum* 18(2): 125–134.

Verdery, Katherine. 1988. A Comment on Goody's Development of the Family and Marriage in Europe. *Journal of Family History* 13(2): 265–270.

Verdon, Michel. 1988. Virgins and Widows: European Kinship and Early Christianity. *Man* 23: 488–505.

Wemple, Suzanne Fonay. 1981. *Women in Frankish Society: Marriage and the Cloister*. Philadelphia: University of Pennsylvania Press.

Williams, Marty Newman, and Anne Echols. 1994. *Between Pit and Pedestal: Women in the Middle Ages*. Princeton, NJ: Markus Wiener Publishers.

Yanagisako, Sylvia Junko. 1987. Mixed Metaphors: Native and Anthropological Models of Gender and Kinship Domains. In Jane Fishburne Collier and Sylvia Junko Yanagisako, eds., *Gender and Kinship: Essays Toward a Unified Analysis*, pp. 86–118. Stanford, CA: Stanford University Press.

Zaretsky, Eli. 1973. Capitalism, the Family, and Personal Life. *Socialist Revolution* 13–14: 69–125.

8

KINSHIP, GENDER, AND
CONTEMPORARY SOCIAL ISSUES

A number of social issues around the world are both influenced by and affecting the intertwining relationships among kinship, gender, and the family. One such topic concerns fairly dramatic changes in family types. Many of the issues surrounding family forms are controversial—disturbing to some and welcome or encouraged by others. These concerns are prominent in the United States but are also seen in other countries. Another relevant topic is domestic or familial violence against women; although the subject has been discussed for some time, it is receiving new global attention. This chapter covers a few of these contemporary issues.

ALTERNATIVE FAMILIES, ALTERNATIVE SEXUALITIES

The United States has long seen the nuclear family of husband, wife, and their biological children as both an ideal and a norm, but today this family form constitutes only about 20 percent of all households (in 1960 it was about 45 percent [US Census Bureau 2010]). Today there are a number of alternative arrangements: divorced single-parent families, blended families, families of never-married mothers with children, and even polygynous families. In addition, over recent decades the United States has seen activism grow among gay and lesbian communities, culminating in a movement for social and legal acceptance of same-sex marriage. Since World War II this activism has been a rocky road to travel. No sooner had outright persecution of homosexuals abated after the McCarthyism of the 1950s than HIV/AIDS was unjustly defined as the "gay disease" in the 1980s. By the opening decades of the twenty-first century, acceptance of homosexuality was much greater, creating a climate that brought same-sex marriage to the fore.

This first case study looks at alternative families in the United States. As we will see, some of these new families are reshaping our cultural ideas of kinship.

CASE 11: NEW AND NOVEL FAMILIES IN THE UNITED STATES

"[Christine's] mother had urged her to start taking birth control pills when she had become sexually active shortly after graduation from high school. Christine had made an appointment at Planned Parenthood in a nearby town, but never kept it. 'It just seemed like a lot of trouble,' she recalled. . . . One night after work, she and Duane, a fellow employee at a fast-food restaurant, went to bed together and used no birth control. He was separated from the mother of his two children, and he and Christine had been flirting off and on for a couple of weeks. They never slept together again, but Christine became pregnant. . . . [She] quit her job, but Duane had already returned to his old girlfriend. Christine never spoke to Duane again, and never told him that her daughter was his" (McKee and Stone 2007: 208–209). *Christine is now raising her daughter on her own. She has joined a growing group of young women in the United States: "never-married mothers," who are single moms not through divorce but through re-maining single while having children.*

"One father said: 'I know it's tough on the kids because they spend at least two days a week with me, and then three days, four days with my ex-wife, and every Saturday and Saturday night or Saturday night and Sunday during the day with my parents, depending on what my schedule is. And the kids are basically living out of a suitcase. It's tough on them that way'" (Jacobson, Leim, and Weiss 2001: 239). *This father is coping with an increasingly common situation: raising children from separate households.*

Bonnie and Sara have been lesbian partners for twenty-seven years. They have three children and two grandchildren. In the spring of 2004, they were legally married in a particular county of Oregon. In 1993 they founded Love Makes a Family Inc. (www.LMF.org), an international organization that supports and gives public voice to lesbian-, gay-, bisexual-, and transsexual-headed families. Bonnie and Sara have been deeply concerned about how the denial of legal marriage for lesbian and gay couples negatively impacts these couples' children. They comment, "For lesbian and gay parents, the studies are in. Our kids are great, but they are hurt by dis-crimination. . . . The children of lesbian and gay parents learn on the playground that they are today's illegitimate children, and they will remain so until their parents can marry." (The Oregonian, *Thursday, May 20, 2004, p. D15)*

As these vignettes illustrate, a great historical transformation in the US family is taking place. This is a transformation away from the ideal of the nuclear family and toward a rising number of and an increasing acceptance of a wide variety of new family forms, new kinds of human relationships, and new ways of perceiving kinship itself. We saw earlier in this book that in American history the nuclear husband-wife-biological-children family was largely a myth, or a reality for only a few for a brief span of time (Coontz 1992), even though it long remained a cultural ideal. Now, however, the US family and family relationships are undergoing such widespread changes that the ideal itself may be fading away. These transformations have been at work both in the United States and in Europe, but so far it is only in the United States that some of these domestic developments have become contested political issues.

Today's families in the United States show considerable variation. Many families are single-parent households, some families are based on partnerships without marriage, an increasing number of marriages are same-sex unions, and an increasing number of same-sex unions (with or without legal marriage) now include children. Here we will take a look at some of these transformations and their implications for kinship and family.

Reproduction Outside Marriage

By 2011, 40 percent of all births in the United States were to unmarried women, up from 5 percent in 1960 (Mundy 2012). In some cases the mothers may be cohabitating with partners (who may or may not have fathered their children) and in other cases they are single mothers raising children on their own. Many other countries, especially in Europe, are also seeing a rise in births outside marriage. What is distinctive about the United States, though, is the large proportion of very young unmarried mothers whose pregnancies were unplanned. Indeed, teenage pregnancy in the United States is the highest among Western developed countries. In 2008 the US teen pregnancy rate was 67.8 pregnancies per 1,000 women ages 15 through 19 (Kost and Henshaw 2012). Generally the US rate is more than twice that of countries such as Canada and England and several times that of many European countries.

In 2001 anthropologist Nancy McKee conducted a study of young, never-married mothers in rural areas of Washington and Idaho. These women had become pregnant while in high school or shortly after graduation. In all cases their pregnancies were unplanned and in all cases the women were unmarried. McKee found that a number of factors were common among these women and likely played a role in their predicaments. These women tended to have rather distant relationships with their parents, especially with their mothers. Many of these women reported that "their mothers had been unable to understand what they were going through as children and adolescents, and that they had been punitive and unsympathetic" (McKee and Stone 2007: 205). While adolescents, all of these women also lacked clear aspirations for their futures and had no ideas about possible careers for themselves. They had never considered abortion (although none of the women were religious) and all of them described sex education in high school as "a joke."

This last point is significant. Notably, "sex education classes stress the Latin names for body parts, describe the interaction of sperm and egg, . . . threaten students with sexually transmitted diseases, and urge celibacy. The classes do not discuss methods of birth control, their efficacy, how to use them or where to get them" (McKee and Stone 2007: 222). Apparently McKee's study was correct to raise the issue of sex education. Indeed a June 2012 report from the Centers for Disease Control and Prevention notes a drop in teenage pregnancy in the United States that may very well be due in part to very recent, more realistic and informative sex education programs inside and outside the classroom (*The Economist*, July–August 2012: 26–27).

Another interesting result was the finding that few of the fathers of the children in these cases considered marriage to their pregnant partners and, for the most part, neither the women nor their families sought marriage either. "The era of the shotgun marriage . . . is apparently at an end" (McKee and Stone 2007: 217). Some of the women had cohabitated with the fathers of their children for a while, but by the time of this study only one of them was still living with her child's father and none of them were married to anyone.

McKee identified four factors behind this lack of interest in marriage that apply to the cases in her study and beyond to US society in general. For one, women are increasingly able and expected to earn a living. The mothers in her study often held low-paying, unskilled jobs, but they were able to support themselves; "they no longer *needed* a man's economic support for survival" (2007: 217). In turn men no longer need women's domestic skills: "Permanent press fabrics, laundromats, prepared foods, and fast food restaurants have taken their places for many Americans" (2007: 218). In addition, illegitimacy is no longer stigmatized, and finally, marriage is no longer needed for easy access to sexual partners.

Divorce and Remarriage

In the United States the divorce rate has hovered around 50 percent over the past three decades, a sixfold increase over what it was in the early 1960s. With this increase in divorce has come an increase in single-parent (usually single-mother) families and, in combination with remarriages, many more families are now "blended" (consisting of stepparents and stepsiblings).

A study in the United States conducted by Jacobson, Leim, and Weiss (2001) explores one dimension of the new blended-family form, namely the fact that in many families following a divorce, children are raised in two separate households. This study, conducted in an area of greater Boston, focuses on mostly white, middle-class families and looks at how parenting between separate households presents challenges to cultural ideas about household boundaries, domestic roles, and the allocation of parental resources. The authors find considerable variation in how easy or difficult adapting to two-household parenting can be for the individuals involved. They conclude that "the two-household family form is not inevitably problematic" (2001: 244). Rather, the families that best adapt to this form are those that accept more permeable household boundaries, develop clear understandings about the movement of children and parental resources between them, and accept more flexible parental roles. Needless to say, a particularly bitter divorce or the feelings of new spouses or partners can hamper a divorced couple's ability to keep household boundaries open and share resources.

Same-Sex Marriages

At midnight on Sunday, May 16, 2004, Massachusetts became the first state in the United States to legalize same-sex marriage. Scores of gay and lesbian couples lined up in front of the Cambridge courthouse to apply for a marriage license. Later in the morning, married same-sex couples left Boston City Hall amid cheers and clapping from the supporting crowd, while a group of protesters demonstrated across the street. The Massachusetts decision was a major historical victory for advocates of same-sex marriage. Currently, same-sex marriages are legal in the additional states of Connecticut, Iowa, New Hampshire, New York, Vermont, and Washington, along with the District of Columbia. Still, many obstacles to legalizing these marriages remain, not least of which is that some groups seek to ban these marriages nationwide through a constitutional amendment. Elsewhere in the Western world, same-sex marriages are legal in Canada, Belgium, Denmark, Iceland, the Netherlands, Norway, Portugal, and Spain.

It is now clear that same-sex partnerships, legal or otherwise, are a vital part of the new family landscape. Many of these couples are also raising children together—some acquired through adoption; some produced through previous heterosexual unions of one or both partners; and today, with the assistance of new reproductive technologies, gay or lesbian couples can produce children biologically related to one partner or even to both partners (see Chapter 9).

Same-sex couples seek through legal marriage access to benefits other married couples enjoy—for example, tax benefits and pension rights. The fact that these benefits could be conferred through some sort of nonmarital civil union suggests that the interest in legal marriage among many same-sex couples goes deeper than this. Anthropologist Ellen Lewin (1998) provides answers to this question of "Why marriage?" for homosexual couples, based on her study of same-sex commitment ceremonies. She notes that while these celebrations take a wide variety of forms, "they all attempt to situate a relationship within a broader community context, to proclaim the authenticity of the relationship in a public manner and to achieve recognition that extends beyond the boundaries of gay/lesbian communities" (Lewin 2004: 11). Many same-sex couples thus seek a legitimization of their relationship that is equal to what is available to other citizens. Noting that while commitment-ceremony "weddings" are rewarding, Lewin adds that "there is nothing quite as powerful as the expression of state approval" (2004: 11).

Another powerful motive behind the push for same-sex marriage concerns the social status of the children of gay and lesbian couples, as noted in the case of Bonnie and Sara above. During public demonstrations against gays in 1992, their youngest remarked, "Mom, they're telling you that you were wrong to have me, but they're telling me that I shouldn't have been born" (*The Oregonian*, Thursday, May 20, 2004, p. D15).

Same-sex marriage advocates face significant opposition in the United States. Some opponents are against homosexuality itself; some are afraid of what they see as "family breakdown," regarding same-sex marriages as threats to social order, somewhat similar to single moms. Some charge that same-sex-marriage advocates are trying to redefine "marriage," away from its standard meaning as a union between a man and a woman. But as we have seen in this book, there is no standard, cross-culturally valid definition of "marriage" in the first place. Not a single characteristic holds across the board for all those many institutions around the world that we would easily label as "marriage"—not legitimization of children, not heterosexual unions, not cohabitation, not even sexual activity. From a global, cross-cultural perspective, those who seek same-sex marriage are not trying to redefine marriage but merely to define it for themselves, in their own interests, as people around the world have always done (Stone 2004a).

Kinship as Choice

In 1991 Kath Weston published a book about how gays and lesbians, often rejected by their own natal families, construct their own families, based on choice. She titled the book *Families We Choose*. But what Weston noted among lesbian families—the new element of choice—now applies as well to the wide variety of new family relationships and new family forms currently developing in the United States. Just as lesbians and gays choose their new families, many stepparents, stepchildren, and stepsiblings now construct real and meaningful kinship with those to whom they are not biologically related by choosing to do so and making a personal commitment to that choice. Many observers note this shift in the construction of Euro-American kinship away from an emphasis on biological relatedness and toward individual choice and will (Stone 2004a, 2004b; Carsten 2004).

At the same time there also seems to be some tension between biology and choice in contemporary American kinship. We will see in Chapter 9 how kin relationships stemming from advances in reproductive technologies are based on choice rather than biology, but the individuals involved also strive to create families that resemble as closely as possible those based on biological ties. In addition, Kaja Finkler (2001) discusses how, alongside the new choice-based kinship, advances in the detection of genetically inherited diseases promote among many people the more traditional notion of kin relationships established through biogenetic connection.

Perhaps as controversial as same-sex marriages in the United States are polygynous unions. These are illegal in every state but do occur among specific religious sects splintered from the Mormon Church. In the media, this practice of polygyny is often associated with abuses against women, especially underage marriage, forced marriage, and the keeping of women in compounds against their will. The following case study corrects some misperceptions about these communities and the role of polygyny within them.

CASE 12: POLYGYNY IN THE UNITED STATES

In spring of 2008, authorities raided a compound of polygynists—a community of Fundamentalist Latter-Day Saints (FLDS) living in their "Yearning for Zion" ranch—near Eldorado, Texas. Scores of adults and some 400 children were removed from the compound, the children becoming wards of the state. Apparently a young girl from within the compound had called Texas Child Protective Services to claim she had been a victim of sexual abuse. By early summer, the Texas Supreme Court had ruled that the authorities had "overreacted" in their raid of the compound and began to return most of the children to the Ranch with their parents.

Not long before this event, Carolyn Jessop had published the book *Escape* (2007), a spellbinding and horrific account of her own escape from an FLDS community. Jessop had been raised in this community, married there at age eighteen, and had eight children before her departure. Her book details incidents of child and wife abuse and the growing religious extremism of the community, then under the influence of Warren Jeffs. Jeffs was in Utah, convicted of being an accomplice to rape, and in July 2008, a Texas grand jury indicted him and four of his followers on charges of felony sexual assault of a child. Jessop's book also covers her own mental anguish through her years of polygynous marriage. She and many others have reported the practice of "placement marriage" in these communities, where young girls, some as young as eleven, are married to much older men. Jessop's own husband was over fifty at the time of her marriage.

The FLDS began as a splinter group of the Church of the Latter-Day Saints (Mormon), which emerged in the United States in the nineteenth century. This group practiced polygyny in the past, beginning in 1843, when its founder and prophet, Joseph Smith, claimed the directive to practice polygyny as a revelation from God. Divine origin aside, this was an expedient move since women converts to the new religion, who sought marriage and children within the Mormon community, vastly exceeded men. Citing polygyny as the reason, US government agencies persecuted Mormon followers after the Civil War; many polygynists were rounded up and jailed. In 1890 a later church leader and prophet banned the practice of polygyny; since this time the mainstream Mormon Church has steadfastly denounced plural marriage. A small group of followers elected to retain the practice, doing so secretly. This group eventually became the FLDS.

The Texas raid and the Jessop book came in the wake of what had been a period of growing tolerance for FLDS polygyny. But with reports of underage marriage and other abuses, the practice of polygyny has again come under fire. This renews a situation where, throughout much of US history and continuing into the 1990s, legal documents and court decisions made polygyny virtually synonymous with abusive relationships, "lack of social duty," and "subversion of good order" (Fox 1997: 22). As we know from several case studies in this book, in societies where polygyny is permitted (the Nuer, Nepalese Brahmans, the Navajo, and others), this view is unwarranted.

From an anthropological perspective, what is interesting and enlightening about FLDS polygyny (at least in the rural areas from where abuses were reported) is how it differs from polygyny as practiced elsewhere in the world. First, there is an issue of magnitude here. In most societies where polygyny is permitted, a few men will have two or a few more wives, though it is true that in some societies, very wealthy men will have more wives and having many wives may be a sign of high status. By contrast, in the FLDS communities some men were reported to have had well over ten or even over fifty wives. As Robin Fox points out, this harem-type polygyny, formerly practiced by some rulers of African kingdoms or emperors of China, was "excessive; a runaway version; almost a parody of a polygynous system" (1997: 38). This runaway style of polygyny inevitably led to one of the reported abuses of the FLDS system: the problem of the "lost boys." There were reports (see, for example, Jessop 2007) that in FLDS communities, hundreds of young males were summarily excommunicated and banished from their homes on charges such as listening to rock music. These boys were simply dumped onto highways to fend for themselves. But, practically speaking, what else could have been done with them? Indeed, if so many women were married to a few older men, most of these young males could not hope to secure wives themselves and would only constitute a threat to the excessive polygyny of the older men.

A second way in which the FLDS communities differ from other polygynous societies is their isolation. This isolation, far more than the practice of polygyny as such, led to male abuses of power and entrapment of women. Jessop reported that as her community grew more religiously extreme and strict, the isolation increased. For example, most books were banned and homeschooling became mandatory. Even before this began, women were not permitted to drive cars with current license plates. That way, were they to try to escape, local police (mostly FLDS members) could easily pick them up and force their return.

A third way in which the polygyny of the FLDS is unique is that in other polygynous societies, monogamy is also permitted. Indeed, as we have seen earlier in this book, in most societies that permit polygyny, monogamy is in fact far more common. In the FLDS, however, polygyny appears to have been more or less mandatory, and was certainly a goal of all households, even though initially, marriage unions started out monogamously. One reason for this is the central religious belief that the practice of polygyny, or "living the principle," was required for the best possible salvation and existence in the afterlife.

Finally, accounts of FLDS communities draw out their patriarchal nature. Again, this is not an automatic result of polygyny as such; polygynous societies may be patriarchal but then so may be monogamous ones (Fox 1997). The FLDS communities emphasized patriarchy through religious doctrines that placed men, and not women, in positions of church leadership and domestic authority and stressed women's salvation through obedience to fathers and husbands. William Jankowiak (2001), who studied an FLDS community, pinpoints what he calls "father glorification" as a core cultural idea and set of practices that bolster and perpetuate the patriarchal, polygynous family in the FLDS. Adoration of fathers is expressed through, for example, public testimonials that glorify the achievements of one's father. In addition, father glorification is brought about by cowives who compete for the husband's attention, drawing their children into their strategies. "By thus cultivating father adoration, mothers hope to demonstrate their superior worth among co-wives and to draw their husband's attention to themselves. . . . Also, as wives focus their attention on their husband, the children, wanting to please their mother and father, follow suit. All this enhances the father's status and esteem" (2001: 277). The result is a culture of male glorification where fathers/husbands become central, powerful figures of domestic units. In sum, FLDS policy is best understood cross-culturally, where we see it as quite unique. Abuses that have been reported within these communities are not the result of polygyny as such but are interwoven with the magnitude and style of the polygyny practiced and the isolation of these communities.

In addition, in some FLDS communities the extreme abuses of Warren Jeffs's groups are absent—where women are not entrapped and many women and men carry out satisfying lives. Janet Bennion (1998) studied one of these, an Allred Mormon polygynous group (formerly known as the Apostolic United Brethren). Bennion shows that most of the converts to this group are Mormon women who feel marginalized within the mainstream Mormon Church. They may, for example, be divorced, single mothers with low prospects for remarriage and with serious financial difficulties. They may join an FLDS community in an effort to secure better socioeconomic status for themselves and their children. In these communities they are easily accommodated into plural marriages. Here they adapt by forging and maintaining strong, supportive relationships with other women, often including their own cowives. As one woman said,

> In monogamy you are tied to a husband for economic sustenance, entertainment, conversation, comradeship, and emotional stimulation. But a polygynous wife is free and independent by necessity and makes her ties with other women. When a monogamous wife doesn't have him [the husband] around, and with no other sisterwives around, she is helpless. Where does she get the friendship, the moral support? A polygynist wife has it all. (Bennion 1998: 96)

Of course, not all polygynous marriages are successful or satisfying. Bennion reports that while most are, "many women, albeit a lesser number, told me that polygyny had ruined their lives, destroyed their self-esteem. . . . Many of these women also said that they would leave except that they would lose their children, their homes, their possessions, and their souls" (1998: viii).

In a later work, Bennion (2004) discusses how both polygyny and its accompanying patriarchy in particular communities in the United States developed as an adaptation to challenging environmental conditions in desert regions. Anthropologist Philip Kilbride and journalist Douglas Page (2012) have recently made the controversial argument that plural marriage (both polygyny and polyandry) should be legalized as marital options in the United States. They suggest that these options are needed since the current pattern of serial monogamy in this country fails to provide viable families within which children's need for stability can be met, as well as adults' need for love, companionship, and commitment. Thus, "plural marriage can, potentially, allow aging widows and widowers to marry men or women already in a committed relationship who they also find attractive; provide an extended and caring family for single parents and their children; [and] reduce the numbers of lonely adults" (2012: viii).

VIOLENCE AGAINST WOMEN

It has been estimated that one in every three women worldwide experiences violence from domestic abuse, rape, or other assault (United Nations Development Fund for Women 2003). This violence occurs in every country but takes different forms within various regions of the world. A great deal of international attention is now focused on this problem. In 1993 the United Nations set forth the Declaration on the Elimination of Violence Against Women. In 2004 Amnesty International launched the Stop Violence Against Women campaign. In the United States, the Violence Against Women Act became federal law in 1994. The next year the Office of Violence Against Women opened within the Department of Justice to provide financial and technical assistance to domestic programs seeking to end domestic violence, dating violence, sexual assault, and stalking. *Violence Against Women* is an international journal seeking to understand the problems and seek solutions. Yet with all this attention the connections between kinship and violence against women have not been widely appreciated.

Some contemporary issues of violence against women that concern kinship are recent, having been brought about by clashes between socioeconomic changes and more traditional structures of kinship and gender. One example comes from my earlier investigation, with Caroline James, of so-called brideburnings or dowry deaths in India (Stone and James 1995). These are cases of married women being murdered (usually burned to death) by their husbands or in-laws on account of the inadequate dowry that they brought with them to the marriage. In India, dowry wealth moves to the groom's family; women are merely vehicles of this property transmission.

A conservative estimate is that 2,000 women per year die from dowry murders in India. Most often in these cases a new bride is first harassed by her in-laws to encourage her parents to deliver more dowry. The bride's parents tend to comply with this in the hope that their daughter will receive better treatment in her new home; however, all too often the point is reached where the parents can deliver no more, and the relationship between the bride and her in-laws comes to a breaking point, resulting in her murder. Typically she is soaked with kerosene and burned, with a report to the police that this was an act of suicide or an accident while the bride was cooking in the kitchen. Often the perpetrators of the crime are not caught or charged and the groom's family then brings in a new bride with a new dowry.

There are many factors behind bride-burning, but my and James's analysis stresses that they arise in part due to socioeconomic changes in India that have led to a loss of female power in their affinal homes. Reports of bride-burning began in the 1970s, when India had shifted from a largely peasant agricultural economy to an urban industrial one. Indian society had become more prosperous and, along with it, more materialistic, with a strong emphasis on a new consumerism. In this shift Indian levels of fertility dropped significantly (as is common under prosperity and urbanization) and, we further suggested, the formerly high value placed on female fertility throughout India had decreased as well. Formerly in India, and elsewhere in South Asia (as covered here in Chapter 3, Case 3), a new bride could move up from her lowly status in her husband's home, escaping from her boot-camp-like experience, through her reproduction. Especially if she bore sons, her status in the household would increase and eventually through her sons' marriages she could become a respected and powerful mother-in-law herself. This source of female power seems to have decreased under India's new socioeconomic conditions. Indeed, one surprising fact about bride-burnings is that so many of the victims had borne children, even sons, or were pregnant at the time of their deaths.

It is not always the case that only women are the victims of social or economic change. For example, both men *and* women in China were negatively impacted by the One-Child Policy that the government began in 1979; further, the impact on women and men has changed over time. The Chinese One-Child Policy was, and remains, very controversial. It began as a government effort to prepare China to transform into a modern, prosperous, global leader (Greenhalgh 2008). It was carried out despite the fact that Chinese culture is strongly patrilineal, with a very clear emphasis on lineage continuity and son preference. Some have seen the policy as draconian, a violation of human reproductive rights, and the cause of both domestic turmoil and individual emotional strife. Further, because of son preference, abortions of female fetuses rose so high that by 1999 China's newborn gender ratio was 120 boys to 100 girls, the highest in the world (Greenhalgh 2008: 1). There have also been reports of female infanticide.

An unexpected result of the One-Child Policy has been that males—growing to adulthood in a cultural context where their ability to marry and construct a family is crucial to their social status and masculinity (Han 2008)—came to so outnumber women that many of them could not secure wives. However, there is evidence that son preference itself is decreasing. Zhang (2007) reports from a village in central China that parents are moving away from a strategy of resisting the One-Child Policy to embracing it. More and more parents are reporting that having only one child is preferable, that having a daughter is as good as having a son, and that daughters can be even more reliable as providers in old age. It could be that, despite all of the criticisms of its problems, the One-Child Policy may in the end enhance the status of Chinese women.

These Chinese and Indian cases are fairly recent. Other cases of violence against women are long-standing, such as female genital mutilation and honor killings. The latter is addressed in the following case study where the interrelationships with kinship and gender are quite clear.

CASE 13: HONOR KILLINGS

In 1960 in a village of Jordan, police discovered that a group of three men were having sex with a young, unmarried woman. On these occasions, they picked her up in a taxi, drove to a resort, and plied her with liquor, apparently without her objection. When the case became known, people of the village and surrounding communities were shocked. The men involved were temporarily jailed and the woman, believed to be pregnant, was released into the custody of her father. Then, "two weeks after the apprehension, the father of the girl took her directly to the front of the house of the guardian of the young men (father of one, uncle of the other) and slew her with his dagger" (Antoun 1968: 684).

This event was an "honor killing," the murder of a girl or woman for the dishonor she brings to her kin with her illicit sexual behavior. Illicit sexual behavior refers to sex on the part of the woman with any man before marriage or, after marriage, with any man other than her husband. With her death, usually carried out by her father or brother or a man representing them, the dishonor she has brought to the larger kin group is nullified. In the case of the Jordanian girl above, village men gathered and publicly cheered this action of the father. After this, one man remarked, "quietly, as if to seal the day's events, that the shame ('*ār*) had now been erased" (Antoun 1968: 684).

Honor killings are regularly reported in the media. In some contexts, actual sexual intercourse need not have taken place; flirtatious behavior or any sign of the woman failing to safeguard her virtue is sufficient to at least place her life at risk. It is estimated that about 5,000 women are honor-killed worldwide each year despite the efforts of many national and international organizations to raise public awareness of these events and initiate reform. Popular accounts sometimes associate honor killings with Arab people, Islam, or the Middle East, but such correlations are incorrect. Honor killings occur among non-Arabs and outside the Middle East (for example, in Turkey and Pakistan) and outside the Muslim world (for example, within Hindu India). Also, in some Muslim countries, such as Indonesia, honor killings are virtually nonexistent.

While we cannot correlate honor killings with specific cultural groups, regions, or religions, anthropologist Diane King (2008) makes the very interesting observation that, as far as we know, honor killings take place only within strongly patrilineal societies, an observation we elaborate below. King investigated honor killings with particular reference to her fieldwork among patrilineal Kurdish people in Iraq. She notes that "it seemed everyone I knew knew *of* cases of honor killings, and many personally knew someone who had been a victim" (2008: 322). Kurdish women of childbearing age seemed to live in fear of honor killings and so adapted to restrictions that would lessen suspicion of any misbehavior:

> In a social milieu in which honor killings are practiced, to create or nurture suspicion about a girl or woman's sexual transgression is to possibly endanger her life. In order to remain above this suspicion, most adolescent girls and women of childbearing age living in small towns of my field site in Iraqi Kurdistan . . . heavily curtail their bodily mobility. A typical female lives with family members, never alone. Nor does she travel anywhere alone, and she is never left home alone. Her household members ensure that if she goes to school or college, she is transported there with kin or in an approved manner such as a school bus. She does not have a job outside the home or one inside the home that would require her to receive nonkin visitors. . . . Social interaction with males who are not her kin does not take place except perhaps for brief conversations in the marketplace. (King 2008: 320–321)

As King notes, areas in which honor killings occur are not only patrilineal but also carry a tradition of *patrogenesis*, whereby men but not women are considered the significant genitors of children. Here King builds upon the work of Carol Delaney (1991), who, as mentioned in Chapter 1, writes about patrogenesis (called by her, "monogenesis") in Turkey and elsewhere. Delaney notes the widespread "seed and soil" metaphors used to describe procreation: Men plant "seed" in the "soil" of the woman's womb. In Iraqi Kurdistan, one interviewee told King, "We say that when people have sex . . . it is like the man plants a seed in a woman" (2008: 326). Women, then, nurture children in the womb, and give birth to children, but do not essentially co-create them. In patrogenic cultures the generation of children's most essential identity is transmitted through males alone, like patrilineal descent itself. So, for example, the offspring of a Kurdish man and an Arab woman would be considered 100 percent Kurdish, not half Kurdish and half Arab (King 2008: 324–325). As with ethnicity, all other categories of primary identity are transmitted through males. The "seed/soil" theory of procreation is ancient, found in both the Bible and the Qur'an, and is widespread in the world. As we saw in Chapter 1, it is a powerful cultural metaphor that easily coexists with knowledge of human biological reproduction and genetic transmission.

A crucial issue in patrogenic cultures is that the *wrong* seed might be planted in the female "soil," and it is at this juncture that notions of honor and the practice of honor killings become salient. A woman's reproductive capacity (woman-as-soil) is the exclusive property of her natal patrilineal kin, the kin groups into which she is born. Rights to her fertility (or rights over this "soil") can be legitimately transferred to another patriline only through proper marriage (or, if the woman marries within her patriline, the rights are transferred to another family). If she has sex with any man before marriage, or if she has sex with any man other than her husband after marriage, potential children of such unions are not legitimate. More pointedly, the female "soil" of the woman's natal patriline has been violated, much as though the earthly territory of the group has been invaded by outsiders. Delaney (1991: 39–40) draws this connection well. Speaking for the Middle East, she maintains that practices such as veiling, seclusion, infibulation, early marriage, and so on are efforts "to enclose the human fields, like the earthly ones, in order that a man may be assured that the produce is his own."

In King's analysis such invasion of female "soil" is a severe affront to the honor (in Kurdish, *namus*) of the male patrilineal group. To her, "honor" in this context is best understood as patrilineal reproductive sovereignty. As she writes:

> Prior to an honor killing, a girl or woman has assumed . . . a social place as *potential* mother. Her body is seen as possibly housing a new person . . . a member of a patriline. But whose patriline? . . . For a new person to be created in the womb/field of the lineage, that lineage must first give a show of its consent in the marriage ritual. . . . A wedding is a sovereignty-affirming event, a chance for lineage "A" to communicate to the watching community that it consents that lineage "B" implant, incubate, and rear new members of its own. A woman who is used, or seen to be open to being used, by another lineage in this way without benefit of the sovereignty-affirming marriage ritual is killed . . . by a member of her lineage. She is killed precisely because she is *of* her lineage, not because she is an outsider or "other" to the perpetuator. It is the fetus that is other. (King 2008: 327)

An honor killing, then, is an assertion of the absolute sovereignty of the patriline over its reproductive soil. In this context, the hymen of a woman becomes a real and a symbolic border of the reproductive territory of the sovereign patriline. "To a great extent, sovereignty has to do with defining borders and keeping out aliens. Where better [place] for a lineage to focus, then, than on the hymen, a convenient border for controlling reproduction?" (King 2008: 328). Women's hymens are the gateways into lineages, boundaries that must be strictly controlled in the name of lineage honor. "An 'honor killing' is a purging of possible un-sanctioned seed along with the plot of reproductive soil in which it may have been planted" (King 2008: 330).

This focus on the hymen is significant. In Iraqi Kurdistan, as elsewhere in the region, men are concerned to have virgin brides and women are concerned to be virgin at marriage, by which is meant to have an intact or unbroken hymen. One woman feared she was technically not a virgin because she had played roughly as a child, running and climbing trees. As she reported to King, "I am very afraid of this. . . . There is not one day, not *one* day, that I do not think about it" (2008: 328). One of the greatest insults one woman can hurl at another is "'I will tear you' (*Ez de tu dirinim*), which literally means, 'I will tear your hymen.' This is a threat more forceful than 'I will kill you' because it means, 'I will obligate your brother to kill you'" (King 2008: 328).

King goes on to draw an illuminating parallel between lineage sovereignty and the state in Iraqi Kurdistan. For many decades Kurdish people have been seeking to form a sovereign state, independent of Iraq and, in its earlier struggles, free of the dictator Saddam Hussein. In March 1991, following the US invasion of Iraq, Kurdish guerrilla forces took their chance, staged a major uprising, and began to shape their new state, defending its borders. Kurdish flags were raised and statues of Saddam Hussein were destroyed. Following this, many outsiders entered Iraq from neighboring countries. Along with some Turkish traders, these were mostly people working with Western relief and development agencies. Although initially this influx of (mostly male) newcomers was welcomed as a sign of free-dom and modernity, by 1995 it was seen as dangerous to upholding honor. King writes, "As interviewees later told me, soon a feeling of sexual vulnerability had settled in" (2008: 332). This was especially true in the border towns of the new, vulnerable state-in-the-making.

King notes that during this period, leaders of the state movement were referred to by kinship terms, as the nation's "father" or "brother," and many people ex-pressed a feeling that all Kurds were now "like one lineage." In one sense this fledgling state with still-vulnerable borders did act like a lineage fearing for its honor: It began to kill women. That these killings took place in the national eu-phoria of the new Kurdish homeland is striking. These were not true honor killings. Most of the women were labeled as prostitutes or were suspected of hav-ing had sexual relations with enemies or outsiders, and their killers were not their fathers or brothers but the ruling guerrilla forces. As one interviewee told King:

In the first years after the uprising, 1991 and 1992, there were killings of women every day! I saw an average of one a day in the court. Her family did not kill her—the *peshmerga* (guerrillas) did, but this was not open. There was a "black list" of the women who had had sexual relations with Baath [Hussein's Iraq] party men. Some were prostitutes, some operated out of fear of the government of Iraq, some were poor, their husbands were off fighting in the war—there were many reasons. The *peshmerga* decided to kill one per day. (2008: 334)

Eventually a Kurdish leader put a stop to this practice. But we can see in these killings the parallel between the lineage, concerned with its reproductive sovereignty, the hymen-borders of its women, and the state, defending both its territorial borders with armies and its conceptual borders with the killing of particular women. As King concludes, "New offspring for the patrilineal state can be gestated in the bodies of women. But new offspring for enemies can be as well. So, women who had threatened the new Kurdish state's sovereignty over its own reproductive processes were eliminated along with any possible fetuses they may have borne" (2008: 335).

And what do Kurdish women think of all this? King elicited interesting remarks from the women among whom she lived and worked in northern Iraq. As we have seen, women seemed to live in fear of honor killings. Additionally, many women expressed to King that the daily restrictions on their behavior to protect their reputation were "suffocating." At the same time, when asked specifically about honor killings, many women voiced the perspective of the male patrilineal body. One said, "My oldest brother Jangir—he is a good man. If I had sex with a boy, he would kill me because he is honorable" (King 2008: 327). Of the peshmerga killings of nonkin women, some women approved. "One woman even waxed nostalgic about them, interpreting that they were no longer carried out as a sign that the Kurdish government had ceased to care about promoting virtue in the society" (King 2008: 334). In any event, women are not just passive spectators in the patrilineal/patrogenic cultural complex that can put their lives in peril. As King notes, there is one way in which women can decidedly influence one another's reputation: through gossip. "For example, a young woman was seen riding in a car with a man unknown to the gossiper. Perhaps the man was an uncle, visiting from out of town. But perhaps not—perhaps he was an illicit lover! And so on" (King 2008: 323). In this way gossip is a powerful weapon that women can and do use against one another.

In this chapter we have addressed some contemporary social issues, showing that our ability to understand them requires contextual knowledge of regional constructions of kinship and family. In the final two chapters of the book we move to a new general topic—challenges to kinship—beginning with the new reproductive technologies covered in the next chapter.

DISCUSSION QUESTIONS

1. What do you see as the future for marriage in the United States and Europe? Will it become obsolete? Why or why not?

2. Honor killings occur in areas that are patrilineal and patrogenic. How, according to Diane King, are these two traits interwoven with the cultural idea that the honor of a kin group depends on the proper sexual behavior of its women? How do King's ideas differ from those of Alice Schlegel and Sherry Ortner (in Chapter 7), who discussed similar cultural concerns with female sexual purity?

3. This chapter has discussed examples of contemporary social issues that concern kinship structures and gender roles. Can you think of other examples?

SUGGESTED FURTHER READING

Jessop, Carolyn (with Laura Palmer). 2007. *Escape*. New York: Broadway Books. This is a fascinating firsthand account of life within an isolated FLDS community.

SUGGESTED CLASSROOM MEDIA

Big Love. 2006–2011. Home Box Office Inc. Many one-hour episodes. This popular TV series focuses on a Utah suburban family of one man and his three wives. In *Big Love* a contrast is drawn between a rural FLDS community, where several abuses occur, and the suburban counterpart, where the polygynist family copes with problems of relationships, childrearing, neighbors, and finances. For classroom use any one of the earlier episodes (or parts of episodes) is recommended.

WEBSITES

www.freshfilm.com/damnedtoheaven. "Damned to Heaven." Provides a video of accounts of former members of Warren Jeffs's Fundamentalist Church of Jesus Christ of Latter-Day Saints community in Arizona. Jeffs was convicted of child sexual assault in Texas in 2011 and is serving a life sentence in prison.

www.nytimes.com/2012/01/30/world/americas/afghan-family-members -convicted-in-honor-killings.html. *New York Times* coverage of an Afghan man and his sons convicted of an "honor killing" in Ottawa, Canada, 2012.

REFERENCES

Antoun, Richard T. 1968. On the Modesty of Women in Arab Muslim Villages: A Study in the Accommodation of Traditions. *American Anthropologist* 70(4): 671–697.

Bennion, Janet. 1998. *Women of Principle: Female Networking in Contemporary Mormon Polygyny*. New York: Oxford University Press.

———. 2004. *Desert Patriarchy: Mormon and Mennonite Communities in the Chihuahua Valley*. Tucson: University of Arizona Press.

Carsten, Janet. 2004. *After Kinship*. Cambridge, England: Cambridge University Press.

Coontz, Stephanie. 1992. *The Way We Never Were: American Families and the Nostalgia Trap*. New York: Basic Books.

Delaney, Carol Lowery. 1991. *The Seed and the Soil: Gender and Cosmology in Turkish Village Society* (Comparative Studies on Muslim Societies, No. 11). Berkeley: University of California Press.

The Economist. 2012. Setting aside Childish Things: America's Teenage Pregnancy Rate Has Hit a 40-year Low. July–August, 26–27.

Finkler, Kaja. 2001. The Kin in the Gene: The Medicalization of Family and Kinship in American Society. *Current Anthropology* 42(2): 235–249.

Fox, Robin. 1997. *Reproduction and Succession: Studies in Anthropology, Law, and Society*. New Brunswick, NJ: Transaction Publishers.

Greenhalgh, Susan. 2008. *Just One Child: Science and Policy in Deng's China*. Berkeley: University of California Press.

Han, Hua. 2008. Living a Single Life: The Plight and Adaptations of the Bachelors in Yishala. In Susanne Brandtstadter and Gonçalo Duro dos Santos, eds., *Chinese Kinship: Contemporary Anthropological Perspectives*, pp. 48–66. New York: Routledge.

Jacobson, David, Joan H. Leim, and Robert S. Weiss. 2001. Parenting from Separate Households: A Cultural Perspective. In Linda Stone, ed., *New Directions in Anthropological Kinship*, pp. 229–245. Lanham, MD: Rowman & Littlefield.

Jankowiak, William. 2001. In the Name of the Father: Theology, Kinship, and Charisma in an American Polygynist Community. In Linda Stone, ed., *New Directions in Anthropological Kinship*, pp. 264–284. Lanham, MD: Rowman & Littlefield.

Jessop, Carolyn (with Laura Palmer). 2007. *Escape*. New York: Broadway Books.

Kilbride, Philip L., and Douglas R. Page. 2012. *Plural Marriage for Our Times: A Reinvented Option?* Santa Barbara, CA: Praeger.

King, Diane E. 2008. The Personal Is Patrilineal: *Namus* as Sovereignty. *Identities: Global Studies in Culture and Power* 15(3): 317–342.

Kost, Kathryn, and Stanley Henshaw. 2012. *US Teenage Pregnancies, Births, and Abortions 2008: National Trends by Age, Race, and Ethnicity*. New York: Guttmacher Institute.

Lewin, Ellen. 1998. *Recognizing Ourselves: Ceremonies of Lesbian and Gay Commitment*. New York: Columbia University Press.

———. 2004. "Why Marriage?" *Anthropology News* 45(5): 11–12.

McKee, Nancy P., and Linda Stone. 2007. *Gender and Culture in America*, 3rd ed. Cornwall-on-Hudson, NY: Sloan Publishing.

Mundy, Liza. 2012. *The Richer Sex*. New York: Simon & Schuster.

Stone, Linda. 2004a. Gay Marriage and Anthropology. *Anthropology News* 45(5): 10.

———. 2004b. Has the World Turned? Kinship and Family in the Contemporary American Soap Opera. In Robert Parkin and Linda Stone, eds., *Family and Kinship: An Anthropological Reader*, pp. 395–407. Malden, MA: Blackwell.

Stone, Linda, and Caroline James. 1995. Dowry, Bride-Burning, and Female Power in India. *Women's Studies International Forum* 18(2): 125–134.

United Nations Development Fund for Women. 2003. *Not a Minute More: Ending Violence Against Women* (UNIFEM report). New York: United Nations.

United States Census Bureau. 2012. *Households and Families: 2012.*

Weston, Kath. 1991. *Families We Choose: Lesbians, Gays, Kinship.* New York: Columbia University Press.

Zhang, Hong. 2007. From Resisting to "Embracing?" the One-Child Rule: Understanding New Fertility Trends in a Central China Village. *China Quarterly* 192: 855–875.

9

KINSHIP, GENDER, AND THE
NEW REPRODUCTIVE TECHNOLOGIES

Home, home—a few small rooms, stiflingly overinhabited by a man, by
a periodically teeming woman, by a rabble of boys and girls of all ages.
No air, no space; an understerilized prison. . . . Psychically, it was a
rabbit hole, a midden, hot with the frictions of tightly packed life. . . .
What suffocating intimacies, what dangerous, insane, obscene relationships between the members of the family group! Maniacally, the mother
brooded over her children . . . brooded over them like a cat over its kit-
tens; but a cat that could talk, a cat that could say, "My baby, my baby"
over and over again.

—*Aldous Huxley*

This passage from Huxley's science-fiction novel, *Brave New World*, gives a
society's comment on its past, a despicable past when humans reproduced
their own offspring and lived in families. In this brave new world, reproduction is entirely state-controlled and carried out in test tubes and incubators.
There is no kinship whatsoever in this new society. There is also no marriage.
Women and men are equally expected to be sexually promiscuous, and sex
is solely for pleasure. But apart from this, rather amazingly, there are few
changes in gender. Women of the brave new world appear passive and fluffy-
headed. Men apparently run the new society and hold all the prestigious or
powerful jobs. In real life, meanwhile, new modes of reproduction are very
definitely challenging conventions of both gender and kinship, as this chapter
will show.

In 1978 the first "test-tube" baby, Louise Brown, was produced in England.
Human conception had taken place inside a petri dish, outside the womb,

and without sexual intercourse. By now thousands of babies have been created in this way, and Louise Brown has herself produced a normal child. About a decade after Brown was born, we began to see cases of "surrogate" mothers and complex legal battles over the fate of their children. In 1987 Mary Beth Whitehead sought custody of a child, the famous Baby M, whom she had borne through a surrogacy contract. She had agreed to bear a child for William Stern, using his donor sperm. Stern's wife, Elizabeth, felt that because she had a mild case of multiple sclerosis, a pregnancy would be too great a risk to her health. The case went through two New Jersey courts. Both awarded custody of Baby M to Stern, although the higher court ruled that the surrogacy contract was invalid.

Surrounded by controversy, these and other New Reproductive Technologies (NRTs) have raised thorny legal and moral issues. They also present a challenge to our deepest ideas and values concerning kinship, and carry profound implications for gender. What are these NRTs, how do they work, and what implications do they have?

THE NEW REPRODUCTIVE TECHNOLOGIES

Reproductive technologies, as such, are not new. Various forms of contraception, abortion, fertility-enhancing concoctions, cesarean surgery, and so on have existed for a long time. As far as I know, every human culture in the world offers local techniques for assisting conception as well as some methods of contraception, effective or not. But the NRTs go beyond promoting or preventing conception, or inducing or ending pregnancy. Some, for instance, provide knowledge about particular reproductive acts, knowledge that humans have never had before. Other NRTs open up reproductive roles that humans have never played before. What follows is a listing of the new technologies with explanations of how they work. The first two are technologies that give us new—and in some contexts, problematic—knowledge.

Determining Biological Fatherhood

Throughout most of human history biological motherhood was taken for granted, but an equivalent "paternal certainty" did not exist. Then, around 1900, some techniques were developed that were capable of specifying, with certainty, who could *not* have fathered a particular child. Thus these tests—for example, the one based on the ABO blood-group system[1]—could exclude individuals from a group of potential fathers but could not determine which particular individual was the actual father.

The new so-called DNA fingerprinting technique has considerably altered this situation. The technique relies on amplifying portions of human DNA in a test tube using the polymerase chain reaction (PCR) and identifying DNA fragments based on restriction fragment length polymorphism (RFLP) and other techniques. DNA can be isolated easily from a small quantity of tissue taken from the individual in question. The general principle here is that human individuals differ in their DNA in many subtle ways and that no two individuals (except identical twins) have exactly the same DNA patterns. The PCR and RFLP techniques are capable of discerning these subtle variations and thus can provide a genetic (DNA-based) "fingerprint" of an individual that corresponds to that individual only, to the exclusion of all others. Genetic fingerprinting is now widely used to determine paternity with a very high degree of certainty, up to 99.99 percent or better. It has also been used to trace the parentage of orphans whose parents were killed and buried in known locales during wars and to identify remains of soldiers killed on a battlefield. Under proper conditions, DNA can survive, even in bones, for thousands of years. Had DNA fingerprinting existed during the life of Anastasia, who claimed to be the sole surviving daughter of Tsar Nicholas II of Russia, her bluff would have been uncovered at the time. In 1995, DNA analysis applied to bone material showed that Anastasia was indeed an impostor.

Determining biological fatherhood may be of great interest or advantage to many individuals in a variety of situations. But what are the broader implications of the fact that this determination can now be made so easily, and so scientifically? Many people have argued that paternity uncertainty in many ways shaped human culture around the globe. They suggest that a whole host of practices in different regions of the world—having to do with female seclusion, restrictions on female behavior, medieval chastity belts, and so on—were all predicated on the principle of paternity uncertainty. But such uncertainty is now a thing of the past. We do not yet know what the long-term consequences may be for women or for men.

The polyandrous Nyinba (Chapter 6) are very concerned with biological fatherhood. But culturally they have constructed a rather efficient and normally satisfying way of designating paternity to husbands. Wives simply announce which husband is the father of a given child, even though in some cases this could not have been scientifically known, or husbands and wives together determine which brother the child most closely resembles. The process of designating paternity gives women a lot of power and, in cases of successful marriages, serves to equitably distribute children to husbands. But what will happen to this system when "real" paternity can be easily and quickly determined through a simple blood test? Will it bring discord between brothers? Will it result in the loss of power and influence for women? And what will happen to women in societies where the accepted punishment for proven infidelity is severe beating or death?

Determining the Sex of the Unborn Child

Techniques for determining the sex of an unborn child are by-products of a technology first developed to screen for genetic defects. These defects are detectable at the chromosomal level. The basic procedure involves harvesting fetal cells *in utero* (from inside the uterus), preparing their chromosomes, and looking at them under a microscope. The resulting chromosome spread is called a *karyotype*, and the process of characterizing chromosomes from an individual is called karyotyping. It turned out to be the case that, while karyotyping chromosomes to detect for genetic defects, technicians found it also very easy to see what sex the fetus was going to be. Karyotyping readily identifies the sex of the fetus since the Y chromosome (unique to males) is very small whereas X is large.

Two techniques are used to sample fetal cells. One is amniocentesis, the process of inserting a needle into the uterus (through the abdomen) and harvesting fluid from the amniotic sac that surrounds the fetus. Fetal skin cells are normally shed into this fluid. Usually only a few cells are present in the fluid, so it has to be cultured *in vitro* (that is, in an artificial environment outside the living organism) to allow for cell manipulation. These cells are then karyotyped. Amniocentesis cannot be applied before the twelfth week of pregnancy since sufficient amniotic fluid is not present until that time.

The other technique, chorionic villus sampling, is less invasive because the abdomen is not punctured. In this case, a sample of chorion is taken by introducing a tube through the vagina into the uterus. The chorion is fetal tissue that lines the uterine cavity and surrounds the amniotic sac. Since this tissue is abundant, no cell culture is necessary and karyotyping can be done right away. There is enough chorion to allow the procedure as early as the eighth week of pregnancy.

In societies that do not express a cultural preference for male or female children, a couple's knowledge of the sex of a fetus is without much consequence. But, as we have seen, some societies strongly prefer male children. In India, for example, amniocentesis is a major social issue. When the test became available, female fetuses were aborted at a very high rate. Many women underwent amniocentesis, either voluntarily or at the insistence of husbands and in-laws, with the idea that their pregnancy would be terminated unless the fetus was male. Many Indian women's organizations have fought to protect women and unborn females from this abuse. In some Indian states amniocentesis is now illegal (except in cases where genetic defects are an issue), but the test is still widely used illegally.

Artificial Insemination and In-Vitro Fertilization

Certain NRTs are used in cases of infertility of an individual or a couple. In males, infertility is usually caused by either sperm defect (low count or immotile sperm cells) or impotence (physiological or psychological). In females, the situation is more complicated. A woman may be sterile, meaning that she is unable to conceive a child, due to absence of ovulation (either no eggs are produced or the egg cannot travel through fallopian tubes that are blocked). However, a sterile woman may still be able to carry and bear a child. Another problem is that a woman may be fertile (able to conceive a child), but the fertilized egg fails to become implanted in her uterus. Some reproductive problems can be corrected by surgery, drugs, or, in some cases of male impotence, psychotherapy. But if these treatments do not work, there are two other procedures that can allow an individual or couple to have a child. These procedures are artificial insemination (AI) and in-vitro fertilization (IVF).

Artificial insemination can be used when a couple seeks to have a child but the male is infertile. In this case the biological father may be an anonymous sperm donor whose sperm is stored in a sperm bank. The sperm bank categorizes sperm according to the physical characteristics of the donors (skin, eye, and hair color; height; and general body features) so that the future parents can roughly determine the looks of their offspring. For example, the parents may seek a child who will look something like its legal father.

Artificial insemination is a simple technique. Donor sperm is simply placed into the uterus of the female at the proper stage of her menstrual cycle. Nature does the rest. Artificial insemination has long been routinely used in animal husbandry to ensure production of animals with desired characteristics. Its average cost ranges from $200 to $400, and its success rate is about 30 percent if fresh sperm is used and about 15 percent with frozen sperm.

Artificial insemination can also be used by women who seek pregnancy without sexual intercourse. For example, a single woman may wish to have a child without involving the biological father beyond anonymous sperm donation. Or a woman may wish to serve as a "surrogate" mother for a married couple who cannot have a child of their own due to the wife's infertility. In this case the surrogate is artificially inseminated with the husband's sperm. The sperm donor is obviously not anonymous, but sexual intercourse between the husband and the surrogate is unnecessary.

The technique of in-vitro fertilization (IVF) is much more complicated and expensive (about $25,000); it also has a lower success rate than AI in cases where fresh sperm is used (about 14 percent). IVF was developed for humans in the late 1970s. In this procedure, immature eggs, or oocytes, are surgically removed from the ovaries of a woman and incubated with sperm in a sterile petri dish in the presence of a nutrient medium. Alternatively, if the sperm cells show poor motility (swimming ability), they can be injected into the egg's cytoplasm (cellular sap) by means of a very fine glass needle (see Image 9.1). This latter technique is called "intracytoplasmic sperm injection" (ICSI). After fertilization occurs, the embryo is allowed to undergo cell division for a few days. The embryo is then removed from the dish and implanted into a woman's uterus, where, if all goes well, it will grow to term.

Usually several oocytes are removed, fertilized in vitro at the same time, and implanted together. Often only one embryo, or none, will continue to

IMAGE 9.1   Photomicrograph of a human egg manipulated with a glass syringe.

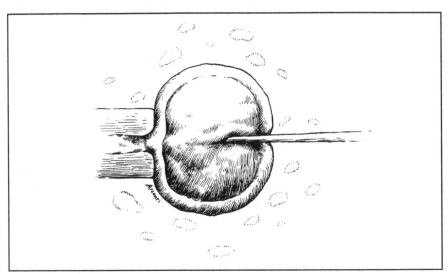

*The object on the left is a holding pipette used to immobilize the egg in a precise position.
The glass needle on the right has penetrated the egg and can be used to inject sperm (as in
ICSI) or a cell nucleus (as in cloning). The needle can also be used to remove the egg's genetic
material by aspiration, prior to injection with a new nucleus. Drawing by Andrew S. Arconti,
author's collection.*

develop. However, cases of multiple births have occurred. Excess embryos
resulting from IVF and not implanted can be frozen and used at a subsequent
time, even many years later. One current problem concerns the fate of all the
frozen embryos now in existence and the question of who has rights over
them. In the United States alone there are tens of thousands of frozen embryos,
and throughout the world, hundreds of thousands.

With both IVF and AI, the biological father can also be the would-be
legal father of the child, or the biological father may be a sperm donor.
With AI, too, one woman may be the legal mother while another woman
is the biological mother. But with IVF, something altogether new happens
to "motherhood." The woman who contributes the oocytes may or may
not be the woman who carries the child and gives birth. Once the eggs of
one woman are fertilized outside the womb, they may be implanted either
back into her or into another woman. This is an important point to which
we will return later.

Table 9.1 summarizes the different forms of AI and IVF, and shows what
options are available depending on the reproductive problem involved. Note
that the "father" (F) is designated as either fertile or sterile, whereas the

"mother" (M) may exhibit different combinations of sterility (unable to conceive) or fertility, and be either able or unable to bear a child. The table indicates the circumstances under which a couple would need a "donor" egg, sperm, or womb. It also shows what genetic connection the child will have with either or both parents, given the various options. In preparing this table I have assumed that it is a couple, rather than an individual, who is seeking a child; that to the extent possible the couple seeks to have a child genetically related to at least one of its members; and that, if possible, the mother seeks to give birth. In real life, some alternative possibilities may also exist. For example, in Case 1 of the table, the mother cannot conceive but can bear a child. Although the table specifies the use of IVF, an actual couple in this situation might elect to avoid the expense and trouble of IVF and use AI with a surrogate mother instead (as in Case 2).

The table also shows three circumstances under which a so-called surrogate mother might be used, along with the different outcomes involved. In Case 2 the surrogate not only carries the child but is the genetic mother, whereas the father is also genetically contributing to the child. In Case 3 the surrogate has no genetic relation to the child, and the child is the genetic product of both parents. Finally, in Case 6, the surrogate has no genetic connection to the child, and the child is genetically related to only one parent, the mother.

TABLE 9.1 NRTs: Contributions of Egg, Sperm, and Womb, with Genetic Outcomes

| | *Donation Needed* | | | | |
Problem	*Egg*	*Sperm*	*Womb*	*Technique*	*Genetic Result*
1. F fertile, M sterile but can bear child	X			IVF	child = 1/2 F
2. F fertile, M sterile and cannot bear child	X		X	AI	child = 1/2 F
3. F fertile, M fertile but cannot bear child			X	IVF	child = 1/2 F + 1/2 M
4. F sterile, M sterile but can bear child	X	X		IVF	child = 0% parents
5. F sterile, M fertile and can bear child		X		AI	child = 1/2 M
6. F sterile, M fertile but cannot bear child		X	X	IVF	child = 1/2 M

Note: F stands for Father, and M for Mother.

As this table shows, IVF can be used to assist reproduction in a greater variety of situations than AI. At the same time, however, it is more problematic than AI. For one thing it is not always safe for women. Depending on her particular role in the process, a participating woman may have to take fertility drugs, some with possible side effects. If she is using or donating her eggs, these must be removed from her through invasive laparoscopy, and if the IVF procedure fails to result in fertilized eggs, it must be performed again. Some women argue that the real beneficiaries of IVF are the highly paid medical professionals who exploit the desperation of childless couples and offer them false hope (Raymond 1993).

CASE 14: NEW REPRODUCTIVE TECHNOLOGIES IN ISRAEL

The NRTs will undoubtedly meet with varied responses in different cultural contexts. A case in point is Susan Kahn's (2000) investigation of these technologies in the Jewish state of Israel. Here there are unique issues surrounding these technologies, reflecting the distinctive meanings of reproduction, kinship, and gender in this setting. To understand these it is important to note a few facts about the Israeli case. First is Israel's intense interest in reproduction, both culturally and politically. For religiously observant Jews, both men and women, reproduction is seen as a religious duty (following the biblical command, "be fruitful and multiply"). There are other motives for having children, or having many children. For example, some Israelis feel that children are vital to preserve and perpetuate a traditional family life, and many Israelis feel that having children is important to compensate for the 6 million Jews killed in the Nazi holocaust. Second, Jewishness is considered to be transmitted exclusively through the mother, or matrilineally. Third, Jewish identity automatically grants one citizenship in Israel. Thus Israeli women are under particular pressure to reproduce since they are the major means through which the Jewish nation can reproduce itself. The effect on women is profound. As a social worker commented to Kahn, "If you're not a mother, you don't exist in Israeli society" (2000: 10).

The importance of reproduction, of reproducing Jews, is reflected in Israel's state policies that, for example, do not financially support family planning services but do offer various subsidies to families with three or more children. And nowhere is state pronatalism more visible than in Israel's policies with regard to the NRTs. Israel, for example, was the first state to legalize surrogate motherhood. Israel's national health insurance subsidizes all the NRTs. In fact, "every Israeli, regardless of religion or marital status, is eligible for unlimited rounds of in-vitro fertilization treatment free of charge, up to the birth of two live children" (2000: 2). Interest in these reproductive technologies is intense, and as a result, Israel has more fertility clinics per capita than any other nation in the world. Israel is now a top country in the research and development of these technologies, and patients from Europe and the Middle East flock to its fertility clinics.

How does use of these technologies play out in Israel? What impact are these technologies having on Israeli constructions of kinship? Kahn's study addresses how these technologies are being used by unmarried women and how the technologies are intersecting with traditional constructions of Jewish motherhood, fatherhood, and the reproduction of Jews.

Kahn found that a small but growing number of Israeli women are choosing to reproduce as single, unmarried women through AI. Significantly, it is socially easier to be an unmarried mother in Israel than in many other places. For one thing, in this Jewish culture, children born to unmarried women are considered fully legitimate. Secondly, there is state support for unmarried mothers, especially in terms of housing, child care, and tax exemptions. There is some stigma against intentional out-of-wedlock reproduction, particularly among the religiously observant, but Kahn heard from one unmarried woman that "it is considered much worse to be a childless woman than it is to be an unmarried mother" (2000: 16). Kahn also found that women who were considering AI, or who had received this treatment, did not see it as their most desirable option, but as a last resort. For example, a childless woman who is divorced or widowed (or who for whatever reason has never married) might feel that she is getting older and does not have the time to delay reproduction until she has formed a new marital relationship.

In Israel, unmarried women who undergo AI can receive sperm only from anonymous donors. Most of these are Jewish. As for the donor's characteristics, the women can choose only the donor's "color," or ethnicity, such as Ashkenazi (Jews of European origin) or Sephardi (Jews of Asian or North African origin). In fact, however, those medical staff who actually match up donor sperm with women AI patients encourage matches along ethnic lines. As one woman commented, "I wanted to try and go for Iraqi sperm or something like that, something dark, but the nurse persuaded me not to. She said she knew the donor for me, he has blue eyes like me, she says he is very nice, very gentle" (2000: 34).

Another woman said, "I had no choice about whose sperm was used. I just know it is medical students, and that they choose someone who looks like me with my background, Ashkenazi, but if a Yemenite woman went in there, they would find her Yemenite sperm" (2000: 35).

Over and over again women reported that they were encouraged to select donors who "looked like them." This encouragement to match egg and sperm ethnically is interesting given that there are known gene mutations among Ashkenazi Jews that can result in genetic diseases in offspring. Donor sperm is screened for one such disease (Tay-Sachs, a terminal genetic disease of the nervous system) but not for the many other disease genes occurring with high frequency among Ashkenazi Jews. Kahn notes that "clearly there is no official policy that mandates the match of Ashkenazi donor sperm with Ashkenazi unmarried women, but the informal practice of sperm selection seems to suggest that it is desirable to observe and maintain ethnic differences in this process" (2000: 37).

In Israel a number of religious fertility clinics will not accept unmarried women patients but do perform a variety of services for married couples, Jewish (orthodox or secular) and non-Jewish. Kahn's observations in one such clinic in Jerusalem revealed how carefully the medical procedures accommodated Jewish law as well as Jewish social and ethical concerns. For example, the Jerusalem clinic employed a number of women (all but one were ultraorthodox women) as special inspectors (called *maschgichot*) to monitor the work of lab technicians who process eggs and sperm. This is done to help prevent any accidental mixings. Kahn writes:

> As one maschgicha put it, "We make sure that Lichtenberg and Silverstein don't get mixed up." Meaning, of course, that they make sure that Lichtenberg's sperm and Silverstein's sperm do not get accidentally mixed up by the lab worker who may inadvertently use the same syringe, pipette, or catheter to handle sperm as she transfers it between test tube and Petri dish. For if Lichtenberg's wife's egg was inadvertently fertilized with Silverstein's sperm, and the resulting embryo was implanted in Lichtenberg's wife for gestation and parturition, then Lichtenberg's wife would give birth to Silverstein's baby. This would obviously give rise to numerous social, ethical, and Halakhic [pertaining to the legal part of the Talmudic literature] questions. (2000: 115)

One such question concerns whether such a mix-up would constitute an adulterous union of sperm and egg.

Another interesting example concerns the care with which a doctor surgically extracts ova from a woman's body. If in the course of this procedure there is some bleeding of the uterus, the woman could be considered *niddah*, or in a state of ritual impurity (as when she menstruates). In this case some rabbis would say that the woman should be prohibited from receiving, a few days later, any embryo produced from her fertilized eggs (as in IVF) since a woman in a state of niddah impurity should not conceive a child. In fact, were a woman to conceive in a state of niddah, her child could be stigmatized as *ben-niddal*, a child of niddah. In the normal course of events, a woman in niddah should take a ritual bath (*mikveh*) seven days after she stops bleeding before she can have sexual intercourse and conceive a child. In the clinic, careful records of each woman's times of niddah and mikveh are kept to ensure that embryos are implanted only at a proper "clean" time of a woman's cycle. Not all rabbis would consider uterine bleeding caused by surgery to place a woman in a state of niddah. But if uterine bleeding does occur, the doctor will tell the patient, who may then consult with her own rabbi to determine whether she can have an embryo implanted.

Of special concern to Israeli rabbis and ordinary citizens alike is how the NRTs affect the kinship status of the individuals who employ them or result from them. In the case of reproduction through egg donation, who is the mother—the woman who donated the eggs or the woman who gestated and gave birth? In the case of AI, rabbis consult Jewish legal sources to figure out who is the father—the man who donated the sperm or the man who has sexual intercourse with the woman (the mother's husband)? These kinds of questions may be raised with regard to the NRTs in many cultures but some additional issues are relevant in Israel. For example, the NRTs raise some problems concerning adultery, which in Jewish law is defined as sexual intercourse between a married Jewish woman and a Jewish man other than her husband. A child conceived of such a union is considered a *mamzer*, the product of an illicit union and therefore unmarriageable. So, if a married woman donates her eggs to another woman (fertilized, let's say, by the other woman's Jewish husband's donated sperm), is this a case of adulterous union between sperm and egg and is the child produced a mamzer? To sidestep this problem, the eggs of unmarried Jewish women are preferred and in high demand. Further, some rabbis question whether it is ethical for any Jewish man to donate his sperm for use by a married Jewish woman not his wife, since this too could be seen as an adulterous union of egg and sperm. Many rabbis argue that a married Jewish woman should accept sperm only from a non-Jewish donor; others argue against this practice, saying it "pollutes" Jewishness.

Things get even more complex in Israel, since intertwined with all these issues is the question of how, with NRTs, is Jewishness transmitted? Thus, if a woman uses eggs donated from a non-Jewish woman, is the child Jewish? Most rabbis argue that the child would be Jewish since a Jewish woman gestated and gave birth to it. Other rabbis say the child would have to be later converted to Judaism in order to be Jewish. But of course, the whole issue of whether one can convert to Judaism is not settled in Israel. As one can imagine, similar problems surround the practice of surrogate mothers. If, for example, a Jewish man and wife produce an embryo through IVF and then use a non-Jewish surrogate mother who gestates and bears the child, is the child Jewish?

These and many other questions raised by the NRTs continue to be discussed and debated in Israel. Many anthropologists (for example, Strathern [1995]) have shown how NRTs in other Euro-American settings have shaken traditional cultural ideas about kinship. Kahn argues that the Israeli case, by contrast, shows that the use of these new technologies "does not necessarily displace a culture's fundamental assumptions about kinship" (2000: 159). Here we see that rabbis and their followers seek to interpret and regulate the NRTs in a way that preserves traditional ideas of kinship and reproduction of Jews. The debates and decisions about the NRTs in Israel clearly do not favor a genetic definition of relatedness, nor have they introduced a new element of "kinship as choice" as in other Euro-American settings.

There are other cases where we can see how strongly cultural traditions influence the local understanding and use of NRTs. For example, in Egypt, in sharp contrast to Israel, the use of NRTs is limited due to financial, technological, and religious (Islamic) considerations (Inhorn 2003). Here, involving third parties (donors) in a couple's reproduction is forbidden due to the implications of adultery. In addition, Egyptian culture strongly stresses patrilineal continuity and male biological paternity (recall from Chapter 3 that this is a region of pronounced lineal masculinity). As a result, cases of male infertility are not remedied through AI of a man's spouse but rather through ICSI (intracytoplasmic sperm injection, covered earlier in this chapter; see Image 9.1) (Inhorn 2003). But in Egypt, even ICSI raises new dilemmas. Males undergoing this treatment fear accidental mixing of their sperm with that of someone else during laboratory procedures. Others are concerned that a child produced by ICSI will be stigmatized if its origin becomes known. And in still other cases the wife of an infertile man may suffer. By the time the husband's condition is known and comes up for treatment, the wife's own fertility may have decreased with the advance of her age. In this case the man may divorce her and take a younger wife (Inhorn 2004).

In nearby Lebanon donor sperm and eggs are available but great secrecy surrounds their use: "The introduction of a third, or even fourth party into the reproductive process is commonly perceived as akin to 'adultery' . . . and thus as potentially ruinous of public reputation, or perhaps as deadly" (Clarke 2007: 10). Indeed one Lebanese doctor insisted that the anthropologist studying fertility treatments sign a confidentiality clause, saying, "There might be honor killings" (Clarke 2007: 10).

Some Additional NRTs

Among the NRTs available, a few are not widely used as yet but may become more prevalent in the future. One, called embryo adoption, would apply to the situation of Case 1 in Table 9.1. Here, the mother cannot conceive but can bear a child. Instead of using IVF with donor eggs, the husband could artificially inseminate another woman who serves as a very temporary surrogate. After a week, the embryo is flushed out of the surrogate's uterus and inserted into the uterus of the mother. Another type of reproductive technology is called oocyte freezing, a procedure in which oocytes, or eggs, are taken from a woman and frozen for later use. So far this procedure has not proven very successful, but if perfected, it could open a whole range of reproductive options. For example, a woman could freeze her oocytes when she is young and healthy and use them later in life when her fertility would otherwise be lower. Technically, she could use them even past menopause. Alternatively, a much older woman could take oocytes donated by a young woman. These could be thawed, fertilized in IVF, and then implanted in the older woman.

Already one fifty-nine-year-old woman has given birth through oocyte donation. Some people are repulsed by the image of very old women giving birth or becoming mothers. Others point out that men have all along been able to reproduce at any age.

Finally, we consider the technique known as cloning, which may one day be applied to human reproduction. Cloning can take several forms, one of which, organismal cloning, is particularly relevant to our discussion. In this procedure, two or more genetically identical organisms are produced, using methods that invariably involve a donor egg devoid of its own nuclear genetic material and a donor nucleus or cell from another or the same individual. With this methodology, sperm is totally unnecessary for the production of an embryo and, ultimately, a mature adult.

Unintended cloning occurs naturally in humans. It produces identical twins, the result of the early splitting of a single fertilized egg into two separate embryos. Identical twins are thus clones of each other. Note that another kind of twins, called fraternal twins, are not genetically identical because they are the result of two different eggs fertilized by two different sperm cells and are thus no more similar or different than ordinary brothers or sisters.

The cloning of animals is not new. An initial success was achieved in the mid-1960s in Great Britain by John Gurdon (1968), who produced clones of the South African clawed toad, Xenopus laevis. Toward this end, Gurdon harvested unfertilized eggs and destroyed their DNA by ultraviolet light irradiation. Next he isolated nuclei (the nucleus is the cellular body that contains the DNA of a cell) from tadpole intestinal cells and injected them into eggs devoid of their own nuclear DNA. Up to 2 percent of the injected eggs developed into mature adults. Note that these toads were clones of the tadpole who donated the intestinal cell nuclei; they were not clones of the individual who donated the eggs.

The first successful cloning of a mammal took place more than thirty years later, in 1997. This was the year in which Dolly, the cloned sheep, was born in Scotland in the laboratory of Ian Wilmut (1998). The event made international headlines because she was cloned from genetic material isolated from adult cells extracted from the udder of a ewe, who was thus the true genetic mother of Dolly. Until then, it was believed that cells or nuclei from fully differentiated organs could not be "reprogrammed" to start embryonic development.

The technique that produced Dolly consisted in harvesting an egg from a donor, removing the genetic material from the egg (by means of a fine glass needle like the one illustrated in Image 9.1, rather than through UV irradiation), and fusing this now enucleated egg with a mature udder cell, containing its own DNA in the nucleus, from a different donor. This egg was then implanted into a surrogate mother, within whom the embryo Dolly developed to term. Dolly, who looked like a perfectly normal sheep, later reproduced through normal mating. Dolly died in 2005 of a viral infection unrelated to the cloning procedure. However, she had developed arthritis at a young age and some of her cellular functions showed signs of premature aging. It is not clear whether her birth through cloning was responsible for this condition.

Shortly thereafter, in 1998, a US/Japanese/British/Italian team announced the cloning of mice, the first of whom was named Cumulina (Wakayama et al. 1998). The method used here differed slightly from the one that generated Dolly. Researchers obtained Cumulina by removing the nucleus of a donor egg through aspiration with a microsyringe and (as in Gurdon's experiment) replacing it with a microinjected nucleus that had been isolated from a cumulus cell. (Cumulus cells are present in adult ovarian tissue.) Thus Cumulina is the result of transferring a new nucleus into an enucleated egg, whereas Dolly is the result of fusing an enucleated egg with a whole cell. Here, too, the manipulated mouse egg was implanted into a surrogate mother and developed normally. Cumulina is of course the clone of the mouse who donated the cumulus cell nucleus and is genetically unrelated to the mouse who donated the egg.

Since then the cloning techniques used to produce Dolly and Cumulina have been successfully applied to goats, cattle, cats, rabbits, rats, and mules, among others.[2] There is no reason to believe that these methods would not work in humans. In the United States, use of federal funds for human cloning for medical or any other purposes was prohibited in 2003. But this is not to say that a full ban on human cloning was implemented. Federal money is not the only source of research support, and other countries might not follow the example of the United States.

One major hurdle to reproductive cloning has been the low rate of success in mammalian cloning: Only a small proportion of the manipulated eggs have developed to maturity, and the rate of abnormal births is high. Thus the risks presented to date by this potential NRT are unacceptable in the case of humans. Nevertheless, there is little doubt that progress will be made in this area.

In one sense, human cloning—if it ever occurs—would be the most radical of the NRTs since it involves asexual reproduction among the members of a sexually reproducing species. All of the other NRTs discussed here, even if they do not rely on sexual intercourse, do rely on the combination of female egg and male sperm. In this respect, cloning is easily the most mind-boggling of the NRTs in terms of its implications for human life.

SOCIAL, LEGAL, AND MORAL IMPLICATIONS

NRTs are becoming available just when other options for reproduction seem to be diminishing in Europe and the United States. Fewer children are now available for adoption both because effective contraception has decreased unwanted births and because a more accepting social climate has allowed more single women to keep their children. At the same time, in the United States about one in six couples suffers some fertility problem (Blank 1990: 13–14). There is some evidence that male sperm count has decreased in the United States and Europe over the past several decades, possibly due to environmental pollution (Swan, Elkin, and Fenster 1997). However, these claims have been disputed and remain controversial (Fisch 2008).

Although NRTs clearly assist the infertile, they are also bringing about some new kinds of social relationships. Some ramifications of these technologies are easy to imagine—and many of these have already occurred. For example, through the use of frozen embryos, two genetic twins could be—and, indeed, have been—born years apart. By means of the same technology, a woman could give birth to her own genetic twin, or to her own genetic aunt or uncle. In 1991 a forty-two-year-old woman in South Dakota, Arlette, gave birth to twins who are her genetic grandchildren. Her own daughter could not bear a child, but she and her husband desperately wanted children. Through IVF, the daughter's eggs were fertilized with the husband's sperm, and later the pre-embryos were implanted into Arlette's uterus. Another woman, Bonny, donated an egg for her infertile sister, Vicki. Bonny's egg was fertilized with the sperm of Vicki's husband and implanted into Vicki's uterus. A male child, Anthony, was born. In this case the genetic mother, Bonny, is a social aunt; her sister, Vicki, gave birth to Anthony, who is her social son but her genetic nephew. Even more disconcerting, through the use of frozen embryos it is also possible for dead people to reproduce. For that matter it is equally conceivable that dead people could be cloned.

Of course the use of NRTs so far has had some happy results, at least for those couples blessed with children they desperately desired. Usually all of the participants in the making of a baby fully agree about its social and legal status. But as we know from the many cases covered in the media, this does not always happen. Baby M was just one such case. Other problems have emerged with the use of frozen embryos. In a famous case of 1989, *Davis v. Davis*, a Tennessee couple attempted IVF because Mrs. Davis was able to conceive but could not bear a child. Nine eggs were fertilized. Two were implanted, unsuccessfully, in Mrs. Davis's uterus, and the remaining seven were frozen for a later try. But then the couple divorced. They went to court over the fate of these embryos. Mrs. Davis wanted to have them implanted, but Mr. Davis wanted them destroyed. He argued that he had a right not to be a father. In the end, Mrs. Davis remarried and requested that the embryos be donated to some other infertile couple. Thus the case was resolved, but it opened the difficult question: Who should have rights over frozen embryos? Or, for that matter, should frozen embryos have any rights, protected by the law?

In another interesting case, this one from Australia, a woman's eggs were fertilized via IVF by an anonymous donor. One of these was unsuccessfully implanted in the woman and the other two were frozen. This woman and her husband then died in a plane crash. It turned out that the couple left a sizable fortune. Should the embryos have rights of inheritance? This was a question that troubled the couple's adult children. Even more pressing, morally speaking, are the larger questions of whether frozen embryos should have rights to be born, or who should decide if, when, and under what circumstances human embryos are to be donated to medical research. Should frozen embryos even be produced in the first place? Certainly, embryo freezing is a useful NRT for infertile couples, and in the case of IVF, a woman is spared repeated laparoscopies through the option of freezing the extra embryos produced the first time. But is embryo freezing a form of irresponsible reproduction? What kind of society, with what views of human life, are we constructing? How should we even think about frozen embryos? Sarah Franklin (1995: 337) argues that the frozen embryo straddles the boundary between science and nature, giving it an ambivalent status such that its identity and meaning will be contested:

> The embryo is a cyborg entity; its coming into being is both organic and technological. Though it is fully human (for what else can it be?) it is born of science, inhabits the timeless ice land of liquid-nitrogen storage tanks. . . . At once potential research material (scientific object), quasi-citizen (it has legal rights) and potential person (human subject), the embryo has a cyborg liminality in its contested location between science and nature.

Moral and legal difficulties also surround the practice of surrogacy, particularly "contract" or "commercial" surrogacy. This form of surrogacy, though permitted in the United States, is illegal in most countries that have laws regulating NRTs (Blank 1990: 157). Some people have severely censured surrogates, calling them "baby sellers." Others have merely wondered what sort of woman would contract to carry a baby for another woman or couple. Surrogates typically receive a fee of about $10,000 for their service. Yet most surrogates insist that they do it not for the money but because they're genuinely motivated to provide a child to an infertile couple. Apparently some women also enjoy the experience of pregnancy and seek to experience it again after they have had all the children they want for themselves. Helena Ragoné's (1994) study of surrogate motherhood in America shows how the surrogate role gives women confidence and a sense of self-importance and worth. These women, she says, are adding meaning to their lives by going beyond the confines of their own domestic situations or their unrewarding jobs to do something vital for others.

Other studies have shown that surrogates are usually not poor women in desperate need of cash but, rather, working-class women. According to Ragoné's (1994: 54) study, the personal income of unmarried surrogates ranged from $16,000 to $24,000, and the average household income of married surrogates was $38,000. Still, in the context of surrogacy the issue of social class and economic inequality is easily raised. The couple seeking a surrogate is generally wealthy, at least wealthy enough to be able to afford a surrogate plus the other expenses ($25,000 or more) that they will pay to doctors and a fertility clinic. But surrogates, though not poor, are not of this privileged social class. They may feel rewarded by the attention, care, gifts, and positive social treatment they receive from the couples they are assisting (Ragoné 1994: 64–66). Is this all well and good, or is contract surrogacy enmeshed in a new type of class exploitation?

In a discussion of surrogacy, Sarah Boone (1994) invokes both racial and class inequality by drawing some disturbing cultural parallels between contemporary surrogate motherhood and the position of black women slaves in an earlier America. Boone describes black slave women as "bottom women" in the gender and racial hierarchy of earlier American society, a hierarchy that placed white males on top, followed by white females and black males. One measure of the "bottom" status of black slave women was wide sexual access to them, for in their position in slave society white male slaveholders could easily exploit them sexually. In addition, black women were themselves considered property and had no legal rights to their children. Meanwhile, "the white woman as top woman became the physically delicate asexual mother/wife, subordinate helpmate" (Boone 1994: 355). Boone asks whether the surrogate mother is another kind of "bottom woman," one whose status is measured not by sexual access to her but by reproductive access to her body: After all, "CCM [commercialized contract motherhood] allows men and privileged women to purchase or rent the gestational capacities of other women in order to produce a genetic heir" (Boone 1994: 358).

A new "top woman" thus emerges here, too, but she is still a wife and the member of a privileged class. Yet this is a "top woman" with a new twist: "Now a career woman in her own right but naturally drawn to motherhood, she is fully appropriate for the more refined roles of genetic contributor and rearer of children," whereas the "bottom woman" surrogate is given "the 'unrefined' work of gestation and childbearing for men and more privileged women who are incapable or unwilling to do this work" (Boone 1994: 358). We may argue that, unlike slave women, surrogates choose their "work" and are not poor or disadvantaged persons. Still, Boone's observations suggest that surrogacy occurs not in a vacuum but in a sociocultural context where it is inseparable from issues of gender and social inequality.

Moral concerns and debates rage on over NRTs. But it is on kinship and gender that these new technologies may yet have their greatest impact.

KINSHIP AND GENDER

We have already seen how the use of frozen embryos confounds some conventional notions of kinship relation. Is the woman who gives birth to her genetic uncle his niece or his mother? What happens to our kinship system when the boundaries of our core concepts of "kin," set long ago by our ancestors and taken for granted for so many centuries, are blurred? Even more jolting, perhaps, is the fragmentation of motherhood that results from the technological ability to separate conception from birth and eggs from wombs (Levine 2008). Robert Snowden and his colleagues (1983: 34) claim that with the advent of NRTs, we now need ten different terms to cover the concepts of "mother" and "father." The terms they propose are as follows:

1. Genetic mother
2. Carrying mother
3. Nurturing mother
4. Complete mother
5. Genetic/carrying mother
6. Genetic/nurturing mother
7. Carrying/nurturing mother
8. Genetic father
9. Nurturing father
10. Complete father

The first three terms cover the distinct stages of conception, gestation, and care for a child. These three aspects of motherhood can be carried out by one, two, or three fewer women. If one woman does all three, she is the "complete" mother. Note that a child could conceivably have five different people as "parents" in this system (1–3 as mothers and 8 and 9 as fathers), even without including stepparents (Blank 1990: 10). But it is really only motherhood that has fragmented as a result of the NRTs, since we have long been accustomed to the idea that a child can have one man as its "genetic" or "biological" father and another as its "nurturing" (or perhaps a better word here might be "legal") father. Similarly, we are familiar with the idea that "legal" or "nurturing" mothers can be different from "natural" or "biological" mothers. What is new is the division of biological motherhood into two parts: conception and gestation.

In comparison to our society, a people like the Nuer (Case 2) would perhaps have had fewer conceptual problems with kinship in relation to the NRTs. For them, legal rights to children were held by fathers (and their patrilineal kin groups), not by mothers. Also, these rights were clearly established by cattle payments, not by concerns with biological fatherhood. Recall that Nuer culture constructed kinship such that children belonged to fathers, defined as the men who paid bridewealth for the mothers.

In the United States, however, ideas about kinship have been based on cultural notions of biology (Schneider 1968). Americans have strongly defined "real" parenthood as biologically based. And they have taken for granted that this way of thinking about kinship is in line with "science." But now science itself has thrown a wrench into the American system of kinship by showing that unitary "natural" motherhood is actually divisible. In the courts and in our own minds we thus face the challenge of reconstructing motherhood and, hence, reconstructing kinship. Will we need to devise a nonbiologically based definition of the mater as the Nuer have done for the pater? Marilyn Strathern (1995) discusses how the NRTs challenge Euro-American notions of "nature" itself as well as fundamental ideas about what constitutes personal "identity." Many other studies have discussed the implications for kinship of the NRTs, especially in European and American culture (see Edwards et al. 1999; Franklin and Ragoné 1998).

We do not know what the future may bring. But what seems to be happening at present is that those involved with the NRTs are not discarding the old cultural ideas about kinship but, on the contrary, are making every effort to preserve the notions of "real" biological parenthood. Toward this end, they are reinterpreting the NRTs and their tricky implications so as to reconcile them with these core cultural notions of biological parenthood and the resulting family ideal (Levine 2008). This process has played out in two very interesting contexts.

One context concerns lesbian couples. Those seeking to have children and to become a family in the conventional sense have of course benefited from the NRTs. At a minimum, one member of the couple may become impregnated with donor sperm. Corinne Hayden's (1995) study shows that some American lesbian couples with children are constructing something truly new in kinship: double motherhood. They are raising their children to perceive that they have two mothers. One way to support this perception is to have the children call both of them "mother." Another way is to hyphenate the co-mothers' names to form the children's surname. In short, these couples seek to raise their children in an environment of parental equality—a process that, in their view, constitutes a true challenge and alternative to the conventional husband-dominant household of the broader US society. Of course, the creation of equal, dual motherhood is confounded by the fact that only one woman can be the biological mother. Even if the lesbian partners themselves perceive their motherhood to be equal, the surrounding society, and courts of law, may not.

In trying to create new forms of kinship and family, lesbian couples are not so much rejecting biology as a basis for kinship as making use of the NRTs to bring their situation in line with biologically based kinship. For example, they may strive for a more equitable double motherhood by getting pregnant by the same donor. In this way, each partner becomes a mother, their children are born genetically related to one another, and they all more closely resemble a family in the conventional sense. Another possibility is for one woman to be artificially inseminated using the sperm of the other woman's brother. Each woman would then have some genetic relation, as well as a conventional kinship relation, to the child. Even more creative is what Hayden (1995: 55) refers to as the "obvious and 'perfect' option for lesbian families: one woman could contribute the genetic material, and her partner could become the gestational/birth mother." Thus even the idea that homosexual unions are "inherently nonprocreative" (Hayden 1995: 56) is challenged, now that a woman can give birth to the genetic child of her female partner. Going a step further, a lesbian couple could combine the last two options: One woman could contribute an egg to be fertilized by the brother (or, for that matter, son) of her lesbian partner, after which the egg would be implanted in her partner.

The other context in which efforts are being made to reconcile the NRTs with core cultural notions, especially American ideas about kinship, concerns surrogate motherhood. As Ragoné (1994: 109) concluded from her study of surrogate mothers in the United States,

> Programs, surrogates, and couples highlight those aspects of surrogacy that are most consistent with American kinship ideology, deemphasizing those aspects that are not congruent with this ideology. Thus, although the means of achieving relatedness may have changed, the rigorous emphasis on the family and on the biogenetic basis of American kinship remains essentially unchanged.

One way in which surrogates and their couples maintain this emphasis is to downplay the relationship between the husband and the surrogate in cases where the surrogate has been impregnated with the husband's sperm. Indeed, since the surrogate is carrying the husband's (and her) child, there are disturbing parallels with adultery. In some surrogate programs the relationship that is given priority and becomes strong is that between the surrogate and the wife. This arrangement is obviously more comfortable for the surrogate; it also allows the wife to feel that she is participating in the process of creating the child. In addition, the wife, or the adoptive mother, in such cases may emphasize her role in the creation of the child as one of intention, choice, and love: "One adoptive mother . . . described it as conception in the heart, that is, the belief that in the final analysis it was her desire to have a child that brought the surrogate arrangement into being and therefore produced a child" (Ragoné 1994: 126).

The NRTs have spurred debates among women in general and feminists in particular over how these technologies are affecting women and relations between the sexes. Some feminists approve of the NRTs precisely because they fragment motherhood and in many ways distance women from "nature" and "natural" reproduction. Their argument is that women have been trapped by their reproductive roles, that their lower status has been due all along to their entrenchment in reproduction and motherhood. According to this view, the NRTs not only expand reproductive choices for individual women and men but can help to liberate women from the inferior status that their bio-logical roles have given them. Other feminists have argued that the legal use of NRTs supports women's right to control their own bodies. They also ap-prove of contract surrogacy because it allows a surrogate to use her body as she wishes for her own economic benefit.

Yet another argument is that the NRTs are potentially good for women but need to be subjected to proper controls and approached with caution (Purdy 1994). Thus, for example, regulations should be implemented to en-sure that surrogate mothers retain control of their pregnancies and, by ex-tension, that contracting fathers not be given rights to say how a surrogate should behave while pregnant, to decide whether she should have a cesarean, to sue her for miscarriage, and so on. With such controls in place, according to this argument, contract pregnancy can considerably benefit infertile women or women with high-risk pregnancies. As for accusations of "baby selling" by surrogate mothers, those taking this position raise an important question: Why are there no parallel objections against the payments made to men who donate their sperm? Laura Purdy (1994: 316) also questions the view that "women can be respected for altruistic and socially useful actions only when they receive no monetary compensation, whereas men—physicians, scientists, politicians—can be both honored and well paid."

Perhaps the strongest feminist criticism of the NRTs has come from Janice Raymond (1993). In her book *Women as Wombs*, Raymond describes the NRTs as a form of "violence against women": Since a male-dominant "med-ical fundamentalism" defines both the problem (infertility) and the cure (the NRTs), application of the new techniques entails "appropriation of the female body by male scientific experts" (1993: xx). Raymond argues directly against the position that NRTs liberate women by freeing them from their previous reproductive roles. On the contrary, she says, the fragmentation of mother-hood, the conceptual wedge that the NRTs place between a woman and a fetus, results in the loss of women's control over reproduction. When the fetus is seen as so separable from a woman, the fetus itself becomes the focus of attention and, in the process, male rights over reproduction are increased: "Reproductive technologies and contracts augment the rights of fetuses and would-be fathers while challenging the one right that women have historically retained some vestige of—mother-right" (Raymond 1993: xi).

Raymond notes that in the case of Baby M, even though William Stern and Mary Beth Whitehead were equally the genetic parents and Whitehead was also the birth mother, Stern was continually referred to in the media as "the father" whereas Whitehead was always "the surrogate." The courts also awarded custody to Stern. About this situation Raymond (1993: 34) writes: "A woman who gestates the fetus, experiences a nine-month pregnancy, and gives birth to the child is rendered a 'substitute' mother. On the other hand, popping sperm into a jar is 'real' fatherhood, legally equivalent, if not superior, to the contribution of egg, gestation, labor, and birth that is part of any woman's pregnancy."

Of course, one could retort that the genetic/birth mother in the Baby M case did sign a surrogacy contract, thus bringing about the whole trouble in the first place. But Raymond's point is that the NRTs are changing our society's perceptions of motherhood and fatherhood, conceptually and legally, and that women may be losing out in the process. Legally speaking, what Raymond (1993: 30) calls "ejaculatory fatherhood" does appear to be gaining ground—in part, perhaps, because ideas about biological fatherhood have not been fundamentally changed by the NRTs whereas ideas about motherhood most definitely have been. In the American biogenetic ideology of kinship, fatherhood is still simple, but motherhood is no longer so.

And what of future reproductive technologies? Human cloning may be a long way off, but it opens up particularly intriguing scenarios with respect to kinship and gender. For example, a woman could donate an egg that, after enucleation, could be injected with the nucleus of one of her own cells. The treated egg could then be implanted into her womb and carried to full term. This woman's baby would of course be a female and the exact clone of herself. In addition, the baby would have no biological father. Yet this woman would be the sole biological mother, since no surrogate would be involved. Further, the woman and her clone would be like identical twins whose births were separated in time by one or more generations. In that sense, a woman could be the sole genetic and biological parent of her own, younger twin sister who is at the same time her daughter. Similarly, male clones would have no genetic mother, only a father who was the donor of the nucleus. In this case, of course, a surrogate mother would be necessary to carry the embryo to term.

DISCUSSION QUESTIONS

1. What moral issues surround (a) the production and use of frozen embryos, and (b) contract surrogate motherhood? What is your position on these issues?

2. How does the use of the NRTs in Israel work to preserve traditional Jewish ideas about kinship?

3. How do the NRTs impact the Euro-American concepts of motherhood, fatherhood, and the parent-child tie?

SUGGESTED FURTHER READING

Ragoné, Helena. 1994. *Surrogate Motherhood: Conception in the Heart.* Boulder, CO: Westview Press. One of the first in-depth studies of surrogate motherhood, how it affects individuals' lives, and its impact on kinship construction in the United States.

Franklin, Sarah. 1997. *Embodied Progress: A Cultural Account of Assisted Conception.* London: Routledge. Explores assisted conception, especially IVF, in Britain, with discussion of implications for cultural constructions of kinship and procreation.

Suggested Classroom Media

That's a Family! 2000. Produced by Debra Chasnoff, Ariella J. Ben-Dov, and Fawn Yacker. Women's Educational Media, San Francisco, CA. Thirty-five minutes. This film is designed for elementary-school children, but it works well for adults, too, and is a pleasure to watch. In the film children themselves describe their own nontraditional families in the United States. These include families of adoption, mixed ethnic families, and families with gay and lesbian parents.

Making Babies. 1999. Produced by Doug Hamilton and Sarah Spinks. Frontline coproduction with Cam Bay Productions. Sixty minutes. This film explores a wide range of NRTs. It raises issues about the changing nature of the family and the commercialization of reproduction.

Websites

www.oregonfertilityinstitute.com/?gclid=CNPO36SAibUCFad_QgodR14 Aag. Oregon Fertility Institute home page. Provides information on NRT services and how they work through this institute.

http://todayhealth.today.msnbc.msn.com/_news/2012/05/28/11883566-a -baby-made-in-india-a-couples-dream-comes-true?chromedomain=usnews &lite. "A Baby Made in India: A Couple's Dream Come True." The site discusses how more US couples are turning to overseas surrogates because it is significantly less costly than in the United States.

Notes

1. All humans are phenotypically either A, B, AB, or O. The A phenotype corresponds to an IAIA or IAIO genotype; the B phenotype corresponds to an IBIB or IBIO genotype; the AB phenotype is always IAIB; and the O phenotype is always IOIO. Let us assume that a child belongs to the A blood group and that its mother is in the O group. This means that the mother is IOIO and the child is either IAIA or IAIO. We know that this child could not possibly have inherited the IA gene from the mother and, therefore, that the IA gene had to have come from the father. Let us assume that a particular man is thought to be the father and that the mother is suing him for child support. The ABO blood test is performed and the man is found to belong to the B group. In other words, the man's genotype is IBIB or IBIO, meaning that he could not have contributed the IA gene; by extension, he could not possibly be the father, and he is excluded. But even if the suspected man turns out to belong to the A group

(making it possible for him to have contributed an IA gene), he is not proven to be the biological father. Indeed, since the whole human population is subdivided into only four blood groups, hundreds of millions of men can be found in each category. But obviously not all A-type men should be suspected, as it would be impossible for the mother to have had sexual intercourse with hundreds of millions of men from all over the planet.

2. Embryo splitting is another example of cloning now routinely used in cattle and potentially applicable to humans. In this technique, a young embryo composed of two, four, or eight cells is disaggregated, and each component cell is forced in vitro to originate a new embryo. The two, four, or eight embryos are of course clones of one another, since they all came from the same original embryo. The embryos are then reimplanted into several surrogate mothers and develop into identical twins, quadruplets, or octuplets, each individual being born to a different surrogate mother. (Note, however, that multiple births are usually not possible in cattle.) In this case, the clones are not identical to either the mother or the father; rather, as noted, they are clones of one another, just like human identical twins.

References

Blank, Robert H. 1990. *Regulating Reproduction*. New York: Columbia University Press.

Boone, Sarah S. 1994. Slavery and Contract Motherhood: A "Racialized" Objection to the Autonomy Argument. In Helen Bequaert Holmes, ed., *Issues in Reproductive Technology*, pp. 349–366. New York: New York University Press.

Clarke, Morgan. 2007. Closeness in the Age of Mechanical Reproduction: Debating Kinship and Biomedicine in Lebanon and the Middle East. *Anthropological Quarterly* 80(2): 402–424.

Edwards, Jeanette, Sarah Franklin, Eric Hirsch, Frances Price, and Marilyn Strathern. 1999. *Technologies of Procreation: Kinship in the Age of Assisted Conception*, 2nd ed. London: Routledge.

Fisch, Harry. 2008. Declining Worldwide Sperm Counts: Disproving a Myth. *Urologic Clinics of North America* 35(2): 137–146.

Franklin, Sarah. 1995. Postmodern Procreation: A Cultural Account of Assisted Reproduction. In Faye D. Ginsburg and Rayna Rapp, eds., *Conceiving the New World Order: The Global Politics of Reproduction*, pp. 323–345. Berkeley: University of California Press.

Franklin, Sarah, and Helena Ragoné, eds. 1998. *Reproducing Reproduction: Kinship, Power, and Technological Innovation*. Philadelphia: University of Pennsylvania Press.

Gurdon, J. B. 1968. Transplanted Nuclei and Cell Differentiation. *Scientific American* 219: 24–35.

Hayden, Corinne P. 1995. Gender, Genetics, and Generation: Reformulating Biology in Lesbian Kinship. *Cultural Anthropology* 10(1): 41–63.

Huxley, Aldous. 1946 [orig. 1932]. *Brave New World*. New York: Bantam Books.

Inhorn, Marcia. 2003. *Local Babies, Global Science: Gender, Religion, and In Vitro Fertilization in Egypt*. New York: Routledge.

————. 2004. Middle Eastern Masculinities in the Age of New Reproductive Technologies: Male Infertility and Stigma in Egypt and Lebanon. *Medical Anthropological Quarterly* 18(2): 162–182.

Kahn, Susan Martha. 2000. *Reproducing Jews: A Cultural Account of Assisted Conception in Israel*. Durham, NC: Duke University Press.

Levine, Nancy E. 2008. Alternative Kinship, Marriage, and Reproduction. *Annual Review of Anthropology* 37: 375–389.

Purdy, Laura M. 1994. Another Look at Contract Pregnancy. In Helen Bequaert Holmes, ed., *Issues in Reproductive Technology*, pp. 303–320. New York: New York University Press.

Ragoné, Helena. 1994. *Surrogate Motherhood: Conception in the Heart*. Boulder, CO: Westview Press.

Raymond, Janice G. 1993. *Women as Wombs: Reproductive Technologies and the Battle over Women's Freedom*. San Francisco: Harper San Francisco.

Schneider, David M. 1968. *American Kinship: A Cultural Account*. Englewood Cliffs, NJ: Prentice Hall.

Snowden, Robert, G. D. Mitchell, and E. M. Snowden. 1983. *Artificial Reproduction: A Social Investigation*. London: Allen and Unwin.

Strathern, Marilyn. 1995. Displacing Knowledge: Technology and the Consequences for Kinship. In Faye D. Ginsburg and Rayna Rapp, eds., *Conceiving the New World Order: The Global Politics of Reproduction*, pp. 346–363. Berkeley: University of California Press.

Swan, Shanna H., Eric P. Elkin, and Laura Fenster. 1997. Have Sperm Densities Declined? A Reanalysis of Global Trend Data. *Environmental Health Perspectives* 105(11): 1228–1232.

Wakayama, T., A. C. F. Perry, M. Zuccotti, K. R. Johnson, and R. Yanagimachi. 1998. Full-Term Development of Mice from Enucleated Oocytes Injected with Cumulus Cell Nuclei. *Nature* 394: 369–374.

Wilmut, Ian. 1998. Cloning for Medicine. *Scientific American* 279: 58–63.

10

THE GLOBALIZATION OF KINSHIP

Consider a few facts about the world in which we now live: There are more Grenadians living in New York City than in the Caribbean country of Grenada. McDonald's restaurants exist in over 100 countries. On any given day some 3 million people fly in airplanes above the earth, moving from one point to another.

These are all examples of what is commonly referred to as "globalization," which, like the NRTs of the previous chapter, is challenging kinship in diverse cultural settings. Although the term is used in a variety of ways, globalization generally refers to the accelerating flow of people, money, goods, and ideas across the globe. This rapid movement is facilitated by contemporary transportation, e-mail, and the Internet. Today we can move our investments or our thoughts from any one point on the planet to another in nanoseconds; our bodies or the products of global factories take a little longer, but everything is on the move, linking us all in new ways, and defying the barriers of nations or cultures.

Standing as powerful symbols of globalization are the Golden Arches of McDonald's, now visible on every continent and in over 26,000 locations. McDonald's is seen as the epitome of an engulfing mass popular culture, originating in North America, but now creating one McWorld while destroying indigenous cultures in its wake. McDonald's has become the target of critics of American cultural imperialism and the centerpiece of an antiglobalization movement. Yet at the same time McDonald's has in many ways altered and adapted to local cultural conditions—serving, for example, a mutton burger in India (Maharaja Mac) where Hindus do not eat beef, and Big Macs without cheese in Israel (to keep meat and dairy products separate). In other ways local consumers change McDonald's on their own, some taking the "fast" out of this fast-food industry. In some East Asian cities McDonald's restaurants are used as places of leisurely dining. In Hong Kong, students stay in them for long periods to study and gossip. What we see with the Golden Arches spreading across the earth is as much a mutation and localization as a globalization (Watson 2006).

Globalization is often, and significantly, associated with the sustaining and deepening of poverty and inequality in the world. Economically, globalization is rooted in the expansion of capitalism, particularly notable after the end of the Cold War. Global capitalism has meant an increasing linking of local, small-scale economies into a broader international economy dominated by multinational corporations. These corporations are oriented toward profits, economic growth, and the commoditization of more and more goods and services. Together with international financial institutions they have fostered a global economy based on what has been called "neoliberalism." Neoliberalism favors unrestricted world trade, privatization, and less interference of governments generally in the economy. These policies clearly benefit the rich but may be devastating for the world's poor. For example, beginning in the 1990s, the World Bank made its loans to developing countries contingent on adopting "structural adjustment." To meet these requirements, poor countries needed to adopt neoliberal economic policies, and to implement these, they needed to cut back social services, including education, public health and sanitation programs, and government antipoverty measures.

This chapter examines the effect of globalization on kinship and family life. One might think, and indeed many have thought, that globalization in general erodes the bonds and structures of kinship. Urbanization and labor migration separate kin, while the mass media introduces new concepts, such as romantic love as a basis for marriage, and new ideals, such as small nuclear families. It has been tempting to assume that the model of the Western world would be followed elsewhere under globalization. The reality, however, appears more complex and convoluted. Much like the Golden Arches' being transplanted to Asia, the forces of globalization everywhere encounter different responses in terms of kinship and family.

KINSHIP, URBANIZATION, AND TRANSNATIONAL MIGRATION

Migration has been an important part of human adaptation since our species' movement out of Africa and settlement of all regions of the planet, beginning 70,000 to 130,000 years ago. We have been and continue to be a species on the move. The shape and the consequences of this movement have varied through different historical periods. While the slow expansion of humans into unoccupied regions was benign, later migrations sometimes set people in brutal conflict, as, for example, in the European migration to the New World, which largely decimated indigenous peoples.

Today human migration assumes a globalizing cast. Human movement is accelerating in volume through both urbanization and the movement of more and more people from more and more countries in international migration, usually for purposes of obtaining work. Both these forms of wage-labor migration may be temporary or "circular," that is, people move back and forth from rural to urban areas in their home country or move in a regular pattern between two or more countries, maintaining ties with and sending remittances to family members back home. This back-and-forth movement between countries is often referred to as "transnational migration." Today transnational migration is largely a flow of people from developing countries to wealthier ones for work, and today women are outpacing men in this migration.

Kinship structures and family ties are closely interwoven with this globalizing migration. A decision to migrate is often made for the sake of economically supporting a family, and the presence of kin abroad frequently encourages one's decision to become a migrant oneself. On the other hand, the availability of certain kin at home may inhibit migration. For example, one study of an economically marginal village in the Caribbean country of Dominica found that while young people generally were strongly motivated to leave the village to seek work elsewhere, young women were far less likely to do so when they had matrikin available in their village (Quinlan 2005). As we saw in Chapter 4, the Caribbean is an area of strong matrifocal kin networks. Matrikin, especially maternal grandmothers, considerably assist young women with child care and other chores. In this rural area, the availability of matrikin was not a factor in male migration.

Also from the Caribbean, Christine Ho (1993) discovered a whole new world of "international families" among Afro-Trinidadian migrants to the United States. These migrants, like others from the Caribbean, are propelled to leave Trinidad for lack of jobs and other opportunities at home. Among them migrant family members are widely dispersed—some may live in Los Angeles, others in New York, still others may live and work in other Caribbean countries, and some stay back in Trinidad. Yet these kin remain intact family units through constant intervisitation, communication, and exchange of people, services, and goods. These international families are not based on coresidence in households but on flexible kin networks. They are tight-knit groups even though their members may all have been dispersed for a decade or more. Moreover, women not only constitute the majority of migrants but they play the most active roles in the financial and social maintenance of these groups. These international families make great use of the Caribbean tradition of "child minding" or informal adoption, where parents rely on kin or friends to care temporarily for their children (either back in Trinidad, elsewhere in the Caribbean, or somewhere else in the United States) until they can resume child care themselves.

The increasing participation of women in transnational migration is seen in other countries, for example, Sri Lanka, where many poor women (representing over 13 percent of working-age women) work for long periods as housemaids in Middle Eastern countries such as Saudi Arabia, Kuwait,

Lebanon, and the United Arab Emirates (Gamburd 2008). In contrast to the matrifocal Caribbean, where women have long assumed primary financial support for families, Sri Lanka is a region where males are expected to be primary providers, with wives subordinate to husbands.

Sri Lankan women who transmigrate do so out of economic desperation. The lack of jobs and low wages have led many women and, if married, their husbands to feel that the woman's working abroad is the only way they can provide food, shelter, and other basics for themselves and their children. Aside from providing daily needs, women migrate to earn money to pay off family debt, buy land, build a house, educate their children, and secure dowries for their daughters or themselves.

To assist this female housemaid migration, husbands and female relatives of migrants take over child care and other household tasks in the migrants' homes. Thus with these married women working not only outside the home but outside the country, and with husbands assuming child care and housework, the more traditional gender roles of husband and wife are reversed. These migrant women are criticized in the Sri Lankan media for abandoning their husbands and children, but studies have shown that children of migrants are generally well cared for. On the other hand, the elevated consumption of alcohol by husbands of migrants may be in part due to the threats to their masculinity that migration of their working wives brings. Males may turn to alcohol (culturally, drinking is a male activity) to reaffirm their masculinity (Gamburd 2008).

These examples show that while kinship and family forms may undergo stress and modification as a result of migration, they remain important and influential. In a similar vein, Daniel Smith (2011), in a title to an article, describes kinship as "stretched and strained but not broken" among the Igbo of Nigeria as they enter an increasingly globalized world. Patrilineal, patrilocal, and organized into traditionally powerful, exogamous kin corporations, the Igbo over the past several decades have experienced increasing economic diversification, urbanization, and labor migration. Education for both women and men has come to be highly valued and seen as crucial to securing good jobs and economically viable futures. In cities Igbo youth are exposed daily to new lifestyles and values through music, films, television, the Internet, and one another. All of these and other forces of globalization are affecting marriage, gender roles, and family formation. But this transformation does not show merely an adoption of external, Western forms of family, or even a lessening of kinship; rather the transformation of kinship is taking its own twists and turns in a way that meshes the old and the new.

On the one hand, modern Igbo marriages show a sharp break with the past and, in some respects, a resemblance to marriage in the Western world. A clear majority of contemporary Igbo marriages are based on personal choice and romantic love, rather than on arrangement by parents and among kin groups. Couples see themselves as independent units rather than as units embedded within lineages, extended families, and local communities. As one young married woman said to Smith, "My father had three wives and 14 children. Often it was every woman for herself. My husband and I have a partnership. We decide things. There is love between us" (2011: 35). On the other hand, a couple's ties to kin and local community remain strong, and final marriage choices still depend on the influence, scrutiny, and consent of the couple's parents and extended families. Virtually all marriages are enacted through specific traditional ceremonies (called *igba mkwu*), which

> involve hundreds of people from and associated with the lineages of the man and woman who are getting married. Extended negotiations of bridewealth, a host of obligatory exchanges, and the tremendous amount of cooperation between the two kin groups that must occur to perform the ceremony successfully instill the respect and mutual obligations that characterize affinal relations in Igboland. . . . There can be no doubt that many people are invested in the marriage. (Smith 2011: 40)

In a similar way, modern marriages appear to be more gender equal than in the past, more of a "partnership," as the woman noted above. However, Smith notes that gender equality is expressed more in the courtship phase of a union; after marriage a patriarchal inequality between husband and wife reemerges. This is seen, for instance, in terms of sexuality or sexual freedom. The situation has changed for Igbo women: In the past female chastity before marriage was expected and valued. Today female education, urbanization, and employment have led to a rising age of marriage for women; this, along with the availability of contraception, has brought about an acceptance of premarital female sexuality (which was always accepted for men). But after marriage there is a clear double standard with regard to marital infidelity. Women are "supposed to be faithful in marriage *and* tolerate men's extramarital affairs" (Smith 2008: 228, original emphasis). Indeed male peer groups encourage male infidelity, and these extramarital affairs are for a man a display of masculinity toward other men.

A mixture of old and new patterns is also seen in terms of reliance on kin and kin networks. On the one hand, Igbos express expanded kin ties as burdensome and seek in some contexts to minimize obligations to their extended family. At the same time they are acutely aware of the continuing importance of kin networks, descent groups, and affinal alliances in securing access to resources in the new global economy. Thus "Igbos gain access to the resources of the state and the wider economy through social networks of reciprocity and obligation that have their roots in the family, the lineage, and the local community" (Smith 2011: 50), and Igbo people "realize that they cannot succeed in contemporary Nigeria if they jettison family and community ties" (Smith 2011: 63).

Finally, many of the stresses and strains involving kinship among the Igbo are reflected in their attitudes toward fertility. Many Igbo today express a need to limit fertility, citing difficult economic times along with the costly necessity of educating children as major reasons. But these attitudes are expressed alongside desires for a relatively high fertility; most people Smith interviewed wanted to have at least four children. Couples also feel pressure from kin to reproduce at this level. Here people are responding to a cultural model whereby "having people" (meaning having kin) is essential to secure access to resources in Nigeria. In this context, a relatively high fertility remains "valued, rational, and collectively promoted" (Smith 2011: 59).

KINSHIP AND TRANSNATIONAL ADOPTION

Among the many people passing over national boundaries and often over continents today are children and infants. These are adoptees, moving from poorer "donor" countries to become members of families in wealthier nations. This movement of children is fairly recent, having become significant only in the latter half of the twentieth century. In the early postwar period, transnational adoptions were sporadic responses to natural disasters, economic crises, and especially wars. For example, following World War II, American families adopted orphans from Germany, Italy, and Greece; Korean children were adopted at the close of the Korean War; and in 1975, through "Operation Babylift," some 3,000 Vietnamese children were adopted in the United States (Kapstein 2003: 2). In these and other cases, the motives for adoption were often humanitarian, with many adoptive parents already having children of their own.

Today the situation is quite different. The transnational flow of children is no longer sporadic or limited to periods of war and other crises; it is ongoing and perpetuated largely by conditions of poverty in donor countries. Today couples or individuals adopt not as a humanitarian act (although this motive may be present, too) but because they desperately seek to have children and are for whatever reason unable to produce their own. And today, although the United States remains the largest receiver of transnational adoptees, dramatically rising numbers of adoptions are now noticeable in European countries.

A number of factors underlie the steady increase in transnational adoptions. In North America and Europe a rise in the age of marriage and increasing postponement of attempts to conceive after marriage has meant that couples have fewer children of their own. Since fertility decreases with age, couples are more likely to be infertile by the time they decide they want children. At the same time few children in these countries are available for domestic adoption due to the availability of contraception and abortion and to the reduction of social stigmas attached to out-of-wedlock births and single motherhood.

At present about 40,000 children are transnationally adopted each year. The United States is followed by France and Italy in receiving the largest number of children from abroad. The highest donor of children is China, followed by Russia and South Korea.[1] The majority of transnationally adopted children are female. China's One-Child Policy and son preference, discussed in Chapter 8, accounts in part for the greater availability of female children for adoption.

This international trade in children has brought a number of problems. One of the most disturbing is the illicit "child trafficking," where adoption rings buy or kidnap children from poor parents to be sold abroad to rich couples. The media has reported several such shocking cases of child trafficking from countries such as Honduras, Guatemala, and Romania, which led to temporary moratoriums on adoptions from these countries over the 1990s. Added to all this have been fears and rumors that infants are purchased or stolen for the use of their vital organs in wealthy nations. There are also fears of the mistreatment of adopted children. In 2012 Russia banned the adoption of children by people in the United States, citing, among other cases of neglect or mistreatment, the death of an adopted Russian child whose adoptive American father left him in an overheated car. Politically this ban was interpreted as retaliation against the United States for its accusations of human rights abuses in Russia.

There are often of course shades of gray between blatant baby-selling and legitimate adoptions. While laws against baby-selling, now widespread around the world, may be officially enforced, bribes to individuals and "donations" to orphanages may occur in the chain from adopters to go-betweens to biological parents. But even the cleanest and most scrutinized and regulated of cases of transnational adoptions raise uncomfortable issues. Given the volume and direction (one way, poor to wealthy) of these child transfers, people of donor countries may express discomfort or a sense of national shame. Similarly, transnational adoptions carry undertones of neocolonialism. Just as in colonial times when ores, minerals, cash crops, and even slaves flowed from disempowered colonies to the wealthy colonial powers for the economic enrichment of the latter, now infants flow over the same route for the emotional and social enrichment of citizens of the same and still wealthiest nations. Finally, one cannot help but reflect upon the issue that these transnational adoptions are made possible by a world economic system that sustains poverty and global inequities.

Transnational adoptions also raise fundamental issues concerning kinship. By what ideas and processes, for example, do children from China, Haiti, or South Korea become incorporated into families of the United States, Norway, or Sweden? One of the most compelling studies of receiving countries is Signe

Howell's (2001, 2009) investigation of transnational adoptions in Norway. Norway is an interesting case: Although it ranks below the United States and some other European countries in the number of transnational adoptees received, it ranks first when adoptions are measured per capita. Norway receives about 700 adoptees per year, largely from China and other Asian countries, but also from Ethiopia and Eastern Europe (former Soviet bloc). By 2004 there were over 17,000 transnationally adopted people in Norway (Howell 2009: 25). As elsewhere in Western Europe, there are virtually no Norwegian children available for adoption.

In general only married heterosexual couples are allowed to adopt in Norway. Overwhelmingly, those couples who adopt are involuntarily infertile; most often they have tried assisted reproduction through various NRTs, considering adoption only when these attempts failed. These people see their childless state as unacceptable; their prime motive for adoption is to become a "normal family" so that they can participate in meaningful sociality with other couples who do have children. In Norway (as elsewhere in Europe) children and family have become increasingly important in recent decades; it is culturally stressed that motherhood and fatherhood are necessary to the happiness and fulfillment of individuals.

As we have seen repeatedly throughout this book, while Euro-Americans emphasize a biogenetic basis of kinship, many other cultures give considerable weight to other bases, or processes, of kinship construction, such as feeding, coresidence, rituals, and so on. Howell places all of these processes of kinship creation, biological or other, into one frame, which she aptly calls "kinning," or "the process by which a fetus or newborn child is brought into a significant and permanent relationship with a group of people, and the connection is expressed in a conventional kinship idiom" (2009: 8). To Howell, kinning is universal, occurring in all societies; it may be enacted by nature (biogenetics), nurture, or law. For Norwegian transnational adoption, only nurture and the law are available, although in Norway as elsewhere in the West, biological connection remains the model along which legal and nurturing kinning are enacted. For example, Norwegian adoptive parents and adoption agency staff refer to two important stages in acquiring an adopted child with the terms "pregnancy" and "birth." "Pregnancy" begins the moment a couple has been approved to adopt and "birth" takes place when they collect the child. As one adoptive mother of a Korean girl commented, "We felt that our daughter was born at Fornebu [Oslo's international airport] on the day that she arrived home" (Howell 2001: 203).

Other kinning efforts include photographing the child in family settings with their grandparents and other relatives and often in places—"a district, valley, fjord or farm" (2001: 213)—in which the parents' own ancestors originated. These photos show the child "in the child's own specially fitted-out bedroom; in front of the open fire in the cabin in the mountains; at

Christmas, on national day, and on birthdays dressed in national [Norwegian] costume . . . with mum and dad, or cousins of the same age" (2001: 213). These photos accompany reports that the couple is required to submit to the donor orphanage, but they also serve as parents' narratives of their child's incorporation into their family. Howell writes, "What the photos in the reports state, again and again is, 'Look, the child is a Norwegian child. We are a typical Norwegian family. We have kin and are connected to places embedded in kin relations'" (2001: 213).[2] In the end, these Norwegian parents do not see adoption as second best, even though it may have been their second choice in the beginning of the process. Nor do they consider their ties to their child as fictive kinship. Howell suggests that Norwegian kinning of foreign children is more appropriately considered a self-conscious kinship.

While adopted children are flowing from Asia, Africa, and Latin America into North America and Western Europe, new ideas about kinship and family are flowing back in the other direction (Howell 2009). This flow of concepts, values, and norms is the other side of what we see as the globalization of kinship. What is being propagated from the West has, in part, to do with ideas about childhood and children, and these ideas have been brought to the foreground through international but Western-dominated efforts to reform and control transnational adoptions. In this respect the most important documents are the United Nations Conventions of the Rights of the Child (UNCRC), crafted in 1989 (ratified by 191 countries)[3] and the Hague Convention on Protection of Children and Co-operation in Respect of Intercountry Adoption, written in 1993 (ratified by 54 countries).

Howell notes a twentieth-century shift in Europe (and North America) in the control over children from private families to public authorities; the UN and Hague conventions on children represent the same kind of movement, but on a global scale. These codifications seek to prioritize "the best interests of the child" in formulating policies and regulations, to be followed by countries engaging in adoptions across borders. Although the UNCRC does not specify what exactly a child's best interests are, in prioritizing these interests, it depicts childhood as special and children as vulnerable. It also depicts children as autonomous individuals with "rights" to be safeguarded. These rights include the right to life, the right to a name and identity, and the right to be raised in a family.

Supporters of the international conventions see this view of children as self-evident, natural, and universal. Anthropologists, however, are quick to point out that views and values of childhood and children are historically and culturally specific. For example, in Peru (see Case 15) children are highly valued but, in contrast with the West, they are valued as companions and caretakers of adults, which "turns the typical North American focus on childcare on its head" (Leinaweaver 2007: 169). In this book we have also seen that adoption is often oriented toward the interests of adults—for example,

in ancient Rome it was done to provide adult males with legal heirs and wor-
shippers of their own souls after death. Even in the West the particular views
of children expressed in the UN conventions did not obtain in the past. For
instance, in Chapter 7 we saw that in colonial North America children, while
desired and no doubt loved, were treated much like servants. And back then
the category of "teenager" did not exist.

However natural and universal they may seem in Europe and North America today, modern conceptions of childhood in the West are of fairly recent
origin, appearing in the late nineteenth and early twentieth centuries. Richard
Robbins (2011) pinpoints how new ideas of childhood as a special developmental period and of children as having special needs came about with the
shifts in industrial capitalism over the turn of the twentieth century. Previously
industries routinely employed children in factories, or families made use of
their labor on farms. Later, and partly due to new laws banning child labor,
capitalists came to realize that "children were to contribute far more to the
national economy as consumers than they ever did as laborers" (2011: 22).
Rather suddenly, it seems, a whole new category of childhood was culturally
and economically visible, a category of little persons full of needs for toys,
needs for new special foods, and needs for new, severely age-graded clothing.
To take but a few measures: Between the opening of the twentieth century
and 1920, the production of toys in the United States increased 1,300 percent;
a baby's clothing industry, nonexistent in 1890, became one of the largest
US industries by 1915 (Robbins 2011: 22). Supporting the trend of meeting
newly perceived needs of children was an army of child psychologists and
educators who informed adults of even further needs of children—private
playrooms and sleeping areas, backyard swing sets, small furniture, even more
toys, and special eating equipment. Without all of these, a child's physical and
mental development would be endangered. Originally targeting parents to
buy these commodities for their children, capitalists quickly learned that they
could increase profits even more by directly targeting children themselves, leaving it to children (through the "nag factor") to influence parental spending.

The core guiding priority of the "best interests of the child" in the international conventions addressing transnational adoption is fully in line with
contemporary Western conceptions of childhood. Underlying this conception
is an expanded spirit of Western individualism—children, like adults, are autonomous individuals full of inalienable individual rights. Missing here is
consideration of any alternative cultural conceptions of persons (children or
adult) as essentially embedded within social relationships, a consideration of
the rights of collectivities rather than just individuals, and any consideration
of the duties as well as rights of any persons. Interestingly, in 1999 a group
of fifteen African countries put in force a document—the African Charter on
the Rights and Welfare of the Child—that Howell interprets as "an act of
resistance on the part of the African states against what they perceive as the

attempted imposition of Western values" (2009: 176) as articulated in the UNCRC. In contrast to the UNCRC, their document presents children as integrated members of communities, not as autonomous individuals, and stresses the duties of children toward adults rather than focusing on children's rights. For example, Article 31 includes the statement that "every child shall have duties towards his family and society, the State and other legally recognized communities and the international community," and that every child shall have the duty to "work for the cohesion of the family, to respect his parents, superiors, and elders at all times and to assist them in case of need" (Howell 2009: 177).

Transnational adoption is growing; it is escalating the flow of children in one direction and ideas of childhood and kinship in another. In this process, kinship is being enacted and understood in new ways everywhere. We have seen especially here the adjustments and "kinning" in countries such as Norway that are major recipients of transnational adoptees. In the following case study we take a close look at the globalization of childhood and kinship from within one donor country, Peru.

CASE 15: CHILD CIRCULATION IN PERU

In the early months of her fieldwork in the town of Ayacucho in Peru, anthropologist Jessaca Leinaweaver encountered a girl in one of the households that she regularly visited:

> When I first met teenaged Reyna . . . I thought she was Cristina's maid. As I read my field notes I can see myself wondering who she was. The notes describe her as "acting like a *muchacha* [maid], answering the phone and the door and running to buy stuff, but also a loved one, who sits around with the group when she's not doing errands—is she related? what is her position? where does she live?" (2008: 81)

As Leinaweaver learns, Reyna is a part of what social scientists call "child circulation," a widespread practice in Peru and other countries in the Andean region. Child circulation is the relocation of a child or young person from his or her natal household to another household. The households may already be related by kinship and, if not, mechanisms will be brought into play to produce a sense of such relatedness, for example, the use of kin terms among participants. Child circulation is usually seen as a temporary arrangement and one that potentially benefits the child, the child's parent(s), and the receiving household. The child typically moves into a household that is better able to provide child care, and very often is more urban. Relocation to a town or city provides both educational opportunities and the chance for the child to assimilate urban life ways and skills, which may ultimately benefit not only the child but, down the road, the child's natal family as well. These benefits to the child are locally expressed as the child's "self-improvement" (*superción*).

In return for these benefits to the child, the receiving household gains from the child's labor—generally housecleaning, laundry, shopping, simply minding the house, and, perhaps, taking care of pets when other members are away. The circulated child may also become a close companion to others in the new house, especially, for example, to an elderly person living alone. Here the motivation is expressed as *acompañar* (to accompany). Finally the child's parents, though they may miss their child, may feel that they cannot provide the child with appropriate care or with educational and other opportunities. Older children often have a say in their relocations and in some cases older children initiate their own circulation.

All of the above-mentioned motivations underlying child circulation were reflected in the case of Reyna, who became a companion to Cristina. Cristina was a widow in her sixties and living alone, her own children having moved away. The initial request for Reyna's circulation came from Cristina's grown sons, who did not want to see their mother alone and unaccompanied. Reyna's father was Cristina's godson; thus there was already a constructed kinship between these households. And Reyna's father was through this link under obligation to Cristina. Finally Reyna's parents were poor, with three other young children at home, and they lived in a small town devoid of social and educational opportunities for youth. The main benefit to Reyna herself was that she could go to high school in Cristina's neighborhood and so "self-improve."

An interesting dimension of child circulation in Peru is the role of the transferred children in establishing or enhancing strong relationships among the participating adults. This role recalls what we saw in Chapter 6 with regard to marriage. In many societies past and present marriage creates alliances between the kin groups of the groom and those of the bride. In a similar way, the parent(s) of a circulated child and the receiving adult(s) of the child's new residence will be drawn together and will establish a new or renewed sense of kinship with one another. This kin-making process is also analogous to that of the institution of godparenthood (noted in the case above) where a child's parents and godparents are drawn into closer association or alliance. In the area of Leinaweaver's work in Peru, a child may have multiple, lifelong godparents, some established at her baptism, others at her marriage, creating a broad web of relationships not only for the child but also for her parents, who will see and treat the child's godparents (their *compadres*, or coparents) as kin.

Like godparenthood, then, child circulation is a kin-creating process among adults. It also, of course, establishes or enhances relatedness between a transferred child and members of her new household. This creation of kinship is processual and is locally articulated through the important cultural concept of *acostumbrar* (to get accustomed). In Leinaweaver's interviews almost all of the people who had experienced being circulated as a child used this word to describe how they had adapted to their new home. "Getting accustomed" is gradually brought about through coresidence, sharing of household tasks, eating together, and so on. For Leinaweaver "*acostumbrarse* is a productive way of thinking about the transformation in behavior, treatment, comfort and sentiment that ultimately results in family" (2007: 169). In this process of forming kinship with members of the new household, the circulated children may also see a lessening of relatedness with kin of their former households. One person who had been transferred as a child told Leinaweaver that the daughters of the new household were like her sisters "because I have now been accustomed many years. . . . My other siblings [of her former natal household] . . . they are my siblings too, but not as much so" (2007: 171).

For all that child circulation may benefit particular individuals and households, it also entails risks and costs. Alongside accounts of successful "accustomings" to new households, Leinaweaver reports that "in fact, most of my interlocuters also made comments that indicated that moving to a new house, although an essential and often beneficial strategy, is often overlaid with a wash of sadness" (2007: 172). Repeatedly she heard from circulated persons that a new arrangement is just "not the same" as living with one's own parents, and she received reports of transferred persons missing their former household members and experiencing other difficulties. In one case a transferred teenage girl reported a successful accommodation, but the girl's birth sister had another view. This sister reported that the circulated girl had been unhappy in her new home until a few years ago. In earlier days,

> she remembered that [her sister] would come home crying, saying that her aunt and uncle [in whose home she now lived] treated her differently than the other girls [their children], that [her aunt's] older daughter hit her, and that they would complain, saying that after buying her clothes and educating her, the least she could do would be this small chore! (Leinaweaver 2007: 172)

There is another dimension to the dark side of child circulation: poverty. Child circulation is, first and foremost, a strategy of the poor and disadvantaged. It is an option that a parent or parents take when they feel that they themselves cannot properly provide for a child. Should their own circumstances improve, they will likely seek the return of their child. Children move upward into better-off households, but however much the individual child or young person may cross class barriers, this individual movement does not break down the barriers but rather reinforces them. "In this way child circulation plays a part in reproducing class relations in Ayacucho" (2007: 167). Another way that it does so concerns the labor that transferred children perform. Most circulated children carry out domestic tasks in their receiving households. This is similar to the labor they would in any case perform in their own households, but in cases where they substantially move up into a better-off, urban family, these chores "come to resemble the work done by a maid in a middle-class home" (2008: 90). Circulated children may also be given a small amount of money called a *propina*, which can mean a "tip," as for a service, but can also mean an "allowance," a payment parents might make to their own child. "This payment situates child circulation in an ambivalent grey area, somewhere between kinship and domestic service, both of which it resembles" (Leinaweaver 2008: 90).

In Peru, and especially in the area of Leinaweaver's work, child circulation increased during the violence, murders, and massive migrations brought about by the conflict between the Shining Path rebels and the Peruvian military from the 1980s through the early 1990s. Here, Maoist militants waged a brutal war with government forces; with atrocities on both sides, an estimated 70,000 people were killed or were "disappeared" during this conflict. This civil war increased the need to relocate children, many of them orphaned, during the danger. Also as a result of this conflict, along with the growing effects of globalization, poverty overall increased and continues to the present time.

Issues of race and gender are also interwoven with child circulation. In terms of race, indigenous Quechua speakers in Peru are generally poorer than the Spanish-speaking population. Often for them, a circulated child will be placed in an environment that will encourage and facilitate the dropping of indigenous markers, such as clothing (for example, woven skirts and felt hats), the speaking of Quechua, the eating of certain foods, and so on. As Leinaweaver notes, "To overcome [poverty] means to become whiter and to shed an Indian way of life" (2008: 110). In this way the "self-improvement" of child circulation is often a rejection of indigenous ways and thus a confirmation of the perceived inferiority of those ways.

As for gender, most circulated children are females. Among families motivated to circulate a child, girls rather than boys assume domestic labor—laundry, ironing, cooking, child care, and housecleaning—and so are valued over boys by receiving households. In addition, parents (and young girls themselves) may see circulation as a step away from other, less desirable possibilities for women. One young circulated girl attending school in town reported that "she was proud to be studying hard rather than working for a living or becoming pregnant like other poor girls her age" (Leinaweaver 2007: 167).

For all its limitations, child circulation is a locally acceptable and long-standing practice aimed at protecting children through kin-building, that is, creating or enhancing ties between households and connecting children with adults in their new locations. Always subject to risks and costs, the vulnerabilities of child circulation are now being exacerbated by the forces of globalization in Peru. Along with the poverty that globalization sustains are the tensions between the local practice of child circulation and state intervention. In this context, the state, having accepted internationalized views of childhood, child abandonment, and adoption standards, often misunderstands and criticizes child circulation. The result is that circulated children may be officially declared "abandoned" and thus adoptable.

Consider the case of Luisa. Her mother died giving birth to her; her father was a poor farmer in his sixties. The father felt he could not provide adequately for his daughter and so placed her into the home of his deceased wife's brother. This man, Luisa's maternal uncle, was also a widower, poor, and he already had two young children at home. A few months after her birth, Luisa became ill and was malnourished. Unable to pay for the medical care she needed, her uncle took her to a local orphanage. In the uncle's understanding, the orphanage would care for Luisa only temporarily; meanwhile he would work to earn money to provide for and educate her. Interestingly, this uncle, like many other poor people in the region, was using the orphanage as though it were a kind of last-chance "receiving family" in the system of child circulation. Many children in orphanages actually have living parents, but the poverty of the parents and lack of other kin able to take in a child will lead them to temporarily place their children with orphanages, planning to retrieve them later in better times.

Once in an orphanage, however, the power of the state steps in and brings with it binding legal determinations of a child's status. A child declared legally abandoned can become internationally adoptable. Thus the risk of using an orphanage for child circulation is that what is locally understood as a temporary relocation may become permanent. The Peruvian state follows its national policy covering abandoned children, which is itself derived from international law encoded in UN policies on children's rights. In other words, the Peruvian state and its representatives have appropriated an external, globalized discourse on children's rights and adoption.

In the eyes of the state, Luisa had been abandoned. An adoption office lawyer filed a document for her stating that "this child is in a state of Material Abandonment and Moral Danger" (2007: 163). The lawyer determined that neither Luisa's father nor her uncle had the economic resources to care for her and that, as widowers, they both lacked a "duly constituted family" (2007: 163). In addition, and adding considerable weight to his determinations, was the fact that Luisa's uncle had left her at an orphanage and that she was malnourished and sick. The legal definition of Luisa's case devalued what Luisa's father and uncle had been trying to do with the strategy of child circulation. As a result, "abandonment proceedings like Luisa's produce legally adoptable children and local strategies of child circulation are defined as inadequate" (Leinaweaver 2007: 174). Peru thus enters the global system of international adoptions—the transfer of babies from poor countries to wealthy ones—discussed earlier in this chapter.

Leinaweaver concludes from her study that child circulations

are ways that poor Ayacuchanos are creatively and purposefully managing their lives, striving for a better future, and building up the multilayered connections that serve them in trying times. When the state intervenes in these relationships, it is infringing on poor Ayacuchanos' abilities to forge kinship ties and to use these ties for survival. (2007: 175)

The circulation of children is common not only in Peru but also in many other countries around the world. As we saw in Chapter 7, a very similar movement of children as temporary apprentices in wealthier households was widespread in Europe in the eighteenth century and also in colonial North America. The practice is also found in West Africa, notably in Benin. In Benin today, however, this practice and understandings of it have shifted under globalization in ways similar to the case of Peru. Erdmute Alber (2011) examines how Benin's entrance into the global economy, with attendant monetization and urbanization, has considerably increased demand for housemaids among urban middle-class families. Young women from rural areas take these low-paying and insecure positions to earn money (needed especially these days to fund their dowries for marriage) and to "open their eyes," or to see the cities and pursue modernity. At the same time the Benin state and related social institutions have adopted a global discourse of "child trafficking." This new discourse was introduced into Benin largely through outside development agencies, foreign children's-rights activists, and the now-globalized media.

In Benin the young housemaids freely choose their work, have no illusions about what to expect, and sometimes leave for towns and cities secretly, without their families' knowledge. But since they often find work through professional brokers and are often under the age of eighteen, the official view from Benin condemns and misconstrues their situations as cases of child trafficking. In Alber's view, seeing these children as victims and their situations as illegal child trafficking prevents us from understanding how Benin's internationally linked economy puts pressure on young girls to pursue low-paying, insecure, and often unpleasant jobs.

CONTINUITIES

Not so long ago many people, including many anthropologists, thought that as societies around the world modernized and industrialized, or as globalization set in, kinship would cease to be so significant and prominent in human affairs. In part this prediction was based on the idea that in so-called primitive societies, kinship and kin networks performed many functions (such as care for the elderly, marriage regulations, legal processes, and political alignments) that had been taken over by social institutions in "more advanced" societies. Thus as "primitive" societies became fewer, their members becoming ethnic minorities within political states, and as "advancement" became more general, kinship would come to have only minimal significance within small nuclear families. Powerful kin groups, complicated clan structures, extended families, and deep lineages would become relics of the past. This clearly has not happened. And in any case the sharp division between "advanced" Western societies and "primitive" others has been largely abandoned.

It is true that kinship systems around the world have changed in their form and structure. And cases could be made for a decrease in the social or political centrality of certain kin groups in particular societies. But overall, kinship has remained a vital aspect of domestic, social, and political life around the globe, as we have seen especially in this last chapter. Equally important is that everywhere we look, ideas and practices concerning kinship are interwoven with and have an effect on gender relationships.

In this book we have examined a variety of ways in which kinship and gender are culturally interrelated. This analysis has involved us in discussions of sexuality and reproduction, and of the interests of many people and groups in exercising control over women's reproductive capacities. We have seen cases, specifically among the Nuer and the Nyinba, in which female sexuality is largely unrestricted but cultural rules allocate a woman's children to her legal husband or husbands and their kinship groups. And among the matrilineal Nayar, female sexuality is unrestrained (except for sexual intercourse before the tali-tying ceremony and at any time with a lower-caste man), but children are allocated to a woman's own kinship corporation under the leadership of her senior matrilineal kinsmen. In all three societies, female sexuality and female fertility are separate social concerns.

We have also seen cases in which a woman's sexuality is, or was, ideally restricted to one man, her husband: Examples include the Nepalese Brahmans, the ancient Romans, the Kurds of northern Iraq, and Europeans in Europe and North America. In these societies, a woman's "inappropriate" sexual behavior (premarital sex or adultery) could result in devaluation of her person, dishonor to her family, and, among the Nepalese Brahmans, devaluation of the woman's future fertility. The Nayar, sharing some of the Hindu caste ideas related to female purity and pollution, also showed this connection between female sexuality and fertility, inasmuch as sex with a lower-caste man would expel a woman and her future children from her caste and kin group. In all of these Eurasian cases we have seen that the concern with female sexual "purity" is interwoven with concerns over property and its transmission, as well as with the maintenance of class and caste divisions; in other words, they are bound up with larger issues of socioeconomic inequality.

Many of the cases discussed in this book have dealt with male-led kin groups seeking control over women's reproduction. We have also seen a few cases where a woman's reproduction was not of much concern to larger groups of kin. Among the Navajo, for instance, although a woman reproduces for her own and her husband's matriclans, clan continuity is not a strong concern. Navajo culture venerates women for their reproductive powers, but it does not punish women for childlessness. Another group, the early Christians in Europe, valued celibacy over reproduction and held that sexuality was equally unspiritual for women and men. As noted in Chapter 7, one historian argues that early Christian women found in Christianity a welcome liberation from both marriage and reproduction.

In this book we have also seen that women's reproductive autonomy varies considerably across cultural groups. In this respect two societies stand out—the Mosuo and the Navajo—with strikingly high reproductive autonomy among women. Both are matrilineal. These are also the societies in which equality between men and women appears to be relatively high in general and where women have considerable access to and control over economic resources. Interestingly, a study by C. H. Browner and Sondra T. Perdue (1988) predicted but did not find an association between women's reproductive autonomy and their autonomy in other spheres of life within one Mexican community. Perhaps the variation among women within this community was too small. I am suggesting that such an association between women's reproductive autonomy and women's exercise of autonomy in other spheres of life would be found cross-culturally. A later study (Browner 2001) showed how economic, institutional, and cultural factors interact to influence women's ability to determine their own reproductive activities in Latino communities in Latin America and the United States. Here, women were more likely to make their own reproductive decisions (against the interests or wishes of their male partners) when they had access to economic resources.

By contrast with the Mosuo and Navajo, in the societies reviewed here that are strongly patrilineal and exhibit a cultural concern with male fertility and lineal masculinity (Nepalese Brahmans, Kurds of northern Iraq), women's reproductive autonomy is low. The Nuer appear to be something of an exception here. Although strongly patrilineal and expressing lineal masculinity, the cultural use of cattle payments to establish fatherhood appears to open options for women—female sexuality is not strongly restricted, women can easily leave husbands, and barren women can enter woman-woman marriage, becoming "fathers" themselves. As with the Nyinba and Nayar, women's sexuality and fertility are separate social concerns among the Nuer.

By and large, white, middle-class Euro-American women have not had to contend with the interests of large kin groups in their reproduction; they have not been under pressure to reproduce for anyone but themselves and their partners. Furthermore, over the centuries, restrictions on their sexuality have relaxed. Yet, paradoxically, these Euro-American women have expressed problems and tensions of their own in the process of trying to reconcile their sexuality, fertility, and personhood in a meaningful and satisfying way. In my view the Euro-American pattern is cross-culturally unusual. Until recently, female sexual behavior was restricted (a double sexual standard was clearly expressed). Yet pressures to bear many children, or bear sons, were not strong; women were not punished or blamed for childlessness, and reproductive autonomy was relatively high. This particular configuration is not found in any of the other case studies in this book. Possibly it was the retention of the double sexual standard (a cultural hangover from an earlier past?) that in North America made women express an uncomfortable fit between their sexuality, fertility, and personhood.

With the emergence of the NRTs, we cannot fail to ask ourselves who we will become, as women, as men, as people, and as kin. But this is not a new question. All human groups throughout history have continually constructed kinship and gender, seeking meaning and identity within these cultural constructions. And along the way, the constructions themselves have been contested between men and women, young and old, powerful and powerless. Now, as we face the development of new (and newer) reproductive technologies, the struggle continues. In this way, perhaps the NRTs are not taking us into a brave new world so much as dealing out new cards in an older dynamic human game of self, kin, and gender definition.

DISCUSSION QUESTIONS

1. Construct a kinship chart showing your relatives (or use the chart you may have constructed following Chapter 1). How many of your living relatives reside in the same town or city as you do? Do any of your relatives live in another country? Have the processes of globalization affected you and your network of kin? If so, in what ways?

2. What different images does the word *globalization* invoke? Can you think of globalization symbols other than McDonald's?

3. If you were to adopt a child from a culture different from your own, would you want this child to be versed in its original culture? Why or why not?

SUGGESTED FURTHER READING

Dorrow, Sara K. 2006. *Transnational Adoption: Cultural Economy of Race, Gender, and Kinship*. New York: New York University Press. An ethnographic study of transnational adoptions proceeding from China to the United States.

Leinaweaver, Jessaca B. 2011. Kinship Paths to and from Europe: A Unified Analysis of Peruvian Adoption and Migration. *Journal of Latin American and Caribbean Anthropology* 16(2): 380–400. This article draws interesting parallels between labor migrants and adoptees of Peruvian origin in Spain in terms of constructions of kinship.

SUGGESTED CLASSROOM MEDIA

Fighting the Tide: Developing Nations and Globalization. 2004. Films for the Humanities and Sciences. DVD. Five-part series, twenty-six minutes each. Covers the effect of globalization in developing countries.

WEBSITES

www.adoption101.com/adoption_information_home.html. "Adoption 101." Provides a wide range of useful information for people wishing to adopt a child, including types of adoption, agencies, processes, legalities, and advice.

www.pstalker.com/migration. Discusses controversial issues surrounding international migration.

http://video.nd.edu/143-immigration-faculty-stories. "Immigration: Behind the Labels." Anthropologist Karen Richman discusses the migration of Mexicans into the United States in terms of economic and cultural issues. A short video is included. University of Notre Dame, Video Channel, 2007.

NOTES

1. With a relatively prosperous economy, South Korea goes against the pattern of adoptable children moving from poor to wealthier countries. Here, the stigma against illegitimacy accounts for children being made available for adoption (Howell 2009: 35n).

2. In most contexts Norwegian parents downplay the biogenetic origins of their transnationally adopted children. But in some contexts this aspect of the child's origins is foregrounded. This is especially the case now since adoption agencies, psychologists, and others in Norway encourage parents to make their adopted children aware of their origins and develop pride in their original culture (Howell 2009: 79–82).

3. The United States, along with Somalia and Ethiopia, has not ratified this UN document; apparently the United States has felt there is too much resistance inside the country to the idea of public authorities interfering in private family matters (Howell 2009: 184n).

REFERENCES

Alber, Erdmute. 2011. Child Trafficking in West Africa? In Ana Marta González, Laurie F. DeRose, and Florence Oloo, eds., *Frontiers of Globalization: Kinship and Family Structures in Africa*, pp. 71–92. Trenton, NJ: Africa World Press.

Browner, C. H. 2001. Situating Women's Reproductive Activities. *American Anthropologist* 102(4): 773–788.

Browner, C. H., and Sondra T. Perdue. 1988. Women's Secrets: Bases for Reproductive and Social Autonomy in a Mexican Community. *American Ethnologist* 15(1): 84–97.

Gamburd, Michele R. 2008. Milk Teeth and Jet Planes: Kin Relations in Families of Sri Lanka's Transnational Domestic Servants. *City & Society* 20(1): 5–31.

Ho, Christine G. T. 1993. The Internationalization of Kinship and the Feminization of Caribbean Migration: The Case of Afro-Trinidadian Immigrants in Los Angeles. *Human Organization* 52(1): 32–40.

Howell, Signe. 2001. Self-Conscious Kinship: Some Contested Values in Norwegian Transnational Adoption. In Sarah Franklin and Susan McKinnin, eds., *Relative*

Values: Reconfiguring Kinship Studies, pp. 203–223. Durham, NC: Duke University Press.

———. 2009. *The Kinning of Foreigners: Transnational Adoption in Global Perspective*. New York: Berghahn Books.

Kapstein, Ethan B. 2003. The Baby Trade. *Foreign Affairs* 82(6): 115–125.

Leinaweaver, Jessaca B. 2007. On Moving Children: The Social Implications of Andean Child Circulation. *American Ethnologist* 34(1): 163–180.

———. 2008. *The Circulation of Children: Kinship, Adoption, and Morality in Andean Peru*. Durham, NC: Duke University Press.

Quinlan, Robert J. 2005. Kinship, Gender, and Migration from a Caribbean Community. *Migration Letters* 2(1): 1–11.

Robbins, Richard H. 2011. *Global Problems and the Culture of Capitalism*, 5th ed. Upper Saddle River, NJ: Prentice Hall.

Smith, Daniel Jordan. 2008. Intimacy, Infidelity, and Masculinity in Southwestern Nigeria. In William R. Jankowiak, ed., *Intimacies: Love and Sex Across Cultures*, pp. 224–244. New York: Columbia University Press.

———. 2011. Stretched and Strained but Not Broken: Kinship in Contemporary Nigeria. In Ana Marta González, Laurie F. DeRose, and Florence Oloo, eds., *Frontiers of Globalization: Kinship and Family Structures in Africa*, pp. 31–69. Trenton, NJ: Africa World Press.

Watson, James L. 2006. *Golden Arches East: McDonald's in East Asia*, 2nd ed. Stanford, CA: Stanford University Press.

Appendix: Kinship Terminology

Human cultural groups have different ways of classifying kin. In most of the United States, for example, people classify MB and FB together under the term *uncle*, whereas in many other societies these two individuals are distinguished by separate terms. For any group we can place an ego on a diagram, trace out various kin from ego, and then label what term ego uses for each of his/her kin. This will show us the classification, or kinship terminology system, for ego's group. In many cases kinship terminology will relate to or reflect kinship practices or cultural ideas about kinship in a particular society. Thus in the United States, people tend to regard MB and FB as the same kind of kin, consistent with the single term *uncle*; it is not important in this bilateral system that one of these kin is related to ego through the mother and the other one through the father.

Despite variation in kinship terminology systems, all of them from around the globe can be grouped into a few major types. This is an intriguing fact in and of itself and it raises questions about why this may be the case. Are there correlations between these major terminology types and other aspects of kinship, such as marriage patterns and rules of descent? Anthropologists over many decades have struggled to answer this question, but so far a neat and consistent fit between kinship terminology systems and some other general variable has not been found (Keesing 1975). For example, Radcliffe-Brown once proposed that kinship terminologies would reflect the kinship "rights and duties" of ego; thus in any one system ego would classify together those kin to whom he owed similar obligations. This is often true of some kinship terms in some systems (as we saw above in the case of the US uncle), but there are too many exceptions and cases where this idea does not appear to apply at all (Fox 1989).

Nevertheless, we can see some patterns relating kinship terminology with other aspects of kinship within a particular society, and a few larger patterns can be seen, even though there may also be a significant number of exceptions. Let's take a look, then, at some of the major types of kinship classification.

FIGURE A.1   Hawaiian Terminology

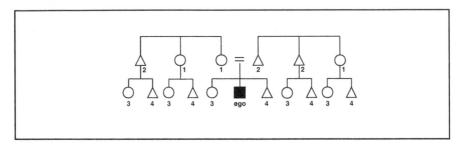

HAWAIIAN

In the Hawaiian system, kin are distinguished simply on the basis of generation and sex. Thus there are very few terms. Ego refers to all female kin of his/her parents' generation by the same term he/she uses for mother; all male kin of this generation are called by the same term as that used for father (see Figure A.1). Similarly in his/her own generation, ego will call all female cousins by the same term used for sister and will label all male cousins with the same term used for brother. Note that in Figure A.1, as on all figures in this appendix, kin who are designated by the same term are labeled with the same number.

Hawaiian systems are found in Hawaii (as the name implies) and in other Polynesian and Melanesian areas, as well as in other parts of the world. There are exceptions but they tend to be associated with societies that lack corporate descent groups (bilateral societies) or have systems of cognatic descent. This is easy to understand since in bilateral/cognatic societies, paternally traced relatives are likely to have the same kind of relationship to ego as do maternally traced ones. In a unilineal system (matrilineal or patrilineal) by contrast, they will have a different relationship to ego. For example, in a patrilineal system FB belongs to ego's own descent group, whereas MB does not.

IROQUOIS

The Iroquois system (named after the Iroquois Indians) is widespread and is strongly (but not universally) associated with unilineal descent. In this system F and FB are called by the same term, M and MZ are called by the same term, but MB and FZ are called by separate terms (see Figure A.2). Then in ego's generation, female parallel cousins are called by the same term as that for sister, male parallel cousins are called by the same term as that for brother, but cross cousins are distinguished by separate terms. In some Iroquois societies, cross cousins are preferred spouses, whereas parallel cousins (classed

FIGURE A.2 Iroquois Terminology

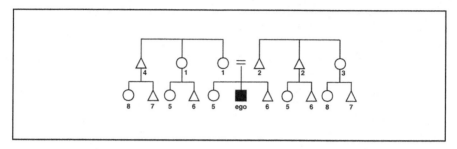

with siblings in the terminology) are prohibited, but there are plenty of exceptions to this.

Some anthropologists refer to a larger kinship terminology category called "Iroquois-Dravidian" with the Iroquois and Dravidian as subtypes within it. The two subtypes make the same terminological distinctions in ego's parental generation and in his/her own generation (cousins), but they differ in how ego classifies other, more removed cousins.

Eskimo

In an Eskimo terminology (named for the Inuit, who were once called Eskimos), ego uses distinguishing terms for members of his/her nuclear family—M, F, B, and Z. Otherwise, in the parental generation there is only a distinction by sex so that MB and FB are called by the same term and MZ and FZ are labeled with the same term. Often in these systems MBW is called by the MZ/FZ term and FSH by the MB/FB term. Ego's cousins are all called by the same term (see Figure A.3) although in some Eskimo systems they may be distinguished by sex. This system should be very familiar to people from the United States and many places in Europe. Aside from its prevalence in North America and Europe, Eskimo terminology is found in many foraging societies around the world. But on a global level the Eskimo system is fairly rare.

The Eskimo system, then, carves out ego's nuclear family and emphasizes individuals within it. Not surprisingly, this system is common in bilateral, neolocal societies where an independent nuclear family dominates the system.

We can examine further one Eskimo system, that found in the United States, to show how the study of kinship terminology can reveal cultural concerns or values. In a now-classic study David Schneider (1980) examined American kinship terms in relation to broader cultural constructions. Schneider drew a distinction between what he called "basic" and "derived" terms. The basic

FIGURE A.3   Eskimo Terminology

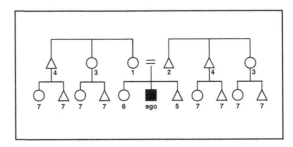

terms are *father, mother, brother, sister, son, daughter, husband, wife, uncle, aunt, nephew, niece,* and *cousin,* whereas the derived terms are basic terms used in conjunction with a modifier. The modifiers are:

> step
> in-law
> foster
> grand
> great
> first, second, etc.
> once, twice (etc.) removed
> half
> ex-

   Combining basic terms with modifiers produces a host of labels for relatives such as *stepdaughter, ex-wife, grandmother, great-grandfather,* and so on. Of course, all of the modifiers are restricted in terms of which "basic" terms they can be combined with. For example, *stephusband* is not possible and the modifier *ex-* can be used only in reference to husband, wife, and other basic terms already modified by *in-law*.

   What Schneider saw in these derived terms—and this becomes important in terms of American cultural values—is that they each have one of two functions. Either they (1) distinguish "blood relatives from those in comparable positions who are not blood relatives" (1980: 22), or (2) mark distance between people. In the first category are the modifiers *step, foster,* and *in-law*. Thus a stepdaughter is distinct from a real daughter, a brother-in-law from a real brother, and so on. The rest of the modifiers are in the second, distance-marking category. Most of these denote a degree of consanguinity; for example, a first cousin is closer than a second cousin, and a half-brother is not as close as a regular brother. Only one modifier, *ex-,* marks distance in another way: "on an in/out basis. Husband is 'in,' ex-husband is 'out'" (1980: 23). Also, all but one of the distance-marking modifiers deal with consanguineal relatives. The exception is, again, *ex-*, which deals exclusively with affinal relatives.

With this observation, Schneider moved to the heart of American kinship: a strong emphasis on or cultural concern with consanguineal or "blood" relationships. As he noted, the first set of modifiers for the derived terms (*step, foster,* and *in-law*) "protects the integrity of the closest blood relatives," and the second set (*great, grand,* etc.) "places relatives in calibrated degrees of distance if they are blood relatives" (1980: 23). Among relatives produced by the second set of modifiers, only affinal relatives can ever be *ex-*, whereas ties of blood can never be severed. The terminological system thus highlights the importance of relationship and closeness through blood in American kinship.

CROW

Crow terminology is associated with matrilineal descent, although several matrilineal societies use another system and Crow terminologies are found in societies that are not matrilineal. In the Crow system (after the Crow Indians) relatives in the parental generation are classified as in the Iroquois terminology, but then we see something new: Some relatives of widely different generations are called by the same term. Thus ego will call his/her BS, MBS, and MMBS by the same term, covering relatives of three different generations. Figure A.4 clarifies what is happening in this system. Here we see that ego calls the unshaded relatives on the diagram (BS, MBS, and MMBS) with the same term (*X*). At first glance this might look odd to an outsider. But notice what all of the relatives on the diagram who are called X have in common with respect to ego. First, all are outside ego's matrilineal group (those within it are shaded); second, all of them are children of male members of ego's matrilineal group.

FIGURE A.4   Crow Terminology

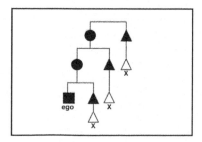

The best way, then, to translate X is "male children of men of my matri-lineage." In Crow terminology, affiliation with matrilineages, and not gen-eration, is what is important about these relatives. In a similar way, in Crow terminology, ego's FZ, FZD, and FZDD will be called by the same term. They are all "women of father's matrilineal group." And ego's F, FB, and FBS are called by the same term, meaning "men of father's matrilineage." Thus the system makes sense in a strongly matrilineal society where matri-lineage affiliation and relation to one's own matrilineage are more important than generation.

Some anthropologists refer to a larger kinship terminology type called "Crow-Omaha," with the Crow and Omaha as subtypes. The Omaha is the patrilineal opposite of the Crow type and indeed is found (with exceptions) in societies with strong corporate patrilineal descent groups. Omaha is the exact reverse of Crow. Here, an ego will, for example, classify ZS, FZS, and FFZS with the same term, meaning "male children of women of my patrilineage."

This discussion has presented a very basic and simplified introduction to kinship terminology systems. Important to note is that these systems are var-ied, but all terminological systems that human groups actually use will fall into a limited set of major types. Also of note is that most of the major types (Eskimo is the exception among the types reviewed here) classify some lineal relatives with collateral relatives (such as F and FB). We have not here re-viewed the variation within these major types, but different societies that use, say, Iroquois terminology also have their own distinctive variations and quirks. What is most important is that, even without a perfect fit between kinship terminology and practice, understanding a people's kinship termi-nology system will help us to see how a people themselves perceive their own kinship.

REFERENCES

Fox, Robin. 1989 [orig. 1967]. *Kinship and Marriage: An Anthropological Perspective.* Cambridge, England: Cambridge University Press.

Keesing, Roger M. 1975. *Kin Groups and Social Structure.* Fort Worth, TX: Holt, Rinehart, and Winston.

Schneider, David M. 1980 [orig. 1968]. *American Kinship: A Cultural Account.* Chicago: University of Chicago Press.

Glossary

affinal related through marriage.

age-set a lifelong affiliation of similar-aged persons who pass through various life stages together as a unit; age-sets are characteristic of East African pastoral societies.

altruistic acts individual behaviors that enhance others' reproductive success while simultaneously reducing one's own.

ambilocal referring to a postmarital residence pattern in which a married couple can choose to live with or near the kin of either the groom or the bride.

amniocentesis a procedure for drawing a sample of amniotic fluid from a pregnant woman by inserting a needle into the uterus; the results provide genetic information about the fetus.

artificial insemination (AI) a process of placing donor sperm into the vaginal cavity of a female at the proper stage of her menstrual cycle in an attempt to achieve pregnancy.

avunculocal referring to a postmarital residence pattern in which a married couple moves to or near the household of the groom's mother's brother(s).

bilateral kinship the recognition of kin connections through both parents; virtually all societies exhibit bilateral kinship.

bilateral society a society that traces kin connections over the generations through both males and females, but without the formation of descent groups.

bridewealth the transfer of wealth from the kin of the groom to the kin of the bride at marriage.

chorion fetal tissue that lines the uterine cavity and surrounds the amniotic sac.

chorionic villus sampling a technique for retrieving chorionic cells from the uterine cavity by introducing a tube into the uterus through the vagina.

clan a group or category of people who claim to share descent through a common ancestor, but whose genealogical links with one another are obscured and no longer traceable; the common ancestor of the group is often a mythical figure.

class endogamy marriage within a given social class.

cloning in the context of this book, the production of genetically identical organisms by artificial means, such as transfer of a donor nucleus to a recipient egg.

cognatic descent descent based on any combination of male or female links.

consanguineal related through descent (or "blood" ties).

corporate group a group of people who collectively share rights, privileges, and liabilities.

cross cousins the children of two opposite-sex siblings.

Crow kinship terminology a type of kinship terminology noted for its merging of relatives of different generations; often associated with matrilineal descent.

descent group a kin group based on descent (patrilineal, matrilineal, or cognatic).

domestic cycle general stages in the process of family reproduction particular to a given society; as domestic groups move through phases of establishment, expansion, and decline, the composition and structure of these groups will fluctuate.

domestic group people who live together and share resources for their subsistence.

double descent the existence in one society of both matrilineal and patrilineal descent groups; each person simultaneously belongs to two descent groups.

dowry wealth that accompanies a bride to her marriage.

embryo adoption the result of artificial insemination achieved by using the uterus of a surrogate, from which the embryo is then flushed and inserted into the uterus of the mother-to-be.

endogamy marriage inside a certain social group or category.

enucleate referring to the action of removing the nucleus of a cell, usually by means of a microsyringe.

Eskimo kinship terminology a type of kinship terminology that emphasizes the nuclear family by giving separate terms for M, F, Z, and B, while grouping together other relatives.

exogamy marriage outside a certain social group or category.

fitness reproductive success; the more fertile offspring a person has, the greater his or her fitness is considered to be.

fraternal polyandry a marriage union in which two or more brothers share one wife.

genitor the biological father of a child.

ghost marriage the practice whereby a patrilineal kinsman takes a wife in the name of a deceased man to have children by the woman in that man's name.

Hawaiian kinship terminology a type of kinship terminology that uses one term for all relatives of the same sex and generation.

hominid a Family-level classification that includes modern humans and their extinct ancestors.

hominoid a Superfamily-level classification of primates that includes apes and humans.

hypergamy marriage of a woman upward into a higher-status group.

inbreeding depression the detrimental effect over time of high levels of inbreeding to the fitness of a population that has a high frequency of deleterious mutations.

inclusive fitness the process whereby an individual enhances his or her reproductive success through altruistic acts that favor the fitness of others who share some genes in common with that individual, as in the case of close relatives.

in-vitro fertilization (IVF) the process of incubating oocytes with sperm in a petri dish to produce a fertilized embryo.

Iroquois kinship terminology a type of kinship terminology in which a single term groups F with FB and M with MZ, while separate terms are used for FZ and MB; cross and parallel cousins are distinguished and parallel cousins are classed with siblings.

karyotype a chromosome spread prepared for microscopic examination.

kin selection the process whereby natural selection acts on inclusive fitness.

kindred a set of relatives traced to a particular ego.

kinship terminology system the set of linguistic terms for kin showing how various kin are distinguished or classified together in a particular culture.

levirate the practice whereby a man marries the widow of his deceased brother.

lineage a group of people who trace their descent to a common ancestor through known links.

matrilineage a group of people who can trace descent from a common ancestor through female links and who can trace the links among themselves.

matrilineal descent descent based on links through females only.

matrilocal referring to a postmarital residence pattern in which a married couple lives in the household or place of the bride's kin; also called uxorilocal.

monogamy marriage between two persons, generally a man and a woman.

mother-in-law avoidance an interaction between a man and his wife's mother characterized by respectful restraint.

multimale, multifemale units groupings of primates that consist of numerous males living and mating with numerous females.

natolocal a residence pattern whereby husbands and wives reside with their own respective natal groups and so do not live together.

neolocal referring to a postmarital residence pattern in which a married couple moves to a new location, living with the kin of neither the groom nor the bride.

nonfraternal polyandry a marriage union in which one woman has two or more husbands who are not brothers.

nucleus the prominent component of living cells, containing genetic material (DNA) bounded by a membrane.

one-male units primate units in which one adult male lives and mates with several females.

oocyte freezing the process of taking oocytes from a woman's uterus and then freezing them for later use.

oocytes immature eggs.

parallel cousins the children of two same-sex siblings.

parental investment the contributions of parents to the fitness of their offspring.

pater the legal father of a child.

patrilineage a group of people who can trace descent from a common ancestor through male links and who can trace the links among themselves.

patrilineal descent descent traced through males only.

patrilocal referring to a postmarital residence pattern in which a married couple lives in the household or place of the groom's kin; also called virilocal.

phratries groupings of two or more clans.

polyandry marriage of one woman to two or more men at the same time.

polygyny marriage of a man to two or more women at the same time.

postmarital residence the location in which a newly married couple will reside.

primogeniture a pattern of inheritance in which only the eldest son receives a patrimony.

sexual dimorphism the external physical differences between males and females.

sexual selection the process by which one sex (usually male) competes for sexual access to the other sex.

sororal polygyny a marriage of two or more sisters to one man.

sororate the practice whereby a man marries the sister of his deceased wife.

totemism the symbolic identification of a group of people with a particular plant, animal, or object.

unilineal descent descent traced through only one sex, as in the case of matrilineal or patrilineal descent.

woman-woman marriage the marriage of a barren woman (who counts as a "husband") to another woman; a genitor is arranged for the "wife," and the barren woman becomes the legal father of the children.

Index